Competition Policy

Competition Policy

An Empirical and Economic Approach

Emmanuel Combe

Foreword by
Philippe Aghion

Wolters Kluwer

Published by:
Kluwer Law International B.V.
PO Box 316
2400 AH Alphen aan den Rijn
The Netherlands
E-mail: international-sales@wolterskluwer.com
Website: www.wolterskluwer.com/en/solutions/kluwerlawinternational

Sold and distributed by:
Wolters Kluwer Legal & Regulatory U.S.
7201 McKinney Circle
Frederick, MD 21704
United States of America
E-mail: customer.service@wolterskluwer.com

ISBN 978-94-035-3731-3

e-Book: ISBN 978-94-035-3751-1
web-PDF: ISBN 978-94-035-3772-6

To Sylvie

About the Author

Emmanuel Combe has been Vice Chairman of the French Competition Authority since 2012 and is a full professor in economics at the University of Paris 1 Pantheon-Sorbonne and at Skema Business School. He is a graduate of the Ecole Normale Supérieure (Lyon) and holds a PhD in economics from the University of Paris 1 Panthéon-Sorbonne. He is a specialist in corporate strategies, new business models, and competition policy. He has published numerous academic articles and books on these different topics.

Table of Contents

List of Figures

Conclusion

List of Tables

Conclusion

Foreword

Competition: as consumers, we love it. It ensures low prices, innovations, and a wide variety of products. As producers and employees, we fear it: competition prevents us from living "the quiet life of monopoly" (John Hicks).

However, competition is first and foremost a formidable stimulus that encourages and motivates one to be ever more efficient.

This cardinal virtue of competition is particularly important today for developed countries, where firms mostly lie at the technological frontier: it is competitive pressure that leads firms to escape from it by innovating. A persistent common wisdom was that competition and intellectual property rights protection would have counteracting effects on innovation incentives: whenever one of them would encourage innovation and growth, the other would discourage it. In fact these two forces are complementary: they both increase the net gain from escaping competition by innovating. This is confirmed by empirical studies showing a positive effect of product market competition on innovation, all the more in economies with better patent protection[1].

If competition is a necessary ingredient for growth, ancient history—let's think of the end of the 19th century in the United States with the emergence of the trusts—as well as more recent history—with the irresistible rise of the digital giants—show that it remains a fragile institution: yesterday's outsiders have a strong incentive, once they have acquired a dominant position, in closing the door in order to block entry of new competitors. Paradoxically, those who were responsible for yesterday's innovations and productivity will become obstacles to future growth. The persistence of their market power is no longer the sign of their intrinsic superiority: it can also result from anti-competitive practices, to the detriment of consumers, well-being and dynamic efficiency.

This is why competition law has been assigned such an important role in modern countries: to detect and sanction anti-competitive practices that prevent the entry of

1. See: Ph. Aghion, C. Antonin, S. Bunel (2021) *The Power of Creative Destruction: Economic Upheaval and the Wealth of Nations*, Harvard University Press, 393 p.

new, as efficient competitors. This law, together with competition authorities, forms the basis of what is commonly called "competition policy."

Emmanuel Combe presents here the different facets of this policy, which is more than a century old in the United States and more than 60 years old in Europe, but which is still too often misunderstood.

In the course of the different chapters, the reader will discover why and how competition policy fights against cartels, those secret and illicit agreements that aim at eliminating all competition on the market; what are the ambivalent effects of a vertical or technological agreement on competition and welfare; what forms an abuse of a dominant position can take, whether it is by excluding rivals or by exploiting clients through excessive prices or discriminatory conditions; why and how competition authorities control mergers & acquisitions.

Emmanuel Combe's book presents several singularities that make it so original and interesting.

First of all, it is based on a constant back-and-forth between economic theory and the experience of the practitioner. Emmanuel Combe was Vice Chairman of the French Competition Authority for 10 years; as such, he systematically illustrates his remarks with examples coming from European or American jurisprudence. Thus, the abuse of dominant position, a rather theoretical notion, takes a very concrete form under his pen, when he reviews various practices such as: tied sales, exclusivity contracts, predatory pricing, refusal to provide access to an essential infrastructure, disparagement of a competitor. In the same vein, the economic analysis of vertical restraints is fed by recent developments, such as Across Platform Parity Agreements (APPAs) or the evolution of selective distribution in the age of online sales. Emmanuel Combe also shows us that public action by competition authorities is today complemented by the rise of civil society, through which the victims of anti-competitive practices seek compensation.

Secondly, this book excels in its ability to bring together the legal approach and economic reasoning, which is quite rare. Thus, in line with the Gary Becker tradition, Emmanuel Combe shows that the economic approach provides a convincing framework in favor of reinforcing the deterrent effect of fines, particularly in the fight against cartels. In particular, he emphasizes the role of criminal sanctions in reducing the incentive for managers to violate antitrust rules. Similarly, with respect to mergers and acquisitions, Emmanuel Combe insists on the need to take better account of efficiency gains, as suggested by the analysis of Oliver Williamson: the harm to competition of a merger must be weighed against the efficiency gains it may generate. On resale price maintenance, the author reminds us that economists call for caution, favoring a "rule of reason" approach rather than a pure prohibition.

Last but not least, Emmanuel Combe's book has the merit of great manuals, that of clarity: it makes sometimes complex concepts accessible, without ever undermining the rigor of the reasoning. For instance, the author explains perfectly, in a simple but always rigorous language, concepts as subtle as the unilateral and coordinated effects, the passing-on approach, the relevant market definition or the optimal sanction theory. Moreover, it gives meaning to public action, by explaining each time the reasons that justify its intervention. The reader will be interested to read the chapter on cartel behavior in which the author shows how inefficient and long-lasting these practices are, which fully legitimizes the corrective intervention of the "visible hand" of public authorities, with leniency programs.

This book should enable students, lawyers and public decision-makers to be better informed. This exercise is to me more essential today than ever: if we want competition policy to remain this precious ingredient at the service of prosperity, we need to explain not only its tools but also, and above all, its profound meaning. This is the contribution and the singularity of this book.

Philippe Aghion
Professor at the Collège de France and at INSEAD

Preface

At a time of increasing public concern regarding high industrial concentration, especially in the digital sector, the question of regulating competition is returning to the forefront: What role can or should competition policy play tomorrow in a free market economy?

To fully understand this debate, one must first know the economic principles of competition. The aim of this book is to provide readers with an economist's viewpoint so that it can be used, for example, by lawyers, in addition to their essential legal expertise, to better understand the objectives and instruments of competition policy.

With this in mind, throughout the book we combine a theoretical approach—with a review of the main microeconomic models and schools of thought on competition and competition policy—and an empirical approach, illustrated by numerous examples of antitrust cases. We believe that this constant back-and-forth between theory and facts will help readers to better grasp complex economic theories through real-life illustrations.

Furthermore, this book can be read without any former mathematical knowledge. It is based on very simple economic formulas and uses graphic illustrations or linear functions.

Finally, each of the book's six chapters can be read independently, which explains why certain key points are reiterated in various chapters.

Chapter 1 begins with a discussion of what economists think about competition: The model of Pure and Perfect Competition is the starting point for any analysis on this subject. It allows us to measure the imperfection of markets and to understand the notion of "*market power.*" This approach, based on market structures, has been enriched and criticized over time, making it possible to fine-tune the analysis and even to question the legitimacy of an antitrust policy.

Chapter 2 provides an overview of competition policies around the world, as well as the legal and institutional framework within which they operate. We show that, with the exception of the American case, competition policy is a recent practice in developed countries—including Europe—and that it is still under construction in emerging and developing countries. We review the various preventive and punitive tools used by antitrust authorities, emphasizing the deterrent role of fines.

Chapter 3 deals with cartels, a practice by which competing firms decide to stop all competition between themselves. We analyze the conditions needed for such agreements to appear and the various forms they can take. We continue by studying the stability of cartels, and then looking at the detection and sanction of these practices, in particular through "*leniency*" programs.

Chapter 4 explores agreements such as vertical distribution or R&D cooperation between competitors that usually have ambivalent effects: While they may reduce competition, they can also lead to efficiencies. We study to what extent and under what conditions these agreements can be authorized by antitrust authorities.

Chapter 5 provides an overview of several behaviors considered to be abuses of dominant positions, such as "*predatory pricing*" or loyalty rebates. While competition may lead to the eviction of some inefficient competitors, it remains to be seen how this "*selection*" process is carried out: Does it result from the intrinsic superiority of some firms over others—the so-called "*competition on the merits*"—or does it express an exclusionary strategy of as-efficient competitors? The task of antitrust authorities is to distinguish between what constitutes an "*abuse*" of a dominant position and simply a case of fierce competition.

Chapter 6 presents merger control, a procedure by which competition authorities examine mergers to ensure they do not lead to excessive market concentration, which could have negative impacts on competition. We return to fundamental concepts such as the "*relevant market*," and we analyze the different possible impacts of mergers on competition and efficiencies.

Acknowledgements

The writing of a book is a solitary exercise but it is enhanced by the valuable contributions of many. I would like to thank Sarah Subremon (Bureau Brandeis Paris), Elodie Camous-Léonard (UGGC Avocats), Guillaume Perret (French Competition Authority), Sylvie Cognet (BNP Paribas), and Constance Monnier (University of Paris 1 Panthéon Sorbonne) for their review and valuable advice. Of course, I remain solely responsible for any errors that may remain.

I also wish to thank Annick Kraitsowits (kraitsowits@yahoo.com) for her valuable translation and insights, Lucy Anderton for her proofreading, Skema Business School and my research laboratory RISE^2 for their constant support.

CHAPTER 1

From Competition to Market Power

It is common to define competition on the basis of its effects: Competition is a market situation in which any profit that is not based on the merits of individual firms cannot be sustained in the long-term. In other words, in a competitive market, a less efficient firm will sooner or later be replaced by new operators. However, while competition can be defined by its consequences, it is more difficult to identify its characteristics.

The most common definition of "*competition*" stems from microeconomics where competition is associated with a specific market structure, that of "*pure and perfect competition.*" In a market with pure and perfect competition, the number of suppliers plays a fundamental role: Given the large number of firms, none of them is powerful enough to have any real market power. Conversely, a monopoly enjoys substantial market power, which leads to higher prices and a loss of total welfare (Section 1).

Between these two polar cases, we find markets characterized by a small number of firms, a situation described as "*oligopoly.*" Cournot's oligopoly model establishes a relationship between market structure and price level: When the number of firms on the market increases, prices tend towards a situation of pure and perfect competition (Section 2). The models of pure and perfect competition, monopoly, and Cournot's oligopoly thus highlight a clear relationship between market structures, defined mainly by the number of firms and the power to set prices (Table 1.1).

Table 1.1 Market Structures and Market Power

Market Structure	*Market Power*	*Lerner's Index**
Pure and perfect competition	Lack of market power: The price is close to the marginal cost c.	L = 0 in the long-term
Simple monopoly	Maximum market power (limited by the price elasticity of demand).	$L = 1/\varepsilon$ (with ε, the price elasticity of demand)
Cournot's oligopoly	Market power decreases with the number of firms.	$L = s_i/\varepsilon$ (with s_i, the market share of a firm i)

* Lerner's index is defined as the ratio of margin (price - marginal cost) to price, i.e.: $(p - c)/p$.

These fundamental microeconomic results were taken up and systematized during the 1950s and 1960s by the Structuralist School (or the Harvard School), through the SCP (Structure-Conduct-Performance) paradigm. This model, which constitutes the framework for understanding competition policy, shows that in a concentrated market, firms that have market power might abuse it, thereby justifying the intervention of the "*visible hand*" of antitrust authorities (Section 3).

However, the relationship between market concentration and market power is not as mechanical and static as the structuralist approach suggests. In particular, there is no systematic relationship between the number of firms and the market power: For example, in a so-called "*contestable*" market, a firm may be alone and not have any market power. A more radical criticism of the structuralist model is made by the Austrian and Chicago Schools: the SCP model is based on a static vision of competition, which does not take into account the dynamics of market structures (Section 4).

SECTION 1 OPPOSING MARKET STRUCTURES: PURE AND PERFECT COMPETITION VERSUS MONOPOLY

In this section, we analyze and compare two opposite market structures: pure and perfect competition and monopoly. We show first that in competitive situations, firms have no market power because the price tends towards the marginal cost. A competitive market leads to a high level of welfare for consumers (§1). On the other hand, a monopoly enjoys strong market power, to the detriment of consumers and total welfare (§2).

§1 The Pure and Perfect Competition Model

Developed at the end of the 19th century, the pure and perfect competition model is a market structure characterized by the fact that suppliers individually have no power over prices; they are "*price takers.*" Demand for each of them is infinitely price elastic: If a firm increases its price above the market price, it loses all of its customers, who immediately switch to another firm. In Figure 1.1, we see that for a market equilibrium price of $5, the quantity offered by a firm—whatever its level—has no influence on the equilibrium price; the demand addressed to it is a horizontal line (i.e., infinitely elastic to the price).

Assumptions of the model: This lack of market power results from the assumptions upon which the pure and perfect competition model is based:

- atomicity: There is a very large number of suppliers on the market;
- free entry and free exit: There are no legal or economic entry barriers. A new player can immediately enter the market. Similarly, a firm that wants to exit the market can do so without bearing any "*sunk costs*";
- homogeneous products: Producers offer goods that are absolutely identical in the eyes of consumers. Price is the only variable that distinguishes one product from another;
- transparency of information: All agents have the same access to information, which is available immediately to all and at no cost. There are therefore no information asymmetries.

On the basis of these assumptions, pure and perfect competition implies that the price tends towards the marginal cost of production, i.e., the cost of producing an additional unit. Indeed, if the price is higher than the marginal cost, new firms enter the market until profits disappear. There are therefore no long-term profits in a market of pure and perfect competition. On the other hand, pure and perfect competition guarantees consumers the lowest possible price, i.e., a price equal to the marginal cost.

Figure 1.1 The Firm's Demand and Total Demand

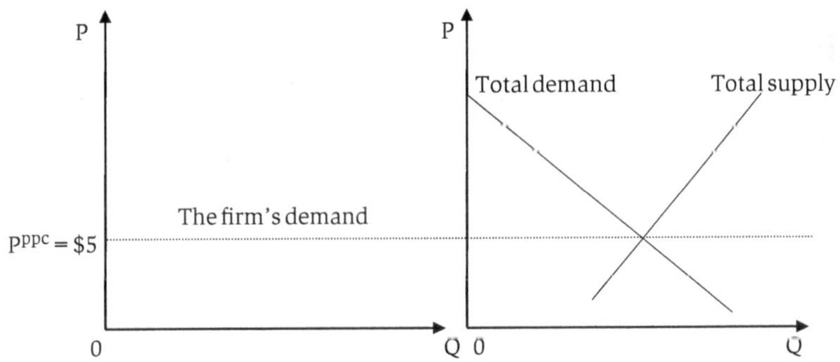

The competitive equilibrium: The fact that the price is equal to the marginal cost can be demonstrated algebraically, with linear functions.

The total demand function takes the following form:

$$P = a - bQ \text{ with } a > c > 0,\ b = 1 \text{ and } Q = \Sigma_{i=1}^{n} q_i$$

Profit (Π) is defined as the difference between total revenue (TR) and total cost (TC):

$$\Pi = \text{total revenue (TR)} - \text{total cost (TC)}$$

The total revenue is the quantity Q multiplied by the price P:

$$\text{Total revenue (TR)} = P \times Q$$

We assume that the total cost (TC) function is linear and consists of a marginal cost c:

$$\text{Total cost (TC)} = cQ \text{ with } c > 0.$$

Profit can therefore be rewritten:

$$\Pi = \text{total revenue (TR)} - \text{total cost (TC)}$$

$$\Leftrightarrow \Pi = (P - c) \times Q$$

(P – c) represents the margin on each unit sold.

From a mathematical point of view, the maximum profit is obtained when the first derivative Π' of the profit is equal to zero (and the second derivative Π'' is negative):

$$\Pi' = 0$$

$$\partial TR/\partial Q - \partial TC/\partial Q = 0$$

$$\Leftrightarrow \text{marginal revenue} = \text{marginal cost}$$

In a perfectly competitive market, no firm has any influence on price, which is therefore considered to be an exogenous variable (i.e., a constant). The profit maximization program is therefore written:

$$\text{Max } \Pi = \text{Max } [PQ - cQ] \text{ with P constant}$$

$$\partial \Pi/\partial Q = 0$$

$$\Leftrightarrow P - c = 0$$

$$\Leftrightarrow P^{ppc} = c$$

We find that in a situation of pure and perfect competition, the equilibrium price P^{ppc} is equal to the marginal cost of production c. We can therefore deduce the total quantity Q^{ppc}:

$$P = a - Q$$

$$\Leftrightarrow c = a - Q$$

$$\Leftrightarrow Q^{ppc} = (a - c)$$

In a market of pure and perfect competition, firms have no market power. The latter is measured with the Lerner's index, defined as the ratio between margin and price. In a situation of pure and perfect competition, the Lerner's index is equal to zero:

$$\text{Lerner index in pure and perfect competition} = (P^{ppc} - c)/\ P^{ppc} = 0$$

The impact of pure and perfect competition on welfare: Let us now analyze the pure and perfect competition equilibrium from a welfare point of view. Total welfare (W) is defined in economics as the (unweighted) sum of consumer surplus (CS) and profits Π_i:

$$W(P) = CS(P) + \sum_{i=1}^{n} \Pi_i(P)$$

Consumer surplus is defined as the difference between each consumer's maximum willingness to pay (i.e., the demand function) and the price paid at equilibrium. In pure and perfect competition, it is equivalent to the gray area in Figure 1.2:

$$CS^{ppc} = [(a - c)(a - c)]/2$$

$$\Leftrightarrow (a - c)^2/2$$

In pure and perfect competition, since the price is equal to the marginal cost, profits are nil.

The total welfare is therefore equal to the consumer surplus:

$$W^{ppc} = (a - c)^2/2$$

We find that in a situation of pure and perfect competition, the total welfare is at its maximum. Indeed, for any price higher than the marginal cost of production, the profit made by firms is less than the loss of consumer surplus. In Figure 1.3, when the price rises above c to reach P_1, profits are equal to area B, i.e.:

$$\sum_{i=1}^{n} \Pi_i = (P_1 - c) \times Q_i$$

Figure 1.2 Pure and Perfect Competition and Consumer Surplus

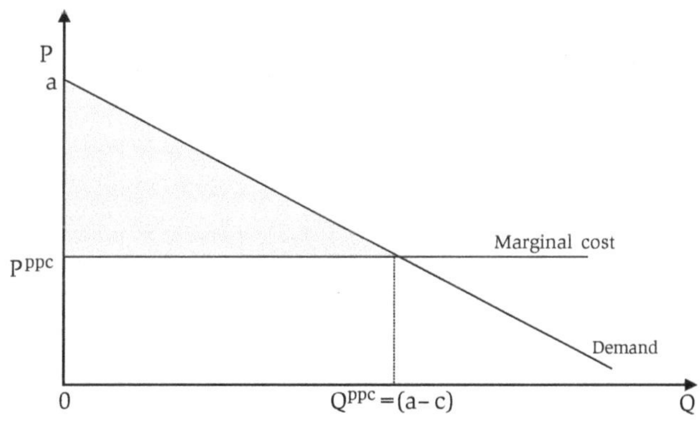

The consumer surplus is now equal to the area A, which corresponds to:

$$CS = (a - P_1)\, Q_1/2$$

We can see that the total welfare has declined, as consumers have lost area (B + D), while firms have gained area B: The net loss is represented by the gray triangle D. This is due to the fact that the price increase has not only led to a transfer of surplus from consumers (who continue to buy) to producers (area B). The price increase has also led some consumers to give up consuming (area D).

The fact that the pure and perfect competition model maximizes the welfare has strong normative consequences:

- industrial concentration can lead to price increases, and can therefore reduce total welfare;
- market power is necessarily to the detriment of consumer surplus, and more generally of total welfare. As pointed out by Armentano (1996): "If economic markets are not perfectly competitive, then there can be no corresponding guarantee that resources would be allocated efficiently. (...). Markets that contain large firms, locational advantages, price discrimination, differentiated products, tie-in sales, promotional advertising, collusion and interdependent rivalry are not perfectly competitive markets, and firms in such markets are said to possess some monopoly power. Consistent with this perspective, such markets might require government antitrust regulation to make them more competitive and more socially efficient."

Figure 1.3 The Impact of a Price Increase on Total Welfare

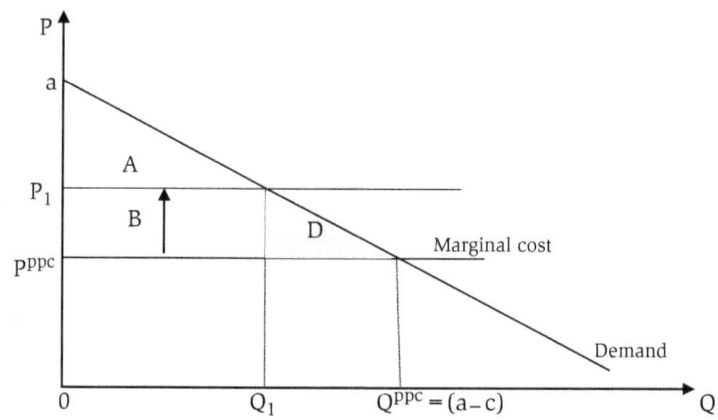

§2 Monopoly and Market Power

In contrast with a market of pure and perfect competition, a monopoly is a market structure characterized by the presence of a single firm, protected by entry barriers (such as a legal monopoly). The monopoly can therefore set a price higher than the marginal cost without fear of consumers turning to other suppliers; it enjoys market power.

The monopoly power: When setting its price, the monopoly must balance between two opposing effects: A price increase above marginal cost allows it to achieve a positive margin on the remaining consumers (margin effect), but it will lose consumers (quantity effect). The price that maximizes the monopoly profit is achieved when these two opposing effects offset each other.

Such a result can be demonstrated algebraically, with linear functions.

The total demand function takes the following form:

$$P = a - bQ \text{ with } a > c > 0,\ b = 1 \text{ and } Q = \Sigma_{i=1}^{n} q_i$$

Unlike in a situation of pure and perfect competition, a monopoly exerts an influence on price; it is "*price maker.*" This means that the price is not a constant but a variable. The total revenue (TR) is therefore written:

$$\text{Total revenue (TR)} = P(Q) \times Q$$

We assume that the total cost (TC) function is linear and consists of a constant marginal cost c:

$$\text{Total cost (TC)} = cQ \text{ with } c > 0$$

The profit function of a monopoly can therefore be rewritten:

$$\Pi = \text{total revenue (TR)} - \text{total cost (TC)}$$

$$\Leftrightarrow \Pi = [P(Q) - c] \times Q$$

$$\Leftrightarrow \Pi = (a - bQ)Q - cQ$$

The maximum profit is obtained when the first derivative of the profit is equal to zero (and when the second derivative is negative):

$$\text{Max } \Pi = \text{Max } [(a - bQ)Q - cQ]$$

$$\Leftrightarrow a - 2bQ - c = 0$$

$$\Leftrightarrow Q^M = (a - c)/2 \text{ with } b = 1$$

The monopoly price P^M is deduced as follows:

$$P = a - Q$$

$$\Leftrightarrow P^M = a - [(a - c)/2]$$

$$\Leftrightarrow P^M = (a + c)/2$$

and the monopoly profit is therefore:

$$\Pi^M = (a - c)^2/4$$

Graphically, the monopoly equilibrium is achieved at the intersection between the marginal revenue and the marginal cost:[2] The monopoly maximizes its profit by producing a quantity Q^M that it sells at a price P^M (Figure 1.4).

Figure 1.4 The Monopoly Equilibrium

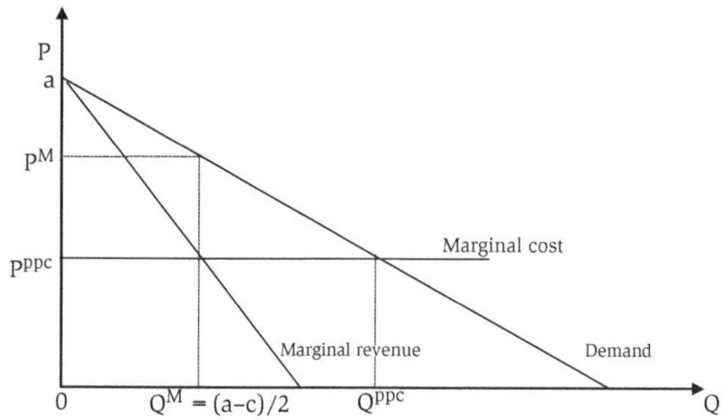

We note that a monopoly situation leads to a higher price than in a perfectly competitive market, and therefore to a lower quantity:[3]

$$P^{ppc} = c < P^M = (a + c)/2$$

$$Q^{PPC} = (a - c) > Q^M = (a - c)/2$$

Market power and price elasticity of demand: The market power of a monopoly is not without limits; it depends on the price elasticity of demand. Indeed, maximizing the profit of a monopoly implies that:

$$\partial (p(Q)Q)/\partial Q = C'(Q)$$

$$\Leftrightarrow p + Q\,(\partial p/\partial Q) = C'(Q) \qquad (1)$$

with C', the first derivative of the total cost, i.e., $\partial C/\partial Q$.

By noting ε the price elasticity of demand,[4] equality (1) is rewritten:

$$p\,(1 + 1/\varepsilon) = C'(Q)$$

$$\Leftrightarrow (p - C')/p = 1/\varepsilon \qquad (2)$$

2. The marginal revenue and the average revenue have the same ordinate. Indeed, the average revenue is defined as the total revenue divided by the quantity, i.e., (a – bQ). The marginal revenue is equal to: (a – 2bQ). The slope of the marginal revenue is twice as steep as that of the average revenue.
3. With a linear demand function, the equilibrium quantity in a monopoly situation is equal to half of that obtained in a situation of pure and perfect competition.
4. The price elasticity of demand represents the change in the quantity demanded as a result of a change in price, i.e., $\varepsilon = (dQ/Q)/(dP/P) = (P/Q)\,(dQ/dP)$. The price elasticity of demand is always negative or nil.

In equation (2), we find that the monopoly market power depends on the price elasticity of demand: when price elasticity is low, the monopoly can raise its price sharply above the marginal cost.

The impact of monopoly on welfare: From a welfare perspective, the monopoly situation implies:

- a transfer of surplus from consumers to the monopoly, measured by area B. This area corresponds to the total profit made by the monopoly (Figure 1.5);
- a "*deadweight loss*": The monopoly profit appears to be lower than the decrease in consumer surplus. Indeed, the consumer surplus is equal to the area (A + B + D) in a competitive situation. In a monopoly situation, the consumer surplus is represented by area A. Consumers have therefore lost (B + D), while the monopoly has made a profit equal to area B: The loss of welfare is therefore equivalent to triangle D and is due to the fact that the increase in price leads some consumers to renounce buying the good.[5] Area D is equal to:

$$(1/2)\ \partial P \partial Q$$

Compared to a situation of pure and perfect competition, the monopoly reduces the total welfare: we speak of the "*allocative inefficiency*" of the monopoly.

Figure 1.5 Monopoly and Welfare

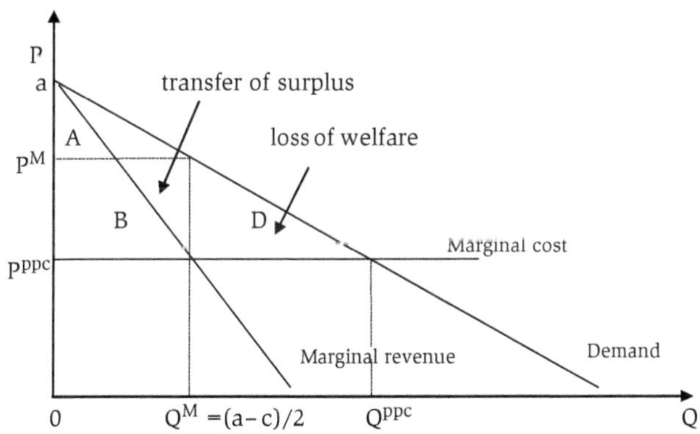

Other costs of the monopoly: Beyond allocative inefficiency, the monopoly can also generate other types of inefficiencies (Posner, 1976):

5. In 1954, Harberger estimated the value of this welfare loss in the case of the American economy. He concluded that the welfare loss was less than 0.1 % of the gross national product of the United States. Subsequent studies lead to different conclusions; for example, Cowling and Muller (1978) estimated the welfare loss at more than 7% of GNP. In the case of France, Jenny and Weber (1980) obtained a welfare loss of 7.4 %.

- *"Productive inefficiency"*: A monopoly may pay less attention to the drift in production costs. Indeed, in a competitive situation, any increase in production costs will lead to market exit. On the other hand, a monopoly can allow its production costs to slip, as it will partially pass on this increase in its price.
- *"Dynamic inefficiency"*: Compared to a firm in a competitive situation, a monopoly that is not threatened by the entry of competitors has less incentive to innovate, because it already receives a rent. Let's take a monopoly on a drug that brings it a profit of \$60. If the monopoly launches a therapeutic vaccine, a substitute for its drug, its profit will increase to \$100. The monopoly's incentive to find the vaccine is therefore equal to (\$100 - \$60), or \$40: The monopoly takes into account the fact that, by innovating, it replaces its own products and cannibalizes the sales of its drug. On the other hand, a firm in a competitive situation has a much stronger incentive to find the vaccine: It is equal to (\$100 - \$0) due to the fact that the firm does not make any profit ex-ante.

Pure and perfect competition and monopoly: A numerical illustration: We can illustrate the results obtained in a pure and perfect competition situation and in a monopoly situation through a numerical example.

Let's assume the following demand function:

$$P = \$\,100 - Q \quad \text{with} \quad Q = \Sigma_{i=1}^{n} q_i$$

The total cost function of each firm is equal to:

$$\text{Total cost (TC)} = 20q$$

In pure and perfect competition, we obtain the following price, quantity and profit (Figure 1.6):

$$P^{ppc} = c = \$20$$

$$Q^{ppc} = 80$$

$$\Pi^{ppc} = 0$$

Figure 1.6 Comparison Between Competition and Monopoly

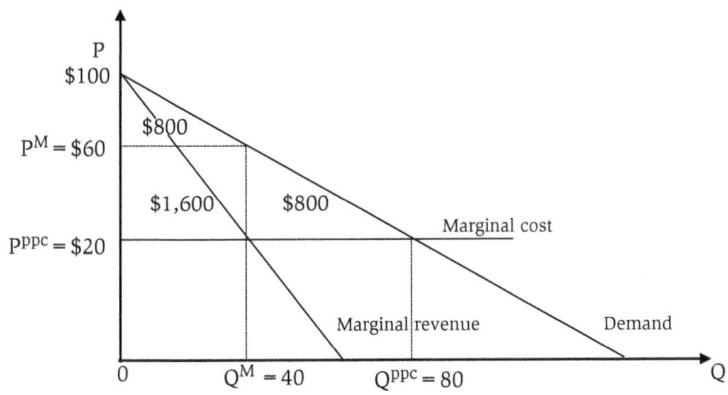

The total welfare in a situation of pure and perfect competition is equal to:

$$W^{ppc} = (100 - 20)^2/2 = \$3{,}200$$

In a monopoly situation, we obtain the following price, quantity and equilibrium profit:

$$P^M = \$60 > \$20$$

$$Q^M = 40 < 80$$

$$\Pi^M = \$1{,}600$$

The total welfare in a monopoly situation is equal to:

$$W^M = \$1{,}600 + (\$100 - \$60)\ 40/2$$

$$W^M = \$2{,}400 < \$3{,}200$$

We note that the monopoly price is higher than the competitive price ($60 > $20) and that the total quantity in a monopoly situation is equal to half of the total quantity in a pure and perfect competition situation. This results in a decrease in total welfare of $800. With linear functions, the loss of welfare is equal to half of the surplus transfer (i.e., the profit of the monopoly):

$$\text{Loss of welfare} = \$800 = 0.5\Pi^M$$

SECTION 2 BETWEEN COMPETITION AND MONOPOLY: COURNOT'S OLIGOPOLY

Between the two polar cases of pure and perfect competition and monopoly, we find intermediate market structures, and, in particular, those characterized by the presence of a small number of firms: oligopoly markets. Among the many models, the one developed by Cournot (1838) establishes an inverse relationship between the number of firms and the price: As the number of firms in the market increases, prices tend towards the marginal cost.

We shall start by analyzing the basic Cournot model with two firms, having the same costs and producing the same products (§1). We shall then study different variations on Cournot's model: We introduce different production costs, different products, and a leader, which makes its decision before the other (§2). We extend Cournot's model to more than two firms in order to show that the number of firms in the market plays a decisive role in how prices and profits evolve (§3).

§1 Cournot's Duopoly

Cournot's equilibrium: Consider two Firms (1 and 2) that produce the same product and must simultaneously choose the quantities they will produce (or their production capacities). It is assumed that each firm determines the quantity that maximizes its profit, taking the quantity of its rival as a given—"*the Cournot conjecture.*" Both firms have the same total cost function (TC), which is linear and with a positive marginal cost:

$$TC_i\ (q_i) = c\ q_i \qquad \text{with } c > 0 \qquad \text{and } i = 1, 2$$

The inverse demand function is also linear:

$$P = a - bQ$$

$$\text{with } a > c,\ b = 1 \text{ and } Q = q_1 + q_2$$

The profit of Firm 1 is written:[6]

$$\Pi_1 = p(Q)\ q_1 - cq_1$$

$$\Leftrightarrow \Pi_1 = (a - q_1 - q_2)\ q_1 - cq_1$$

Profit maximization leads to:

$$\Pi'_1 = 0$$

$$\Leftrightarrow a - 2q_1 - q_2 - c = 0$$

$$\Leftrightarrow q^*_1 = (a - q_2 - c)/2$$

$$\Leftrightarrow q^*_1 = (a - c)/2 - q_2/2 \qquad (1)$$

Equation (1) is the reaction function of Firm 1: It expresses the quantity that Firm 1 will produce, taking into account the quantity produced by its competitor Firm 2. Graphically, the reaction function of Firm 1, noted R_1, is a decreasing line.

6. The reasoning is, of course, symmetrical for Firm 2.

Figure 1.7 The Reaction Function of Firm 1

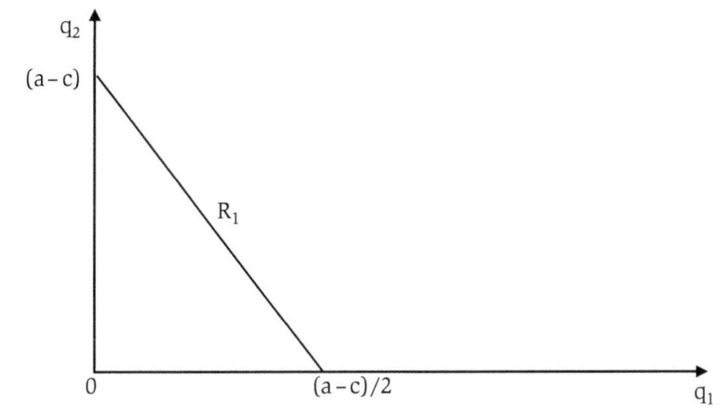

When Firm 2 doesn't produce anything, Firm 1's best response is to produce the monopoly quantity (a – c)/2, as we see on the x-axis (for $q_2 = 0$) of Figure 1.7. Symmetrically, Firm 1 will produce nothing if Firm 2's output is equal to that obtained in a pure and perfect competitive market, namely (a – c), as we can see on the y-axis (for $q_1 = 0$).

By symmetry, we obtain the reaction function of Firm 2:

$$q^*_2 = (a - c)/2 - q_1/2$$

The reaction function of Firm 2 is shown in Figure 1.8. When Firm 1 doesn't produce anything, Firm 2's best response is to produce the monopoly quantity (a – c)/2, as we can see on the y-axis (for $q_1 = 0$). Symmetrically, Firm 2 will produce nothing if Firm 1's output is equal to that obtained in a perfectly competitive market, namely (a – c), as we can see on the x-axis (for $q_1 = 0$).

Figure 1.8 The Reaction Function of Firm 2

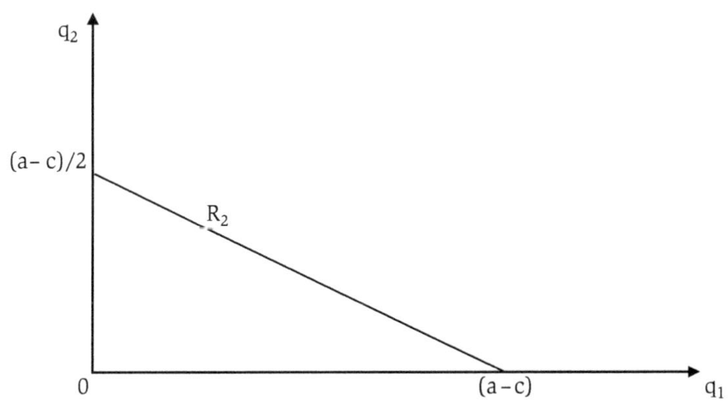

Cournot's equilibrium (also called a "*Cournot-Nash equilibrium*,"[7] by reference to game theory) corresponds to the intersection of the two reaction functions (Figure 1.9): At point E, each firm will produce the Cournot's quantity q^{cour}. Graphically, we see that the total quantity in a Cournot's model is greater than the quantity of a monopoly (a - c)/2 but less than the quantity produced in a perfectly competitive market (a - c); Cournot's duopoly is an intermediate market structure between pure and perfect competition and monopoly.

Figure 1.9 Cournot's Equilibrium

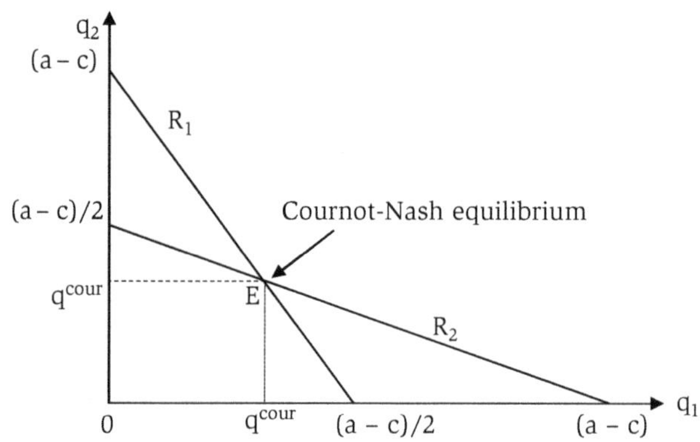

Algebraically, Cournot's equilibrium can be calculated from the two reaction functions:

$$q^*_1 = (a - c)/2 - q_2/2$$

$$q^*_2 = (a - c)/2 - q_1/2$$

By replacing q^*_1 in q^*_2 (or vice versa), we obtain the Cournot's quantities for each firm:

$$q^{cour}_1 = q^{cour}_2 = (a - c)/3$$

We then obtain the price, total quantity, and total profit in a Cournot's situation:

$$p^{cour} = (a + 2c)/3$$

$$Q^{cour} = 2(a - c)/3$$

$$\Pi^{cour} = 2(a - c)^2/9$$

Comparing Cournot's model to a competitive or monopoly situation: Compared to pure and perfect competition, a Cournot's duopoly reduces the total quantity

7. A Nash equilibrium is a situation in which no player has a unilateral interest in changing its choice; given the choice of other players, this is its "*best re.*"

produced. With linear functions, Cournot's supply is equal to two-thirds of the quantity in a pure and perfect competition situation:

$$Q^{cour} = 2(a - c)/3 < Q^{ppc} = (a - c)$$

The price in Cournot's model is therefore higher than the pure and perfect competitive price:

$$P^{cour} = (a + 2c)/3 = c + (a - c)/3 > P^{ppc} = c$$

Compared to a monopoly, a Cournot's duopoly offers a higher total quantity and therefore a lower price:

$$Q^{cour} = 2(a - c)/3 > Q^{M} = (a - c)/2$$

$$P^{cour} = (a + 2c)/3 < P^{M} = (a + c)/2$$

The sum of the duopoly profits is less than those in a monopoly situation:

$$\Pi^{cour} = 2(a - c)^2/9 < \Pi^{M} = (a - c)^2/4$$

Cournot's duopoly is, strictly speaking, an "*intermediate market structure,*" between pure and perfect competition and monopoly, whether in terms of price, total quantity, or profits (Figure 1.10).

Figure 1.10 Cournot's Duopoly as an Intermediate Market

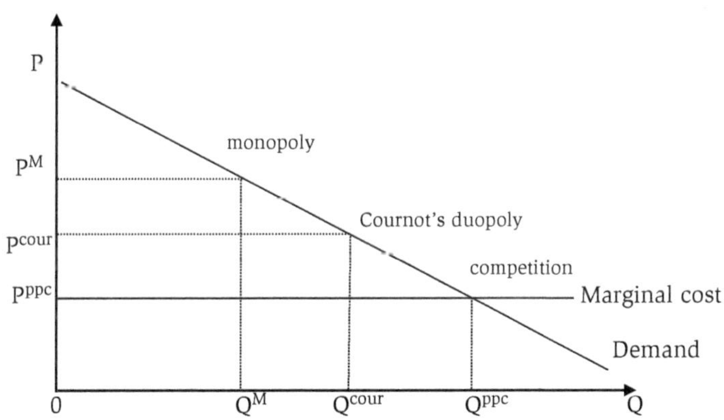

Cournot's duopoly: A numerical illustration: We can illustrate the results obtained in Cournot's duopoly through a numerical example.

Let's assume the following demand function:

$$P = \$100 - Q \quad \text{with } Q = q_1 + q_2$$

The total cost function of each firm is equal to:

$$\text{Total cost (TC)} = 20q$$

In Cournot's duopoly, we obtain the following price, quantity and total profit (Figure 1.11):

$$P^{cour} = \$46.7$$

$$Q^{cour} = 53.3$$

$$\Pi^{cour} = \$1{,}423$$

Figure 1.11 Cournot's Equilibrium: A Numerical Illustration

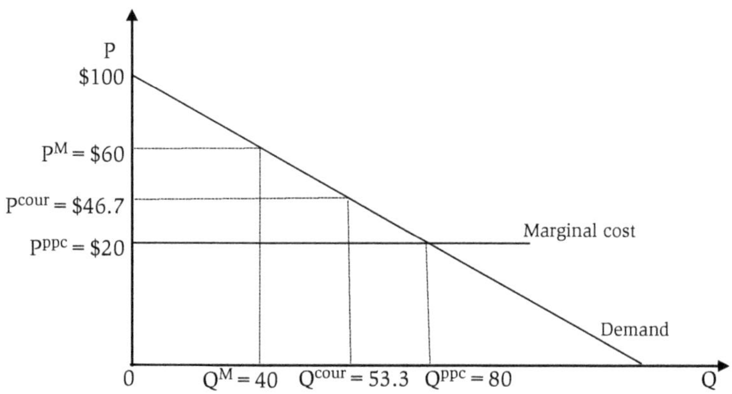

The total welfare is equal to:

$$W^{cour} = \$1{,}423 + (\$100 - \$46.7) \times \$53.3/2$$

$$W^{cour} = \$2{,}845.4$$

We note that Cournot's price is higher than the pure and perfect competition price but lower than the monopoly price. Similarly, the total quantity in Cournot's model is greater than the monopoly quantity, but less than the quantity obtained in a perfectly competitive market. Regarding total welfare, it is higher than in a monopoly situation but lower than the total welfare achieved in a perfectly competitive market:

$$P^{cpp} = \$20 < P^{cour} = \$46.7 < P^{M} = \$60$$

$$Q^{M} = 40 < Q^{cour} = 53.3 < Q^{cpp} = 80$$

$$W^{M} = \$2{,}400 < W^{cour} = \$2{,}845.4 < W^{cpp} = \$3{,}200$$

The transition from a monopoly to a Cournot duopoly can be explained intuitively. When Firm 1 is alone on the market, there is no competitive pressure on it and it makes a high profit of $1,600. The entry of Firm 2 has a double negative effect on the profit of Firm 1:

- Firm 1 is now under competitive pressure from the newcomer, which reduces the total profit on the market from $1,600 to $1,423, a decrease of $177.

- Firm 1 must share the market and therefore the remaining total profit; this effect represents a decrease of \$711.5 in its profit.

The entry of Firm 2 into the market therefore reduced the profit of Firm 1 from \$1,600 to \$711.5, a decrease of \$888.5.

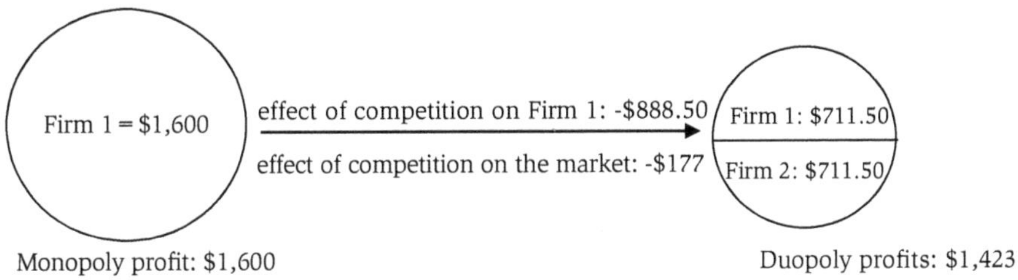

§2 Variations on Cournot's Duopoly

Cournot's duopoly with asymmetric costs: Until now, we have assumed that the two firms had the same marginal cost c. If we introduce different costs, the total cost (TC) function of each firm becomes:

$$TCi\ (qi) = c_i\ qi \quad \text{with } c_i > 0 \text{ and } i = 1, 2$$

After profit maximization, we obtain the reaction functions of both firms:

$$q^*_1 = (a - 2c_1 + c_2)/3$$

$$q^*_2 = (a - 2c_2 + c_1)/3$$

We see that a firm with a lower cost than its competitor will have a higher level of production and a higher profit. For example, if Firm 1 is a "*high cost*" firm and Firm 2 is a "*low cost*" firm, the latter will produce more. In our previous numerical example, if $c_1 = \$30$ and $c_2 = \$20$, we obtain the following equilibrium quantities:

$$q^*_1 = (100 - 60 + 20)/3 = 20$$

$$q^*_2 = (100 - 40 + 30)/3 = 30$$

Cournot's duopoly with differentiated products: We have so far assumed that Firm 1 and Firm 2 both offer an identical product. If we introduce product differentiation, the demand function of Firm 1 is:

$$P_1 = a - \beta q_1 - \gamma q_2 \quad \text{with } \beta, \gamma \geq 0$$

The coefficient β measures the degree of product differentiation: When β tends towards γ, the two products are close substitutes. Indeed, Firm 1's product is impacted in the same way by an increase in the quantity q_2 of its competitor as by an increase in its own quantity q_1. On the other hand, when the coefficient γ tends towards zero, the two products are barely substitutable: If $\lambda = 0$, the two products are completely independent.

The same reasoning applies to Firm 2, whose demand function can be written:

$$P_2 = a - \beta q_2 - \gamma q_1 \text{ with } \beta, \gamma \geq 0$$

For simplicity, we assume that the marginal production cost is zero.
The profit function of Firm 1 is then written:

$$\Pi_1 = (a - \beta q_1 - \gamma q_2)\, q_1$$

Maximizing the profit of Firm 1 implies:

$$\Pi'_1 = 0$$

$$\Leftrightarrow a - 2\beta q_1 - \gamma q_2 = 0$$

$$\Leftrightarrow q^*_1 = (a - \gamma q_2)/2\beta$$

Similarly, for Firm 2, profit maximization implies:

$$q^*_2 = (a - \gamma q_1)/2\beta$$

By integrating the reaction function q^*_1 into q^*_2 (or vice versa), we obtain the following Cournot's equilibrium:

$$q_1^{\,cour} = a/\,(2\beta + \gamma)$$

$$p_1^{\,cour} = a\beta/\,(2\beta + \gamma)$$

$$\Pi_1^{\,cour} = (a^2\beta)/\,(2\beta + \gamma)^2$$

We find that as product differentiation increases, so do prices and profits. On the other hand, when the products are perfectly substitutable ($\beta = \lambda$), we find the same result as in the case of a Cournot's duopoly with homogeneous products (and a zero marginal cost). We therefore see that the intensity of competition depends on the degree of product differentiation: If product differentiation is high, competition between firms is low.

A duopoly with a leader: In a Cournot's duopoly, it is assumed that both firms make their decisions at the same time; it is a simultaneous game. We can also study the case in which one of the two firms, called "*leader*," decides before the other; this leader/follower model is the Stackelberg (1934) duopoly.

Let's take two Firms 1 and 2, with the same marginal cost of production c. The demand function is linear:

$$P = a - bQ \quad \text{with } b = 1$$

Firm 1 chooses its production level before Firm 2. We therefore have a two-stage sequential game:

Firm 1 chooses q_1

↓ stage 1

Firm 2 sets q_2

↓ stage 2

Firms 1 and 2 are in competition

To solve this sequential game, we must apply the method of "*backward induction,*" consisting of starting from the second stage of the game and going back to the first stage.

In the second stage, the profit function of Firm 2 is:

$$\Pi_2 = (a - Q) - cq_2$$

$$\Leftrightarrow \Pi_2 = (a - q_2 - q_1)\, q_2 - cq_2$$

Maximizing the profit of Firm 2 at the second stage provides the reaction function q^*_2:

$$\Pi'_2 = 0$$

$$\Leftrightarrow a - 2q_2 - q_1 - c = 0$$

$$\Leftrightarrow q^*_2 = (a - c)/2 - q_1/2$$

In the first stage, Firm 1 anticipates the reaction of Firm 2 and integrates it into its profit function:

$$\Pi_1 = [a - (q_1 + q^*_2)]q_1 - cq_1$$

$$\Leftrightarrow \Pi_1 = [a - (q_1 + (a - c)/2 - q_1/2)]q_1 - cq_1$$

Maximizing the profit of Firm 1 implies:

$$\Pi'_1 = 0$$

$$\Leftrightarrow a - 2q_1 - (a - c)/2 + q_1 - c = 0$$

$$\Leftrightarrow q^{stack}{}_1 = (a - c)/2 > q^{cour}{}_1$$

We infer the quantity of Firm 2, which is the "*follower*":

$$q^*_2 = (a - c)/2 - q_1/2$$

$$\Leftrightarrow q^*_2 = (a - c)/2 - [(a - c)/2]/2$$

$$\Leftrightarrow q^{stack}{}_2 = (a - c)/4 < q^{cour}{}_2$$

We notice that there is a "*first mover advantage*": Firm 1 takes advantage of the fact that it sets its production level first to produce more than it would have produced in a Cournot's duopoly model. It sets a quantity that is equal to that of a monopoly. Firm 2, on the other hand, sets a lower production level than it would have set in a

Cournot's model; it produces half as much as Firm 1. The profit of Firm 1 is twice that of Firm 2. It is higher than in the Cournot's model, while that of Firm 2 is lower:

$$\Pi^{stack}_1 = (a - c)^2/8 > \Pi^{cour}_1 = (a - c)^2/9$$

$$\Pi^{stack}_2 = (a - c)^2/16 < \Pi^{cour}_2 = (a - c)^2/9$$

We also notice that the equilibrium in the Stackelberg's model is more competitive than in the Cournot's model, because the total production is higher (and therefore the price lower):

$$Q^{stack} = 3(a - c)/4 > Q^{cour} = 2(a - c)/3$$

$$P^{stack} = (a + 3c)/4 < P^{cour} = (a + 2c)/3$$

§3 From Duopoly to Cournot's Oligopoly

Cournot's analysis based on a duopoly can be generalized to more than two firms.

Cournot's equilibrium with N firms: Suppose we have N firms (with $N \geq 2$), all having the same marginal cost c. The inverse demand function is linear:

$$P = a - bQ \quad \text{with } Q = \Sigma_{i=1}^{n} q_i$$

With $b = 1$ and taking Firm 1 from the N firms, we can rewrite the demand function as follows:

$$P = a - bQ_{-1} - bq_1$$

with Q_{-1} being the sum of the quantities of all firms other than Firm 1.

As before, Firm 1 maximizes its profit by taking the quantity Q_{-1} as an exogenous factor:

$$\Pi_1 = [a - (Q_{-1} + q_1)]q_1 - cq_1$$

Maximizing the profit of Firm 1 implies:

$$\partial \Pi_1/\partial q_1 = 0$$

$$\Leftrightarrow (a - Q_{-1} - 2q_1 - c) = 0 \qquad (1)$$

As the firms are identical, we have $q_1 = q_2 = \ldots q_N$ and the equality (1) can be rewritten:

$$q_1 = q_2 = q^{cour} = (a - c)/(N + 1)$$

We notice that when N increases, the quantity each firm supplies decreases. When N tends towards $+\infty$, the quantity each firm produces becomes infinitesimal, as in a situation of pure and perfect competition:

$$lim_{N\to+\infty} q^{cour} = lim_{N\to+\infty} \frac{a-c}{N+1} = 0$$

The total quantity on the market is equal to:

$$Q^{cour} = Nq^{cour} = [N/(N + 1)] (a - c)$$

When N increases, the total quantity on the market increases and tends towards the quantity produced in a situation of pure and perfect competition:

$$lim_{N\to+\infty} Q^{cour} = lim_{N\to+\infty} (\frac{N}{N+1})(a-c) = (a-c)$$

The equilibrium price in Cournot's model is:

$$P^{cour} = (a + Nc)/(N + 1)$$

When N increases, the Cournot's price tends towards the marginal cost, i.e., towards the cost in a situation of pure and perfect competition:

$$lim_{N\to+\infty} P^{cour} = lim_{N\to+\infty} \left[\frac{a}{N+1} + \frac{Nc}{N+1}\right] = c$$

The profit of a firm is equal to:

$$\Pi^{cour} = (a - c)^2/(N + 1)^2$$

We notice that a firm's profit depends on the number of firms on the market. Indeed, when N tends towards $+\infty$, the profit of each firm tends towards zero:

$$lim_{N\to+\infty} \Pi^{cour} = lim_{N\to+\infty} \frac{(a-c)^2}{(N+1)^2} = 0$$

In Cournot's oligopoly model, the number of firms in the market plays a decisive role in the evolution of price and profits.

We can now compare Cournot's model with the two polar cases—pure and perfect competition and monopoly—taking as a variable the number of firms in the market (Figure 1.12). A monopoly situation may correspond to one firm in the market or several firms that form a perfect cartel (dotted line); in this case, the price P_M is high compared to the marginal cost c, regardless of the number of firms in the market. On the other hand, in a situation of pure and perfect competition (e.g., a Bertrand's competition between two firms or a single firm on a perfectly contestable market; *see* below), the price P_C is low and equal to the marginal cost c. Between these two polar cases, we find that the Cournot's price decreases when the number of firms N increases and tends asymptotically towards the pure and perfect competitive price.

Figure 1.12 Price Evolution and Number of Firms

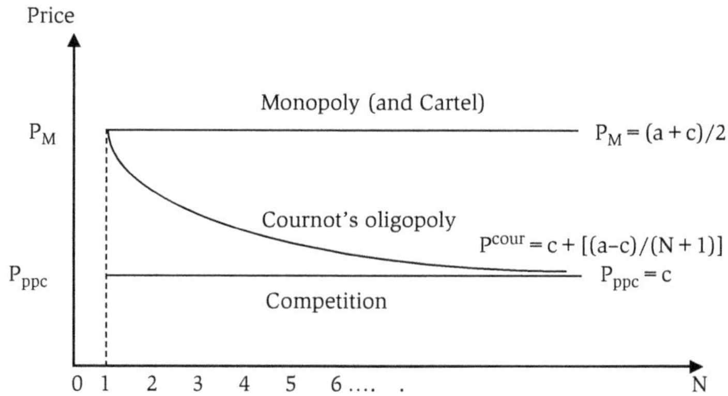

Cournot's oligopoly: A numerical illustration: We can illustrate the impact on prices of the Cournot's model with N firms, through a numerical example.

Suppose that N = 3 and the marginal cost of each firm is \$20. The demand function is linear:

$$P = 100 - Q$$

Cournot's equilibrium gives the following results:

$$q^{cour} = (100 - 20)/4 = 20$$

$$Q^{cour} = (3 \times 20) = 60$$

$$P^* = \$40$$

$$\Pi^{cour} = \$1{,}200, \text{ or } \$400 \text{ per firm}$$

If a new competitor enters the market, the number of firms increases from N = 3 to N = 4, resulting in an increase in total production, but a decrease in production for each firm already in the market and a decrease in price and profits:

$$q^{cour} = (100 - 20)/5 = 16$$

$$Q^{cour} = (4 \times 16) = 64$$

$$P^{cour} = \$36$$

$$\Pi^{cour} = \$1{,}024 \text{ i.e., } \$256 \text{ per firm}$$

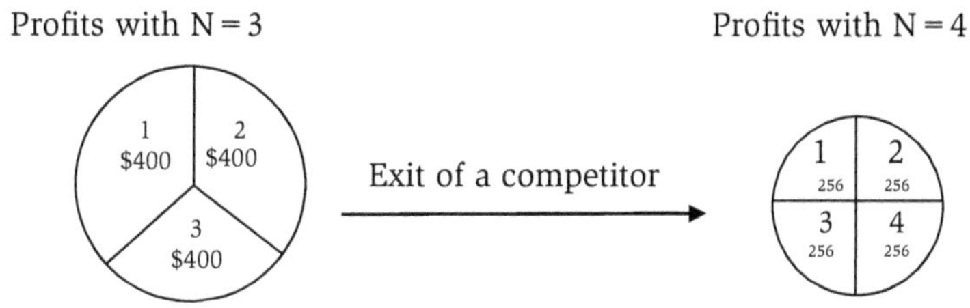

Conversely, if a competitor exits the market, for example after a merger, the market becomes a duopoly and we find the previous results. The decrease in the number of firms reduces the total production but increases the production of the two remaining firms—their price and their profits:

$$q^{cour} = (100 - 20)/3 = 26.60$$

$$Q^{cour} = (2 \times 26.60) = 53.30$$

$$P^{cour} = \$46.70$$

$$\Pi^{cour} = \$711.50 \text{ per firm}$$

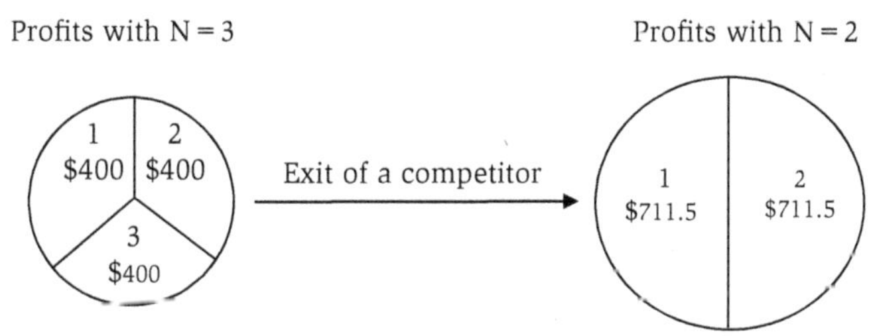

The impact of the number of firms on welfare: Let us now consider the implications that the Cournot's model with N firms has on welfare. The consumer surplus is equal to:

$$CS^{cour} = N^2(a - c)^2/2(N + 1)^2$$

We can see that the consumer surplus increases when the number of firms increases and gets closer to the pure and perfect competition level:

$$lim_{N\to+\infty} CS^{cour} = lim_{N\to+\infty} \frac{N^2(a-c)^2}{2(N+1)^2} = (a-c)^2/2$$

The total profit is equal to:

$$\Pi^{cour} = N(a - c)^2/(N + 1)^2$$

The total profit decreases continuously (to reach zero) as the number of firms increases:

$$lim_{N\to+\infty} \Pi^{cour} = lim_{N\to+\infty} \frac{N(a-c)^2}{(N+1)^2} = 0$$

The total welfare increases as the number of firms increases, which means that the positive effect of a price decrease on consumer surplus outweighs the negative impact on profits:

$$W^{cour} = [(a - c)^2/ 2b]\ [(N^2 + 2N)/(N + 1)^2]$$

$$\partial W^{cour}/\partial N > 0$$

Cournot's model with a fixed cost: We have seen that in Cournot's oligopoly model, the total welfare and consumer surplus always increase with the number of firms. However, this result is based on the assumption that firms do not incur a fixed cost of entry.

Suppose now that each firm bears a fixed cost F in addition to its marginal cost c:

$$TC(q_i) = cq_i + F \text{ with } i = 1, 2, \ldots N \text{ and } F > 0$$

If the consumer surplus is not affected by the fixed cost, the total profit is modified:

$$\Pi^{cour} = [N(a - c)^2/(N + 1)^2] - NF$$

We can therefore note that the total welfare does not increase continuously with the number of firms; there is an optimal number of firms that maximizes the welfare. This is due to the fact that an increase in N has two opposite effects:

- on the one hand, consumer surplus increases because prices decrease;
- on the other, firms' profits decrease and can even become negative, as each firm bears a fixed cost.

There is therefore a trade-off between allocative efficiency (a lower price due to a greater number of firms) and productive efficiency (a greater number of firms reduces economies of scale).

The profit function of a firm in Cournot's model is equal to:

$$\Pi_i^{cour} = (p^{cour} - c)q_i^{cour} - F$$

$$\Leftrightarrow = \left(\frac{a + Nc}{N+1} - c\right)\left(\frac{a-c}{N+1}\right) - F$$

$$\Leftrightarrow = \frac{(a-c)^2}{(N+1)^2} - F$$

The maximum number of firms in the market is such that the profit for each firm is positive or equal to zero (but never negative):

$$\Pi_i^{cour} - F \geq 0$$

$$\Leftrightarrow N \leq \frac{(a-c)}{\sqrt{F}} - 1$$

The maximum number of firms (N) depends on three main factors:

- marginal cost (c): The lower the marginal cost, the higher the number of firms;
- market demand (a): The higher the demand, the higher the number of firms;
- fixed costs (F): When fixed costs are high, few firms can remain profitable and stay on the market.

If we use the previous numerical example (a = \$100; c = \$20), the number of firms decreases with the level of the fixed cost F:

- if the fixed cost is \$25, the maximum number of firms is 15;
- if the fixed cost is \$100, the maximum number of firms is 7;
- if the fixed cost is \$1,600, we are in a situation of natural monopoly, since there is only room for one firm.

Cournot's oligopoly: A case study: Cournot's analysis can be applied to a specific market: The 3G mobile phone market in France after the entry of a fourth operator in 2012, Free Mobile. A simulation of the entry effects was carried out in 2009 by the French Treasury Department, based on a Cournot modeling with linear functions.

In this simulation, the marginal cost of a mobile operator is equal to c. The price of a mobile phone subscription before the entry is equal to p_0 and the number of subscribers is q_0 (Figure 1.13). After the entry of the fourth operator, the price drops to p_1. The decrease in price leads to an increase in subscriptions to q_1. The consumer surplus increases by the area (A + B); the producer surplus decreases (the area A is lost), but is partially offset by an increase in quantities with the arrival of new customers (area C). The total welfare therefore increases and is equivalent to the surface area (B + C).

Figure 1.13 Impact of the Entry of a Fourth Mobile Phone Operator

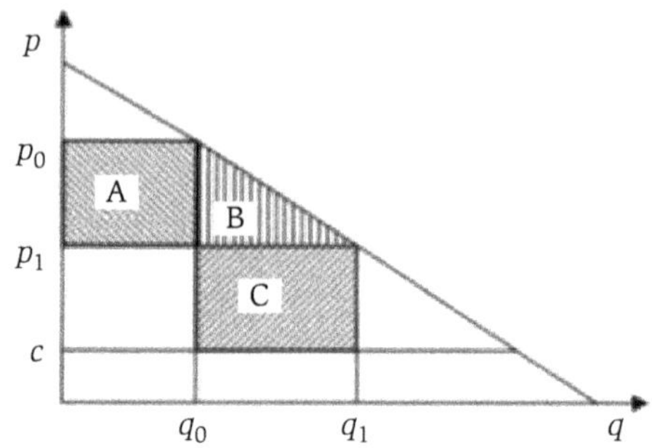

Source: Directorate general of the Treasury (2009).

By setting the value of several parameters (in particular, by taking a price elasticity of demand equal to –1), the study concludes that the entry of Free Mobile should reduce prices by 7%. This price decrease leads to a reduction in profits by €852 million per year for the three incumbents, and an increase in the consumer surplus of €1,224 million per year (Table 1.2). The total welfare therefore will increase by €373 million per year. On the other hand, the change from four to five operators would be less effective for the welfare: The net gain would be only €155 million per year.[8]

Table 1.2 Impact on Welfare of the Entry of a Fourth and Fifth Operator

Impact in Millions of Euros/Year	*From 3 to 4 Operators*	*From 4 to 5 Operators*
Change in annual consumer surplus	1,224	643
Change in operators' annual surplus (excluding fixed network investment cost)	-852	-488
Change in total welfare	372	155

Source: Directorate general of the Treasury (2009).

8. In retrospect, Free Mobile's entry in 2012 led to a price decrease of around 25% over two years, which was greater than that forecast in the model.

SECTION 3 MARKET STRUCTURE AND MARKET POWER: THE STRUCTURALIST APPROACH

Based on these microeconomic analyses, a school of thought called the "*Harvard School*" (or, "*Structuralist School*") was developed during the 1950s-1970s under the impetus of authors such as Bain (1956) or Mason.

This School tried to establish a causal (but indirect) link between market concentration and market power:[9] If a market is highly concentrated, firms are likely to have strong market power. The extent of entry barriers and the degree of product differentiation will also play a key role in assessing firms' market power.

The Structuralist School has strong implications on competition policy: The primary objective of antitrust authorities is to limit market concentration and to maintain a certain distribution of market power, thereby avoiding anti-competitive behaviors.

We'll start by presenting the well-known SCP model, which summarizes the structuralist approach (§1). We'll continue by examining different empirical tests that verify the relevance of the SCP model (§2).

§1 The SCP Model

The structuralists' views can be presented through the well-known SCP model:

- market structures (S) are characterized by the number of firms, market share distribution, the degree of product differentiation, and the height of entry barriers. When there are few firms on the market—when market concentration, product differentiation, and entry barriers are high—the market structure will be close to that of a monopoly. Conversely, if the market is fragmented and poorly concentrated, products homogeneous, and entry barriers low, the market structure will be similar to that of a perfectly competitive market;
- conduct (C) refers mainly to the pricing and investment strategies of firms: Behaviors of firms depend on market structures;
- performance (P) expresses the firm's market power and is measured by the margin rate or the Lerner's index.

9. This filiation does not mean that structuralists explicitly claim to be part of the microeconomic tradition. Rather, it is the result of a convergence of views, which the Chicago authors rightly pointed out: "The tie-in between a structuralist approach to competition and a perfectly competitive perspective ought to be made explicit. The market-structure approach to competition assumes that structure determines the behavior of firms in the industry and that behavior determines the quality of the industry's performance. But this is precisely the perspective of the perfectly competitive benchmark school. Perfect competition theory assumes the same sort of one-way determinism between structure, conduct and performance. (...) An attack on the perfectly competitive perspective, therefore, is an attack on the entire structuralist methodology" (Armentano, 1996).

The structuralist authors try to establish a causal link between these three parameters: The characteristics of market structures (S) determine the conduct of firms (C), which explains their performance (P):

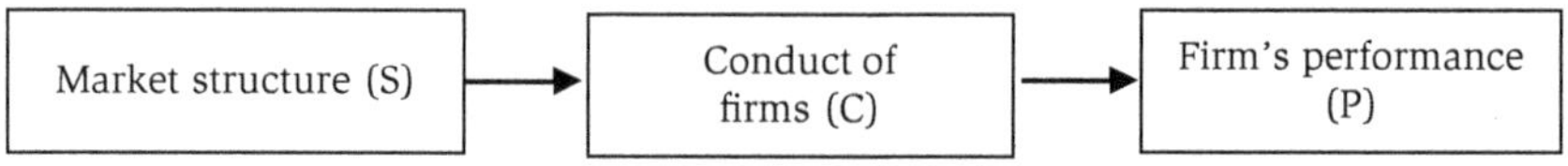

A generalization of the SCP model: The relationship between market structure, behavior and performance can be found in the oligopoly theory (Cowling & Waterson, 1976).

Let us consider a Cournot's oligopoly with N firms ($N \geq 2$) producing a homogeneous good. The demand function is:

$$P(Q) \text{ with } Q = (\Sigma q_i) \text{ and } i = 1, \dots N$$

The profit function of a Firm i is:

$$\Pi(q_i) = P(Q)q_i - C_i(q_i) \qquad (1)$$

With C_i, the total cost of a Firm i.

Profit maximization implies (first-order condition):

$$P(Q) + q_i (\partial p/\partial Q)(\partial Q/\partial q_i) - C'_i = 0 \qquad (2)$$

with $C'_i = \partial C_i/\partial q_i$

$\partial Q/\partial q_i$ represents the variation in the total quantity resulting from the variation in the quantity produced by a Firm i. This expression can be divided in two elements: The production q_i of a Firm i and the total production Q_j of other firms. We can write:

$$\partial Q/\partial q_i = \partial (\Sigma q_i)/ \partial q_i = \partial q_i/\partial q_i + \partial Q_j/\partial q_i = (1 + a_i)$$

a_i represents the "*conjectural variation*," i.e., the anticipation of a Firm i on the competitor's reaction to a variation in its own production level. In Cournot's model, since each firm takes the production of its competitor as a given, we have: $a_i = 0$.

Equation (2) can be rewritten:

$$p(Q) + q_i(\partial p/\partial Q)(1 + a_i) - C'_i = 0 \qquad (3)$$

For a Firm i, Lerner's index is therefore equal to:

$$(p - C'_i)/p = s_i(1 + a_i)/\varepsilon \qquad (4)$$

with s_i the market share of a Firm i and ε the price elasticity of demand.

We find that market power increases with market share, for a given level of price elasticity and conjectural variation.

At the sector level, the average margin is equal to:

$$\frac{\sum_{i=1}^{n} pq_i - \sum_{i=1}^{n} C'_i q_i}{pQ} = \frac{\sum_{i=1}^{n} s_i(1+a_i)q_i}{Q} \qquad (5)$$

Let us take as a measure of concentration the Herfindahl index (noted H):

$$H = \sum_{i=1}^{n} s_i^2$$

with $s_i \in [0, 1]$, $i = 1, 2, \ldots, n$

The H index is between 1 in the case of a monopoly and 0 in the case of a perfectly competitive market.[10] The H index takes into account both the number of firms and the distribution of market shares: For a given number of firms, as the distribution of market shares increases, so does the Herfindahl index.[11]

As $s_i = q_i/Q$, equality (5) can be rewritten:

Market structure (S)

Conduct (C)

$$\frac{\sum_{i=1}^{n} pq_i - \sum_{i=1}^{n} C'_i\, q_i}{pQ} = \frac{H(1 + a_i)}{\varepsilon}$$

Performance (P)

We find that the performance (P), measured by the average margin rate, is an increasing function of the market concentration, measured by H; as market concentration increases, so do margin rates. H also depends on the conduct (C) of firms in the market through the conjectural variation.

However, the margin rate is limited by the price elasticity of demand; in a monopoly ($H = 1$ and $a_i = 0$), we find a well-known result: The monopoly power is limited only by the price elasticity of demand ε. When the market is oligopolistic, the value of the price elasticity of demand can be interpreted as an indicator of the degree of product differentiation; a low price elasticity of demand means that substitutability between products is limited, which increases the margin rate.

10. Indeed, in a competitive sector, $H = n(1/n^2) = 1/n$. The H index is developed in detail in Chapter 6.
11. By using the variance of market shares (noted σ^2), the H index can be rewritten: $H = n\sigma^2 + 1/n$.

§2 Empirical Tests of the SCP Model

The SCP model has generated a lot of empirical tests.[12] Considering the difficulty of observing a firm's conduct (C), the SCP model tests establish a direct relationship between the structural characteristics of markets (S) and the firm's performance (P):

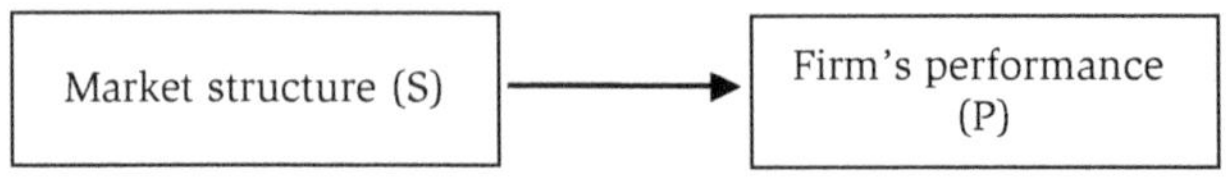

Bain's pioneering study: Bain (1951, 1956) was one of the first to empirically assess the influence of entry barriers and industrial concentration on market power. In accordance with the oligopoly theory, Bain postulates that market power increases with the degree of market concentration and the height of entry barriers. In a 1956 statistical study of a sample of 20 manufacturing industries, Bain measured market concentration using the concentration ratio (CR), defined as the sum of the market shares (rated s) of the M largest firms, over a total of N firms, i.e.:

$$CR_m = \sum_{i=1}^{M} s_i \; x\, 100$$

with $s_i \in [0, 1]$ and $i = 1, \ldots, M, M + 1, \ldots, N$

Bain uses the CR_4 ratio, i.e., the sum of the market shares of the four largest firms in each industry. Because the marginal cost is difficult to estimate, a firm's performance is not directly measured by the Lerner index but by taking earnings per share. Bain analyzes the entry conditions in each industry, distinguishing three types of obstacles:

- economies of scale: If the optimal minimum size is high compared to the market size, entry of new competitors is unlikely. Indeed, a newcomer faces a dilemma: If it enters with the optimal minimum size, it risks causing prices to fall; if it enters with a small production capacity, it suffers a cost disadvantage compared to the insiders;
- product differentiation: In a market with highly differentiated products, consumers are loyal to existing brands, which hinders the entry of a new competitor. Indeed, the newcomer must either make a brand investment to become known by consumers, or lower its prices to attract them;
- absolute cost advantage: When an incumbent firm controls scarce inputs, entrants cannot access the market with the same cost conditions.

After identifying the three main entry barriers, Bain makes a (relative) assessment of their level in each industry and distinguishes three groups: industries with high barriers, substantial barriers, and low barriers. Bain links, for each group, the

12. For an exhaustive study, we refer to Weiss (1987).

concentration ratio and the profit rate and obtains two results that confirm the SCP paradigm (Table 1.3):

- the profit rate is on average higher in industries with high entry barriers;
- within each group, the profit rate increases with the degree of market concentration.

Table 1.3 Bain's Results

Industry	*Profit Rate (in %)*	*Concentration Ratio (CR_4)*
High barriers		
Automobile	23.9%	90%
Cigarettes	12.6	90
Spirits	18.6	75
Typewriters	18	79
Ink pens	21.8	57
Average	**19**	**78**
Substantial barriers		
Copper	14.6	92
Steel	11.2	45
Agricultural machinery	13.4	36
Petroleum refining	12.9	37
Soap	15.8	79
Shoes	13.4	28
Gypsum	15.4	85
Metal containers	10.7	78
Average	**13.4**	**60**
Low barriers		
Preserves	9.8	27
Cement	14.3	30
Flour	10.1	29
Butcher's shop	5.1	41
Rayon	18	78
Low-cost shoes	11	28
Pneumatic tires	12.7	77
Average	**11.6**	**44**

Source: Bain (1956).

Econometric studies of the SCP model: Following Bain's pioneering study, econometric tests were conducted on individual data sets and at the industry level in the 1960s-1970s. In particular, Collins and Preston (1969) studied the relationship between market concentration and profitability in a sample of 417 American manufacturing industries, distinguishing between consumer and production goods industries. Unlike Bain, the authors did not explicitly consider entry barriers, assuming that a high market concentration was the result of high entry barriers. The equation tested is:

$$\text{Price-cost margin} = a_1 + a_2CR_4 + a_3K$$

The variable K represents the capital intensity of the industry, i.e., the ratio of capital to total sales. Indeed, the price-cost margin must be higher in highly capital-intensive industries, since it includes the return on capital. Collins and Preston obtain the following results for consumer goods industries:

$$\text{Price-cost margin} = 17.36 + 0.199^{*}\ CR_4 + 0.103\ K \qquad R^2 = 0.38$$

(*) statistically significant result at 1%.

We note that the coefficient of the concentration ratio CR_4 is high and statistically significant: A 10% increase in the concentration ratio increases the price-cost margin by 1.99% on average.

For the manufacturing goods industries, the impact of market concentration on the price-cost margin appears to be lower and less significant:

$$\text{Price-cost margin} = 19.48 + 0.033^{*}\ CR_4 + 0.133\ K \qquad R^2 = 0.26$$

(*) statistically significant result at 10%.

Indeed, a 10% increase in concentration ratio only increases margins by 0.33%. Collins and Preston explain this result by the fact that entry barriers are lower in goods-producing industries, given the low level of product differentiation.

Several econometric studies have taken into account entry barriers (which Collins and Preston do not do), particularly those related to economies of scale and product differentiation. Most of these studies concludes that product differentiation (measured by the ratio of advertising expenditure to turnover) has a strong influence on market power, while market concentration as such has a positive but more limited influence. For instance, Strickland and Weiss (1976) study the determinants of the price/cost margin on a sample of manufacturing industries, introducing a measure of economies of scale (the optimal minimum size relative to the total output, noted MES) and product differentiation (the ratio of advertising expenditure to turnover, noted ASR), in addition to capital intensity (KSR). In the consumer goods industries, the authors find a strong impact of product differentiation (ASR) and optimal minimum size (MES) on the price-cost margin:

$$\text{Price-cost margin} = 17.83 + 0.095\ CR^{*}_4 - 0.004\ KSR + 1.396\ ASR^{**} + 0.520\ MES^{***}$$

(*) statistically significant at 10%.
(**) statistically significant at 1%.
(***) statistically significant at 5%.

For production goods, the regression also highlights the role of product differentiation (SRP), while the variable measuring economies of scale (MES) does not appear significant:

$$\text{Price-cost margin} = 17.23 + 0.06\ CR^{*}_{4} + 0.119\ KSR^{**} + 1.778\ ASR^{**} - 0.142\ MES$$

(*) statistically significant at 10%.

(**) statistically significant at 1%.

The implication for competition policy: In the SCP paradigm, market structures play a decisive role; if there are few firms in the market and entry barriers as well as product differentiation are high, then firms will have high market power.

In addition, concentrated markets are conducive to anti-competitive behaviors. For example, in a market with few players (S), firms may adopt tacit or explicit collusion (C), which will result in high performance (P):

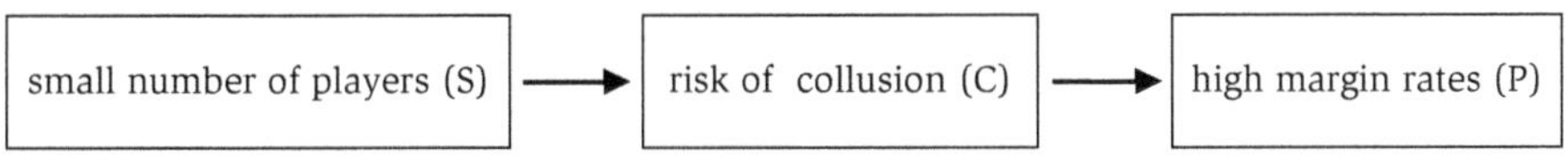

Similarly, in a highly concentrated market (S), a dominant firm may exclude efficient competitors from the market—for example, by charging predatory prices (C)—which will ultimately result in higher performance (P):

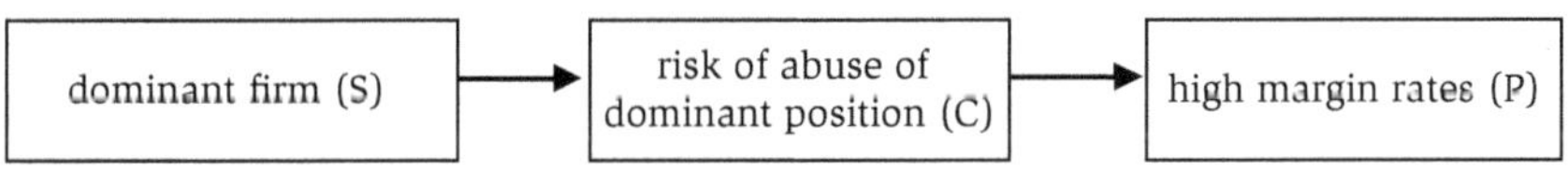

Since market power results from both market structures (S) and firms' conduct (C), competition authorities may intervene at two levels:

- regarding market structures, competition authorities must limit the level of concentration, in particular by controlling mergers;
- regarding anti-competitive behaviors, large firms must be closely monitored when markets with high entry barriers are concentrated, in order to prevent collusion or abuse of dominant positions.

The SCP paradigm calls for an interventionist policy, focused on the diffusion of market power; all market power is suspicious, because it reduces consumer surplus and total welfare.

SECTION 4 BEYOND MARKET STRUCTURES

While the structuralist approach is the main basis for analyzing competition, it has, over time, been both enriched and criticized, sometimes in a radical way.

A first enhancement was to go beyond the idea that the intensity of competition is necessarily related to the number of firms in the market. For example, a single firm may charge a competitive price if it is threatened by the entry of newcomers, as the "*contestable markets*" theory emphasizes (§1).

A second enhancement concerns consumer surplus: Its level depends on price but also on other parameters, such as the quality or variety of products. In addition, consumer surplus is only one element of the total welfare; some firms' strategies can reduce consumer surplus while increasing total welfare, such as a merger that lowers production costs (§2).

The structuralist approach has also been radically criticized by the Chicago School, which is based on the contributions of the Austrian School of the early 20th century (Hayek, Schumpeter, Von Mises): The SCP paradigm is based on a static approach, leading to artificially opposing competition and monopoly. The result is a profound questioning of the legitimacy of antitrust policies (§3).

§1 Market Atomicity Enhancements

In both the pure and perfect competition model and the SCP model, the market atomicity hypothesis is central: A competitive market is characterized by the presence of a large number of firms. However, atomicity is not always necessary to achieve a perfectly competitive equilibrium, as shown by the Bertrand's duopoly and the theory of "*contestable*" markets.

Pure and perfect competition with two firms: Bertrand's duopoly: Oligopolistic competition is not limited to the well-known Cournot or Stackelberg models. In particular, Bertrand's duopoly (1883) shows that if competition is based only on price, without any capacity constraints, a perfectly competitive equilibrium could be achieved with only two firms in the market.

Consider Firms 1 and 2, which have the same total cost function:

$$TC(q_i) = cq_i \quad \text{with} \quad i = 1, 2 \text{ and } c > 0$$

The two firms must simultaneously set their prices P_1 and P_2; they have no capacity constraints. We assume that their products are perfectly identical; the only choice criterion for consumers is the price.

The demand function is linear:

$$P(Q) = a - Q$$

with $a > 0$, $a > c$ and $Q = q_1 + q_2$.

When both firms set the same price ($P_1 = P_2$), each firm gets half the market, i.e.:

$$q_i = (a - P)/2$$

If $P_1 \neq P_2$, the demand is exclusively for the firm with the lowest price:

$$q_1 = (a - P) \text{ and } q_2 = 0 \text{ when } P_1 < P_2$$

$$q_2 = (a - P) \text{ and } q_1 = 0 \text{ when } P_1 > P_2$$

With these hypotheses, we can show that the only equilibrium is the situation of pure and perfect competition:

- neither firm will set a price $P_1 = P_2 < c$: Each firm would make losses. The equilibrium price is necessarily equal to or greater than c;
- if $P_1 > P_2 > c$: Firm 1 sells nothing and therefore will set a price slightly lower than P_2 to make a positive profit;
- if $P_1 > P_2 = c$: Firm 2 will set a price P_2 higher than c but lower than P_1 (and symmetrically);
- if both firms charge the same price, $P_1 = P_2 > c$: It is not an equilibrium, since each firm will lower its price to capture the entire market.

We conclude that the only possible price is:

$$P_1 = P_2 = c$$

We obtain the famous "*Bertrand paradox*": Both firms charge a price equal to the competitive price and obtain zero profits.[13]

We see that the intensity of competition in a market does not necessarily depend on the number of firms but on the nature of competition; price competition, without capacity constraints, leads to a result similar to that of pure and perfect competition, without the atomicity condition.

The Bertrand's equilibrium (also called "*Bertrand-Nash equilibrium*" by reference to game theory) can be illustrated graphically. Figure 1.14 shows the reaction function of Firm 1 as a function of Firm 2's price. If Firm 2 charges a price P_2 higher than the monopoly price P_M, Firm 1's best response is to charge a monopoly price P_M. If Firm 2 charges a price P_2 such as $P_M > P_2 > c$, the best response for Firm 1 is to set a price $P_1 = P_2 - \varepsilon$ (with ε positive and close to zero) in order to capture all consumers (graphically, it corresponds to a slight shift to the left of the first bisector). If Firm 2 sets a price $P_2 < c$, Firm 1's best response is to set a price $P = c$.

13. For a discussion of the assumptions of Bertrand's model, *see* the Annex at the end of this chapter.

Figure 1.14 The Reaction Function of Firm 1 in Bertrand's Duopoly

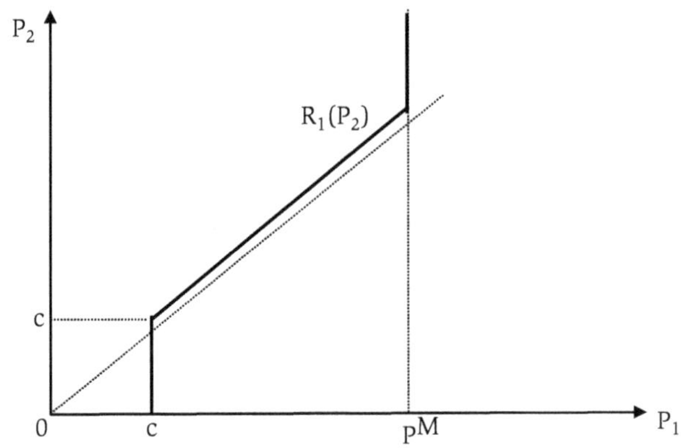

A symmetrical reasoning can be done with Firm 2 (Figure 1.15).

Figure 1.15 The Reaction Function of Firm 2 in Bertrand's Duopoly

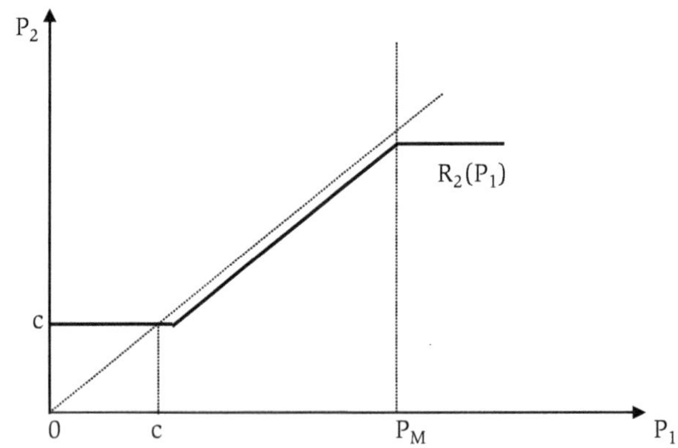

At the intersection of the two reaction functions, we obtain the Bertrand's equilibrium (Figure 1.16):

$$P_1 = P_2 = c.$$

Figure 1.16 Bertrand's Equilibrium

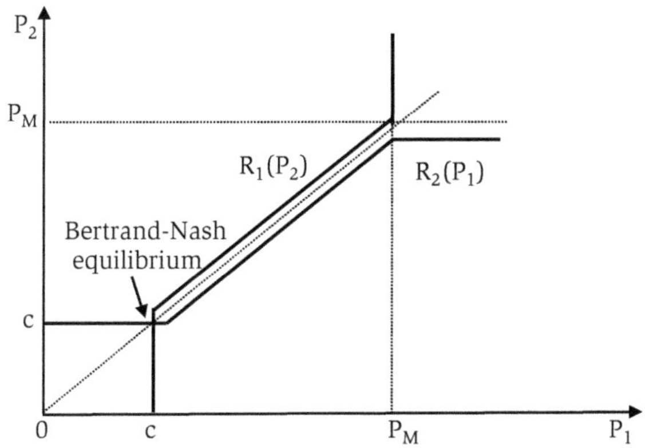

Pure and perfect competition with a single firm: A contestable market: Under certain assumptions, a competitive equilibrium can be obtained even if there is one firm on the market. Indeed, the theory of "*contestable*" markets shows that a firm threatened by the entry of newcomers has no choice but to charge a price equal to the marginal cost (or to the average cost, in the presence of a fixed cost); to achieve a competitive equilibrium, what counts is less the number of firms on the market than the threat of entry of new competitors (Baumol, Panzar & Willig 1982).

A market is contestable when three conditions are met:

- new firms have access to the same production function as incumbents;
- entry costs can be recovered if the new firm exits from the market: There are no "*sunk costs.*" For example, if a firm enters the airline market, it must bear the fixed cost of purchasing an aircraft; however, this cost is not a sunk cost because there is a secondary market to resell the aircraft;
- the entry delay is shorter than the one required by the incumbent to modify its prices.

Consider the case of a firm operating in a contestable market with economies of scale (Figure 1.17). If it charges a price P_1 higher than the competitive price P^*, a competitor will enter the market by offering a price slightly lower than P_1. The incumbent, fearing the entry of a new competitor, has no choice but to set a price P^*: In a contestable market, a single firm loses its monopoly power.

Figure 1.17 The Contestable Market Equilibrium

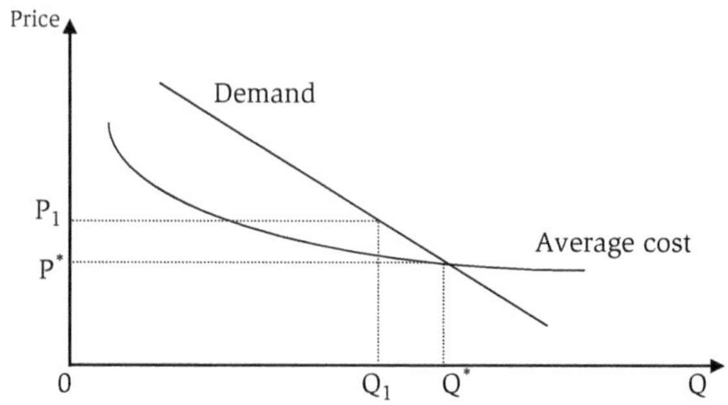

An illustration of a contestable market: The theory of contestable markets is rarely found in its purest form in the real economic world. However, it can be considered that some markets—in which entry and exit barriers are low—are close to a contestable market.

This is the case of the airline industry, which has given rise to several empirical studies on the role of potential competition. For example, Morrison (2001) studied the impact that the entry of Southwest Airlines had on the ticket prices of competing airlines in the United States. When Southwest entered a new route from A to B, with the same departure and arrival airports as its competitors, the latter lowered their ticket prices by 46.2 % (Table 1.4). However, Morrison showed that this competitive impact was not limited to routes directly competing with Southwest Airlines but was extended to the entire market, through the so-called "Southwest effect." There were two cases:

- Case 1: If Southwest is already present in airports A and B, without operating flights between A and B, its presence alone forces competitors to reduce their prices by 33 %; they fear that Southwest may fly from A to B in the near future.
- Case 2: When Southwest is present at substitutable departure or arrival airports without being on the A-B route, competitors still, surprisingly, reduce their prices preventively by 13.1 %. For instance, at the end of 2006, Southwest opened a base at Washington D.C. airport in order to fly to Chicago O'Hare. At Chicago airport, Southwest already operated flights to Cleveland. It was therefore possible for the low-cost airline to open a direct line between Washington and Cleveland. Competitors anticipated this eventuality by adjusting their prices downwards on the Cleveland/Washington route. This effect follows the contestable markets theory: The possibility of a new firm entering the market forces incumbent firms to take into account this potential competition and adjust their prices downwards as a protective measure.

Table 1.4 Fare Adjustments of Established Airlines to Southwest's Presence

Category	*Variable*	*Coefficient*	*Standard Error*	*Effect on Fares*
Actual Competition	At-At-Server	-0.620	0.023	-46.2%
	At-Neat-Server	-0.306	0.023	-26.4%
	Near-Near-Serves	-0.167	0.029	-15.4%
Potential Competition	At-At-Does not Serve	-0.401	0.027	-33.0%
	At-Near-Does not Serve	-0.140	0.033	-13.1%
	Near-Near-Does not Serve	0.188	0.033	20.7%
	At-Far-Serves	-0.125	0.021	-11.8%
	Near-Far-Serves	-0.067	0.024	-6.5%

Source: Morrison (2001).

The degree of market contestability is now largely integrated by competition authorities, particularly in the field of mergers.

Thus, in France, when Air Liberté was acquired by AOM French Airlines (2000), the French authorities explicitly invoked the market contestability to authorize the merger. In particular, although the new entity AOM-Air Liberté was alone on two air routes (Paris Orly–Perpignan and Paris Orly–Toulon-Hyères), the French authorities estimated that the threat of entry would deter any attempt to increase the price, because Air France held 49.3% of the slots at Paris Orly Airport. These slots were not assigned to a specific route: Air France could freely use them to fly wherever. It was therefore possible for Air France to use some of its slots to compete with the new entity on the Paris Orly–Toulon-Hyères and Paris Orly–Perpignan routes: "If the new entity does not take into account this competitive pressure and increases its tariffs, it will lead to the entry of a competitor into the market, which will have the effect of reducing fares to the equilibrium price" (free translation).

§2 Consumer Surplus Enhancements

In the structuralist approach, any price increase above the marginal cost leads to a reduction in consumer surplus. However, the consumer surplus does not only depend on the price; it also includes other parameters such as the variety or quality of products.

Consumer surplus, beyond prices: In the standard microeconomic approach, consumer surplus depends on the quantity consumed and the price paid. However, other variables, such as the product's quality, can also have an impact on consumer surplus.

Let's assume that the demand for a product not only depends on its price, but also on the level of presale service: For example, some individuals are more likely to buy a computer if the seller can offer them advice before their purchase.

We assume that the purchase of the product and the consumption of the service are two separate acts: For example, a consumer asks Distributor 1 for advice and then buys the product from Distributor 2. Distributor 1's efforts will therefore have benefited its competitor. Providing presale service is costly for the distributor: For example, it has to invest in ongoing staff training or in efficient product presentation (explanatory brochures, in-store demonstrations, etc.).

If competition between distributors is based solely on price, none of them will provide presale service. Therefore, some consumers will not buy the product. This non-cooperative result is to the detriment of the producer because it will sell fewer products.

To overcome this situation, the producer can impose a minimum resale price on its distributors, higher than the competitive price. In this case, distributors will be encouraged to offer the presale service; indeed, because they can no longer compete by lowering their prices, they will compete on the quality of their service. Consumers will pay more and this will reduce their surplus; but in return, the quantity consumed will increase, as presale service has increased.

From consumer surplus to total welfare: As we have seen, the total welfare (W) represents the sum of the consumer surplus and the profits:

$$W(p) = CS(p) + \Sigma\Pi_i(p)$$

In the typical microeconomic approach, welfare decreases when the price rises above the marginal cost, because the additional profit does not compensate for the loss of consumer surplus. However, it is not always the case; for instance, when a firm implements a strategy of price discrimination, consumers' surplus decreases but welfare can increase.

We can illustrate this case with a monopoly, which produces at marginal cost c. The monopoly decides to apply a "*first-degree discrimination*" strategy: It consists of making each consumer pay his or her reservation price (i.e., the maximum price he or she is willing to pay). In this case, the monopoly increases the quantities until it reaches the marginal consumer whose reservation price is equal to the marginal cost: The monopoly offers the same quantity as in a situation of pure and perfect competition (Figure 1.18).

However, unlike in a competitive market, where all consumers pay the same price P_{ppc}, only the marginal consumer is charged that price. The consumer surplus in a pure and perfect competition (grey area) is entirely transferred to the monopoly: The welfare is equal to the monopoly profit. From a welfare point of view, this situation is equivalent to the one in a perfectly competitive market: The monopoly, by perfectly discriminating between consumers, has not led to a reduction in welfare.

Figure 1.18 First Degree Discrimination and Welfare

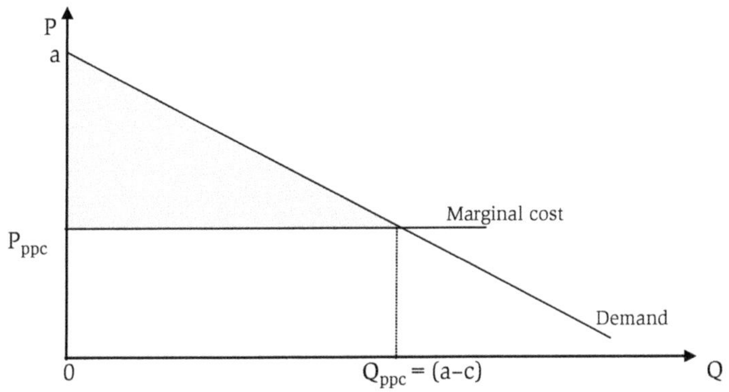

Another example can be found in the analysis of mergers; as Williamson (1968b) pointed out, a merger can improve the total welfare, while having a negative impact on the consumer surplus, if it significantly reduces the marginal cost.

Suppose two firms with the same marginal cost c_1 compete in a Bertrand duopoly (Figure 1.19). Before they merge, the two firms sell the total quantity Q_1 at price P_1; they make no profit since the price is equal to the marginal cost. The two firms decide to merge, which has a double effect:

- the marginal cost decreases from c_1 to c_2 as a result of efficiencies;
- the price increases from P_1 to P_2, as the new entity is now a monopoly.

The merger results in a monopoly profit, equal to the margin multiplied by the quantity Q_2:

$$\Pi = (P_2 - c_2)\, Q_2$$

Before the merger, the consumer surplus is equal to the abd area; since profits are nil, the total welfare is also equal to the abd triangle. After the merger, the consumer surplus decreases as consumers pay more: They've lost the area (A + D). However, the merger also increases profits by an amount equal to the area (A + B). If we add the producer's profits with the consumers' losses (i.e., A + B – C – D), we obtain an area equal to (B - D).

The final impact of the merger on welfare therefore depends on the comparison between the area B and the area D:

- if D > B, the merger decreases the total welfare;
- if D < B, the merger increases the total welfare, even if it reduces the consumer surplus.

Figure 1.19 The Trade-Off Between Market Power and Efficiency Gains

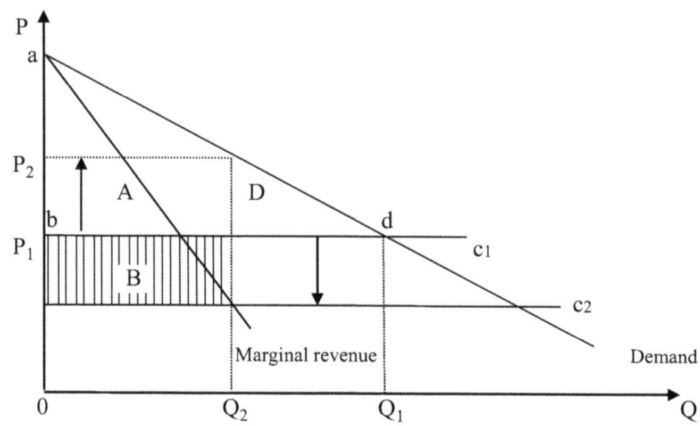

If we apply a welfare criterion, a merger that harms consumers but leads to strong efficiencies should be authorized. However, we will see in Chapter 6 that consumer surplus remains the main analytical criterion for competition authorities.

§3 The Radical Criticism of the SCP Model

The structuralist approach has been radically challenged by the Chicago School (Posner, Stigler, Bork), which extends the criticism of the pure and perfect competition model carried out by the Austrian School in the first half of the 20th century.

A dynamic approach to competition: The structuralist approach is based on a static view of competition in which a monopoly is the perfect antithesis of competition. Another view, whose inspiration can be found in the Austrian School [*see* in particular: Von Mises (1896), Hayek (1948), Rothbard (1962) or Schumpeter (1942)], considers competition to be a continuous process of selecting firms that are the most efficient and innovative.

According to Schumpeter, price competition encourages an "escape competition effect," pushing firms to innovate in order to achieve a temporary monopoly situation. However, this monopoly situation will not last: The innovative firm will quickly be imitated and price competition will return.

The dynamics of a market is similar to a continuous process of "*creative destruction*." As in sports, firms are constantly competing in the market to win over consumers with new products or more-efficient production methods. From this perspective, profit is simply the reward for the technological or commercial superiority of the "*surviving*" firms. This reward is transitional, since market forces (through imitation) will quickly restore prices close to production costs, through the entry of new players. As Armentano points out (1996): "Business competition is always a dynamic process, not a given static state of affairs, in which suppliers continually strive to offer improved alternatives to market participants. Unlike the perfectly competitive world, competition is a process of discovering opportunities for profit, and then adjusting market conditions so that these opportunities tend to be exploited."

Figure 1.20 The Schumpeterian Dynamics of Competition

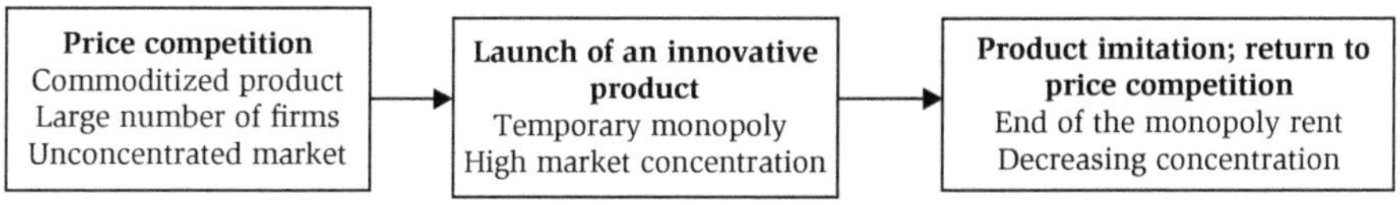

Market concentration is the result of a selecting process of the most-efficient firms. In this sense, market concentration attests to the intensity of competition; competition and monopoly are therefore the two inseparable aspects of market dynamics. As Lepage (1989) notes: "When a firm is particularly efficient and succeeds in reducing its costs beyond what its competitors can do, it will generate high profits, but it will also tend to gain a greater market share. If it has a sufficient capacity to innovate constantly and challenge competitors in time, this will result in both a high concentration rate and higher than average profits. In this case, the correlation between concentration and profits is not an indication of insufficient competition, but on the contrary, the result of the presence of an over-competitive firm" (free translation).

Similarly, from a dynamic perspective, entry barriers mentioned by structuralist authors are not insurmountable: An entry barrier is only high for a new entrant if it wants to enter with a product or technology similar to that which already exists on the market. However, a newcomer may bypass an entry barrier by launching an innovation on a different market from the one in which incumbents operate. Excepting legal barriers, entry barriers are therefore relative and not absolute obstacles.

Unlikely anti-competitive behaviors: Structuralists have stressed the role of anti-competitive conducts (parameter C) in explaining a firm's performance (P). For example, Bain estimated that on concentrated markets the strong performance of firms could be the result of a collusion with competitors. The Chicago School insists on the low success rate of a collusive strategy.

According to Stigler (1964), cartels are unstable because each firm has an incentive to deviate from the collusive agreement. Let us consider two firms, A and B, competing in a Cournot duopoly. The two firms can form a cartel in order to obtain a monopoly profit (Figure 1.21). When they compete, each firm makes a profit of $3. When they form a cartel, the total profit (equal to $10) is higher than the competitive profit and is equally distributed between the two firms ($5 each). If one of the two firms cheats by granting a secret discount to its customers while its competitor maintains the cartel price, it makes an even higher profit; indeed, customers turn to the firm with the low price. In this case, the cheating firm makes a profit of $9, while its competitor doesn't earn anything.

Let's solve the simultaneous game shown in Figure 1.21 by eliminating the dominated strategies.[14] If Firm B complies with the cartel agreement, the best strategy for Firm A is to cheat ($9 > $5). Similarly, if Firm B cheats, Firm A's best response is to also cheat ($3 > $0); whatever Firm B's strategy, the choice to respect the agreement is always dominated for Firm A by the choice to cheat. Firm B, anticipating that Firm A will always cheat, must choose between respecting the agreement or cheating: It will also prefer to cheat ($3 > $0).

This is a well-known configuration in the non-cooperative game theory, known as the "*prisoner's dilemma*": While it would be collectively advantageous to respect the agreement (with a total gain of $10), the rationality leads to a less advantageous situation for both players ($3 < $5) and collectively (total gain of $6 and not $10). According to this analysis, cartels would therefore be doomed to instability.

Figure 1.21 Cartel and Prisoner's Dilemma

		Firm B	
		Does not cheat	Cheats
Firm A	Does not cheat	($5, $5)	($0, $9)
	Cheats	($9, $0)	($3, $3)

NB: for each payment, the first gain is that of Firm A, and the second, that of Firm B.

The Chicago School also shows that some abusive practices, such as a "*predatory pricing*" strategy, are doomed to fail. A predatory pricing strategy consists of a dominant firm temporarily lowering its price in order to drive out an equally efficient competitor, before increasing its price to a higher level than before. This strategy is based on sacrificing short-term profits with the intent of recovering this loss in the long term.

Economists such as McGee (1958) or Bork (1993) have questioned the credibility and profitability of this type of strategy, which are, according to them, part of a "myth":

- it does not prevent the entry of new firms into the market once the predator raises its price. This entry is all the more likely, as the production capacity of the victim can be bought back. The gains from a predatory pricing strategy would therefore be at best short-term gains;

14. A strategy is said to be "*dominated*" for an agent X if it provides him with an ever lower gain than another strategy, regardless of the choice of the other agents with which X interacts.

- other strategies allow firms to obtain more-sustainable monopoly positions, such as a merger;
- predatory pricing cannot work when competitors know that this is a temporary strategy (perfect information assumption) and that they have access to the credit market. Indeed, in this case, they can borrow, which defeats the predatory strategy. From the lender's point of view, the commitment to lend is low risk: the mere promise of a credit line deters the predator to launch a price war; therefore, the victim doesn't use the credit line;
- customers (especially if they are firms) have an incentive to help the victim if they fear that they will then face a monopoly.

With these theoretical arguments, Chicago economists show that predatory pricing law is unnecessary and can even be exploited by inefficient firms: The law would encourage them to file complaints against efficient firms, with the sole aim of obtaining compensation. Antitrust legislation would then have the undesirable effect of deterring efficient firms from lowering their prices too aggressively. More fundamentally, according to the Chicago School, the condemnation of predatory pricing practices is based on a misunderstanding of competition, which is based on frequent episodes of "*price wars*," particularly to launch new products or to conquer new consumers.

The inversion of the SCP model: Since competition is a dynamic process, the relationship between market structures (S) and performance (P) must be analyzed over the long term and not at a given moment in time: The empirical tests of the structuralist authors would not be relevant, since the relationship is not tested within a time period.

More fundamentally, the Chicago School questions the SCP model, in which market structures (S) determine firms' performances (P).

For Demsetz (1974), the relationship must be reversed: It is the conduct (C) and performance (P) of firms that determine market concentration (S), and not the other way around (Figure 1.22). For example, imagine a firm launches an innovative or better product on the market. It will conquer consumers, quickly achieve higher margins than competitors, and thus acquire a dominant position. In this case, the strong market concentration is the result, and not the cause, of the superior performance of certain firms. As Demsetz points out: "A phenomenon that is likely to generate fairly persistent differences in accounting rates of returns is the fact that some products are more efficiently produced by firms possessing a large share of the market, while in other industries large market shares are not necessary for efficiency. Those firms that first act on the belief that large scale is an advantage, and that invest in the marketing and production techniques prerequisite to executing the move to large scale, will possess a competitively secured advantage in timing and in obtaining early consumer acceptance that will be difficult to overcome in a short time period. The market may not have grown large enough to accommodate more than a handful of such firms. These firms can produce at lower unit cost than smaller firms. They are superior in this respect, and they command an economic rent for achieving primacy."

Figure 1.22 The SCP Relationship Revisited

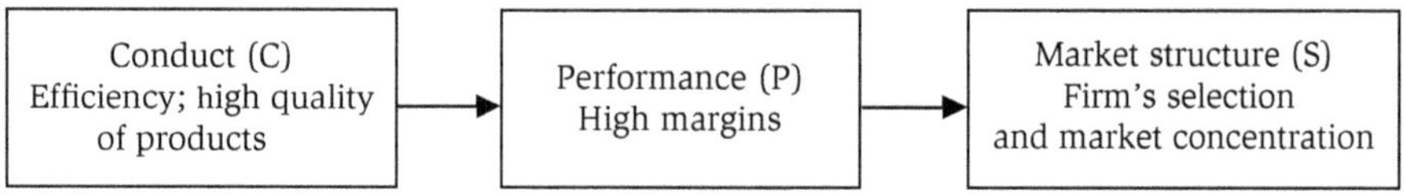

The Chicago School therefore seriously challenges antitrust policies: If the market is able to correct its own imperfections, competition policies become useless at best, at worst harmful to competition, by protecting inefficient firms and curbing the process of "*creative destruction.*"

Enhancing the structuralist approach: Faced with these radical challenges, the structuralist approach has experienced a second youth from the 1980s onwards with the "*new industrial economy*"; the hypotheses of the Chicago School have been examined and challenged, using in particular game theory and information asymmetries. This "post-Chicago" trend shows that cartels are not necessarily unstable practices, that predatory pricing practices can work under certain conditions, or that exclusivity agreements can lead to the eviction of an equally efficient competitor (Table 1.5). The post-Chicago School argues for a case-by-case approach, rather than on per se principles (prohibiting or authorizing).

Chapters 3-6 are essentially based on this new industrial economy, which restores legitimacy to antitrust action.

Table 1.5 Competitive Strategies: Two Opposing Approaches

	Chicago School	*New Industrial Economy ("Post Chicago")*
Predatory prices	Unlikely practice.	Possible in case of asymmetry in size, access to the financial market or information.
Cartels	Unstable by nature, given the incentive for each member to "cheat."	Cartels can be stable, if the practice is repeated.
Vertical agreements	Mutually beneficial for firms and consumers.	Case-by-case approach. Possibility of restricting competition through a vertical agreement.
Exclusivity agreements, discounts, tying	Mutually beneficial for firms and consumers.	Possibility of excluding an equally efficient competitor.

	Chicago School	*New Industrial Economy ("Post Chicago")*
Mergers	Source of efficiency gains.	Case-by-case approach: Balancing efficiency gains with reduction in competition.
Role of antitrust authorities	At best useless; harmful, as it can restrict efficient firms.	Necessary tool to fight against cartels and abuses of dominant position. Case-by-case approach.

Review Topics:

Compare pure and perfect competition and monopoly.
Detail the economic analysis of oligopoly.
What is the role of the number of firms in determining market power?
Describe the SCP paradigm and its implications for competition policy.
What are the main critics of the SCP paradigm?

Recommended Readings:

Dominick Armentano, *Antitrust and Monopoly: Anatomy of a Policy Failure* (The Independent Institute, 1996).
Robert Bork, *The Antitrust Paradox* (The Free Press, 1993).
Dennis Carlton and Jeffrey M. Perloff, *Industrial Economics* (De Boeck, 2015).
Israel Kirzner, *Competition and Entrepreneurship* (University of Chicago Press, 1973).
Richard Posner, *Antitrust Law: An Economic Perspective* (University of Chicago Press, 1976).
Oz Shy, *Industrial Organization: Theory and Applications* (The MIT Press, 1996).
Jean Tirole, *Industrial Organization* (Economica, 2015).
Leonard Weiss (ed.) *Concentration and Price* (The MIT Press, 1987).

ANNEX: SOLUTIONS TO THE BERTRAND'S "PARADOX"

Bertrand's paradox can be solved by challenging the assumptions of the model.

- Heterogeneity of costs:

Suppose that the two firms have different marginal costs: For example, $c_2 > c_1$. Two configurations must be considered:

- if $c_2 \leq p^M{}_1$, Firm 1 set a price of c_2 and remains alone on the market;
- if $c_2 > p^M{}_1$, Firm 1 charges a monopoly price $p^M{}_1$.

- Product differentiation:

Suppose that the products are no longer homogeneous: A firm that sells at a higher price (than its competitor) loses only a part of the demand. Let us consider the following demand functions:

$$D_1 = a - P_1 - \beta P_2$$

$$D_2 = a - P_2 - \beta P_1$$

with $1 > \beta > 0$.

We note that the demand to a firm is a decreasing function of its own price and that of its rival. The profit function of Firm 1 is:

$$\Pi_1 = (a - P_1 - \beta P_2)(P_1 - c)$$

The reaction function of Firm 1 is:

$$\partial \Pi_1 / \partial P_1 = 0 \Rightarrow P_1 = (a + \beta P_2 + c)/2 \qquad (1)$$

Similarly, for Firm 2, we get:

$$P_2 = (a + \beta P_1 + c)/2 \qquad (2)$$

By substituting (2) in (1), the equilibrium price is:

$$P_1 = P_2 = c + \frac{1 - (1 - \beta)c}{(2 - \beta)}$$

We find that the equilibrium price is higher than the marginal cost.

- Production capacity constraint:

In 1897, Edgeworth pointed out that the introduction of a capacity constraint helps to overcome the "*Bertrand's paradox.*" Indeed, if both firms charge the same price but more than the marginal cost, no firm has an interest in lowering its price if the production capacities are full.

- Repetition of the game:

In Bertrand's duopoly, the situation in which $P_1 = P_2 > c$ does not constitute an equilibrium, because each firm has an incentive to reduce its price if its competitor maintains its price. Nevertheless, if the price game is repeated over an infinite horizon, any price $P_1 = P_2 > c$ can become an equilibrium, if firms are sufficiently patient

CHAPTER 2

Competition Policy: Main Evolutions and Instruments

In 2019, more than 130 countries in the world had adopted competition laws that included at least some provisions on cartels (Aydin et al., 2016). We will start by presenting how competition policies originated in the United States in 1890, and how they have spread throughout the world (section 1). Then, we will detail the legal framework in which competition authorities operate and study their role in fighting anti-competitive practices such as cartels and abuses of dominant position. We will pay particular attention to the economic approach of sanctions, initiated by the Nobel Prize G. Becker (section 2). We'll conclude this chapter by reviewing the various types of sanctions being imposed today, other than public fines; for example, the infringement of competition laws has given rise to private actions initiated by victims ("private enforcement") and, similarly, in some countries, to the development of a criminal legal arsenal in order deter individuals from engaging in hardcore cartels (section 3).

SECTION 1 ADOPTING COMPETITION POLICIES THROUGHOUT THE WORLD

Competition policies are recent in most developed countries, except in the United States, where antitrust policies date back to the 1890 Sherman Act. In Europe, the first antitrust policies appeared in 1957 when the European Common Market was established, and then gradually spread throughout the Member States from the 1980s onwards.

With regards to emerging and developing countries, competition policies started being implemented in the 2000s, often under the impetus of international organizations (such as the International Monetary Fund), or as part of a regional economic integration process. Hence, in 2008, China adopted the Anti Monopoly Law, which introduced all the provisions of a competition law in a "*socialist market economy.*" Today, many developing countries have put in place competition policies, but their effectiveness remains limited, with the exception of Kenya.

We can therefore conclude that over the last 50 years, competition policies have been adopted throughout the world but still need to be implemented further in most developing countries. This progressive spread of competition policies raises an essential question: Is a competition policy a prerequisite for a developing country to move to the next stage of its development?

§1 The American Tradition

The founding act: The Sherman Act (1890): In the field of competition policy, the United States and Canada are pioneering countries; the first competition laws were passed by 15 U.S. states in the 1880s[15] before a federal antitrust policy was introduced in 1890 with the Sherman Act. This legislation relating to collusion and market monopolization was born in a particular historical and political context:

- several American states had already adopted similar provisions, but their scopes were limited to intra-State trade;
- the years spanning 1870-1880 were marked by a strong wave of industrial concentration, giving rise to "giants" in sectors such as oil, steel, electricity and railways. In particular, Standard Oil Company's practices in the U.S. oil market attracted the attention of the public authorities, and in 1888, a senator launched an investigation against this "*Trust*."[16] Other investigations followed—in particular involving the Sugar Trust and the Whiskey Trust;
- a rising "*populist*" rhetoric developed during the 1890 legislative elections, based on the defense of consumers, and small agricultural and manufacturing producers. The American public opinion was concerned about the growing concentration of economic power in the hands of a few large firms. Politicians pointed out the risk that strong market concentration represented a threat to the democratic process itself, as Senator Sherman stated, "The popular mind is agitated with problems that may disturb social order, and among them none is more threatening than the inequality of condition of wealth, and opportunity that has grown within a single generation out of the concentration of capital into vast combinations to control production and trade and to break down competition."

This concern regarding industrial concentration was not however shared by economists at the time; indeed, during the period spanning 1885-1920, authors such as Ely (1900), Clark (1912), or Davenport (1919) emphasized the efficiency gains resulting from industrial concentration (DiLorenzo & High, 1988). It was not until the

15. In the United States, federal and state competition law coexist. In the event of a conflict, federal law prevails. In this chapter, we will focus on federal law alone.
16. The "Trust" refers to a mechanism by which shareholders entrust their securities to a trustee and waive their voting rights in exchange for higher dividends.

late 1930s that American economists took a more favorable view of antitrust laws (Kirat & Marty, 2019).

While the first cartels were condemned shortly after the Sherman Act—including the Trans-Missouri and Addyston Pipe cases in 1898—large conglomerates were not really targeted until the beginning of the 20th century. It was only after the financial crises of 1902-1903, and then 1907-1908, that antitrust authorities prosecuted large American trusts. During his two terms, from 1901 to 1908, President Theodore Roosevelt earned himself a "trust busting" reputation as his government multiplied regulatory reforms and antitrust prosecutions: After the Northern Securities Company's case in 1904, the federal government opened a case against the Standard Oil Company in 1906. It took five years of proceedings, but, in 1911, Standard Oil was convicted of having violated Section 2 of the Sherman Act. The U.S. Department of Justice (DOJ) ordered the company's dismantlement into 33 independent firms, which gave rise to Exxon, Mobil, Chevron, American and Esso.

The Clayton Act (1914): A second legislative step was taken in 1914 with the adoption of the Clayton Antitrust Act and the Federal Trade Commission (FTC) Act, and the creation of the FTC, an administrative authority in charge of competition and consumer protection. The adoption of these texts, which dealt with discriminatory practices and controlling mergers, has often been analyzed as a political response to the fears of the public opinion shocked by financial scandals and the Sherman Act's ineffectiveness in fighting against market concentration. Indeed, cartel practices, sanctioned by the Sherman Act, had given way to horizontal and vertical mergers, particularly during the period spanning 1895-1904. In this context, the Clayton Act was passed to discourage mergers between large firms.

Ramirez and Eigen-Zucchi (2001) assessed the impact of the Clayton Act on American firms by comparing the evolution of the cumulative stock market returns of two portfolios: one composed of shares of large firms, the second including shares of small firms. This empirical method assumed that capital markets would immediately incorporate legislative changes into share prices. This was the case: The Clayton Act was "bad news" for large firms, because it limited their development and their search for market power through mergers. The period studied was between Woodrow Wilson's presidential election in November 1912, which corresponds to the beginning of the Clayton Act bill, and when the bill became law in January 1914. Figure 2.1 shows the cumulative returns of the two portfolios; it appears that the cumulative return (risk adjusted) of the small business portfolio outperforms that of large firms by 9%. The stock exchange therefore anticipated that the Clayton Act would have a negative impact on the profitability of large firms.

A study of the senators' votes during the Clayton Act adoption confirms the previous result. Ramirez and Eigen-Zucchi (2001) apply the "*Public Choice*" theory, which supposes that laws redistribute wealth among economic actors. Broadly speaking, the Clayton Act affects three interest groups: farmers, large firms and small producers. The law is rather favorable to agricultural interests since Section 6 of the Clayton Act partially exempts this sector from the application of antitrust laws by allowing farmers to form cooperatives. On the other hand, the Clayton Act negatively affects large industries, in particular by discouraging horizontal mergers. In accordance with the Public Choice's theses, the senators' votes reflected their electors' interests: Senators in favor of the Clayton Act were in the Southern states, traditionally oriented towards agriculture and small industry, while those opposed to the text were mainly located in the Northern industrialized states.

Figure 2.1 Cumulative Return on Two Stock Portfolios During the Clayton Act Adoption (1912-1913)

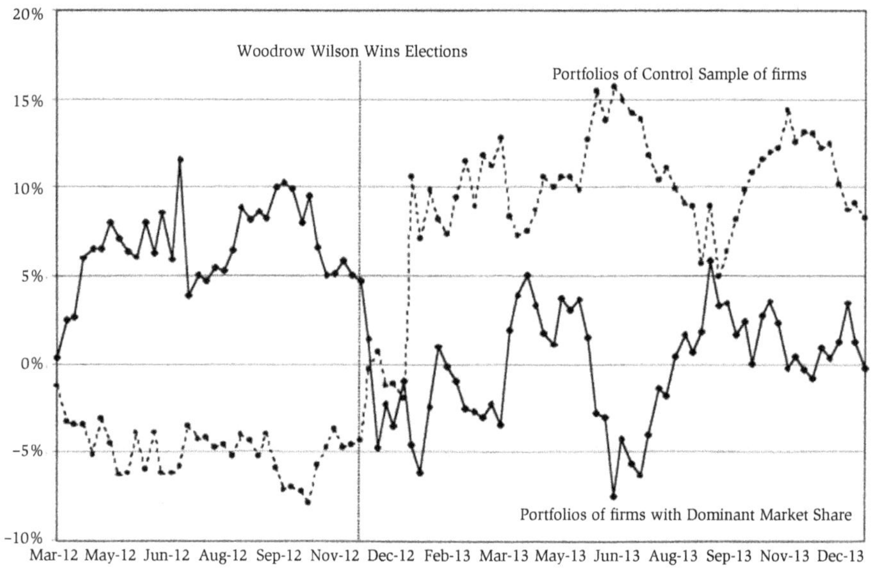

Source: Ramirez and Eigen-Zucchi (2001).

For more than a century, the Sherman Act and the Clayton Act have been the two main pillars of the American antitrust policy, although they have been amended over time (Table 2.1):

- The Robinson-Patman Act (1936), adopted in a context of conflict between small independent retailers and store chains, amends Section 2 of the Clayton Act: Any practice of price discrimination that has the effect of restricting competition is considered illegal.
- Section 7 of the Clayton Act only concerned the acquisition of a firm through equity investments. Its scope was extended in 1950 with the adoption of the Celler-Kefauver Act. Later, the Hart-Scott-Rodino Antitrust Improvements Act introduced in 1976 a system of prior and mandatory notification of mergers.

Table 2.1 Antitrust Legislation in the United States—Main Dates

- 1890: Adoption of the Sherman Act
- 1914: Adoption of the Clayton Act (price discrimination, tying, cross-directors, mergers, etc.), the Federal Trade Commission Act and creation of the Federal Trade Commission
- 1933-1938: The National Industrial Recovery Act suspends antitrust laws
- 1936: Adoption of the Robinson-Patman Antitrust Improvements Act, which amended Section 2 of the Clayton Act
- 1950: Adoption of the Celler-Kefauver Act on merger control (which supplements Section 7 of the Clayton Act)
- 1968: Publication of the first Mergers Guidelines
- 1978: Adoption of the Hart-Scott-Rodino Act on prior notification of mergers
- 1982: New Merger and Acquisition Guidelines, which are more flexible than those adopted in 1968
- 1984: Adoption of the National Cooperative Research Act (NCRA), which authorizes R&D joint ventures under certain conditions through a notification system; publication of the Non-Horizontal Merger Guidelines
- 1993: The NCRA is replaced by the National Cooperative Research and Production Act (NCRPA)
- 1993: Adoption of a new leniency program
- 1995: Publication of the Antitrust Guidelines for the Licensing of Intellectual Property
- 2000: Publication of the Antitrust Guidelines for Collaborations Among Competitors
- 2004: Adoption of the Antitrust Criminal Penalty Enhancement and Reform Act, which increases criminal penalties
- 2010: Publication of new Horizontal Merger Guidelines
- 2020: Publication of new Vertical Merger Guidelines

The main antitrust cases in the United States—anti-competitive agreements and abuses of dominant position—are presented in Table 2.2.

Table 2.2 Key Antitrust Cases in the United States

- 1892: Trans-Missouri (cartel)
- 1898: Addyston Pipe (collusion in calls for tender)
- 1911: Standard Oil; American Tobacco; DuPont (market monopolization)
- 1927: Trenton Potteries (cartel)
- 1945: Alcoa case (margin squeeze initiated by a monopoly)
- 1956: Bridge (market monopolization)

- 1961: General Electric (collusion in calls for tender)
- 1962: Brown Shoe Co. (blocking a vertical merger)
- 1967: Utah Pie Co. (predatory pricing)
- 1969: Opening of investigation against IBM (market monopolization; closed with no charges)
- 1971: Opening of investigation against breakfast cereal leaders (market monopolization; closed with no charges)
- 1975: Rank Xerox (market monopolization)
- 1974: Opening of investigation against AT&T (market monopolization)
- 1984: Dismantling of AT&T
- 1986: Zenith (dismissal of a predatory pricing charge)
- 1994: First investigation against Microsoft (closed by settlement)
- 1997: Investigation against Microsoft (closed by settlement)
- 1999: Vitamins (cartel)
- 2000: American Airlines (predatory pricing charge rejected)
- 2008: Rambus convicted of misuse of its patents (market monopolization)
- 2015: Record $3 billion fine against the Exchange rate cartel
- 2019: T-Mobile/Sprint mega merger is authorized
- 2000-2019: Numerous cartel convictions with sanctions exceeding $1 billion (car parts, LCD screens, Libor, etc.); few cases of market monopolization but opening in September 2019 of an investigation against Google by 50 Attorneys General
- 2019: Opening of an investigation against Amazon by the FTC

Antitrust laws have been applied over time by the DOJ and the FTC in a fluctuating manner. We can identify three main waves, particularly in the field of market monopolization.

A first wave of investigations took place during the period spanning 1906-1920, with the 1911 condemnation of American Tobacco and Standard Oil. During the 1929 crisis and the Great Depression, the Roosevelt administration adopted the 1933 National Industrial Recovery Act (NIRA), which put antitrust activity on hold until 1938 (*see* below). It was only just before World War II that Roosevelt reactivated the antitrust arsenal, in particular, with the opening of an investigation against the American aluminum giant, Alcoa.

A second and long wave of antitrust investigations took place during the years 1945-1970. Many large American firms such as IBM or Kellogg's were accused of market monopolization. Structuralist theses were in vogue; the primary objective of antitrust authorities was to preserve an effective competitive market structure, rather than to analyze the effects of practices on prices and consumer surplus. In particular, several antitrust decisions that were adopted were in line with the structuralist's thinking:

- in 1945, in the Alcoa case, U.S. courts established that a practice of margin squeeze (although favorable to consumers) should be prohibited as it strengthened a monopoly position;
- in 1962, in the Brown Shoe Co. case, the U.S. Supreme Court confirmed that the antitrust authorities should block a vertical merger if it creates a risk of market foreclosure;
- in 1967, in the Utah Pie Co. case, the U.S. Supreme Court confirmed that a selective fall in prices below costs was proof that a predatory pricing strategy had been applied.

During the 1980s, there was a decline in the number of investigations initiated by the U.S. government, particularly under the Reagan and George H. W. Bush administrations. Two developments explain this shift in the antitrust policy. First, in a context marked by the fear of a "Japanese technological domination," the priority was given to strengthening the United States' external competitiveness. In particular, an MIT report entitled "Made in America" showed that the Japanese economy was less concerned by antitrust law than the U.S. economy and called for a relaxation of competition law in the United States. Then, the Reagan era marked the triumph of the Chicago School's theses, which reconsidered firms' strategies in a more favorable light: For example, the Zenith case (1986) marked the refusal to consider any aggressive pricing as a predatory pricing. Similarly, the 1982 publication of The Merger and Acquisition Guidelines by the Reagan administration marks a strong shift from the 1968 Guidelines: The cursor was moved from the preservation of a competitive market structure to the analysis of a merger impact, namely, on prices.

During the Clinton era, from 1993 to 2001, a third wave of antitrust actions took place. The U.S. authorities opened investigations against large firms, such as the two trials against Microsoft in 1994 and 1998. At the same time, the fight against cartels was relaunched with the adoption of an incentive leniency program for firms (1993) and individuals (1994).

Since the 2000s, while antitrust activity in the field of cartels has remained strong—with a record fine in 2015 against the Exchange Rate cartel—market monopolization cases have been relatively rare, with the exception of the 2008 Rambus case. Since the election of Donald Trump, antitrust activity seems to have stalled; the number of new cases opened is at its lowest level since the 1990s (Figure 2.2). Several studies conclude that the decline in antitrust activity in the United States since 2000 has led to a strong industrial concentration, which is not observed in Europe (see for example: Gutierrez and Philippon [2018]).

Figure 2.2 Number of Antitrust Investigations in the United States (1990-2018)

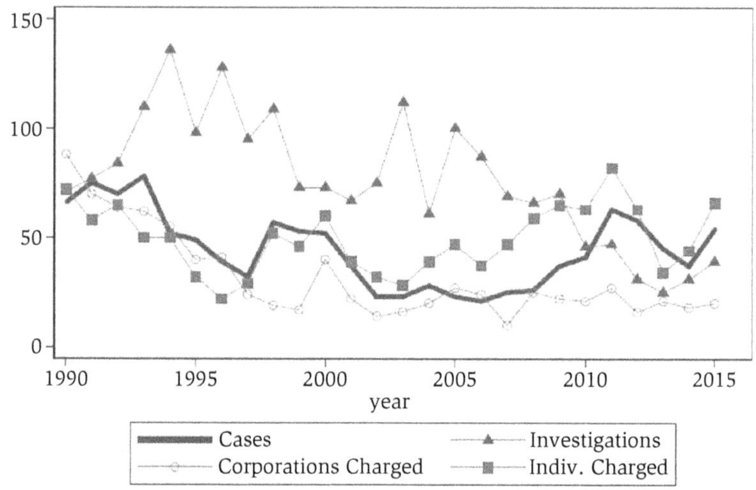

Source: Gutierrez and Philippon (2018).

How can we explain this cyclicality in the enforcement of U.S. antitrust laws, even though the regulatory framework has remained fairly constant over time?

A first explanation was sought in the political alternation between Republicans and Democrats, the latter being more inclined to launch investigations against large firms. Suggested by Posner (1970), this approach has not led to conclusive results: The political party of the elected president and the composition of the Congress do not significantly influence the zeal of antitrust authorities.

A second line of research focused on the role of macroeconomic conditions: Is antitrust activity pro-cyclical or counter-cyclical? According to the interest group theory (Peltzman, 1976), antitrust interventions should be pro-cyclical: When the economy goes into recession, profits fall and firms can experience financial difficulties, leading to a relaxation of antitrust vigilance. Moreover, according to Posner (1970), financial resources of antitrust authorities are more limited during recessions. Conversely, antitrust violations are more frequent during downturns (e.g., collusion behavior), which should lead antitrust to be more active. The Ghosal and Gallo (2001) study confirms the counter-cyclical nature of antitrust interventions: Their econometric test, which covers all antitrust cases opened by the DOJ during the 1955-1994 period, reveals an inverse and significant relationship between different indicators of economic activity (such as stock market indices, unemployment rate, firm profit levels, and Gross Domestic Product) and the level of investigations by antitrust authorities.

An instructive period: The antitrust laws during the New Deal: Following the 1929 crisis, the Roosevelt administration enacted the NIRA in 1933, which put antitrust activity on hold until World War II. The aim of the NIRA was to stop the fall in prices by allowing firms to limit competition in return for wage increases negotiated with unions. The Code of Fair Competition thus put antitrust laws on pause: As early as 1934, more than 500 industries decided to engage in practices of imposed resale prices and minimum prices and to form cartels. Although the NIRA was declared unconstitutional by the U.S. Supreme Court in 1935, antitrust authorities continued to "turn a blind eye" to collusion practices. Cole and Ohanian (2003) measured the impact of the NIRA on the economic crisis during the period spanning 1933-1939[17] by comparing the observed situation ("data" in Figure 2.3) with a situation in which the U.S. economy had remained competitive ("competitive model").

Figure 2.3 Observed and Simulated Production Trends in the United States

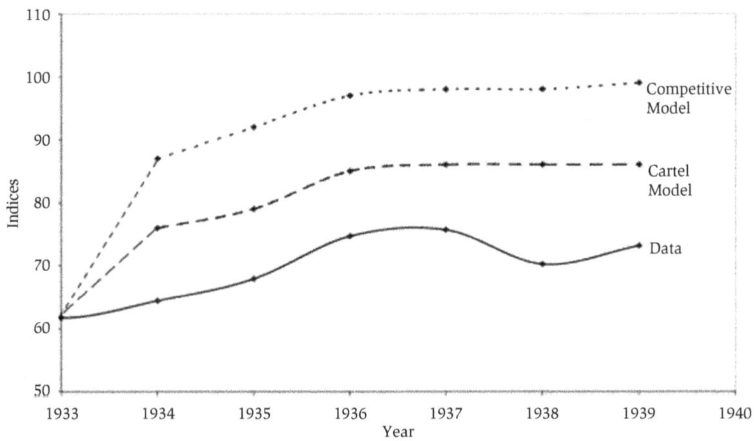

Source: Cole and Ohanian (2004).

They conclude that more than half of the gap between observed and simulated output is explained by the cartelization of the economy and the resulting wage increases ("cartel model"); far from facilitating the end of the Great Depression, the NIRA only prolonged it, by delaying structural reforms.

§2 Europe: The Impetus of the Common Market

From the ECSC to the EEC: The foundations of the European competition policy date back to the creation of the European Coal and Steel Community (ECSC), which was ratified in 1951 and came into force in 1953. The Federal Republic of Germany joined France, Italy, and the three Benelux countries to create a common market for coal and steel; this meant the abolition of customs duties and quantitative restrictions; and the

17. It should be recalled that the GDP per capita (in real terms), which was 39% lower than its trend in 1933, was still 27% lower in 1939.

prohibition of discriminatory measures, subsidies, or aids granted by European States. In particular, the ECSC put an end to cartel practices (both domestic and export) prevailing in France and Germany in the coal and steel industry. Article 65 of the Treaty prohibits agreements between firms that have the effect of restricting competition within the common market. Similarly, Article 66(7) of the Treaty deals with abuses of dominant position. In this sense, the ECSC Treaty is, according to Jean Monnet's words, "the first European antitrust law."

A new decisive step was taken with the creation of the European Economic Community (EEC), following the Treaty of Rome in 1957. Article 2 of the Treaty sets out the aims of this economic integration project: "The Community shall have as its task, by establishing a common market and progressively approximating the economic policies of Member States, to promote throughout the Community a harmonious development of economic activities, a continuous and balanced expansion, an increase in stability, an accelerated raising of the standard of living and closer relations between the States belonging to it."

Article 3 sets out the means to achieve these objectives and refers in particular to competition rules, which are presented as a necessary instrument of integration: "(...) the activities of the Community shall include, as provided in this Treaty and in accordance with the timetable set out therein:

> (f) the institution of a system ensuring that competition in the common market is not distorted."

Three main articles will form the pillars of the European competition policy:

- Article 85 on agreements between firms (now Article 101 TFEU).
- Article 86 on abuse of dominant position (now Article 102 TFEU).
- Article 92 on State aid (now Article 107 TFEU).

It should be noted that, unlike the ECSC (through Article 66), the European competition policy did not originally have a merger control system; as early as 1973, the Commission proposed to adopt specific rules in this area, but it only came into force after 1990.

From Regulation 1/2003 to ECN+: The early 2000s saw a major reform of the European competition policy, with the 2004 adoption of Regulation 1/2003:

- While the European Commission retains an exclusive competence for the control of state aid and mergers with a European dimension, each European Union (EU) Member State directly applies Articles 101 (cartel) and 102 (abuse of dominant position). A European Competition Network (ECN) is put in place, gathering the Commission and the national competition authorities. It allows consultations, collaboration and exchanges of information in the application of Articles 101 and 102.

- The system of "prior notification" of agreements gave way to a system of "legal exception": Firms must assess the lawfulness of their agreements themselves.[18]

In 2014, the Damage Directive was introduced in Europe; it promotes private enforcement actions while preserving the effectiveness of the public enforcement.

In 2019, a new impetus was given to the European competition policy through the ECN + Directive, which allows national competition authorities to implement competition law in a more effective way. This Directive obliges each Member State to ensure that its national competition authority has the necessary guarantees of independence, resources, and power to set fines in order to ensure the effectiveness of Articles 101 and 102. In particular, the Directive strengthens the deterrence aspect of competition policy by allowing antitrust authorities to impose "effective, proportionate and dissuasive fines."

Table 2.3 Competition Policy in Europe: Key Dates

- 1953: The ECSC Treaty comes into force
- 1957: Signing of the Treaty of Rome
- 1962: Implementation of Regulation n° 17, enhancing the effectiveness of antitrust policies
- 1990: Merger regulation come into force
- 2004: The new Regulation 139/2004 on merger control and Regulation 1/2003 on the application of Articles 101 and 102 come into force
- 2006: The Commission publishes its notice on immunity from fines and reduction of fines in cartel cases
- 2009: The Commission publishes a Communication on abusive exclusionary practices by dominant firms
- 2010: The Commission publishes its Exemption Regulation 330/2010 on vertical agreements and its exemption regulation 1217/2010 on R&D agreements
- 2011: The Commission publishes its Guidelines on horizontal cooperation agreements
- 2014: The Commission publishes its Exemption Regulation 316/2014 on technology transfer agreements
- 2014: The Commission adopts the Damage Directive on actions for damages following infringements of competition law
- 2019: Entry into force of the ECN + Directive which strengthens the role of national competition authorities
- 2020: The Commission proposed new rules for the digital economy with the Digital Market Act.

The main antitrust cases—in the fields of cartels and abuse of dominant position—that have marked the EU history are presented in Table 2.4.

18. Regarding the functioning of the legal exception system, *see* Chapter 4 on conditional agreements.

Table 2.4 Key Antitrust Cases in Europe

- 1979: Hoffmann-La Roche (abuse of dominant position; exclusivity contract)
- 1985: Akzo (abuse of dominant position; predatory pricing)
- 1991: Tetra Pak (abuse of dominant position; predatory pricing)
- 1999: British Airways/Virgin (abuse of dominant position; loyalty discount)
- 2002: Michelin case (abuse of dominant position; loyalty discount)
- 2001: Sanction against the Vitamins cartel
- 2004: Microsoft I case (abuse of dominant position; tying sales)
- 2007: Telefonica case (abuse of dominant position; margin squeeze)
- 2008: Sanction against the Flat Glass cartel; for the first time, a sanction exceeds €1 billion
- 2008: Microsoft II case (non-compliance with commitments)
- 2009: Intel case (abuse of dominant position; loyalty rebates)
- 2012: Sanction against the TV and computer screen cartel
- 2016: Sanction against the Truck cartel
- 2017-2019: Three sanctions against Google for several abuses of dominant position

Delays in implementing at a national level: For a long time, antitrust policies have occupied a minor place in the national legal system of European countries, even after the birth of the European common market.

This low appetite for competition rules is largely due to ideological and historical reasons: The implementation of a competition policy requires countries to adhere to the market economy, which does not correspond to the traditions in many European countries. For instance, countries such as France have long favored the direct intervention of the State in the economy, particularly after World War II. In Europe, certain anti-competitive practices were tolerated and even encouraged during World War II: Under the Nazi regimes, for example, cartels flourished.

It was in 1947 that Germany adopted for the first time in Europe a competition legislation[19] under the pressure of the Allies, who wanted to reshape the German economy and rebuild it on sound foundations. Far from remaining theoretical, the antitrust policy quickly played an essential role in Germany, by basing itself on the "ordo-liberal" thinking, developed since the 1930s by authors such as Walter Eucken. Indeed, during the inter-war period, the Ordo-Liberal School (also known as the Fribourg School) developed a "*social liberalism,*" based on values such as the entrepreneurial freedom and the regulation of competition; the objective was to build a market economy which would benefit the society as a whole. This vision, which broke with the authoritative and corporatist vision of Nazism, was favorably received after 1945 by political figures such as Ludwig Erhard, the Chancellor Adenauer's

19. In fact, Germany adopted a law on cartels in 1923, mainly to limit hyperinflation. This law does not prohibit cartels as such but establishes a registration system.

Minister of Economy. In 1957, it led to the adoption of a competition law and creation of an independent competition authority, the *Bundeskartellamt* (Federal Cartel Office).

Except for the German case, European countries did not have any real competition policy until the 1980s: It was the EU that encouraged the implementation of an antitrust policy at the Member State level. For example, while Spain has had a competition legislation since 1962, it was after its accession to the EU in 1986 that it applied a genuine competition policy with the 1989 adoption of the Competition Act.

The case of the Netherlands is quite singular: Historically, cartels had always been tolerated. It was only after 1993 when the SPO (a Construction association) was explicitly condemned by the European Commission for horizontal price fixing that an independent competition authority was established in 1998.

The European impetus is also reflected in the national competition policies put in place in the former Eastern Bloc countries (Poland, Hungary, etc.) after their accessions to the EU. The negotiations included an important section on competition policy: Eastern countries had to adopt a legislative framework in line with the European rules and to make their competition policies more effective.

An illustration of reticence: The French case: The French case is very instructive. It illustrates the reluctance to accept a competition policy fully independent from political power. After World War II, reconstruction was carried out in a forceful and directive way, spurred on by the State and in a context of strong price controls.[20] The Ordinance of December 1986 marked a decisive step in France's "long march" towards having an autonomous competition policy. The Competition Council, an independent administrative authority, was created and the general principle of "freedom to set prices" was introduced. In May 2001, the New Economic Regulations (NRE) Act amended certain provisions of the 1986 Ordinance to bring it in line with European law: In particular, financial penalties were increased and the prior notification of mergers became mandatory.

However, the final decision in merger cases still remained in the hands of the Minister of the Economy; an important part of competition policy was therefore still outside the decision-making power of the Competition Council. In February 2009, following the Law on the Modernization of the Economy (LME), the Competition Authority was created to replace the Competition Council. Two important changes were made:

(1) merger control was transferred to the Competition Authority and is no longer under the control of the Minister. However, once the Authority has taken a decision on a case, the Minister of the Economy can still overturn the decision on the "grounds of general interest other than competition," such as the competitiveness of firms, or to maintain employment. In practice, the Minister used this mechanism only once during the 2008/2018 period, when Cofigeo acquired William Saurin in 2018;

20. For more on the history of competitive ideas in France since Colbert, we refer to Chapter 1 of Bosco and Prieto's book (1993).

(2) the Competition Authority may give its own opinion on any competition issue and make recommendations to improve the competitive functioning of markets.

§3 Implementing a Competition Policy in Emerging and Developing Countries

Since the 1990s, many emerging and developing countries have implemented a competition policy that covers at least anti-competitive agreements. In many cases, this policy is part of a program of structural reforms (privatizations, budgetary stabilization, etc.), initiated by international organizations (such as the IMF) after an economic crisis or as a result of a country's accession to a regional organization. Even though competition policies have been adopted around the world, their effectiveness appears to be unequal and differs greatly between countries.

Differences per region: In South America, few countries have a genuine and effective competition policy. This situation is the result of strong State interventionism (such as protectionist policies, price controls, nationalizations) and can be explained by the reluctance of politicians to entrust competition policy to an independent authority. However, countries such as Chile and Brazil have an effective antitrust arsenal: In Brazil, the Real Plan was launched in 1994 to stabilize an economy battered by hyperinflation. A structural reform program was adopted, including the creation of an independent antitrust agency: the Brazilian Competition Authority (CADE). We can also mention the case of Mexico: Since the 1982 debt crisis, the Mexican economic policy has moved towards a State disengagement, accentuated by its entry into the North American Free Trade Agreement (NAFTA) in 1990. After implementing a program of openness to international trade and foreign direct investments, deregulation, and privatization, the Mexican government adopted the Federal Economic Competition Law (FLEC) in 1993 and created a competition authority, the Federal Economic Competition Commission (FTC).

In Asia, several emerging countries have adopted competition policies, such as India, which, in 2003, enacted the Competition Act and created the Competition Commission. Other Asian countries have implemented antitrust policies as part of IMF structural reform programs, after the 1998 economic crisis. For example, Indonesia enacted a law on unfair and monopoly practices in 1999. More recently, China, on the economic catch-up path, implemented an antitrust arsenal in 2008 with the adoption of the Anti Monopoly Law, which introduces all the provisions of a competition law. For example, in 2014, the Chinese competition authority imposed a $200 million penalty on several Japanese automotive suppliers that had formed a cartel in China.

On the African continent, the situation is quite mixed. In North Africa, while Maghreb countries (Algeria, Morocco, and Tunisia) have adopted competition laws, their effectiveness remains rather low in practice. In sub-Saharan Africa, several countries now have effective competition policies, such as Kenya, which adopted the Competition Act in 2012 and strengthened the power of its competition authority. Most of the competition laws in force in sub-Saharan Africa have been enacted within the framework of the Common Market for Eastern and Southern Africa (COMESA), which adopted competition rules in 2013.

Competition policy: The result of a catching-up process?: The question of whether a competition policy in a developing or emerging country should be implemented remains open: Are competition policies prerequisites and necessary conditions for economic development, or is the implementation of such a policy rather a step in a catch-up process? Several arguments have been put forward to advocate a late and differentiated implementation (compared to developed countries) of competition policies in developing countries (Singh & Dhumale, 1999):

- economic take-off often requires State intervention, both as a coordinator of economic decisions and as a public investor. Close links between public authorities and private firms are strong during this catch-up phase. This situation is not conducive to an effective and independent competition policy;
- competition policy is costly, and its effectiveness on a national level may be limited if anti-competitive practices are carried out by foreign firms (e.g., international cartels);
- according to Kovacic et al. (2016), it takes at least 20-25 years for a competition policy to become effective, due to the learning curve;
- an effective competition policy requires human resources that developing countries often lack, as elites prefer to embrace more lucrative careers in the private sector (Aydin et al., 2016);
- competition policy may not be sufficient to stimulate private initiative if there are no private incentives to invest and no entrepreneurship spirit: As Bienaymé (1998) notes, competition policy: "does not have the power to encourage the population itself to redouble its initiatives. Entrepreneurship cannot be decreed; it is simply encouraged by provisions to defend free access and open markets. Competition law creates safeguards more than it directly stimulates competition" (free translation from French);
- many developing countries are characterized by a political and economic oligarchy, which has no interest in establishing antitrust rules. Indeed, most lucrative economic sectors (such as oil, raw materials, heavy industry) are in a monopoly situation; the monopoly rents often benefit a small minority of people with privileged ties with the political power (Géradin & Petit, 2003). In the absence of structural political reforms (democratic elections, emergence of a class of entrepreneurs, etc.), competition policy is likely to remain ineffective;
- many informational barriers limit the effectiveness of competition policy. Analyzing the cases of Kenya and Zambia, Boadu and Olofinbiyi (2003) show that high inflation makes it difficult to demonstrate collusive prices, while the large informal sector makes the definition of "relevant markets" more complex;

- economic take-off implies a high accumulation of capital and therefore high profit expectations for investors. Too much competition can limit the profitability of projects and challenge the process of capital accumulation and the adoption of new technologies.

The idea that competition policy should be "put to sleep" when a country makes its economic catch-up can be illustrated by the Japanese case, which did its economic catch-up in the 1950/1960s.[21] Competition policy in Japan began in 1947, driven by the United States (which then occupied the country) with the adoption of The Antimonopoly Act and the creation of the Japan Fair Trade Commission. The Allies had to dismantle the large Japanese companies (the *zaibatsus*), which had played a decisive role during the war. The Antimonopoly Act covers the main areas we can find in the American antitrust policy:

- Section 3 condemns restrictive trade practices (such as cartels) and market monopolization behaviors.
- Section 19 regulates unfair commercial practices, such as refusal to sell, discriminatory prices, and, more generally, vertical restraints.
- Chapter 4 prohibits mergers where they have the effect of restricting competition.

However, in practice, the 1947 text remained poorly applied before the 1980s: Competition policy was long subservient to MITI's (Ministry of International Trade and Industry) industrial policy (Amsden & Singh, 1994). Okimoto (1989) summarizes the place given to competition policy in Japan's catch-up process in these terms: "The Japanese government takes a more pragmatic approach to antitrust enforcement, one that makes allowances for national goals such as industrial catch-up. It takes into account other collective values and extenuating circumstances in weighing enforcement decisions against the letter and spirit of antitrust laws. Included here are such considerations as economies of scale, enhanced efficiency, optimal use of scarce resources, international competitiveness, heightened productivity, business cycle stabilization, industrial orderliness, price stabilization and economic security."

Cartel exemption regimes from The Antimonopoly Act dominated after World War II. In 1953, an Amendment to The Antimonopoly Act allowed "recession cartels" and "rationalization cartels," while resale price maintenance (RPM) practices may be allowed in certain circumstances. During the period spanning 1953-1994, 1,379 cartels benefited from an exemption scheme. In terms of industrial concentration, the former *zaibatsus* quickly recovered to form *keiretsus*, and the MITI greatly encouraged this process of industrial concentration in key industries, as noted by Amsden and Singh.

21. A fairly similar reasoning could be applied to the case of South Korea, which caught up economically in the 1970s and 1980s. Long protected and controlled by the State, organized around large conglomerates (*chaebols*), the Korean economy has evolved since 1990s towards a free market economy. Today, South Korea has an effective antitrust arsenal, quite similar to that in force in the United States, particularly in the criminal repression of cartels.

It is only at the end of the catch-up period and under the pressure of foreign countries (calling for a greater opening of the Japanese market to imports)[22] that Japan gradually implemented a real competition policy. For example, it was not until 1984 that the first cartels were sentenced to financial penalties, while the 1990s saw a strengthening of criminal sanctions (1992) and a gradual abolition of cartel exemptions (1997 and 1999).

Competition policy: A preliminary condition for economic take-off?: A second approach considers competition policy as a prerequisite for economic development. First, several empirical studies on the relationship between competition and growth show that competition improves productivity and the incentive to innovate (Nickell, 1996; Aghion et al., 2009). Buccirossi et al. (2011) directly tested the impact of competition policy on the aggregate productivity growth on a sample of 12 OECD (Organisation for Economic Co-operation and Development) countries and 22 industries over the period spanning 1995-2005. They demonstrate the direct relationship between the harshness of antitrust policies and productivity growth: Productivity growth is high when competition policies are strict (Figure 2.4). They also show that the impact of a competition policy is higher when the country is lagging behind from a technological point of view. This result is particularly true for developing countries that must fill the technological gap.

Figure 2.4 The Impact of Antitrust Policy on Economic Growth

Effective competition policy + legal system

↓

Encouraging firms to compete and to reduce costs
(rather than forming a cartel or abusing of their dominant position)
Entry of new competitors

↓

Productivity gains

↓

Economic growth

Second, in the context of World Trade Organization (WTO) negotiations (such as the Uruguay Round), most developing countries have gradually opened their economies to imports and foreign investment, particularly from developed countries. However, in the absence of any competition policy, developing countries may be victims of anti-competitive practices initiated by foreign firms, without having the legal framework to prosecute them. For example, the impact of an international cartel on a developing country is twofold:

22. The United States began bilateral discussions known as the Structural Impediments Initiative in 1989: The United States asked Japan to strengthen competition rules in order to facilitate American firms' access to the Japanese domestic market.

- at the level of final and intermediate consumers (who use the product as an input), the price of imported products increases;
- local firms can take advantage of an international cartel to align their prices upwards (with a so-called "umbrella policy"). They may also suffer from an international cartel blocking the access to developed countries by using public strategies (anti-dumping duties) or private strategies (threats of price war in case of entry, locking of the distribution system, etc.).

Third, cartels or abuses of dominant position can particularly affect the poorest consumers, especially when they involve essential products. For example, in 2013, the OECD notes that "[c]artels and boycotting agreements have been discovered and prosecuted in the baking, milling, sugar and milk industries in developing countries. Anti-competitive practices are endemic in public transportation markets such as bus and taxi services, on which many poor consumers depend. The cement industry, on which so much public infrastructure—including public housing—relies, is riddled with cartels and abuse of dominant positions. These problems are not specific to a small group of countries but rather are widespread throughout the developing world."

Anti-competitive practices can also prevent low-income people from increasing their incomes (e.g., by undertaking small-scale ventures) if markets are cartelized or closed by exclusivity agreements.

Finally, since the 1990s, developing countries have been engaged in extensive privatization programs, including network industries (gas, electricity, etc.), and foreign private investors have acquired many public firms. The absence of a genuine competition policy can alter the effectiveness of these programs, because the gains from privatizations depend on the intensity of competition in the market, rather than on capital ownership (Singh & Dhumale, 1999; Boadu & Olofinbiyi, 2003).

SECTION 2 THE LEGAL AND INSTITUTIONAL FRAMEWORK

We start by clarifying the legal framework in which antitrust authorities operate (§1), before presenting the institutional framework (§2). We finish by analyzing the effectiveness of antitrust sanctions (§3).

§1 The Legal Framework: Competition Law

Competition policy covers three main areas, which are found in all OECD countries, although the procedures and review criteria may differ (Table 2.1):

- restrictive agreements between firms, both horizontal and vertical;
- abuses of dominant position. These first two components constitute the core of what is called an "antitrust" policy, whose scope is narrower than "competition policy";
- the control of mergers.

Beyond these common provisions, competition policies sometimes have specific features—e.g., Europe with the State aid notification regime.

Restrictive agreements: A first field of competition policy concerns agreements—both horizontal and vertical—between undertakings aimed at restricting competition: Broadly outlined, agreements that have the sole effect or object—like cartels—of restricting trade are prohibited, while other forms of agreements are assessed according to a "rule of reason" (in the United States) or an exemption regime (in Europe).

Cartel practices in the United States fall under Section 1 of the Sherman Act (1890), which states: "Every contract, combination in the form of trust or otherwise, or conspiracy, in restraint of trade or commerce among the several States, or with foreign nations, is declared to be illegal. Every person who shall make any contract or engage in any combination or conspiracy hereby declared to be illegal shall be deemed guilty of a felony, and, on conviction thereof, shall be punished by fine not exceeding $10,000,000 if a corporation, or, if any other person, $350,000, or by imprisonment not exceeding three years, or by both said punishments, in the discretion of the court."

At the level of the EU, we find similar provisions in paragraph 1 of Article 101 TFEU:

> 1. The following shall be prohibited as incompatible with the internal market: all agreements between undertakings, decisions by associations of undertakings and concerted practices which may affect trade between Member States and which have as their object or effect the prevention, restriction or distortion of competition within the internal market, and in particular those which:
>   (a) directly or indirectly fix purchase or selling prices or any other trading conditions;
>   (b) limit or control production, markets, technical development, or investment;
>   (c) share markets or sources of supply;
>   (d) apply dissimilar conditions to equivalent transactions with other trading parties, thereby placing them at a competitive disadvantage;
>   (e) make the conclusion of contracts subject to acceptance by the other parties of supplementary obligations which, by their nature or according to commercial usage, have no connection with the subject of such contracts.
> 2. Any agreements or decisions prohibited pursuant to this Article shall be automatically void.

Abuse of dominant position: The second component of competition policy deals with "abuse of dominant position," a term that covers both exclusionary and exploitative practices. In the United States, Section 2 of the Sherman Act condemns attempts to monopolize the market: "Every person who shall monopolize, or attempt to monopolize, or combine or conspire with any other person or persons, to monopolize any part of the trade or commerce among the several States, or with foreign nations, shall be deemed guilty of a felony, and, on conviction thereof, shall be punished by fine not exceeding $10,000,000 if a corporation, or, if any other person, $350,000, or by imprisonment not exceeding three years, or by both said punishments, in the discretion of the court."

At the European level, the abuse of dominant position falls under Article 102 TFEU: "Any abuse by one or more undertakings of a dominant position in the common market or in a substantial part of it by one or more undertakings shall be prohibited as incompatible with the common market in so far as it may affect trade between Member States.

Such abusive practices may include, but are not limited to, the following:

(a) directly or indirectly impose unfair purchase or sale prices or other unfair trading conditions,
(b) limit production, markets or technical development to the detriment of consumers,
(c) apply unequal conditions to equivalent services to trading partners, thereby placing them at a competitive disadvantage,
(d) make the conclusion of contracts subject to the acceptance by the partners of additional services which, by their nature or according to commercial usage, are not related to the subject matter of those contracts."

Merger control*:* The third part of competition policy concerns merger control. Unlike the antitrust action (cartel, abuse of a dominant position), which is retrospective, merger control is preventive: Firms must declare their merger project before carrying it out.

In the United States, merger control is essentially governed by Section 7 of the Clayton Act, which states: "No person engaged in commerce or in any activity affecting commerce shall acquire, directly or indirectly, the whole or any part of the stock or other share capital and no person subject to the jurisdiction of the Federal Trade Commission shall acquire the whole or any part of the assets of another person engaged also in commerce or in any activity affecting commerce, where in any line of commerce or in any activity affecting commerce in any section of the country, the effect of such acquisition may be substantially to lessen competition, or to tend to create a monopoly [...]."

In the European case, the merger control was not included in the Treaty of Rome, and this provision was added in 1990, with the Regulation 139/2004: "Concentrations which would significantly impede effective competition in the common market or a substantial part of it, in particular as a result of the creation or strengthening of a dominant position, must be declared incompatible with the common market."

Beyond these three pillars of competition law, which are found in all OECD countries, Europe has adopted a specific legislation on state aids: They are prohibited when they may distort competition within the EU and must be notified in advance. Established since the Treaty of Rome, this system, which only exists in Europe, aims to avoid a "subsidy race" between States, each of them being tempted to subsidize its "national champions": A prisoner's dilemma situation would occur, leading to a multiplication of public subsidies in Europe.

Paragraph 1 of Article 107 TFEU stipulates that: "Save as otherwise provided in the Treaties, any aid granted by a Member State or through State resources in any form whatsoever which distorts or threatens to distort competition by favoring certain undertakings or the production of certain goods shall, in so far as it affects trade between Member States, be incompatible with the internal market."

An aid can be qualified as a "State aid" if four criteria are cumulatively met:

- the aid is granted from public resources of a European State;
- it gives the firm a selective advantage;
- it distorts competition;
- it is likely to affect trade between Member States.

Since 2001, the Commission has adopted several exemption regulations allowing Member States to grant certain categories of aid without prior notification when they meet specific criteria. However, they must still inform the Commission of any such aid schemes. Thus, an aid that is granted on the basis of these exempted schemes and that complies with all the conditions is presumed to be compatible with the internal market.

Table 2.5 The Main Areas of Competition Policy

Object	*United States*	*European Union*
Agreements	- Section 1 of the Sherman Act - Section 3 of the Clayton Act	Article 101 of the TFEU Treaty
Abuse of dominant position	- Section 2 of the Sherman Act - Section 2 of the Clayton Act (discrimination)	Article 102 of the TFEU Treaty
Merger control	- Clayton Act, section 7 - Celler-Kefauver Act - Hart-Scott- Rodino Act	Regulation n° 139/2004
State aid		Articles 107 and 108 of the TFEU

The role of guidelines: In order to increase legal certainty and make their decisions more predictable, competition authorities publish guidelines (Table 2.6) on various competition policy topics: merger control, licensing agreements, etc. Their aim is to provide an overview of the rule of law at the time of the guidelines' publication. For this reason, guidelines are regularly revised to take into account changes in antitrust authorities' practice: For example, in the field of merger control, the U.S. Guidelines have been amended five times since 1968.

Table 2.6 The Main Guidelines in the United States and Europe

Purpose of the Guidelines	*United States*	*Europe*
Licensing	Antitrust Guidelines for Licensing of Intellectual Property (2017)	Guidelines on Technology Transfer Agreements (2014)
Horizontal agreements	Antitrust Guidelines for Collaboration Among Competitors (2000)	Guidelines on Horizontal Cooperation Agreements (2011)
Vertical restrictions	Guidelines in 1985 repealed in 1993	Guidelines on Vertical Restraints (2010)
Calculation of fines	U.S. Sentencing Guidelines (2011), included in the Primer Antitrust (2019)	Guidelines on the Method of Setting Fines (2006)
Merger control	Non-Horizontal Merger Guidelines (1984) Horizontal Merger Guidelines (2010) Vertical Merger Guidelines (2020)	- Communication on the relevant market (1997) - Horizontal Merger Guidelines (2004) - Communication on Acceptable Remedies (2008) - Non-Horizontal Merger Guidelines (2008)

Rules applied to assess anti-competitive behaviors: When assessing the lawfulness of a practice under competition law, competition authorities can use two different approaches.

A first approach, used in the United States, consists of analyzing the firm's behavior according to a "per se" rule or a rule of reason. According to the per se rule, conduct is prohibited or permitted in principle without the need for a case-by-case analysis. For example, cartel behavior is prohibited per se by U.S. authorities; no justification can be given to exempt them. This prohibition of price fixing was first stated in the United States in the Trans-Missouri case (1897) and then reaffirmed in the Trenton Potteries (1927) and Socony-Vacuum Oil (1940) cases.

Unlike the per se approach, the "*rule of reason*" consists of balancing the effects of a practice that negatively affects competition with other positive effects. For example, a selective distribution agreement between a producer and its distributors can be accepted even if it restricts competition; the nature of the product (strong brand image, etc.) can justify the need to select the resellers and this restriction can be beneficial to consumers. Similarly, an R&D agreement between competitors or a merger is not prohibited as such; its approval by antitrust authorities is the result of a balance between competitive risks and economic efficiencies.

The dichotomy between the per se approach and the rule of reason is not immutable, and the processing of certain practices has evolved over time. Thus, with regards to resale price maintenance (RPM), the United States has evolved from a per se prohibition approach to an approach based on the rule of reason: In 1997, in the Leegin case, the Supreme Court opened a breach in the almost 100-year-old prohibition of the minimum resale price. In this case, Leegin, which was not in a dominant position, applied a minimum resale price in order to encourage its distributors to offer service to end customers. Following an action brought by a distributor wishing to offer rebates, Leegin was ordered to pay "*treble damages*" and this decision was confirmed on appeal. However, the Supreme Court overturned the decision on the grounds that the imposition of a minimum resale price could benefit consumers by promoting competition through services.

The Supreme Court therefore invited judges to treat minimum resale prices according to a rule of reason—in particular, when the producer does not have a dominant position—rather than applying, on principle, a prohibition.

In Europe, anti-competitive practices are analyzed according to two approaches: the offense by object or the offense by effect. A practice constitutes an offense by object when it is sufficiently harmful to be considered unlawful, without the need to demonstrate its alleged anti-competitive effects. But unlike the per se approach, an offense by object does not exclude that the practice can then be exempted. For example, in Europe, if a resale price maintenance (RPM) constitutes an offense by object, it may nevertheless be exempted in certain very specific cases, e.g., when a new product is launched on the market.

Conversely, an infringement by effect requires an analysis of the potential or actual effects of the practice before determining whether it is unlawful. When an antitrust practice negatively affects competition, whether by object or by effect, it can sometimes get exempted. Indeed, paragraph 3 of Article 101 TFEU states:

> However, the provisions of §1 may be declared inapplicable:
>
> - any agreement or category of agreements between companies,
> - any decision or category of decisions of associations of undertakings and,
> - any concerted practice or category of concerted practices, which contribute to improving the production or distribution of products, or to promoting technical or economic progress, while reserving for users a share of the resulting benefit, and without:
>   (a) impose restrictions on the undertakings concerned which are not indispensable for achieving these objectives,
>   (b) to give such undertakings the possibility, in respect of a substantial part of the products in question, of eliminating competition.

Until 2004, in order to benefit from an exemption, agreements had to be notified to the Commission, but this procedure gave way to a so-called "*legal exception*" system: Since the adoption of Regulation 1/2003, firms must now assess the lawfulness of their agreements themselves under Article 101 TFEU. In order to clarify the conditions under which an agreement can automatically be exempted, the Commission has adopted several "*block exemption*" regulations, which we will discuss in Chapter 4.

§2 The Institutional Framework: The Role of Competition Authorities

The implementation of a competition policy is first entrusted to competition authorities, who aim to maintain the public economic order. A competition authority pursues several goals: advisory, preventive, corrective and punitive. This subsection is dedicated to reviewing these roles one by one and then to comparing how sanctions are determined in both the United States and in Europe.

The central role of competition authorities: An antitrust policy is mainly implemented by a competition authority, which is unlike any sectoral regulator:

- its scope covers all firms and sectors within a geographical territory, unlike sectorial regulatory authorities, which are specific to an industry;
- the intervention of a competition authority is by definition discontinuous: It intervenes on a case-by-case basis, when an anti-competitive practice has been detected, or when there is a merger project. On the one hand, competition authorities are less exposed to the risk of bias and "regulator capture" unlike a sectorial regulator. On the other hand, they have less access to the firm's cost structure information;
- with the exception of merger control cases, antitrust authorities' investigations can be quite long, given the difficulty of collecting evidence;
- in Europe, competition authorities have high degrees of independence from the political power.

In the case of the United States, competition policy is implemented both by the U.S. DOJ through its Antitrust Division and by a specialized agency, the FTC, created in 1914. The status of the two agencies differs significantly: The DOJ is an emanation of the executive power while the FTC is an administrative authority with a certain degree of independence. They each have different roles: The FTC ensures compliance with the prohibitions set out in the Clayton Act and the FTC Act, while the DOJ ensures the application of the Sherman Act and has the power to initiate criminal proceedings. Another difference distinguishes the FTC from the DOJ: In the case of an infringement of the federal competition laws, the DOJ acts before federal courts while the FTC has its own judicial panels. Regarding merger control, the two authorities share tasks, in particular, according to their sectorial competences.

At the European level, the European Commission is in charge of the competition policy through the Directorate General for Competition (DG Comp). The Commission's decisions can be challenged before the General Court, and an appeal can be brought before the European Court of Justice (ECJ).

The implementation of competition rules in Europe has undergone major changes since 2004, with the adoption of the Regulation 1/2003:

- the Commission no longer has an exclusive competence to apply Articles 101 and 102. This competence is now shared with the national competition authorities;

- a ECN (European Competition Network) has been set up, bringing together the Commission and the competition authorities of the Member States. It allows consultations, collaboration, and exchanges of information between competition authorities in the application of Articles 101 and 102 TFEU. The Commission is at the head of the network.

Preventive function: Competition authorities exercise a preventive function through the "*prior notification*" system.

Thus, in the case of mergers and acquisitions (M&A), firms must notify the antitrust authorities about their projects before implementing them; this is an ex-ante control. For example, during the period spanning 2009-2018, the EU received between 300 and 400 merger notifications each year, while the U.S. authorities were notified of 1,000-2,000 drafts (Figure 2.5). Once the authorities have examined the project, they have three options:

- accept unconditionally;
- give a conditional acceptance: For example, if the firms accept some "commitments" such as reselling certain assets to competitors;
- forbid the merger: For example, in February 2019, the European Commission blocked the merger between Alstom and Siemens in the high-speed train and rail-signaling sector.

Chapter 6 details the merger control procedure.

Figure 2.5 Merger Notifications in Europe and the United States (2010-2020)

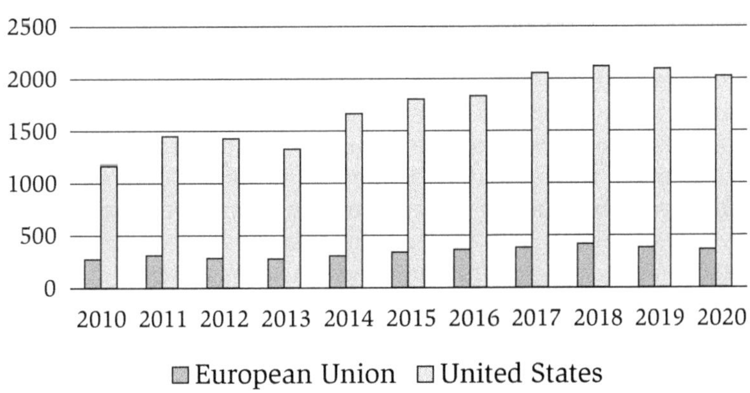

Source: Made by the author using data from the European Commission and the FTC.

While merger notification is found in most antitrust laws, the EU was characterized until 2004 by a prior notification system for agreements between firms. This system was replaced in 2004 by a "*legal exception*" procedure. Now firms must assess themselves whether their agreements restrict competition or not; if so, they must prove ex post that the competitive restriction is offset by efficiency gains in order to obtain an "*exemption.*"

There were several reasons for moving from a (ex-ante) preventive control system to a (ex-post) retrospective system:

- the notification of agreements involved significant legal and transaction costs for firms;
- the notification system resulted in a substantial bureaucratic burden for the Commission, with very lengthy decision-making delays;
- firms have learned "the rules of the game" in Europe since 1957. This learning process no longer justified maintaining an ex-ante control;
- it is more effective to allocate the Commission's limited resources to cartel detection and enforcement.

While the notification of agreements has disappeared in Europe, State aids must be notified to the European Commission, thereby ensuring that the aids do not distort competition within the Union. Aids granted on the basis of non-notified schemes and exceeding a certain threshold are illegal and must be reimbursed. Thus, in July 2015, the Commission ordered electric utility company EDF to reimburse €1.3 billion to the French State, which had granted it an unjustified tax exemption in 1997.

Corrective function: In Europe, a firm suspected of abusing its dominant position or having concluded a vertical agreement can end the investigation process by committing to change its behavior and resolve the "*competition concerns*" identified by the competition authority. At the European level, Article 13 of the Regulation 1/2003 states: "Where, in the course of proceedings which might lead to an agreement or practice being prohibited, undertakings offer the Commission commitments such as to meet its concerns, the Commission should be able to adopt decisions which make those commitments binding on the undertakings concerned. Commitment decisions should find that there are no longer grounds for action by the Commission without concluding whether or not there has been or still is an infringement. (...). Commitment decisions are not appropriate in cases where the Commission intends to impose a fine."

A commitment procedure does not imply any acknowledgement of guilt, but it legally obliges the firm to respect its commitments. If not, non-compliance can lead to sanctions. For example, in 2013, the European Commission sanctioned Microsoft with a fine of €561 million for failing to comply with its commitments.

Punitive function: Regarding anti-competitive practices (cartels, abuse of dominant position), competition authorities can impose sanctions on firms when they commit an infraction. Different punitive instruments can be used:

- an injunction to cease: Antitrust authorities may require firms to stop the offending practice, to return to the previous state, or to change their behavior, possibly under threat of penalty. Thus, in March 2004, the European Commission ordered Microsoft to disclose to its competitors the information necessary to ensure the interoperability of their software with Windows and to offer OEMs (Original Equipment Manufacturer) a version of Windows that doesn't include Media Player;

- an order of publication: For example, in France, the Competition Authority can order the publication of a summary of the decision in the newspapers, which publicly stigmatizes the offender and his behavior;
- dismantling measures: This provision exists only in the United States. It has been used only in extreme cases of abuse of dominant position such as in the Standard Oil case in 1911 or against AT&T in 1984;
- financial penalties: Antitrust authorities may impose a fine on a firm that infringes the law. We develop this point in the following two subsections.

Setting antitrust sanctions in the United States: In the United States, the maximum level of penalty is set by the Sherman Act at $100 million for a firm. However, in practice, American authorities may deviate from this ceiling by imposing sanctions of up to twice the unlawful gain made by the offender or twice the loss suffered by the victims. Concerning the calculation of the penalty, the U.S. Sentencing Guidelines (2011), which are included in the Primer Antitrust (2019), recommend a two-step approach.

First, a base amount is determined on the volume of trade affected by the practice. The choice to use the volume of sales ensures the proportionality of the penalty and also facilitates the calculation:

> "The Commission determined that tying the offense level to the scale or scope of the offense is important in order to ensure that the sanction is in fact punitive and that there is an incentive to desist from a violation once it has begun. The offense levels are not based directly on the damage caused or profit made by the defendant because damages are difficult and time-consuming to establish. The Commission determined, however, that volume of commerce is an acceptable and more readily measurable substitute. Volume of commerce, rather than loss, serves as the basis for offense level calculation because damages are difficult and time-consuming to determine, and the scale or scope of the offense as measured by the volume of commerce is an acceptable proxy for the harm caused by the defendant's conduct."

A surcharge factor is applied to the volume of trade affected by the practice if it exceeds $1 million. The increase coefficient can be particularly dissuasive (Table 2.7).

Table 2.7 Coefficient of Penalty, According to the Volume of Trade Affected by the Practice

	Volume of Commerce (Apply the Greatest)	*Adjustment to Offense Level*
(A)	More than $1,000,000	add **2**
(B)	More than $10,000,000	add **4**
(C)	More than $50,000,000	add **6**
(D)	More than $100,000,000	add **8**
(E)	More than $300,000,000	add **10**
(F)	More than $600,000,000	add **12**
(G)	More than $1,200,000,000	add **14**
(H)	More than $1,850,000,000	add **16**[25]

Source: Primer Antitrust (2019).

Once the volume of trade has been determined, the U.S. authorities retain a proportion of this volume, which is fixed at a flat rate of 20%.

The basic amount of the penalty is therefore equal to:

Basic amount of the penalty =
(volume of trade affected) × adjustment coefficient × 20%.

The U.S. authorities adjust this amount by a multiple between 0.05 and 4 in order to take into account the firm's "*degree of guilt*":

Final amount of the penalty = Basic amount × [0.05; 4].

Over the period spanning 2011-2020, the total amount of sanctions imposed by the U.S. antitrust authorities reached $9 billion, culminating in 2015 with the imposition of a $3 billion sanction against the Exchange Rate cartel (Figure 2.6).

Figure 2.6 Evolution of Antitrust Sanctions in the United States (2011-2020)

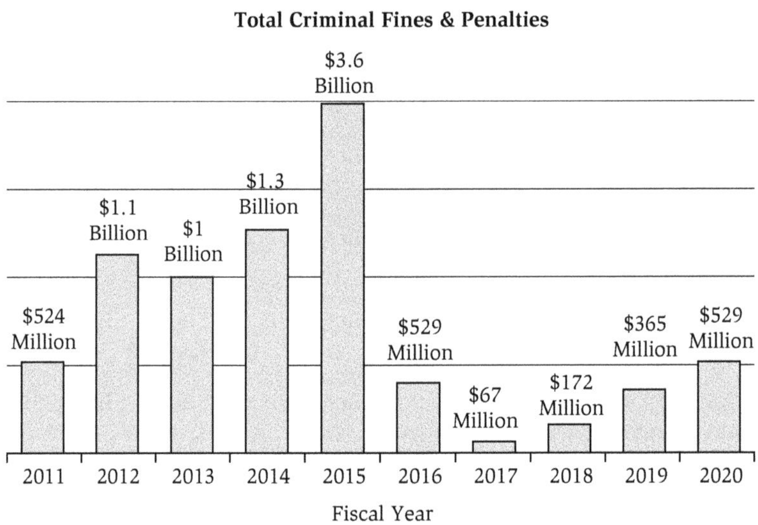

Source: U.S. Department of Justice, Antitrust Division (2021).

Setting antitrust sanctions in Europe: In Europe, fines are capped at 10% of the firm's annual and worldwide turnover. The method used to calculate penalties is presented in the Guidelines on the Method of Setting Fines and is calculated in two steps. A basic penalty amount is first calculated; it is equal to a percentage of the value of sales affected by the practice, multiplied by the number of years of infringement. This percentage can be as high as 30% of annual sales. Whatever the duration of the infringement, an "*entry fee*" is applied in the case of cartels, which is between 15% and 25% of annual sales. This entry fee may also be applied to other infringements, and not only cartels. Once the basic amount has been calculated, the penalty can be increased or decreased, depending on any aggravating or mitigating circumstances; in particular, recidivism may lead to a penalty increase of up to 100%. On the other hand, settlement or leniency procedures may lead to a reduced fine.

While penalties in Europe remained low for a long time in absolute terms, they've increased very sharply from the 2000s (Figure 2.7), especially in the case of cartels. During the period spanning 1990-2020, a total of €30.1 billion were imposed in fines, with €29 billion having been imposed after 2000. In the period spanning 2015-2020, the Commission imposed no less than €9.5 billion in cases of abuse of dominant position, including three sanctions against Google for a total of €8.2 billion.

Figure 2.7 Amount of Sanctions Imposed by the European Commission on Cartels (1990-2020; Million Euros)

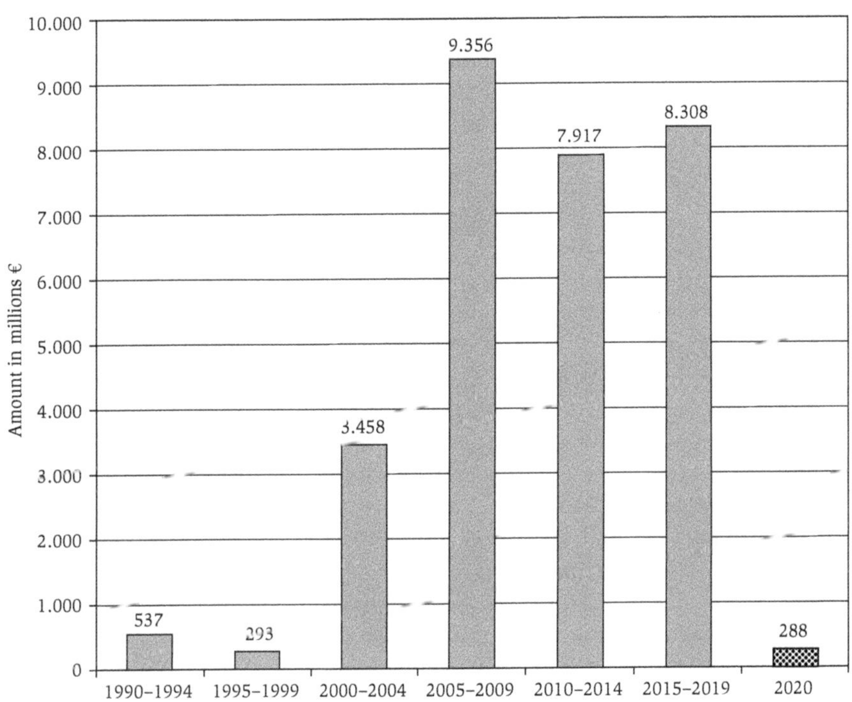

Source: DG Competition (2021).

A wide range of procedures: The processing of anti-competitive practices such as cartels or abuses of dominant position is divided into several phases: After a referral (the filing of a complaint), a contradictory investigation phase is conducted, which can lead to a statement of objections, before the competition authority makes a final decision (rejection, dismissal, sanction, injunction, etc.). During the investigation of an antitrust case, different procedures can be used.

First, some countries, such as France, have specific procedures, known as "*interim measures*": Investigating a case can be very long, in regards to the plaintiff's urgency, and the plaintiff may request that the competition authority ensure that the offensive conduct is stopped, pending the final decision. For instance, Article L 464-1 of the French Commercial Code provides that: "The Competition Authority may [...] take such protective measures as are requested or as it deems necessary. Such measures may only be taken if the practice seriously and immediately affects the situation of the general economy, or that of the sector concerned, or the interests of consumers or the plaintiff. They may include the suspension of the practice concerned as well as an injunction to return to the previous state. They must remain strictly limited to what is necessary to deal with the emergency" (free translation).

The granting of interim measures is subject to two cumulative conditions: a likely infringement of competition law, and the existence of a serious, irreparable and immediate injury for the plaintiff. The measures adopted must be limited to what is strictly necessary (according to a proportionality principle).

Second, to overcome the difficulties of collecting material evidence in the case of cartels—because firms can conceal or even destroy evidence of their secret practices—many countries have set up "*corporate leniency programs*": Sanctions are reduced for firms that disclose their participation in a cartel or facilitate investigations. The extreme case is a total exemption from penalties for the first firm to report its participation in a cartel. The United States has had this type of program in place since 1978; the EU, since 1996. This instrument, which is very effective in Europe, will be studied in detail in Chapter 3.

Third, when it is proven that a firm has infringed the competition rules, the firm may conclude a "*settlement*" with the antitrust authorities, wherein the firm renounces to contest the accusation in exchange for a reduced fine. In Europe, the settlement procedure was introduced in 2008, and allows a firm that has participated in a cartel to benefit from a 10% reduction in penalties if it does not contest the statement of objections. For the Commission, a settlement allows to speed up the sanction process. A settlement is different from a commitment decision in that:

- a settlement decision does establish an infringement and requires an admission of guilt, whereas a commitment decision does not establish an infringement and does not require any admission of guilt;
- a settlement decision simply requires a "*cease and desist*" of past practice, whereas a commitment decision requires the firm to do what it has agreed to do;
- a settlement procedure is only available for cartels, whereas commitment decisions are appropriate in all antitrust cases except for cartels.

§3 The Effectiveness of Antitrust Sanctions: An Economic Approach

Should the role of a sanction be simply to punish the offender or to equally deter future offenders? What would be the optimal level of the sanction? This subsection reviews how to calculate both optimal sanctions and the optimal level of detection.

The deterrent role of sanctions: The penalties imposed by antitrust authorities have two objectives. First, to punish a breach of competition rules by confiscating the illicit profit; second, to deter any would-be offenders by sending a clear signal to the market that competition law violations are not part of a "*sound economic strategy.*" The economics of crime, developed by Becker (1968) provides a useful framework to understand this deterrent role.

When a firm chooses to engage in an anti-competitive practice, its choice is based on a comparison between gains and costs. If the firm is risk neutral, the firm will not break the law if the expected cost is greater than the illicit gain. The expected cost is itself composed of two terms, the anticipated sanction and the probability of being detected:

$$\text{expected cost} > \text{illicit gain}$$

$$\Leftrightarrow (\text{monetary sanction} \times \text{probability of detection}) > \text{illicit gain} \qquad (1)$$

If we take the point of view of antitrust authorities, the sanction must be at least equal to:

$$\text{optimal monetary sanction} \geq \frac{\text{illicit gain}}{\text{probability of detection}} \qquad (2)$$

We can explain this principle with a numerical example. Suppose several firms form a cartel in order to increase the price by 20% from $5 to $6. At a price of $5, the quantity sold is 100 units. At the cartel price, the quantity decreases to 80 units (Figure 2.8).

Figure 2.8 Cartel: A Transfer and Loss of Surplus

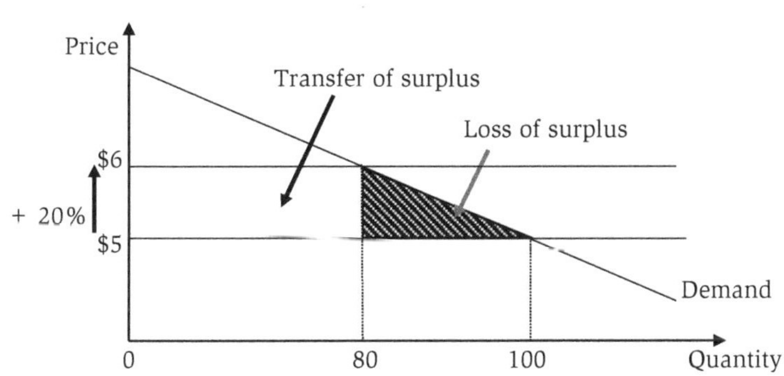

A cartel leads to a transfer of surplus from consumers (who continue to buy the product) to the cartel. This transfer corresponds to the illicit gain (also called "*overprofit*"), and is measured by the grayed-out rectangle: Its value is equal to (\$6 - \$5) × 80 = \$80.

Suppose that the probability of detection is 25% (or 0.25). In this case, the optimal sanction that deters the firm from violating the law is at least equal to:

$$\textbf{optimal monetary sanction} \geq \frac{80\$}{0.25}$$

$$\Leftrightarrow \textbf{optimal monetary sanction} \geq \$320$$

We see that the "*optimal sanction*" has several interesting properties:

- the amount of a sanction is strongly related to the illicit gain;
- it must always be higher than the illicit gain, because the probability of detection is lower than 100%. For an abuse of dominant position, the probability of detection is higher than for a cartel that, by definition, is a secret practice;
- the sanction has a deterrent function: It is set in such a way that no firm has financial incentive to break the law. If firms are well informed and convinced that the optimal sanctions will be applied ex-post, they no longer have any ex-ante incentive to transgress the law. Law enforcement is no longer necessary, as there are no longer any offenders. While antitrust authorities do not strictly apply this approach, the general deterrence principle is now clearly acknowledged, as reflected in the preamble of the European Commission's Guidelines on the Method of Setting Fines (2006): "(...) the Commission must ensure that its action has the necessary deterrent effect. Accordingly, when the Commission discovers that Article 81 or 82 of the Treaty has been infringed, it may be necessary to impose a fine on those who have acted in breach of the law. Fines should have a sufficiently deterrent effect, not only in order to sanction the undertakings concerned (specific deterrence) but also in order to deter other undertakings from engaging in, or continuing, behavior that is contrary to Articles 81 and 82 of the EC Treaty (general deterrence)."

For antitrust authorities, there is a trade-off between the amount of the fine and the probability of detection: If the probability of detection is low, sanctions must be high. And as detection is costly, it is more efficient to combine a low probability of detection with a very high sanction.

However, this solution raises practical difficulties:

- a high sanction increases the adverse effect of a mistake;
- firms may not have the financial capabilities to pay very high fines;

- a sanction that has been set high because the probability of detection is low implies that the firms that have been caught pay for those that have not.

In reality, antitrust authorities use sanctions and the probability of detection in a complementary way. Indeed, the probability of detection is not exogenous; it depends on the tools the competition authorities possess to detect infringements. For example, leniency programs (*see* Chapter 3) are an efficient way to increase the probability of cartel detection.

While providing a useful guide, Becker's analysis of sanctions has several limitations. First, the amount of the fine is based only on the illicit gain. However, the amount of a penalty should also depend on the intrinsic seriousness of the practice, whatever its effects on the illicit gain. This is particularly true for cartels.

Second, the criterion for setting a fine is not limited to the unlawful gain. An anti-competitive practice that drives up prices also leads to a reduction in demand. In Figure 2.8, the cartel practice does not only transfer surplus from consumers to producers; it also leads to a loss of welfare: As the price has risen by 20%, consumers who used to buy at a competitive price no longer buy at a cartel price. This loss of surplus is represented by the hatched triangle and its value is equal to: (\$6 - \$5) × 20 × 0.5 = \$10.

If we consider that the role of an antitrust policy is to protect the consumer's surplus, the sanction must include, in addition to the unlawful gain, the loss of surplus. In our numerical example, the optimal monetary sanction therefore becomes:

$$\text{optimal monetary sanction} \geq \frac{\$80 + \$10}{0.25}$$

$$\Leftrightarrow \text{optimal monetary sanction} \geq \$360$$

The cost of detection: We have so far discussed the effectiveness of sanctions without taking into account the cost of an antitrust action. This cost includes both the cost of detecting an illegal practice and the cost of investigating a case. Once this cost is introduced, the objective is no longer to detect all offenses but to focus on those that are most damaging to the economy.

Suppose that the marginal cost of detecting an anti-competitive practice is constant (or increasing). The marginal benefit of detection decreases over time as the antitrust authorities detect the most-harmful infringements first, and then smaller less important ones. The optimal level of detection is achieved when the marginal cost of a new investigation is equal to the marginal benefit of an antitrust intervention.

In Figure 2.9, the horizontal axis represents the total number of anti-competitive practices, the number of which has been arbitrarily set at 100. On the Y-axis, we represent the marginal cost of an antitrust investigation (C_m) as well as the marginal benefit resulting from an antitrust investigation (B_m). The optimal level of investigation is determined by the equalization of marginal cost and marginal gain: In our example, if the marginal cost is C_1, only the 60 most important cases should be investigated. It would not be efficient to detect all anti-competitive practices, as the marginal cost of detection would be higher than the marginal benefit to the society.

Figure 2.9 The Optimal Level of Antitrust Detection

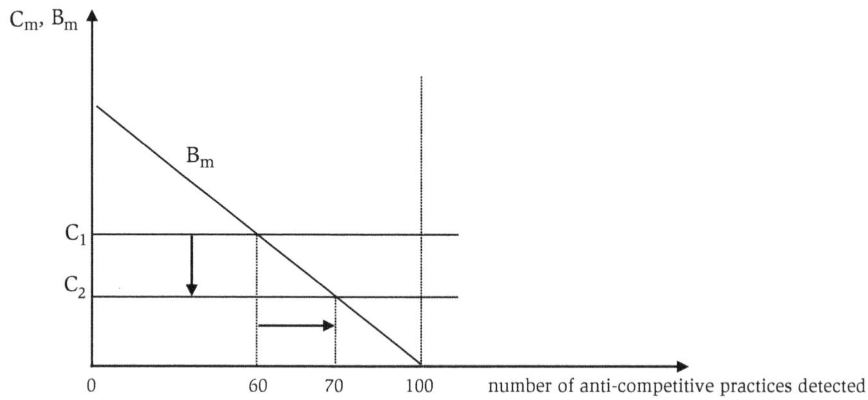

A decrease in the marginal cost leads to an increase in the number of cases investigated. This is the case when competition authorities set up:

- a leniency policy, which reduces the detection's costs of a cartel;
- a settlement policy, which reduces the costs of processing a case.

In Figure 2.9, a reduction in the marginal cost of investigation from C_1 to C_2 results in an increase in the number of investigations from 60 to 70.

SECTION 3 FROM PRIVATE ACTIONS TO CRIMINAL SANCTIONS

Competition policy is not limited to fines imposed by antitrust authorities. First, victims of anti-competitive practices can claim compensation for damages suffered. If private claims are different from public sanctions, they contribute to increasing the total cost of infringing competition law; indeed, the firm will not only have to pay a fine in the name of "*public enforcement*," but it will also have to compensate the victims *("private enforcement")* (§1). Economic analysis is particularly important in quantifying the amount of injury suffered; the aim is to build a counterfactual (*"but for")* scenario, i.e., the situation that would have prevailed if the anti-competitive practice had not taken place (§2).

Second, a competition policy can take the form of criminal proceedings against individuals who have been personally involved in practices such as cartels. Although this criminal procedure has been implemented in the United States since the 1990s, it remains ineffective throughout the rest of the world, despite the adoption by some countries of a criminal legal arsenal (§3).

§1 The Rise of Compensation Claims

A practice developed in the United States: In the United States, compensation claims are encouraged under the Clayton Act (Section 4) and are frequent. The victim of an anti-competitive practice can really play the role of a "*private policeman.*" The amounts of compensation can sometimes even be higher than the antitrust sanctions: For example, in the Lysine cartel, the U.S. authorities imposed a fine of $98.5 million on cartel members. The compensations obtained by the victims during the 1996-2010 period amounted to $82.5 million (Connor et al., 2012).

Several factors can explain the strong development of private actions in the United States:

- the amount of damages goes beyond the simple restitution of the illicit gain; Section 7 of the Sherman Act and Section 4 of the Clayton Act state that the victim can claim compensation for up to three times the damage suffered. However, this punitive system has been amended in the case of a leniency program: The Antitrust Criminal Penalty Enhancement and Reform Act (ACPERA), adopted in 2004, limits the amount of compensation to a single damage (known as "*detrebling*") for the first firm that cooperates with antitrust authorities;
- the American model is largely based on the "*class action*" system; several plaintiffs can join their claims for compensation in the same case (which implies that the claims are similar) and entrust their defense to a single lawyer. This procedure has the advantage of encouraging many victims who have suffered a minor damage at the individual level (but high at the global level, given the large number of victims) to take action; if it is not profitable to file a complaint alone, pooling claims allows victims to achieve economies of scale;
- the remuneration of lawyers facilitates civil proceedings: Contingent payments (payment is only made if the proceedings are successful, on the basis of a percentage of the compensation obtained by the victim) are frequent.

A more recent development in Europe: Compared to the U.S. case, compensation claims are still limited in other OECD countries. For example, in Europe, during the period spanning 2006-2013, only 25% of all infringements condemned by the Commission gave rise to compensation claims. However, as early as 2001, the ECJ recalled in its Courage ruling that any person who has suffered damage as a result of an anti-competitive practice can claim compensation.

The situation is changing in Europe with the Directive 2014/104/EU[23] on damages, which aims to promote actions for compensation:

23. The directive was transposed in France by Order No. 2017-3030 of March 9, 2017.

- in order to give victims better access to the proof of damages caused, national courts may require authorities to disclose evidence, while ensuring that such disclosure orders are proportionate;
- a final decision of a competition authority ruling that an infringement of competition law took place automatically constitutes a proof of fault ("*follow on*" system). The victims then have to demonstrate the harm they suffered and the causal link with the offense. The private action can also be conducted autonomously ("*stand-alone*" system), but the victim must in this case prove the fault;
- if an infringement has led to a price increase that has been passed on, the people who have ultimately suffered the damage can claim compensation;
- some safeguards ensure that the fear of compensation claims does not discourage firms from cooperating with competition authorities through leniency programs.

In addition, the European Commission encourages Member States to set up a system of "*class action*," in order to encourage a large number of victims who have suffered a minor individual damage to claim compensation. This mechanism is particularly useful for consumers or small businesses; for example, in the case of the Truck cartel (2016) in Europe, the victims of the practices were potentially thousands of road haulage firms—and in particular Small and Medium-sized Enterprises (SME)—that purchased trucks.

§2 Calculating Damages

The logic of compensation consists of creating a scenario describing where the victim would be if the offense had not occurred. This right to compensation covers not only the loss suffered ("*damnum emergens*") but also the loss of earnings ("*lucrum cessans*"), and includes the payment of an interest rate.

In order to obtain compensation, the victim must prove that: An infringement of antitrust laws has been committed; the infringement has caused a personal damage; and the damage results directly from the offense.[24] Economic analysis plays an essential role in civil actions because it helps solve three issues:

- who are the real victims of an anti-competitive practice? Indeed, a direct victim may have passed on all, or part of, the extra price to downstream customers; the latter then become the "*indirect victims*" of the practice. We deal in detail with this question of "*passing on*" in Chapter 3;
- what is the nature of the damage suffered by the victim? The damage is different in an exclusionary abuse, compared to a cartel;

24. The reader may find it useful to read the *Practical Guide on the Quantification of Damage*, published in 2013 by the European Commission. In July 2019, in order to encourage actions for compensation, the European Commission also published guidelines on "passing on" (a concept that we develop in Chapter 3).

- what is the extent of the damage suffered by the victim? It is necessary to build a counterfactual scenario. The aim is to reconstitute the market as it should have been if the practice had not taken place, and to compare this "counter-factual" situation with the observed situation in order to calculate the amount of injury caused.

The nature of the damage: The nature of the damage depends on the type of anti-competitive practice. In the case of a cartel, the injury is mainly represented by the "*extra price*" paid during the practice. If we use the previous numerical example, the extra price corresponds to the illicit gain (also called "*overprofit*"), measured by the gray rectangle in Figure 2.8: Its amount is equal to ($6 – $5) × 80 = $80. The reasoning is essentially the same if the practice is an exploitative abuse as an "*excessive price.*"

In the case of an exclusionary abuse, the injury is a "*loss of profit*" for the competitor, resulting from a decrease in volumes. For example, a firm that is victim of a disparagement practice will have a lower market share. The firm will first calculate the turnover lost due to the exclusionary practice:

$$\text{(theoretical volume} \times p^*) - (\text{observed volume} \times p^*) = \text{lost revenues}$$

Second, the victim has to adjust the loss because the decrease in volumes leads to a cost reduction. The loss of profit is therefore equal to:

$$\text{Lost revenues} - (\text{total cost with theoretical volume} - \text{total cost with observed volume}) = \text{lost profits}$$

The choice of a counterfactual scenario: To build a counterfactual scenario, there is no single approach. Four main methods can be used.

A first approach is to take as counterfactual a market that is similar but not affected by the practice: It is a comparative approach ("*yardstick*"). For example, the comparison can be made between countries that have the same structural characteristics (same market size, same number of competitors, etc.). Suppose a cartel has developed in Country A, and that the price observed during the practice was $8. In Countries B, C, and D—those comparable to Country A but that have not been affected by the cartel—the observed prices are respectively $6, $5 and $6. The average price on the three comparable markets is therefore $5.3. The price differential between Country A and the average of the other three countries can be considered the extra price imposed by the cartel in Country A (Figure 2.10). The result of this method, which we can apply to similar countries or markets, depends on the choice of the appropriate comparator; it is rare that two countries or two markets are absolutely identical.

Figure 2.10 The Market Comparison Method

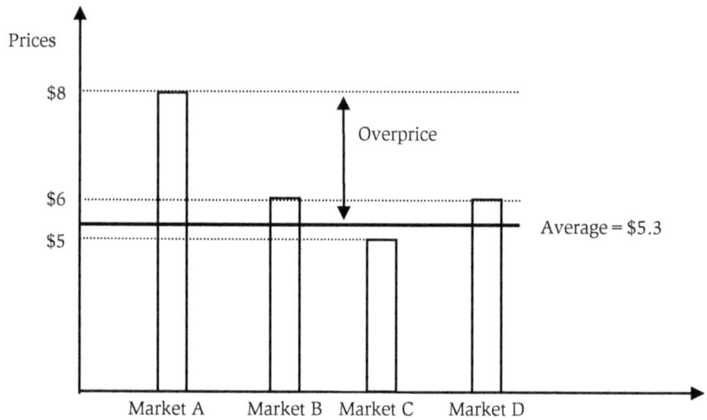

A second method consists of taking as counterfactual the market before or after the practice (a so-called "*before and after*" method). In the case of a cartel or an excessive price, if the price declines once the practice has ended ("*after*" method), the price differential can be interpreted as a measure of the "*overcharge.*" Similarly, if the price is lower before the cartel begins ("*before*" method), the price increase can be interpreted as the extra price imposed by the cartel.

This method can be applied with econometric tests on time series or by using a simple "*interpolation*" rule, consisting of linking the prices before and after the period of the practice. In Figure 2.11, we see that the price, while fluctuating in the short term, fluctuates around a constant and increasing trend both before and after the practice. On the other hand, during the cartel period, the price increases abnormally compared to the trend. An interpolation method consists of reconstituting the price that should have prevailed in the absence of the cartel by linking points A and B, either by straight line or oscillation (dotted line). The difference between the observed price and the reconstituted price is a measure of the "*overprice.*"

To make comparisons over time, it is necessary to ensure that the start and end dates of the practices are relevant:

- a cartel can be set up after a severe price war: The reference price will then be too low and will overestimate the damage suffered by victims;
- symmetrically, the end of a cartel does not necessarily imply a rapid and strong price fall if firms replace explicit collusion with tacit collusion. In this case, the damage suffered by victims will be underestimated.

Figure 2.11 The Interpolation Method

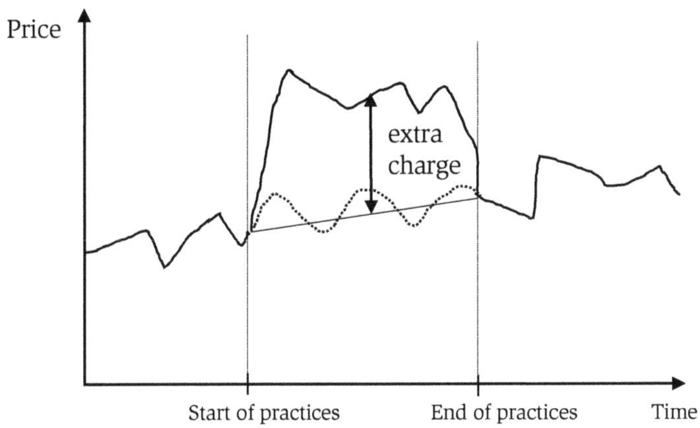

The price difference between periods may also be explained by other factors than the anti-competitive practice. For example, if production costs increased during the cartel period, a part of the price increase does not result from the cartel; an econometric model including a multitude of demand and cost factors can measure and isolate the role played by the cartel in the price increase.

The first two methods can be combined together in order to make a comparison over time and between two different markets. This "*difference in difference*" method is a combination of the two methods and eliminates the previous bias. Consider a market A that has been affected by a cartel practice and for which price data is available before the practice (Table 2.8). A first subtraction can be made between the price P'_A observed during the practice and the price observed before the practice: P_A. But this price difference may be due to other structural factors that are unrelated to the cartel and have affected all similar markets. We can take a similar market B, unaffected by the practice, and carry out the same operation: We subtract the price P'_B observed in market B during the practice in market A from the price P_B in market B before the practice takes place in the market A. The injury suffered in the market A is equal to the difference between these two differences, i.e.:

$$\text{Damage} = (P'_A - P_A) - (P'_B - P_B)$$

Table 2.8 The Method of "Difference in Differences" (DID)

	Price Before the Practice	*Price During the Practice*	*Difference*
Market A (affected market)	P_A	P'_A	$(P'_A - P_A)$
Market B (unaffected market)	P_B	P'_B	$(P'_B - P_B)$
Difference in differences			$(P'_A - P_A) - (P'_B - P_B)$

A third method consists of building up a counterfactual market based on cost and demand parameters. For example, suppose that Firm A abuses its dominant position by foreclosing Firm B from the market. Firm B is as efficient as Firm A.

The inverse demand function is equal to:

$$P = \$100 - Q \text{ with P the price and Q the total quantity}$$

The total cost function of each firm is equal to:

$$\text{Total cost (TC)} = 20q \text{ with q, the individual quantity}$$

After the exclusion of Firm B, Firm A behaves as a monopoly (Figure 2.12). The monopoly equilibrium is:

$$P^M = \$60$$

$$Q^M = 40$$

$$\Pi^M = \$1{,}600$$

In order to obtain compensation, Firm B should rebuild the market structure that would have prevailed if the abuse had not taken place. If the counterfactual market is a Cournot's duopoly, the price, quantity and profits would be equal to:

$$P^{cour} = \$46.7$$

$$Q^{cour} = 53.3$$

$$\Pi^{cour} = \$1{,}423 \text{ or } \$711.5 \text{ per firm.}$$

Firm B can therefore estimate that the loss of profit due to the exclusion is equal to $711.5 per period. Similarly, the clients of Firm B can argue that in a Cournot duopoly, the price would have been $46.7 and not $60.

The result of the counterfactual strongly depends on the counterfactual chosen. Firm A can defend itself by arguing that the competition is mainly price based, and that the "*right*" structural model is a Bertrand duopoly with homogeneous products: In this case, if Firm B enters the market, the price would be equal to the marginal cost (i.e., P = $20) and Firm B would have made no profit. Therefore, Firm B cannot claim compensation. Conversely, Firm A's consumers will argue that they've suffered a very high damage, in view of the large price gap between the monopoly situation and Bertrand's duopoly situation.

Figure 2.12 A Counterfactual Based on the Market Structure

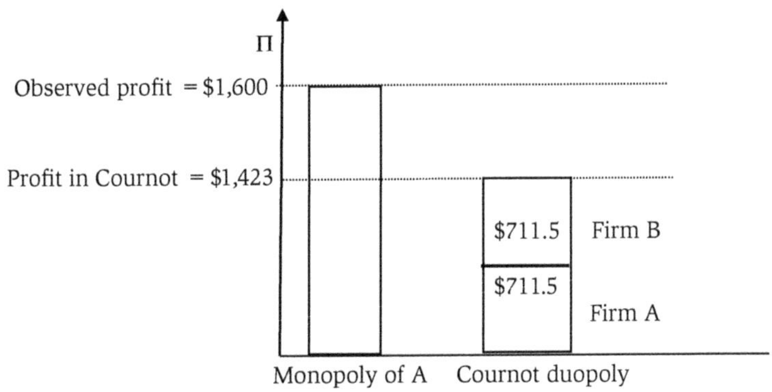

A fourth and final method uses accounting and financial data to assess the damage suffered by a victim. For example, in the case of a cartel, the unit cost of production with a reasonable profit margin can be used to estimate the counterfactual price.

Each method can be implemented with different techniques, ranging from the simplest (e.g., average calculations) to the most complex such as econometrics. The choice of a technique will depend largely on the quality and volume of available data. In particular, economists often use econometrics, which consists of explaining a variable (in this case, the rise in price or the fall in volumes) by using several explanatory variables. The objective is then to distinguish and quantify the influence of each factor.

§3 The Criminalization of Cartels

In addition to antitrust sanctions and private actions, some countries have introduced criminal provisions against individuals, mainly when they have participated in a cartel. Worldwide, 25 jurisdictions have a more or less developed criminal arsenal against competition violations in 2019 (Table 2.9). In practice, however, only the United States uses criminal sanctions against individuals.

Table 2.9 Example of Countries with Criminal Provisions Against Individuals

Country	*Date of Adoption of Criminal Sanctions; Last Reform*	*Nature and Ceiling of Criminal Sanctions*
France	Reform in 2001 to increase the maximum sentence and fine	Up to €75,000 in fines and up to 4 years in prison
United States	Sherman Act of 1890 Reform in 2004 to increase the maximum sentence and fine	Up to $1 million in fines and up to 10 years in prison
Canada	Criminal Law of 1889 Reform in 2010 to increase the maximum sentence and fine	Up to $25 million in fines and/or a prison sentence of up to 14 years
Australia	Introduction of criminal sanctions in 2009	Up to 10 years in prison or $340,000 in fines
South Korea	Reform in 2012 to increase the maximum sentence and fine	Up to 3 years in prison
Japan	Penalty in 1992 Reform in 2009 to increase the maximum sentence and fine	Up to 5 years in prison

The American exception: In the United States, the Sherman Act (1890), reinforced in 2004 by the Antitrust Criminal Penalty Enhancement and Reform Act, provides for a penalty of up to $1 million and 10 years' imprisonment. This legal arsenal is applied in major cartel cases; during the period spanning 2011-2020, 433 individuals—American or non-American[25]—were prosecuted for participating in cartels, and a large majority of them were sanctioned with a fine, a prison sentence, or house arrest (Figure 2.13).

25. In 2014, the U.S. DOJ obtained the first extradition of an Italian business executive accused of having played a decisive role in an international agreement on marine hoses, which affected the American territory.

Figure 2.13 Criminal Proceedings Against Firms and Individuals in the United States (2011-2020)

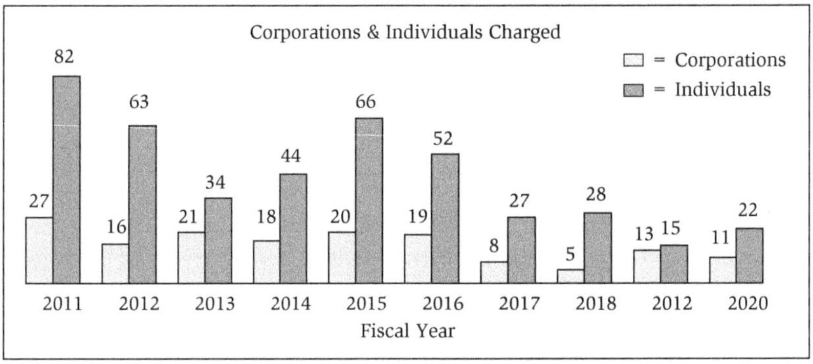

Source: U.S. DOJ, Antitrust Division (2021).

The use of criminal prosecution in the United States is partly due to cultural factors: Cartels are considered "*conspiracies*" and are subject to strong moral condemnation by the public opinion. In a 2014 memo entitled Individual Accountability for Corporate Wrongdoing, the prosecutor Deputy Attorney General Sally Yates summarized the American philosophy of criminalizing cartels as follows: "One of the most effective ways to combat corporate misconduct is by seeking accountability from the individuals who perpetrated the wrongdoing."

Some economic arguments can also explain the criminalization of most serious anti-competitive practices. In particular, managers may have personal interests in organizing cartels in order to rapidly increase profits: Their "performances" will boost their paychecks, indexed on short-term performance indicators, or will speed their internal or external careers. In the long term, however, this strategy does not create value for shareholders; once the cartel has been detected, the sanction imposed by antitrust authorities will ultimately be borne by shareholders. From this perspective, criminal sanctions against managers reduce the potential conflicts of interest between shareholders and managers: They provide an incentive to maximize profits by using lawful strategies (innovation, etc.). We will develop this point in detail in Chapter 3.

Poor enforcement in other countries: Unlike the United States, countries with criminal legislation against cartels do not really use it. For example, in the United Kingdom, since the 2002 adoption of the Enterprise Act, only six prison sentences and six disqualifications of executives have been imposed throughout the period spanning 2003-2019.

Similarly, in France, while Article L. 420-6 of the French Commercial Code provides for a prison sentence for any person who fraudulently takes "a personal and decisive part in the design, organization or implementation" of a cartel in practice, it is rarely applied. On average, two criminal sentences per year are imposed in the form of fines or suspended prison sentences. The weak enforcement of criminal law outside the

United States is mainly due to the fact that cartel practices are not considered as being morally condemnable by society as a whole.

Review Topics:

What are the different fields of competition policy?
Compare the implementation of competition policies in the United States and Europe.
Do emerging and developing countries need a competition policy?
How can one evaluate the effectiveness of antitrust sanctions?

Recommended Readings:

Herbert Hovenkamp, *Principles of Antitrust* (Foundation Press, 2017).
William Kovacic and Carl Shapiro, *Antitrust Policy: A Century of Economic and Legal Thinking* (Journal of Economic Perspectives 43-60, 1999).
E. Thomas Sullivan (ed.), *The Political Economy of the Sherman Act: The First One Hundred Years* (Oxford University Press, 1991).
Gary Becker, *Crime and Punishment: An Economic Approach* (Journal of Political Economy 169-217, 1968).

ANNEX: ANTITRUST LEGISLATIONS (EXCERPTS)

1. U.S. antitrust laws

Sherman Act, §1

Every contract, combination in the form of trust or otherwise, or conspiracy, in restraint of trade or commerce among the several States, or with foreign nations, is declared to be illegal. Every person who shall make any contract or engage in any combination or conspiracy hereby declared to be illegal shall be deemed guilty of a felony, and, on conviction thereof, shall be punished by fine not exceeding $10,000,000 if a corporation, or, if any person, $350,000, or by imprisonment not exceeding three years, or by both said punishments, in the discretion of the court.

Sherman Act, §2

Every person who shall monopolize, or attempt to monopolize, or combine or conspire with any other person or persons, to monopolize any part of the trade or commerce among the several States, or with foreign nations, shall be deemed guilty of a felony, and, on conviction thereof, shall be punished by fine not exceeding $10,000,000 if a corporation, or, if any other person, $350,000, or by imprisonment not exceeding three years, or by both said punishments, in the discretion of the court.

Clayton Act, §2

It shall be unlawful for any person engaged in commerce, in the course of such commerce, either directly or indirectly, to discriminate in price between different purchasers of commodities of like grade and quality, where either or any of the purchases involved in such discrimination are in commerce, where such commodities are sold for use, consumption, or resale within the United States or any Territory thereof or the District of Columbia or any insular possession or other place under the jurisdiction of the United States, and where the effect of such discrimination may be substantially to lessen competition or tend to create a monopoly in any line of commerce, or to injure, destroy, or prevent competition with any person who either grants or knowingly receives the benefit of such discrimination, or with customers of either of them.

Clayton Act, §3

It shall be unlawful for any person engaged in commerce, in the course of such commerce, to lease or make a sale or contract for sale of goods, wares, merchandise, machinery, supplies, or other commodities, whether patented or unpatented, for use, consumption, or resale within the United States or any Territory thereof or the District of Columbia or any insular possession or other place under the jurisdiction of the United States, or fix a price charged therefor, or discount from, or rebate upon, such price, on the condition, agreement, or understanding that the lessee or purchaser thereof shall not use or deal in the goods, wares, merchandise, machinery, supplies, or other commodities of a competitor or competitors of the lessor or seller, where the effect of such lease, sale, or contract for sale or such condition, agreement, or understanding may be to substantially lessen competition or tend to create a monopoly in any line of commerce.

Clayton Act, §7

No person engaged in commerce or in any activity affecting commerce shall acquire, directly or indirectly, the whole or any part of the stock or other share capital and n° person subject to the jurisdiction of the Federal Trade Commission shall acquire the whole or any part of the assets of another person engaged also in commerce or in any activity affecting commerce, where in any line of commerce or in any activity affecting commerce in any section of the country, the effect of such acquisition may be substantially to lessen competition, or to tend to create a monopoly.

No person shall acquire, directly or indirectly, the whole or any part of the stock or other share capital and n° person subject to the jurisdiction of the Federal Trade Commission shall acquire the whole or any part of the assets of one or more persons engaged in commerce or in any activity affecting commerce, where in any line of commerce or in any activity affecting commerce in any section of the country, the effect of such acquisition, of such stocks or assets, or of the use of such stock by the voting or granting of proxies or otherwise, may be substantially to lessen competition, or to tend to create a monopoly.

2. European antitrust law (agreements and abuse of dominant position)

Article 101

(ex Article 81 TEC)

1. The following shall be prohibited as incompatible with the internal market: all agreements between undertakings, decisions by associations of undertakings and concerted practices which may affect trade between Member States and which have as their object or effect the prevention, restriction or distortion of competition within the internal market, and in particular those which:
   (a) directly or indirectly fix purchase or selling prices or any other trading conditions;
   (b) limit or control production, markets, technical development, or investment;
   (c) share markets or sources of supply;
   (d) apply dissimilar conditions to equivalent transactions with other trading parties, thereby placing them at a competitive disadvantage;
   (e) make the conclusion of contracts subject to acceptance by the other parties of supplementary obligations which, by their nature or according to commercial usage, have no connection with the subject of such contracts.
2. Any agreements or decisions prohibited pursuant to this Article shall be automatically void.

3. The provisions of paragraph 1 may, however, be declared inapplicable in the case of:
   - any agreement or category of agreements between undertakings,
   - any decision or category of decisions by associations of undertakings,
   - any concerted practice or category of concerted practices, which contributes to improving the production or distribution of goods or to promoting technical or economic progress, while allowing consumers a fair share of the resulting benefit, and which does not:
     (a) impose on the undertakings concerned restrictions which are not indispensable to the attainment of these objectives;
     (b) afford such undertakings the possibility of eliminating competition in respect of a substantial part of the products in question.

Article 102

(ex Article 82 TEC)
Any abuse by one or more undertakings of a dominant position within the internal market or in a substantial part of it shall be prohibited as incompatible with the internal market in so far as it may affect trade between Member States.
Such abuse may, in particular, consist of:

(a) directly or indirectly imposing unfair purchase or selling prices or other unfair trading conditions;
(b) limiting production, markets or technical development to the prejudice of consumers;
(c) applying dissimilar conditions to equivalent transactions with other trading parties, thereby placing them at a competitive disadvantage;
(d) making the conclusion of contracts subject to acceptance by the other parties of supplementary obligations which, by their nature or according to commercial usage, have no connection with the subject of such contracts.

Article 107

(ex Article 87 TEC)

1. Save as otherwise provided in the Treaties, any aid granted by a Member State or through State resources in any form whatsoever which distorts or threatens to distort competition by favoring certain undertakings or the production of certain goods shall, in so far as it affects trade between Member States, be incompatible with the internal market.
2. The following shall be compatible with the internal market:
   (a) aid having a social character, granted to individual consumers, provided that such aid is granted without discrimination related to the origin of the products concerned;

(b) aid to make good the damage caused by natural disasters or exceptional occurrences;
(c) aid granted to the economy of certain areas of the Federal Republic of Germany affected by the division of Germany, in so far as such aid is required in order to compensate for the economic disadvantages caused by that division. Five years after the entry into force of the Treaty of Lisbon, the Council, acting on a proposal from the Commission, may adopt a decision repealing this point.

3. The following may be considered to be compatible with the internal market:
   (a) aid to promote the economic development of areas where the standard of living is abnormally low or where there is serious underemployment, and of the regions referred to in Article 349, in view of their structural, economic and social situation;
   (b) aid to promote the execution of an important project of common European interest or to remedy a serious disturbance in the economy of a Member State;
   (c) aid to facilitate the development of certain economic activities or of certain economic areas, where such aid does not adversely affect trading conditions to an extent contrary to the common interest;
   (d) aid to promote culture and heritage conservation where such aid does not affect trading conditions and competition in the Union to an extent that is contrary to the common interest;
   (e) such other categories of aid as may be specified by decision of the Council on a proposal from the Commission.

Article 108

(ex Article 88 TEC)

1. The Commission shall, in cooperation with Member States, keep under constant review all systems of aid existing in those States. It shall propose to the latter any appropriate measures required by the progressive development or by the functioning of the internal market.
2. If, after giving notice to the parties concerned to submit their comments, the Commission finds that aid granted by a State or through State resources is not compatible with the internal market having regard to Article 107, or that such aid is being misused, it shall decide that the State concerned shall abolish or alter such aid within a period of time to be determined by the Commission.

   If the State concerned does not comply with this decision within the prescribed time, the Commission or any other interested State may, in derogation from the provisions of Articles 258 and 259, refer the matter to the Court of Justice of the European Union direct.

   On application by a Member State, the Council may, acting unanimously, decide that aid which that State is granting or intends to grant shall be considered to be compatible with the internal market, in derogation from the provisions of Article 107 or from the regulations provided for in Article 109, if such a decision is justified by exceptional circumstances. If, as regards the aid in question, the Commission has already initiated the procedure provided for in the first subparagraph of this paragraph, the fact that the State concerned has made its application to the Council shall have the effect of suspending that procedure until the Council has made its attitude known.

If, however, the Council has not made its attitude known within three months of the said application being made, the Commission shall give its decision on the case.

3. The Commission shall be informed, in sufficient time to enable it to submit its comments, of any plans to grant or alter aid. If it considers that any such plan is not compatible with the internal market having regard to Article 107, it shall without delay initiate the procedure provided for in paragraph 2. The Member State concerned shall not put its proposed measures into effect until this procedure has resulted in a final decision.
4. The Commission may adopt regulations relating to the categories of State aid that the Council has, pursuant to Article 109, determined may be exempted from the procedure provided for by paragraph 3 of this Article.

CHAPTER 3

Fighting Against Cartels

"Our competitors are our friends; our customers are our enemies."
Statement by a member of the Lysine cartel,
cited in OECD (2000).

In July 2016, the European Commission imposed a record €2.9 billion fine on six truck manufacturers for price fixing and passing on to customers the costs of complying with environmental standards. In addition to this first sanction, another truck manufacturer was fined €880 million on September 2017 for the same practices. In total, the Commission sanctioned the Trucks cartel to a total fine of €3.8 billion. This exemplary decision is one on the long list of international cartels sentenced in Europe since the early 2000s: the Vitamins cartel (2001), the Elevators cartel (2007), the Windscreens cartel (2008), the Computer and Television Screens cartel (2012), and so on.

A cartel is an explicit and secret agreement between competitors that has the sole objective of removing the competitive pressure that normally exists between them. It is the most formalized form of coordination between firms; it goes beyond a simple "*concerted practice*" consisting of exchanging strategic information, without going so far as to jointly set the price. Thus, the cartel aims to create a monopoly and thereby represents the exact opposite of competition, which is characterized by the decision-making autonomy of each firm and a strong uncertainty about the behavior of competitors (Figure 3.1).

Figure 3.1 Degree of Coordination and Uncertainty

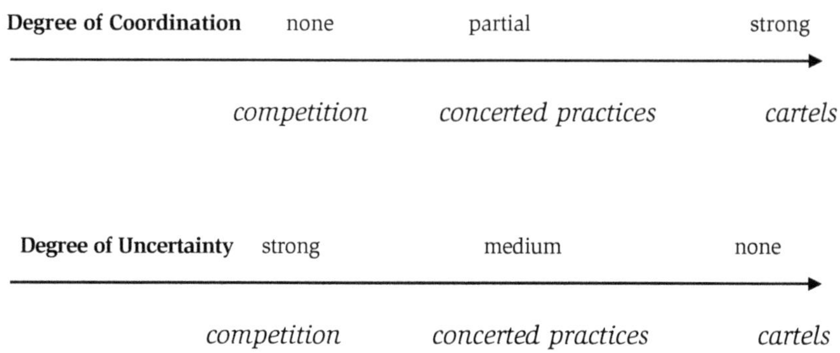

After having drawn a portrait of cartels (Section 1), we will explore under which conditions this practice could be stable over time (Section 2). We'll examine how antitrust authorities fight against cartels by imposing public sanctions; we use the theory of "*optimal sanctions*," which offers a powerful analytical framework to understand the rationale of fines (Section 3). Beyond antitrust sanctions, we'll analyze the role of criminal sanctions against individuals and private actions for damages (Section 4). We will end this chapter by studying how antitrust authorities detect cartels, using tools such as leniency programs (Section 5).

SECTION 1 HOW ARE CARTELS FORMED?

In this section, we'll first study the reasons that lead a firm to form a cartel (§1). We'll identify the main factors that are favorable to the creation of cartels by using both economic theory and empirical studies (§2). Finally, we'll examine how firms organize a cartel, by setting a price together, by allocating quotas or markets (§3).

§1 Why Do Firms Form Cartels?

In Chapter 1, we highlighted that when several firms compete in a Cournot oligopoly, the total profit is always lower than the monopoly profit:[26]

$$\Sigma\Pi_{ppc} = 0 \leq \Sigma\Pi_{OLIGOPOLY} < \Pi_{MONOPOLY}$$

Indeed, in Cournot's model, when the number of firms increases, total profit decreases. It tends towards zero as the number of firms is high, i.e., as we reach a situation of pure and perfect competition (N represents the number of firms):

26. The exact level of total oligopoly profit will depend on variables such as the type of competition (Cournot or Bertrand), the degree of product differentiation, and the number of firms.

$$lim_{N \to +\infty} \Pi^{cour} = lim_{N \to +\infty} \frac{N(a-c)^2}{(N+1)^2} = 0$$

The decrease in total profit when N increases is due to the fact that each firm exerts a competitive pressure on the others, which reduces prices and profits.

Therefore, in an oligopoly situation, firms have a "natural" incentive to collude either to increase their profits (by creating an offensive cartel) or to avoid them plummeting, after the entry of a new competitor (by creating a defensive cartel).

An offensive cartel: The purpose of an offensive cartel is to increase the total profit by explicitly coordinating the behavior of competing firms. A "*perfect*" cartel would thus lead to a situation of monopoly.

For example, two firms A and B are competing in a Cournot duopoly; each one makes a profit of \$30. If the market were a monopoly, the profit would be equal to \$100. The incentive to form a cartel is therefore equal to:

$$\$100 - (2 \times \$30) = \$40.$$

By setting a monopoly price, each firm can obtain an additional profit of \$20:

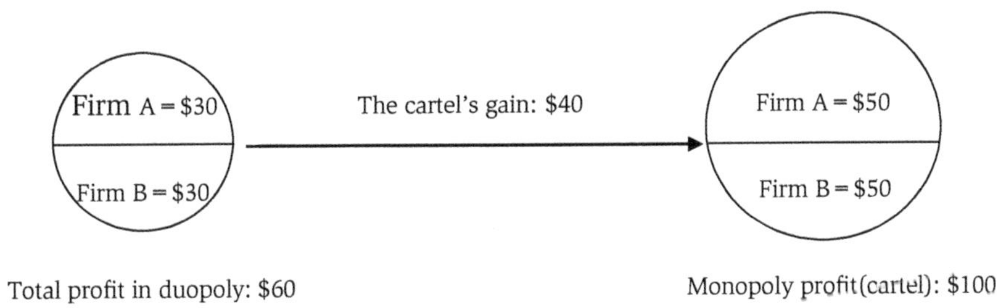

A defensive cartel: The symmetrical situation of a defensive cartel can also be considered: Firm A in a monopoly situation in its domestic market is threatened by the entry of a competitor, Firm B (coming from another country). The entry of Firm B will therefore change the market from a monopoly to a duopoly: The price and profit of Firm A will decrease because it will have to share the total profit.

For example, if the monopoly profit is \$100, the entry of a competitor reduces the total profit to \$60, which will be split in two (if both firms have the same production costs). The entry of Firm B reduces the profit of Firm A from \$100 to \$30, i.e., a decrease of \$70 (\$40 due to the competitive effect; \$30 due to the sharing of the remaining profits). In this case, Firm A has a strong incentive to convince Firm B not to enter its market in return for a similar strategy in Firm B's market; this market sharing agreement leads to maintaining a monopoly in each country.

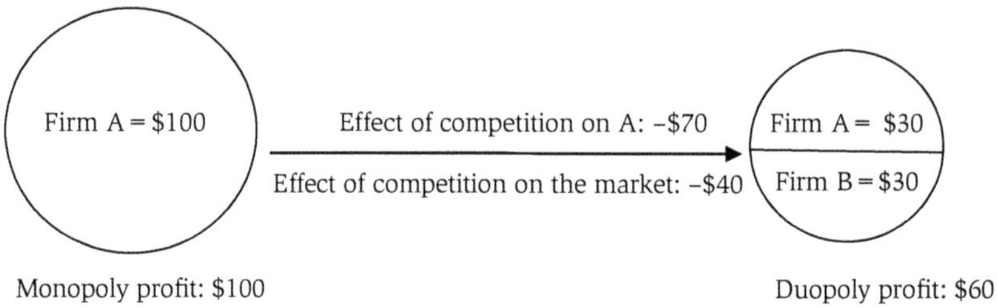

A similar situation consists of agreeing with a competitor not to enter the market by paying it off. This type of cartel was observed in the pharmaceutical sector in the United States and Europe during the 2000s; faced with the expirations of their patents and the entry of generics, some firms have paid off the newcomer (for instance, by licensing the newcomer to produce their products) in order to avoid facing head-on competition (Table 3.1).

This mechanism can be explained through a simple example: A monopoly A makes a profit of $100 per period; with the entry of Firm B, the market becomes a duopoly. The total profits decrease to $60, i.e., $30 per firm. Firm A, therefore, has a strong incentive to pay Firm B so that it does not enter the market: Firm A is willing to pay between $30 and $70 to avoid the entry of Firm B. For example, if Firm A offers Firm B a compensation of $40, this situation is mutually advantageous: Firm B obtains a higher profit than it would have obtained by entering the market ($30). Firm A keeps a profit ($100 - $40, or $60) that is twice as much as it would have obtained if Firm B had entered the market.

This type of agreement may involve a license transfer from A to B in exchange for a delay to launch a generic product. These *"pay for delay"* agreements have given rise to several antitrust cases in the pharmaceutical sector (Table 3.1). For instance, in 2014, the European Commission imposed a fine of €427 million on the Servier laboratory (also for an abuse of dominant position) and on five generic manufacturers: They had decided to delay the launch of a cheaper version of a cardiovascular drug on the market in exchange for payments and license transfers.

Table 3.1 Example of "Pay for Delay" Agreements (European Commission)

Agreement	*Objective*	*Antitrust Sanctions*
Fentanyl case (2013)	Johnson & Johnson produces fentanyl. In 2005, its patent on fentanyl patches expired in the Netherlands and Novartis' Dutch subsidiary Sandoz was about to launch a generic fentanyl patch.	€16 million

Agreement	*Objective*	*Antitrust Sanctions*
	J&J and Novartis concluded an agreement to delay the entry into the Dutch market of a cheaper generic version.	
Citalopram case (2013)	Lundbeck colluded with its competitors to delay the launch of cheaper generic versions of citalopram, an antidepressant.	€93 million for Lundbeck; €52 million for the generic drug producers
Perindopril case (2014)	Servier and five generic manufacturers agreed to delay the launch of cheaper versions of a cardiovascular drug, perindopril, used to reduce high blood pressure.	€427 million in total (including a €330 million for the abuse of its dominant position)
Modafinil case (2020)	Cephalon's best-selling product Modafinil is a medicine used for the treatment of excessive daytime sleepiness. After the patent expired in Europe in 2005, Cephalon entered into an agreement implying that Teva, a generics company, would not enter the market with a cheaper version in exchange for cash payments.	€60.5 million

§2 Factors Favoring Cartel Formation

If the aim of a cartel is to either increase profits or prevent their decline, we need to understand why empirically all firms don't engage in such practices. We will first identify the main factors that are favorable to the formation of cartels, basing our work on both economic theory and empirical studies that have been carried out on existing cartels.[27] However, these factors must be considered with caution; they are neither necessary nor sufficient conditions, as it is quite difficult to draw a typical profile of a cartel. We will show that cartels are more frequent when the market is concentrated, when products are intermediary products, when entry and exit barriers are high, and when firms participating in the cartel are similar.

A concentrated market*:* Cartels generally develop in markets with a small number of suppliers (an oligopoly) or with firms that have strong market shares. It is easier to reach an agreement when there are few firms on the market, as negotiation

27. For clarity, we distinguish between conditions conducive to the formation of cartels and those conducive to their stability (Section 2). Of course, in reality, the decision to collude takes into account both types of conditions simultaneously.

costs are limited, or when a few leaders dominate the market, with small firms aligning their behavior with the leaders.

The empirical research of Combe and Monnier (2012), based on a sample of 111 cartels detected by the European Commission between 1969 and 2009, confirms this, as it shows that the average number of participants in a cartel is 7.7 and that it is even limited to 5 in a sector such as the chemical industry (Table 3.2).

Table 3.2 Average Number of Participants by Sector

Sectors	*Number of Participants (on Average)*
Metallurgy and non-metallic products	12.1
Machinery and Equipment (M&E)	8.1
Paper, cardboard, rubber and plastic industries	13.6
Textile, construction	12.8
Chemical Industry	4.8
of which:	
Basic chemical industry	5.1
Pharmaceutical industry	3.2
Other chemical products	5.6
Services (trade, financial services and transport)	6.8
Food, beverages and tobacco products	5.5
Overall average	**7.7**

Source: Combe and Monnier (2012).

However, cartels involving a large number of firms have been observed: In this case, professional bodies, such as unions or associations often play the role of the cartel leader or "*facilitator*."

Intermediary products*:* While a cartel may concern products purchased directly by final consumers, a majority of cartels are formed with firms providing inputs. Combe and Monnier (2012) show that more than two-thirds of cartels detected in Europe have taken place in sectors such as metallurgy, chemicals, machinery, and equipment manufacturing or materials (Table 3.3). If we consider the 10 largest fines imposed by the European Commission (until 2019), a similar observation can be made: Most cartels, like the Trucks or Elevators cartels, have primarily affected products used as inputs by other firms. This characteristic can be explained by two main factors:

- professional customers have a low price elasticity, at least in the short term. They have no choice but to buy the products even if the price increases. They can also transfer the extra price onto their downstream customers. Therefore, being part of a cartel is very profitable because the price increase is not offset by a significant drop in demand;

- intermediary products such as cement or vitamins are characterized by a certain homogeneity: These ingredients will be integrated into a final product, which will be differentiated. It is therefore easier to set prices when the products are similar in both features and uses.

Table 3.3 The Main Sectors Affected by Cartels in Europe

Sectors	*Number of Cases (%)*
Metallurgy and non-metallic products	16
Machinery and Equipment (M&E)	12
Paper, cardboard, rubber and plastic industries	11
Textile, construction	5
Chemical Industry	29
of which:	
Basic chemical industry	12
Pharmaceutical industry	7
Other chemical products	10
Services (trade, financial services and transport)	16
Food, beverages and tobacco products	12

Source: Combe and Monnier (2012).

Entry/exit barriers*:* The presence of entry/exit barriers (legal or economic) is a favorable condition for a cartel to emerge. Without barriers, any attempt to raise the price above the competitive level quickly leads to the entry of new firms. Cartel members themselves can deter the entry of new competitors by erecting strategic barriers. For instance, in December 2001, the European Commission sanctioned several breweries that had formed a cartel in Luxembourg: The cartel's members had colluded to block access to new breweries that were not members of the cartel.

Similarities between cartel members: The similarity between firms, whether in terms of production costs or size, facilitates the cartel's formation. An identical cost structure makes threats of retaliation credible if a member "cheats": Since firms are symmetrical, they can impose identical sanctions on each other.

§3 Various Types of Collusion

To obtain higher profits, cartel members can use different methods. We will identify the different forms of collusion, even if, in practice, cartels may use several of them simultaneously (Table 3.4). We'll study successively price fixing agreements, basic point systems, market or customer allocations, bid rigging, quotas allocation, and collective boycott.

Table 3.4 Collusive Practices Used by Cartels

Practice	*Principle*
Price fixing	Firms agree directly on a given price or a price increase, or on a common formula to calculate the price.
Basing point system	Firms agree on a base point from which a base price is calculated; the final price is the base price plus transportation costs.
Market or customer allocation	Firms divide markets geographically or per customer.
Bid rigging in calls for tender	During a call for tender, firms designate in advance the winner but submit "fake" bids, to give the appearance of competing against each other.
Quotas	Firms collectively decide to reduce production in order to raise prices; they allocate quotas, based on the marginal production costs of each firm; possibility of *"side payments."*
Collective boycott	Firms agree to prevent a competitor from entering the market, principally by colluding with suppliers upstream.

Setting a common price or tariff increase: Joint pricing is the most immediate and common form of cartel: Firms can determine together a sale or purchase price, a price target, a tariff increase, a margin, a maximum discount level, payment terms, transport and delivery costs, or a floor price. Empirical studies show that, depending on the case, firms can set a single price for the entire market—as done by the Lysine cartel in the United States—or several prices, depending on the type of customer, as observed in the Carbon and Graphite Products cartel, or according to geographical areas.

The setting of a common price is more difficult when there are different variants of the same product, in particular in terms of quality; in this case, cartel members must clearly specify the type of product on which they agree in order to avoid any attempts to "cheat" (consisting, for example, of respecting the cartel price but offering the customer a product of higher quality). In more complex cases, the cartel can develop a pricing formula or price scale that incorporates different product characteristics.

Basing point system: For firms selling heavy products such as steel, agreeing on a set price can sometimes be a bit trickier; as factories are not located in the same place and transport costs are high, the final price can differ greatly depending on the location of customers and the firm's factories.

The solution to this issue is to agree on a common reference location—a *"base point."* Then, a *"base price"* is set at this point and the final price given to consumers is equal to the base price plus transportation costs. As a result, regardless of the cartel member and its location, the final delivery price will always be the same.

This system was applied, for example, in the United States in the 1920s by members of the Steel cartel. Pittsburgh was used as the base point: The base price from

Pittsburgh was set at $40 per ton and then transport costs were added on. So, for example, the transportation cost from Pittsburgh to Chicago was $7.6 per ton; a single common delivery price to Chicago was then set at $47.6 per ton, regardless of the factory's location.

Market allocation: Dividing markets into geographical regions is another form of collusion: Each cartel member is granted a territory, generally its country of origin or its "historical" location. This practice is quite frequent in Europe, given the fragmentation of countries before the European common market was set up; firms were in dominant positions in their domestic market. Thus, to avoid mutual market penetration, firms entered into a "*non-aggression pact*": Each member would not enter the market of its foreign competitor.

In Europe, the cement cartel is a good illustration of this kind of agreement: During the 1980s, 33 European cement producers and nine business associations set up a general market-sharing agreement to protect domestic markets and control the flow of cement exports and imports in Europe. More recently, in 2012, the French Competition Authority sanctioned a Franco-German Flour cartel aimed at limiting access to national markets: The level of Franco-German exports of flour was determined in advance by cartel members.

A geographical market allocation makes it easier to detect a cheating behavior; in the case of the Vitamins cartel (fined in 2001), Hoffmann-La Roche, the largest producer of vitamin B2, detected Takeda's deviations by simply using the Japanese government's export data.

Customer allocation*:* The allocation of markets may also be done according to customers: Each cartel member is assigned a category or a list of customers and promises not to contact competitors' customers. This allocation of clients is generally based on historical precedence: Each firm is assigned customers it already has in its portfolio, thereby "*freezing*" market shares. In the case of the Luxembourg Brewery cartel, four firms had divided up the "*horeca*" market (hotels, restaurants and cafés). The cartel was based on an agreement signed in 1985: Each party agreed not to supply beer to any customer who was already linked to another supplier by an exclusive purchasing contract, called a "*beer tie.*" The durability of the beer tie was reinforced by a consultation mechanism: Before supplying a new customer, the cartel member had to check beforehand whether the customer was already linked to another supplier by a beer tie. In case of non-compliance, financial penalties were imposed.

Call for tender and bid rigging*:* A call for tender is a procedure whereby a client (called "*contracting authority*") puts several firms (called "*bidders*") in "*competition for the market*" (in distinction from "*competition in the market*"). This procedure is frequent in the case of public entities, such as local authorities (school canteen contracts, school milk contracts, historical monument renovations, school bus pick-ups). The firm that offers the most attractive price wins the contract. The call for tender encourages participants to offer the lowest possible price, because everybody fears that their competitors will underbid them in order to win the contract.

For example, if a contracting authority estimates that the cost of building a school is $1 million, it is likely that bidders will offer a price close to this amount. The profit of the successful bidder will then be ... zero, since the price only covers its costs (this situation is sometimes referred to as "the winner's curse"). Bid rigging consists of firms colluding to decide in advance who shall be the winner and the price at which he will win the bid. In our example, Firm A colludes with Firm B so that the latter will win the contract at a set price of $1.2 million. In order to simulate competition between the two firms, Firm A submits a bid at a higher price, for example at $1.3 million. This practice is referred to as "*phantom bidding*" or "*fake bidding.*" Firm A agrees to lose the market to Firm B, as long as, in return, it is allowed to win another tender of an equivalent size in the near future.

Quotas: One way of organizing a cartel is to agree on quotas so that the total production will be close to that of a monopoly; each member is then allocated a maximum quantity to produce. From a theoretical point of view, the optimal allocation of quotas must be based on the marginal production costs of each firm. If firms have the same costs, each of them is allocated an identical quota, equal to the monopoly quantity, divided by the number of cartel participants. On the other hand, if firms do not have the same production costs, the firm with low production cost will be allocated a high quota. As a result, an inefficient firm (with a high marginal cost) will have to reduce its production, sometimes to the point of making a lower profit than in a competitive situation; in this case, the most efficient firm must compensate for it with a profit transfer called "*lateral payment.*"

In practice, quotas are usually allocated according to each member's historical sales data: Each firm is allocated a quota according to the market share it has when the cartel is formed.

Collective boycott: Another form of cartel consists of agreeing with its competitors to boycott the entry of a new firm into the market by putting pressure on upstream suppliers.

In 2002, the French Competition Council sanctioned several distributors of optical products in the Lyon area; they'd organized a collective boycott of suppliers in order to stop them from supplying a newcomer. Indeed, an optical store, Optical Center, had set up in Lyon and was offering 20%-40% discounts on optical products, including on those of prestigious brands. Faced with this competitive threat, 40 opticians met and launched a campaign to boycott suppliers of the brands listed at Optical Center. Several trade retaliation measures against these suppliers were initiated: orders were cancelled, their products were no longer presented in stores, etc. Once the suppliers had joined the boycott of the new entrant, the cartel became both horizontal and vertical.

The role of trade associations*:* Firms in the same sector may sometimes take advantage of their professional body to implement a cartel. Unions or associations facilitate collusion by regularly bringing together all the producers of an industry; these meetings offer the perfect opportunity for firms to set the cartel's goals and structure (organized around price fixing or quota setting, etc.).

For example, in the case of the Lysine cartel, the meetings of the professional association served as a cover-up for cartel members to secretly conduct their illicit practice. In their study on 111 cartels in Europe, Combe and Monnier showed that in 25% of the cases, a trade organization took part in the cartel, particularly when the cartel had a large number of members: one-third of cartels with more than 10 members, and all cartels with more than 16 participants, relied on such an organization. For example, the European Cement Federation (Cembureau) was in charge of organizing the Cement cartel dismantled in 1994, which brought together 33 producers and 9 business associations.

SECTION 2 CARTEL STABILITY

Following the work of Nobel Prize winner George Stigler (1964), it has been argued that cartels are inherently unstable structures: Once the decision to increase prices has been made, each cartel member has an individual incentive to cheat in order to gain market shares and profits. Therefore, Stigler argues, under such conditions that there is no need to fight against cartels, as, by nature, they are doomed to fail (§1). However, this argument seems questionable both empirically and theoretically: We'll demonstrate that, under certain conditions, a cartel can be stable over time (§2). We'll then identify the main conditions that can favor the stability of a cartel (§3).

§1 Cartels: Unstable by Nature?

There are many historical examples of cartel members cheating and thus leading to the implosion of the cartel. For instance, in the rail sector, the 1870s cartel of major American firms never really worked, despite the fact that the cartel could easily enforce its price and tonnage distribution agreements and that there wasn't yet any antitrust legislation at the time in the United States to stop them: "In continuing to try to make the cartel work, Fink's organization had almost as much trouble with the weak cooperative roads (and even some of the stronger ones) as he did with the uncooperative ones controlled by speculators. Traffic managers and freight agents developed new subterfuges for evading the published rates. These included false billing regarding weight or amounts shipped or distances sent and improper classification of freight moved. [...] By 1884, nearly all the railroad managers and most investors agreed that even the most carefully devised cartels were unable to control competition" (Chandler, 1977, pp. 141-142).

This example shows that each cartel member has an individual interest in lowering its price just below the price set by the cartel in order to make additional profits. If all cartel members behave in the same way, the only way out is ... a return to fierce competition.

The "prisoner's dilemma" theory: The intrinsic instability of a cartel can be addressed by using game theory, and, more particularly, the famous *"prisoner's dilemma."* This story states that even though two entities would benefit from working together, they each do what benefits themselves as individuals rather than do that which is best for the group. The result is that both entities lose out.

In the matrix in Table 3.5, two firms A and B are represented. When they compete against each other, each makes a profit of $30, and the total profit is therefore $60. If they form a cartel, they will reap the benefits of a monopoly situation, i.e., gain a total profit of $100 (or $50 per firm).

Once the agreement is concluded, each firm faces a strategic conundrum: respect the cartel price or cheat and lower its price.

If they both respect the agreement, they will both make a profit of $50. However, if one of the two cheats while its rival behaves fairly, the first one will increase its profits to $80, while the second will lose all its customers and see its profits shrivel to $0.

The profit Π_d (equal to $80) gained by a cheating firm is, by definition, greater than the profit $\Pi_{m/2}$ (equal to the monopoly profit shared between the two firms, i.e., $50 per firm) earned in a cartel situation. When both firms cheat, we return to a competitive market situation, and the profit of each firm Π_C is equal to $30. So, we have:

$$0 < \Pi_C < \Pi_{m/2} < \Pi_d$$

What is the result of this game? If Firm A respects the agreement, the best strategy for Firm B is to cheat since $80 > $50; if Firm A does not respect the agreement, for Firm B, there would be no benefit in respecting it either, since $30 > $0. Thus, whatever the choice of Firm A, Firm B will always cheat. As a result, Firm A, anticipating that Firm B will cheat, will do the same thing. Each firm considers that its best strategy is to cheat (to maximize its profits and/or minimize its losses), regardless of what its rival does. As a result, both lose out and the final outcome is a return to a competitive market situation and profits equal to ($30, $30). This result shows that cartels are doomed to fail because of the opportunistic behavior of each member.

One can note that if the prisoner's dilemma is repeated in an iterative process over several periods, the end outcome doesn't change. Indeed, suppose that the two firms decide to agree to fix their prices for four consecutive periods. In the last period, as the game is nearly over, the two firms will cheat. By reasoning with "*backward induction*," the best choice in the before-last period will also be to cheat. One can easily understand that the two firms will cheat right from the beginning of the game.

Table 3.5 Cartel and Prisoner's Dilemma

	Firm B	
Firm A	Respects the price	Cheats
Respects the price	($50, $50)	($0, $80)
Cheats	($80, $0)	**($30, $30)**

N.B.: In each box, the first digit corresponds to the profit of Firm A and the second to the profit of Firm B.

Empirical studies*:* If cartels were by nature unstable, as predicted by the prisoner's dilemma, their lifespans would be very short: Cartels would explode shortly after having been created, and the market would return to a situation of pure and perfect competition. However, empirical studies show that the average lifespan of a cartel isn't equal to zero. The results presented in Table 3.6 show that:

- on average, convicted cartels in Europe have lifespans of 7.3 years. More generally, empirical studies find average lifespans to be between 5 and 8 years (*see* Combe and Monnier's 2012 study);
- the life expectancy of cartels varies greatly; some cartels fall apart rapidly (such as the French Beef cartel, sanctioned in 2003 by the European Commission and which lasted less than three months), while others manage to last for several decades.[28]

It's difficult to interpret these results and qualify a lifespan as being short or long, as we do not have an established time reference framework. According to the European Commission's Guidelines on the Method of Setting Fines (1998), an infringement of less than five years is considered to be of short duration. Conversely, any infringement that has lasted "*over five years*" is considered to be of long duration. On the basis of this standard, nearly two-thirds of cartels in Europe can be qualified as long-term cartels.

Table 3.6 The Life Expectancy of Cartels

	Average Duration	*Median*	*Number of Cases*
Combe and Monnier (2012)	7.3	5.7	111
Bolotova et al (2007)	8.61	nc	395
Veljanovski (2007)	6.5	nc	30
Levenstein and Suslow (2006b)	7.5	nc	72
Zimmerman and Connor (2005)	6.3	4.4	166
Dick (1996)	5.3	nc	111

28. The Organic Peroxides cartel sanctioned by the European Commission in 2003 and the Gas cartel sanctioned in 2009 had lasted almost 30 years.

	Average Duration	*Median*	*Number of Cases*
Bryant and Eckard (1991)	6.3	4.8	184
Griffin (1989)	7.3	nc	54
Eckbo (1876)	4.6	nc	52
Posner (1970)	7.5	nc	989

Source: Combe and Monnier (2012).

§2 Cartel Stability over Time

Beyond this empirical observation, it is important to understand how cartels stabilize themselves over time. To do this, we will repeat the prisoner's dilemma over an indefinite (or infinite) number of periods. We will see that when the game is repeated over an infinite horizon, it is possible, under certain conditions, for the cartel to become stable as none of the firms have an incentive to cheat anymore.

The prisoner's dilemma repeated over an infinite horizon*:* In the section above, we assumed that the two firms formed a cartel to play once or over a finite number of periods. Now let us assume that firms A and B have agreed on an infinite or indefinite number of periods (they do not know a priori the end date of the game). In a situation of "repeated game," firms A and B adopt the following rule: "I will respect the cartel price, as long as my partner does the same; if my partner cheats in period T, I will no longer respect the cartel price and I will always cheat from T + 1 to infinity."

This rule, known as the "*trigger strategy*," consists of punishing the partner who cheats in T by immediately applying a competitive price in the following period and all those thereafter (Figure 3.2).

Figure 3.2 Punishing Defection: The Trigger Strategy Rule

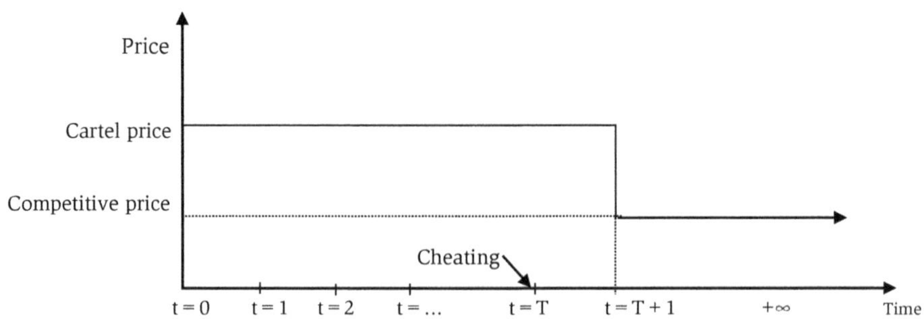

To correctly compare the gains of a firm when it cheats and when it sticks to the collusive price, we need to take into account the fact that gains depreciate over time: $1

tomorrow will be worth less than \$1 today. To measure the depreciation over time, economists use a "*discount factor.*" The discount factor, noted δ is between 0 and 1:

- when it is close to 1, it means that the future is only slightly devalued since \$1 tomorrow is almost as valuable as \$1 today. For example, if $\delta = 0.95$, \$1 is worth in two periods: $0.95^2 = \$0.90$;
- if it is close to zero, it means that the value of \$1 depreciates very quickly over time. For example, if $\delta = 0.2$, \$1 in two periods is no longer worth more than $0.2^2 = \$0.04$.

Let's compare the gains of the two possible strategies available to Firm A (the same reasoning applies to Firm B). If Firm A never cheats, it earns $\Pi_{m/2}$, half a monopoly profit (i.e., \$50) over each period. Given the depreciation over time, the gains must be discounted. Remember that the sum of $1 + \delta + \delta^2 + \delta^3 + \ldots + \delta^n$ is a geometric sequence, the result of which is $1/(1 - \delta)$.

The discounted gain when Firm A respects the deal and therefore does not cheat is:

$$\$50 + \delta\$50 + \delta^2\$50 + \ldots = \$50/(1 - \delta) \qquad (1)$$

If Firm A cheats in T, it makes a gain of \$80 in T but then, from T + 1 to infinity, it will only make a competitive profit of \$30 in each following period. The total cheating gains, if Firm A cheats from T to infinity is therefore:

$$\$80 + \$30\,\delta/(1 - \delta) \qquad (2)$$

Firm A has no incentive to cheat if (1) > (2):

$$\$50/(1\text{-}\delta) > \$80 + \$30\,/(1\text{-}\delta)$$

$$\Leftrightarrow \delta > \delta^* = 3/5$$

with δ the discount factor, and δ^* the critical discount factor.

The value of the critical discount factor δ^* can equally be calculated with the following formula:

$$\delta^* = (\Pi_d - \Pi_m/2)/(\Pi_d - \Pi_c)$$

$$\Leftrightarrow \delta^* = (\$80 - \$50)/(\$80 - \$30)$$

$$\delta^* = 3/5$$

We can represent on a horizontal axis the different values of the discount factor (Figure 3.3). We see that if the firm has a discount factor of less than 3/5 (e.g., 2/5), it will cheat. Conversely, if its discount factor is greater than 3/5 (e.g., 4/5), it has no incentive to cheat.

Figure 3.3 The Value of the Discount Factor: Its Impact on the Incentive to Cheat

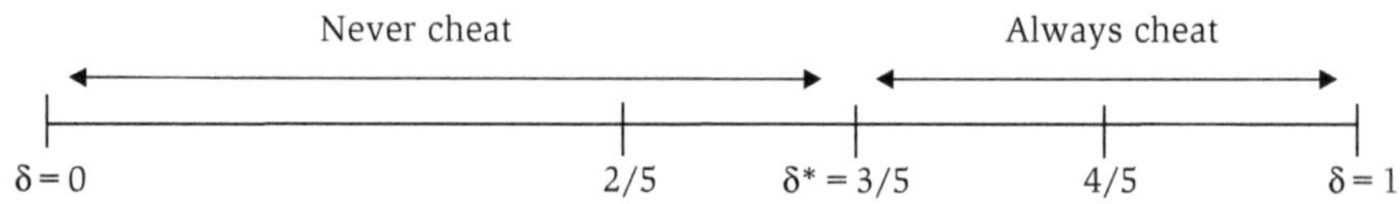

Intuitively, one can see that the choice to cheat or not will depend on the weight given to future gains, and, therefore, on each firm's short-term or long-term preferences: If the future is highly depreciated, a firm will prefer to cheat to make an immediate profit, even if it will then be punished. On the other hand, the cartel is stable if each cartel member sufficiently values future gains; this "*patient*" behavior itself depends on several parameters, such as:

- the financial situation of the firm: A firm in bankruptcy or heavy debt will highly value the current earnings and be more likely to cheat. A cartel is therefore more likely to be stable if it includes firms with a low probability of bankruptcy or a low debt ratio, such as old and/or large firms;
- the market growth or decline: When the market enters a phase of decline, firms are tempted to deviate from the cartel price because future punishments will take place on a smaller market.

Changes in the discount factor: The value of the discount factor δ^* depends on three parameters: the cartel profit, the competitive profit and the cheating profit.

If all three parameters change, the value of the discount factor will change too. Let's take the matrix of Table 3.5 and assume this time that the competitive profit is $10 (instead of $30), as shown in Table 3.7. In other words, the firm that cheated in T will earn a profit of $10 per period after T + 1. We can therefore consider that reducing the competitive profit is equivalent to increasing the punishment against the cheater.

Table 3.7 Cartel and Harsher Punishments

	Firm B	
Firm A	Respects the price	Cheats
Respects the price	($50, $50)	($0, $80)
Cheats	($80, $0)	**($10, $10)**

N.B.: In each box, the first digit corresponds to the profit of Firm A and the second to the profit of Firm B.

We immediately see that since the competition profit is lower, each firm has less incentive to cheat (Figure 3.4). The critical discount factor δ^* is now equal to:

$$\delta^* = (\Pi_d - \Pi_m/2)/(\Pi_d - \Pi_c)$$

$$\Leftrightarrow \delta^* = (\$80 - \$50)/(\$80 - \$10)$$

$$\Leftrightarrow \delta^* = 3/7$$

Figure 3.4 Harsher Punishments: Their Impact on the Incentive to Cheat

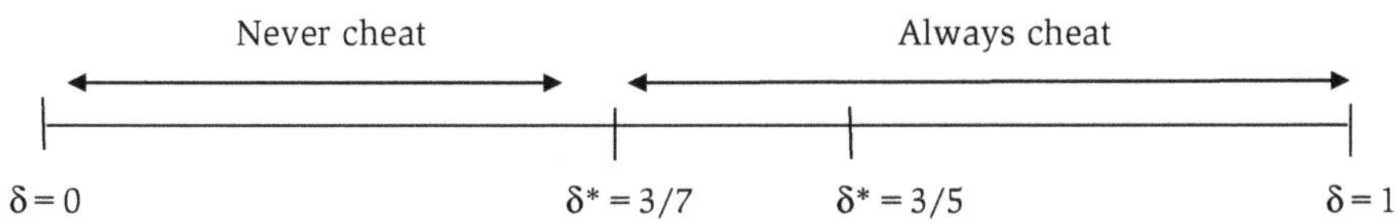

Let us take the matrix from Table 3.5 and now assume that the cheating profit is reduced from \$80 to \$60, as shown in Table 3.8.

Table 3.8 Cartel and the Decrease in Cheating Profits

	Firm B	
Firm A	Respects the price	Cheats
Respects the price	(\$50, \$50)	**(\$0, \$60)**
Cheats	**(\$60, \$0)**	(\$30, \$30)

N.B.: In each box, the first digit corresponds to the profit of Firm A and the second to the profit of Firm B.

We see immediately that since the gain from cheating is lower, each firm has less incentive to cheat (Figure 3.5). The critical discount factor δ^* is now equal to:

$$\delta^* = (\Pi_d - \Pi_m/2)/(\Pi_d - \Pi_c)$$

$$\Leftrightarrow \delta^* = (\$60 - \$50)/(\$60 - \$30)$$

$$\Leftrightarrow \delta^* = 1/3$$

Figure 3.5 Drop in Cheating Profits: Its Impact on the Incentive to Cheat

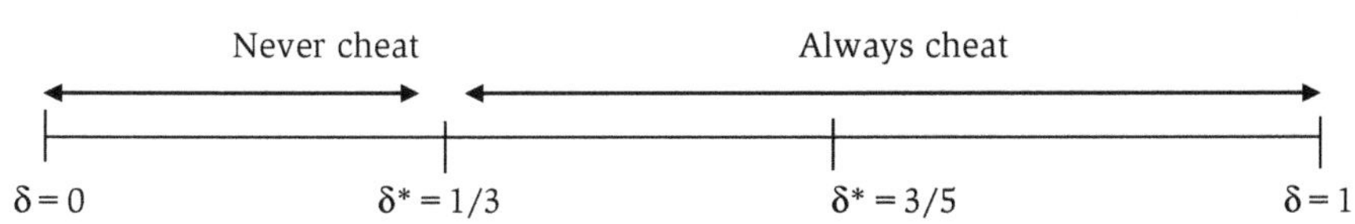

§3 Factors and Practices Favoring Cartel Stability

We have seen that a cartel can become stable if cheating members are harshly punished or if cheating produces only limited gains. In practice, this means that a cartel must be able to very quickly detect any signs of cheating in order to punish the defector immediately. We can identify the main market characteristics and practices that favor a cartel's stability over time.

Market conditions: Market characteristics influence the stability of cartels and partially determine the ability of cartels to detect and punish all deviant members early on:

- detecting deviant behavior is easier when there are few cartel members. When there are many firms, each firm benefits from a low profit, which increases incentive to cheat. On the other hand, the punishment for deviant behavior appears to be more severe when there are more firms on the market;
- in a transparent market, firms that cheat are quickly detected, which is the case in most B2C (Business to Consumers) markets;
- cheating is less profitable when transactions are frequent because punishments can be implemented quickly;
- dispersion of demand facilitates collusion: For example, a concentration of demand may be characterized by large orders that encourage sellers to offer discounts to win contracts;
- since the stability of a cartel depends on the extent of the retaliation, multi-market contacts promote collusion;
- the nature of competition affects the stability of the cartel. Price competition (such as in a Bertrand's competition) reinforces the severity of the punishment compared to quantity competition (such as in a Cournot's competition), but also offers higher profits in case of cheating. However, it is shown that, in general, price competition (à la Bertrand) is less conducive to a stable agreement than quantity competition (à la Cournot).

Practices that promote cartel stability: The stability of a cartel can be enhanced by implementing certain key practices to better detect and punish potential cheaters: exchanging information; establishing monitoring mechanisms, commercial clauses, or compensation mechanisms; and even threatening members with a price war.

Information exchange. As prices are not always transparent, particularly in B2B (Business to Business), cartel members may be encouraged to offer secret discounts to customers. To avoid such cheating and detect it early, cartel members can exchange information about transactions on a regular basis.

For example, in Europe and the United States, firms in the Vitamins cartel had set up a mechanism to ensure compliance with the commitments and held regular meetings where they exchanged monthly or quarterly data on sales, volumes and prices charged. These meetings were supplemented by weekly phone contacts. By comparing sales and allocated quotas regularly, they could monitor each member's commitment and, if necessary, punish any deviant behavior.

Similarly, in the Endive cartel (2012), sanctioned by the French Competition Authority, members used a software information exchange system, called Infoclar, which centralized in real time the prices producers charged, and allowed each member to check that they were in line with prices collectively decided. As the information collected did not remain anonymous, cheaters were immediately identified when an anomaly (price difference) arose and were subjected to punishment and retaliation measures.

Exchange of information can thus be done at different levels: at the global, regional, or local level, or at the level of each client. In the context of the Vitamins cartel, the exchange of information was mainly based on regional data. In the Carbon and Graphite Products cartel, the members exchanged information about the prices charged and the turnover generated by each customer.

Monitoring mechanisms. To ensure the veracity of the news transmitted and the compliance with agreements, some cartels have set up specific surveillance mechanisms. For example, cartels have used external auditors or professional associations (as in the cases of the Lysine cartel, Vitamins cartel, and Citric Acid cartel). In the Plumbing Tube cartel (2004), sanctioned by the European Commission, firms engaged in unilateral price monitoring to avoid relying solely on competitors' statements. The sales force of one of the firms was used to collect information on the prices charged by other cartel members.

Commercial clauses. Some commercial clauses, such as the best price clause, can enhance the stability of a cartel. The best price clause states that a customer who identifies a lower price will obtain the same price or a refund of the difference. This clause allows cartel members to detect any deviations by using customers as a source of information.

In 2002, for example, the French Competition Council sanctioned a cartel in the distribution of household electrical and electronic products: The producer Akai and its distributors (Darty, FNAC, Conforama, and others) had jointly set the price and created a system to monitor cheaters based on a clause that refunded consumers any price difference.

Similarly, the "most-favored customer" clause stipulates that all customers will be treated in the same way and that existing customers will benefit from any future price reduction. This clause limits the profitability of a price decrease, since the firm that deviates will have to compensate its previous customers.

Compensation mechanisms. In terms of punishment, cartel firms can set up compensation schemes. Thus, in the Citric Acid cartel, sanctioned by the European Commission in 2001, firms selling above their quotas had to compensate other cartel members who had not reached their quotas. In practice, if a firm exceeded its quota in a given year, it was forced the following year to buy the equivalent of its quota overrun from other firms.

The threat of a price war. The cartel's stability can be insured by threatening price wars or retaliation in the case of cheating. Thus, in the Copper Plumbing Tube cartel, sanctioned by the European Commission in 2004, cartel members adopted aggressive trade practices against cheaters: Each time a participant made an offer to a customer allocated to another producer and/or did not respect the agreed price, it was obliged to justify itself and risked punishment.

In most cases, retaliation measures are targeted at cheaters and do not trigger general price wars. In the Medical and Industrial Gases cartel sanctioned by the European Commission in 2013, the cartel established a list of customers that could be used to implement retaliatory measures against possible cheaters. Having these lists of potential "*targets*" allows the cartel to achieve an "*equilibrium of terror.*" If some still try to cheat, an extended retaliation campaign is launched—in all territories and not just in the market where the deviation took place. For instance, cross-border retaliation was frequent in order to hit cheaters harder in their domestic markets, where appropriate targets were easier to find.

SECTION 3 CARTELS AND ANTITRUST SANCTIONS

Because cartels increase prices and reduce the total welfare, they're prohibited by antitrust laws (§1). We'll analyze the legal framework set up in the United States and Europe to fight against these illicit practices (§2). We use the theory of "*optimal sanctions*" to determine the appropriate level of public fine that should be imposed on firms in order to deter them to form a cartel (§3), and we apply this analytical framework to the European case.

§1 Why Sanction Cartels?

Cartels are prohibited by antitrust laws because they lead to artificial price increases without any compensation for customers, who buy the same products as before but at more expensive prices; they are therefore inefficient practices. A cartel reduces the total welfare and doesn't just transfer surplus from consumers to firms. The cartel does not lead to any reduction in costs and it freezes all incentive to innovate. Moreover, as we have seen in Section 2 above, cartels can become stable if their members are able to monitor and punish "cheating" behaviors.

Price increases ("*overcharges*") induced by cartels can be significant. Thus, the empirical study by Boyer and Kotchoni (2015) on a large sample of 1119 cartels, highlights three results (Table 3.9):

- average price increases are in the order of 16%-17%, whether in the United States or Europe;
- international cartels lead on average to higher overprices (19.49%) than domestic cartels (15.29%);
- roughly a third of cartels succeed in imposing price increases of more than 50%.

Table 3.9 Estimated Price Increases in Europe and the United States

		All Cartels	*OE > 0%*	*0% < OE < 50%*	*OE ≥ 50%*	*Cartels Before 1973*	*Cartels After 1973*
All locations	Mean	17.52	18.89	13.62	35.28	17.87	17.39
	Median	14.05	14.35	13.63	34.23	13.45	14.22
	Prop.%	100.00	92.77	70.18	22.59	28.50	71.50
US	Mean	16.45	18.13	13.73	34.70	17.92	15.76
	Median	14.01	14.27	13.75	32.52	13.94	14.14
	Prop.%	30.00	27.23	21.52	5.71	9.64	20.36
EU	Mean	17.75	18.97	13.08	34.16	17.70	17.79
	Median	13.78	13.90	13.32	32.55	13.40	14.03
	Prop.%	33.48	31.34	22.59	8.75	13.39	20.09
Domestic	Mean	15.29	16.80	13.26	37.00	16.86	14.59
	Median	13.40	13.55	13.32	35.80	13.40	13.39
	Prop.%	46.79	42.59	36.25	6.34	14.46	32.32
International	Mean	19.49	20.67	13.99	34.61	18.90	19.70
	Median	15.44	15.64	14.03	33.91	13.67	15.52
	Prop.%	53.21	50.18	33.93	16.23	14.02	39.20

Source: Boyer and Kotchoni (2015).

These price increases lead to a transfer of surplus from customers to cartel members, but also to a loss of welfare, as some customers give up buying products because of higher prices. These two effects are illustrated in Figure 3.6.

Suppose that several firms are in competition, with a market price equal to \$5. At a price of \$5, the quantity sold is 100 units. They decide to form a cartel to increase the price by 20%. At the cartel price (\$6), the quantity decreases to 80 units. The cartel practice has two effects on the market:

- a transfer of surplus from customers who continue to buy the product and now pay more to cartel members. This surplus transfer corresponds to the illicit gain (also called overprofit) measured by the grayed-out rectangle: Its amount is equal to (\$6 − \$5) × 80 = \$80. It is neutral in terms of welfare;
- a loss of total welfare: Since the price has risen by 20%, some customers who bought at the competitive price no longer buy at the cartel price. This "*loss of surplus*" is represented by the hatched triangle and its amount is equal to: (\$6 − \$5) × 20 × 0.5 = \$10. The surplus loss will depend on the price elasticity of demand: The more elastic the demand, the greater the loss of surplus.

Figure 3.6 Cartel: A Transfer and Loss of Surplus

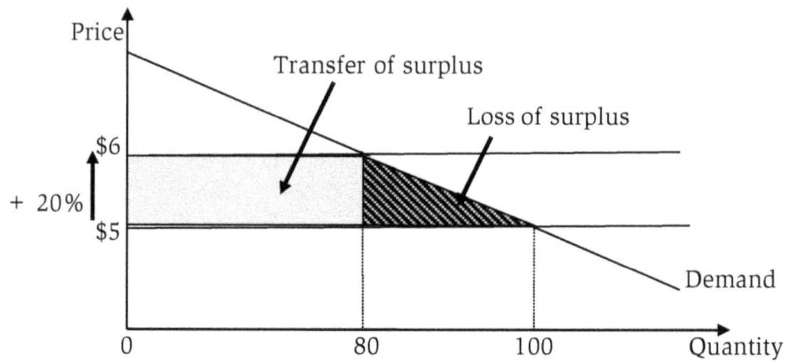

Beyond this static inefficiency, cartels can also generate dynamic inefficiency: As firms are no longer subject to the stimulus of competition, their incentive to innovate and lower production costs is reduced. The economy is thus deprived of efficiency gains that firms would have developed if they'd had to compete with each other.

§2 Public Sanctions: The Legal Framework

As cartels are inefficient and sustainable practices, they are prohibited by antitrust laws. Today more than 90 jurisdictions around the world prohibit such practices, and the fight against cartels is the key objective of antitrust policies.

The American case: In the United States, horizontal agreements to restrict competition fall under Section 1 of the Sherman Act (1890), which states that: "Every contract, combination in the form of trust or otherwise, or conspiracy, in restraint of trade or commerce among the several States, or with foreign nations, is declared to be illegal."

Following the Trans-Missouri (1897) and Trenton Potteries (1927) cases, the American authorities found that cartels were subject to a per se approach: Nothing could ever justify such anti-competitive practices. The Sherman Act, implemented by the Antitrust Division of the U.S. DOJ, sets the maximum amount of sanction at $100 million for firms. However, antitrust authorities may in practice circumvent this maximum by imposing sanctions of up to twice the cartel's unlawful gain or twice the loss suffered by the cartel's victims. Regarding the calculation of the penalty, the U.S. Sentencing Guidelines (2011) recommend that it be set at 20% of the volume of sales affected by the cartel.

Since the 2000s, American authorities have sentenced several large international cartels to heavy fines, such as the Vitamins cartel ($875 million) or Liquid Crystal Displays cartel ($1.4 billion). Over the past ten years, the total sanctions that the DOJ has imposed on cartels has reached $9 billion, excluding actions for compensation and penalties imposed on individuals (Figure 3.7).

Figure 3.7 Antitrust Sanctions Against Cartels in the United States (2011-2020)

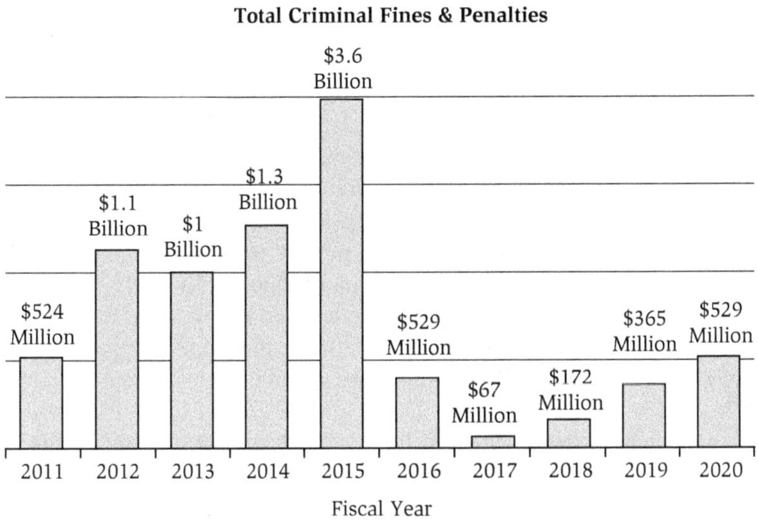

Source: Antitrust Division, Department of Justice (2021).

The European case: In Europe, anti-competitive agreements are prohibited by Article 101 TFEU:

> 1. The following shall be prohibited as incompatible with the internal market: all agreements between undertakings, decisions by associations of undertakings and concerted practices which may affect trade between Member States and which have as their object or effect the prevention, restriction or distortion of competition within the internal market, and in particular those which:
>   (a) directly or indirectly fix purchase or selling prices or any other trading conditions;
>   (b) limit or control production, markets, technical development, or investment;
>   (c) share markets or sources of supply;
>   (d) apply dissimilar conditions to equivalent transactions with other trading parties, thereby placing them at a competitive disadvantage;
>   (e) make the conclusion of contracts subject to acceptance by the other parties of supplementary obligations which, by their nature or according to commercial usage, have no connection with the subject of such contracts.
> 2. Any agreements or decisions prohibited pursuant to this Article shall be automatically void.

Although cartels are not prohibited per se in Europe, in practice, they are always sanctioned; they are considered as restrictions of competition by object and cannot be exempt from a sanction. Moreover, the effect (potential or actual) of a cartel on the market is presumed.

Anti-competitive agreements are sanctioned up to a maximum of 10% of firms' worldwide total turnover. The amount of the penalty is determined according to the Guidelines on the Method of Setting Fines (2006). First, a basic penalty amount is calculated: It is equal to a percentage of the value of sales affected by the cartel, multiplied by the number of years of the infringement. This percentage can be as high as 30% of annual sales. Then, the infringer is fined an additional "*entry fee,*" regardless the cartel's duration: Its amount is between 15%-25% of the value of annual sales. This is done to deter firms from participating in a cartel, even for only a short period. Once the basic amount has been calculated, the fine may be increased or decreased depending on any aggravating or mitigating factors. Indeed, if the firm is a repeat offender, the Commission can increase the fine by up to 100%. On the other hand, settlement or leniency procedures can lead to a reduction in fines.

While cartel fines in Europe have long remained low in absolute terms, they have grown strongly since the 2000s (Figure 3.8), particularly following the publication of the Guidelines on the Method of Setting Fines in 2006.

Figure 3.8 Total Sanctions Imposed by the European Commission Against Cartels (1990-2020; Million Euros)

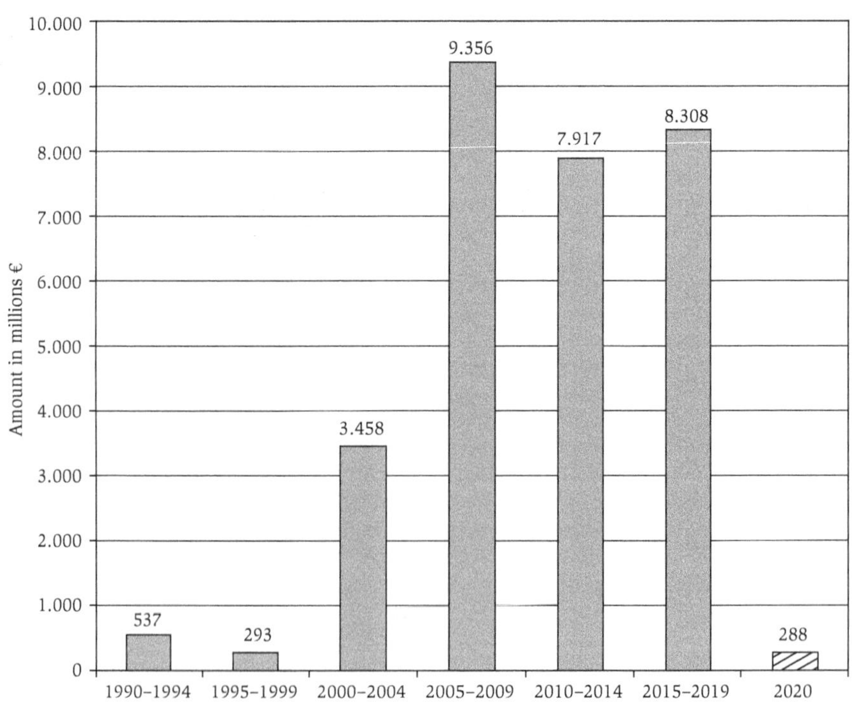

Source: DG Competition (2021).

In particular, the European Commission has imposed fines in excess of €1 billion (Table 3.10), as in the Carglass (€1.1 billion) or Truck (€3.8 billion) cartels.

Table 3.10 The 10 Largest Sanctions Imposed by the Commission Against Cartels

Year	*Case Name*	*Amount in €*
2016 and 2017	Trucks	3,807,022,000
2012	TV and computer monitor tubes	1,409,588,000
2013 and 2016	Euro interest rates derivatives (EIRD)	1,276,433,000
2008	Carglass	1,185,500,000
2019	Forex	1,068,879,000
2014	Automotive bearings	953,306,000
2007	Elevators and escalators	832,422,250
2001	Vitamins	790,515,000
2010 and 2017	Airfreight (incl. re-adoption)	785,345,000
2013 and 2015	Yen interest rate derivatives (YIRD)	669,719,000

Source: DG Competition (2021).

The case of concerted practices: Another form of collusion between competing firms is "*concerted practices,*" which consist of exchanging strategic information between competitors.

In its Guidelines on Horizontal Cooperation Agreements, the European Commission states "[that] an exchange of information can [...] constitute a concerted practice if it reduces strategic uncertainty in the market and thus facilitates collusion, i.e., if the data exchanged are of a strategic nature. Consequently, the exchange of strategic data between competitors amounts to concerted action, in that it reduces the independence of competitors' behavior on the market and their incentive to compete" (paragraph 61).

When they concern past historical information, the exchanges of information are assessed according to their actual effects on competition, which depends on two sets of criteria: on the one hand, the economic conditions prevailing in the market (in particular, the level of transparency, the degree of market concentration, the symmetry of firms), and, on the other hand, the characteristics of the information exchanged (in particular its aggregated or individualized nature, its age, or the frequency of exchanges).

In the English Tractors case (1998), the ECJ maintained that the regular exchange of information regarding the sales of tractors in the United Kingdom constituted an anti-competitive agreement in so far as it infringed on the principle of autonomy of conduct. In France, in 2005, the French Competition Authority also sanctioned six Parisian palaces for exchanging confidential commercial information in an oligopolistic market, thereby artificially increasing market transparency. When the exchange of information between competitors is regarding future prices, then they are treated as "*restrictions by object*," as the ECJ pointed out in the T-Mobile (2009) and Banana (2013) cases.

§3 Antitrust Sanctions: An Economic Approach

From an economic perspective, what should be the right amount of fines imposed on a cartel? The theory of "*optimal sanctions*" offers a powerful analytical framework for answering this question. After having outlined the fundamentals of this theory, we will apply it to cartels in Europe in a context characterized by the increase in sanctions since the 2000s. Finally, we will underline the limits of such an approach, particularly with regards to legal criteria.

The theory of optimal sanctions: The starting point of the optimal sanctions theory is quite intuitive: An economic actor (a firm as well as an individual) will break the law if the gains reaped are greater than the costs (Becker, 1968). This principle refers to the notion of rationality, wherein one always balances costs and benefits before making a decision.

In the case of a cartel, quantifying the benefit of infringement is easy: It's the difference between the cartel price and the competitive price, multiplied by the volume of sales. In Figure 3.6 above, this illicit overprofit is measured by the gray rectangle and is equal to:

$$(\$6 - \$5) \times 80 = \$80$$

Cartel members know that they will be sanctioned and heavily fined if antitrust authorities catch them. The cost for the firm is therefore divided into two distinct elements: the fine and the probability of being caught.

Suppose that the firm is "*risk neutral*"; when it decides to join a cartel, it will weigh up the expected gains against the expected costs. The firm will not risk breaking the law if the expected costs are higher than the illegal gains:

$$\text{expected cost} > \text{illegal gain}$$

$$\Leftrightarrow (\text{fine} \times \text{probability of detection}) > \text{illegal gain} \quad (1)$$

If we take the antitrust authorities' point of view, the penalty must be at least equal to:

$$\text{optimal monetary sanction} \geq (\text{illegal gain}/\text{probability of detection}) \quad (2)$$

In our numerical example, if the probability of detection is 25% (i.e., 0.25), the optimal monetary penalty that deters the firm from breaking the law must be at least equal to:

$$\text{optimal monetary sanction} \geq \$80/0.25$$

$$\text{optimal monetary sanction} \geq \$320$$

We see immediately that the optimal sanction has several characteristics:

- the amount of the fine depends on the overprice and the value of sales affected by the cartel. It means that the high or low level of a sanction makes no sense, strictly speaking: The amount of the sanction is directly proportional to the illicit gains made by the cartel;
- the sanction must always be greater than the illicit gain, because the probability of detection is less than 100%;
- the lower the probability of detection, the higher the sanction should be. For antitrust authorities, there is a trade-off between the harshness of the sanction and the detection rate. Detection being costly, the economic approach advocates acting on the sanction rather than on the probability of detection: The optimal policy is therefore to set low probabilities of detection associated with strong sanctions (compared to what can be earned with illicit gains);
- the sanction has a deterrent function: It is set in such a way that no firm has financial incentive to break the law. The objective of an optimal sanction is not only to strongly punish firms that are caught (individual deterrence), but also to send a clear message of deterrence to any firms that may be tempted to form a cartel (general deterrence). It can even be considered that if firms are informed and convinced that optimal sanctions will be applied ex-post, they will no longer have any ex-ante incentive to break the law: Law enforcement is no longer necessary as there will no longer be any offenders.

Limitations of the optimal sanctions theory: While it provides a powerful theoretical framework, the optimal sanctions theory nevertheless has several limitations, particularly when confronted with what is put into practice by competition authorities.

First, the optimal sanction does not take into account the intrinsic seriousness of the cartel practice: A cartel without illicit gain should not be sanctioned. This approach does not correspond to real life: Antitrust authorities consider cartels serious enough to be sanctioned simply because they exist, whatever their effects.

Second, the theory of optimal sanctions only allows antitrust authorities to calculate monetary sanctions. However, today, in addition to fines, competition authorities may also impose non-monetary sanctions, such as the publication of their ruling to inform the market (as done in France, for example). It is difficult in this case to quantify the value of such a sanction, as one cannot precisely assess the negative effect the publication will have on a firm's reputation.

Third, the theory of optimal sanctions requires a calculation of the illicit gains: This task often leads to numerous disputes regarding the exact quantum of the sanction that should be imposed. In practice, competition authorities are not required to quantify precisely the extent of the overprice, but only to demonstrate it exists, thereby allowing them to take a more qualitative approach.

Fourth, the optimal sanction approach can lead to an extreme case where public authorities choose a very low probability of detection (to avoid detection costs), and therefore impose fines close to infinity as a deterrent. Take, for example, our numerical example presented above: If the probability of detection is only 1 %, the amount of the sanction for an illegal gain of $80 would be ... $8,000. The sanction would be completely disproportionate compared to the illicit gain, and so would not be socially acceptable.

Fifth, the theory of optimal sanctions does not focus on the nature of the sanction but only on the amount of the penalty due. However, in real life, being sanctioned by competition authorities is not, for a firm, the same as being sued for civil damages. A sum imposed by a competition authority has a greater deterrent effect than the same sum paid in compensation to a victim, as the process is more public.

Finally, the optimal sanction does not take into account the loss of welfare (i.e., $10 in our numerical example) and the harm done to the economy. This is because the potential infringer bases its decision on the potential illegal gains and not on potential total damages. However, the role of a competition authority should be to take into account the total impact on the market, and not just the amount of illegal profits made by the cartel.

The ability to pay: If strictly applied, the theory of optimal sanctions could lead to fines that are not financially sustainable for firms, thus driving them to bankruptcy. It would be a paradox if antitrust sanctions lead to a reduction of competition in the market. To avoid this situation, competition authorities can use two safeguards:

- the maximum amount of the sanction is limited to a percentage of the firm's turnover; in Europe, it is legally capped at 10% of its worldwide turnover;
- when calculating the penalty, the specific financial situation of the firm is taken into account. Thus, at the European level, the Guidelines on the Method of Setting Fines (2006) state that, in exceptional circumstances, the Commission may reduce a firm's penalty if the latter proves that the fine is likely to endanger "irreparably the economic viability of the firm concerned" beyond the "mere finding of an unfavorable or loss-making financial situation." Similarly, in France, the Guidelines on the Calculation of Penalties (2011), published by the French Competition Authority, stipulates that a firm may request a reduction in penalties, but it has to justify the existence of particular financial difficulties at the time of the decision.

These principles have been applied on many occasions; for example, the European Commission has reduced, sometimes very significantly, the amount of the penalty to take into account the critical financial situation of a firm (Table 3.11). The most emblematic case is that of the Cathode Ray Tube cartel, where one of the participants, the French firm Technicolor, received an 85% reduction in the fine, decreasing its penalty from €219 million to €38 million.

Similarly, in France, the French Competition Authority has reduced sanctions on several occasions. These have sometimes been substantial when firms were able to demonstrate their financial fragility. For example, the 80% reduction granted to GAD in the Breton Pork cartel (2013), or the 35% reduction for the Grands Moulins de Strasbourg in the Flour cartel (2012), illustrate this point.

Table 3.11 Sanction Reductions and Firms' Inability to Pay (EU)

Cartel	*Total Penalty*	*% of Reduction due to Inability to Pay*
Cathode Ray Tubes cartel (2012)	€1.4 billion	85% for a firm (Technicolor)
Window Hardware Stores cartel (2012)	€86 million	45% for a firm
Bathroom Sanitary Facilities cartel (2010)	€622 million	25% for two firms and 50% for three firms
Pre-stressed Steel cartel (2010)	€269 million	25%, 50%, 75% for three firms
Phosphate Producers cartel (2010)	€175 million	70% for a firm
International Removals cartel (2008)	€32.7 million	70% for a firm

Optimal sanctions theory: How it is applied in Europe*:* Despite these limitations, the optimal sanctions theory provides a useful analytical framework for assessing ex-post whether the sanctions imposed by competition authorities have been sufficiently dissuasive. Combe and Monnier (2011, 2013) compared the sanctions imposed by the European Commission on 64 cartels between 1969 and 2009 with the amount of the fines that should have been given according to the optimal sanction theory. The aim was to determine whether the increase in sanctions from the 2000s onwards led the European Commission to impose excessive sanctions. To do this, the authors estimated the illicit gain obtained by each cartel on the basis of four parameters:

- the extra price imposed by the cartel: For the exercise, it is assumed that the price increase was of 17.5%, in accordance with the results of the Boyer and Kotchoni (2015) study;
- the price elasticity of demand, which negatively affects the amount of the illicit gain. Indeed, if customers are very price sensitive, the price increase leads to a significant reduction in the quantities purchased, which reduces the amount of the illicit gain. On the basis of numerous empirical studies, a range of elasticity with a minimum level equal to 0 (when demand is completely inelastic to price) and a maximum level at –2, is used;
- the size of the market affected by the cartel behavior: The larger the market and the longer the cartel has lasted, the greater the illicit gains are;
- the competitive margin before the cartel. Indeed, if the competitive margin is high, the price increase resulting from the cartel leads to a reduction in the

quantities purchased (except when the price elasticity of demand is zero) in which firms obtained a positive margin. The higher the competitive margin, the lower the illicit gain. In Figure 3.9, the firm realizes a competitive margin (with a price P_C) equal to the sum of the areas (B + C). In a cartel situation, by charging a P* price, the illicit gain obtained is equivalent to area A, from which area C—which represents the margin lost on customers who have given up consuming—must be subtracted.

Figure 3.9 Impact of the Competitive Margin on Cartel Profit

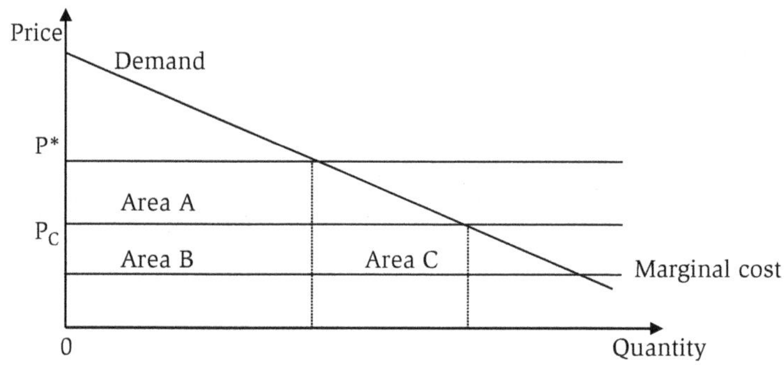

Source: Combe and Monnier (2013).

The probability that a cartel will be detected is set at 15%, which corresponds to a multiplier coefficient of 7.15%, is in line with the results of the empirical studies that Bryant and Eckard (1991) and Combe et al. (2008) did.

On the basis of these different parameters, two types of sanctions are calculated according to the level of price elasticity and the probability of detection (Table 3.12):

- sanctions relative to illicit gain: The fine is limited to the amount of illicit gains made by firms. The probability of detection is therefore assumed to be at 100%;
- optimal sanctions: As there is only a 15% probability of detection, the fines are higher. They are equal to the amount of illicit gain made by the firm, plus an additional punitive penalty.

Taking into account the two extremities of price elasticity of demand, each type of sanction includes an upper limit (when the price elasticity is zero) and a lower limit (when the price elasticity is equal to -2).

Table 3.12 Sanctions Depending on the Probability of Detection and the Price Elasticity of Demand

	15% Probability of Detection	*100% Probability of Detection*
Zero elasticity	Maximum punitive fine	Maximum sanction relative to illicit gain
Elasticity of -2	Minimum dissuasive fine	Minimum sanction relative to illicit gain

Source: Combe and Monnier (2013).

A first scenario—the most business friendly—corresponds to a very high price elasticity of demand (equal to -2). Figure 3.10 shows, for each cartel, the relationship between the sanction imposed by the European Commission and the unlawful gain. If this ratio is less than one, it means that the European Commission's sanction is less than the minimum illicit gain made by the cartel. It appears that this ratio exceeds one in only 30 cases out of 64: At best, half of the sanctions reach or exceed the minimum amount of the cartel's illicit gain.

Figure 3.10 Fine Given Divided by the Lowest Optimal Fine (ε = -2)

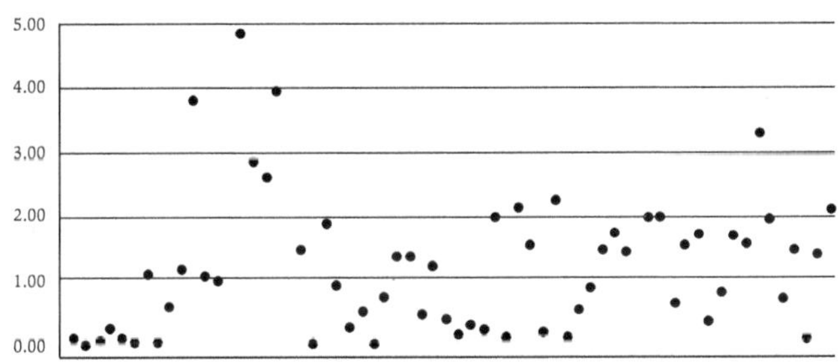

Source: Combe and Monnier (2013).

The second case, where the elasticity of demand is zero, corresponds to the maximum gain that firms can achieve with the cartel. Figure 3.11 shows the relationship between the sanction imposed by the European Commission and the maximum unlawful gain of the cartel. This ratio provides a first indication of the European Commission's deterrence policy. Indeed, if the ratio is higher than one, it means that the penalties exceed the maximum illegal gain. This situation occurs in only 25 out of 64 cases. In other cases, the European Commission's fines are below the maximum amount of unlawful gains.

Figure 3.11 Fine Given Divided by the Lowest Optimal Fine (ε = 0)

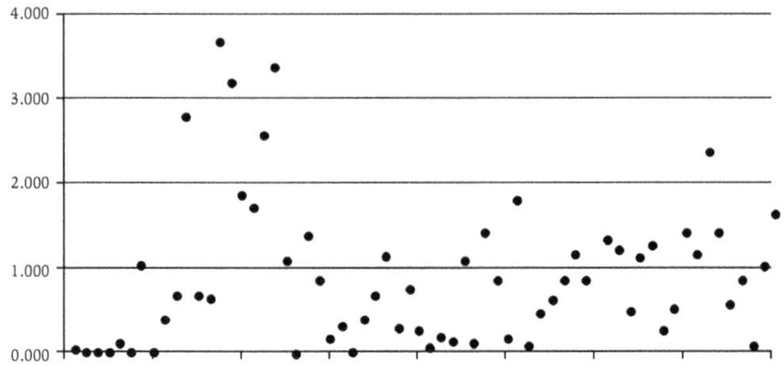

Source: Combe and Monnier (2013).

Taking into account the probability of detection, Figure 3.12 represents the relationship between the sanction imposed by the European Commission and the sanction that should be imposed to deter cartel formation in the best-case scenario for firms (demand elasticity equal to -2). If this ratio is higher than one, it means that the penalties paid by firms exceed the minimum dissuasive penalty. Over the entire period, only one sanction is above the lower limit. For the remaining 63 cases, the sanctions are still below the lower limit, and most of them remain far from the bottom of the range.

Figure 3.12 Fine Given Divided by the Dissuasive Fine (ε = -2)

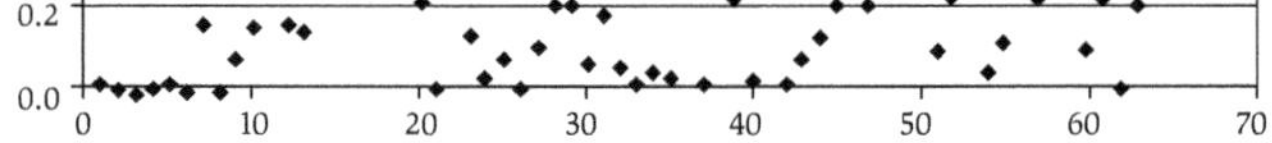

Source: Combe and Monnier (2013).

Figure 3.13 shows the relationship between the sanction imposed and the upper limit of the range (price elasticity of zero demand) in the least favorable case for firms. If the ratio is higher than one, it means that the penalties paid by firms exceed the maximum dissuasive penalty. No penalties are above this ceiling.

Figure 3.13 Fine Given Divided by the Lowest Optimal Fine (ε = 0)

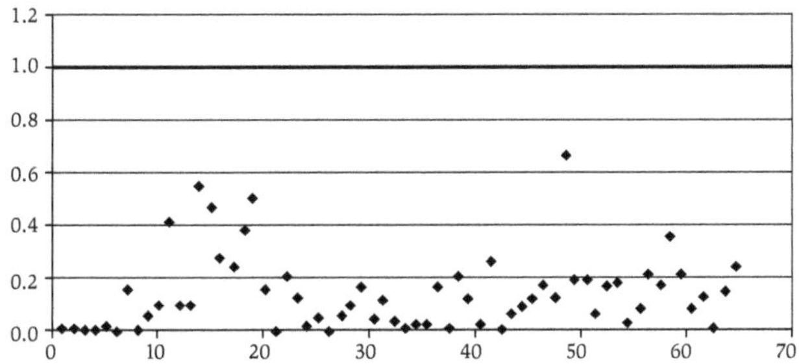

Source: Combe and Monnier (2013).

On the basis of these results, we can conclude that the European Commission, although it has become harsher in recent years, has not crossed the red line of "*over-dissuasion.*" In other words, fines were probably too low in the past, and their increase from the 2000s onwards has simply brought them closer to the optimal level, without ever exceeding it. In other words, the fact that the European Commission has been stricter since the 2000s does not mean that it has become too strict.

SECTION 4 CARTELS: BEYOND ANTITRUST SANCTIONS

In addition to fines against firms, some countries such as the United States have put in place criminal sanctions against individuals who have taken part in a cartel. We'll explain the rationale behind this kind of sanction, by using the "*corporate governance*" approach (§1). Public action also does not exclude victims from suing cartel members in efforts to claim compensation for the damage they have suffered (§2).

While these two types of actions are of a different legal nature, they contribute to increasing the total amount of sanctions that cartel members may have to pay.

§1 The Opportunity for Criminal Sanctions

In 2019, 25 countries in the world had a legal system to provide for the criminal prosecution of individuals participating in a cartel. Thus, countries such as Ireland (in 1996), the United Kingdom (in 2002), or Australia (in 2009) have introduced criminal sanctions, but their effectiveness remains limited in practice. In the United Kingdom, the *Enterprise Act* of 2002 led to five firm prison sentences and three "*director disqualification*" orders during the period spanning 2003-2018.

Similarly, in France, if Article L. 420-6 of the *French Commercial Code* has provided for a prison sentence of up to four years and a fine up to €75,000 "for any individual who illegally takes a personal and decisive part in the conception, organization or implementation" (free translation) of a cartel, it is rarely applied. We observe that in France an average of only two criminal sentences per year has been given, as a fine or as a suspended prison sentence.

The only country that actually prosecutes individuals is the United States: The Sherman Act (1890), strengthened by the 2004 adoption of the Antitrust Criminal Penalty Enhancement and Reform Act, provides for a penalty of up to $1 million and 10 years in prison for individuals. This legal arsenal has been applied since the 1990s in major cartel cases; during the period spanning 2010-2019, 392 individuals, American or non-American, were prosecuted for participating in a cartel. Of them, 251 were sentenced to prison terms of 17 months on average, and 84 were sentenced to house arrest. The American courts have also broadened the scope of criminal liability, prosecuting several employees of the same firm: In the Vitamins cartel, six executives of Hoffmann-La Roche were charged. Moreover, since the Vitamins cartel (1999), no fewer than 50 non-U.S. leaders have been extradited to the United States, where they've served prison sentences for participating in major international cartels.

Table 3.13 Individuals Prosecuted for Cartel Practices in the United States (2010/2019)

Case Results

Criminal Fines & Penalties Imposed	*2010*	*2011*	*2012*	*2013*	*2014*	*2015*	*2016*	*2017*	*2018*	*2019*
Individual: Total Individual Fines ($000)	$4,373	$1,522	$2,141	$3,069	$2,016	$369	$5,245	$1,017	$10,795	$2,138
Number of Individuals Fined	19	25	31	29	24	15	31	34	53	22

Confinement

Incarceration	*2010*	*2011*	*2012*	*2013*	*2014*	*2015*	*2016*	*2017*	*2018*	*2019*
Number of Individuals Sentenced	37	39	55	39	35	15	36	52	59	25
Number of Individuals Sentenced to Incarceration Time	29	21	45	28	21	12	22	30	21	22
Average Number of Days of Incarceration	898	502	747	750	787	402	330	262	285	179

Other Confinement[1]	*2010*	*2011*	*2012*	*2013*	*2014*	*2015*	*2016*	*2017*	*2018*	*2019*
Individuals Sentenced to Other Confinement	6	12	4	5	7	2	5	19	21	3
Average Number of Days of Other Confinement	216	173	135	162	181	180	120	201	154	222

Source: U.S. Department of Justice, Antitrust Division (2020).

1. Includes house arrest or confinement to a halfway house or community treatment center.

The fact that the U.S. authorities do not hesitate to prosecute individuals is explained by the strong moral condemnation of cartels in the American society, which are considered as a "*conspiracy against the market.*"

To understand the legitimacy of criminal sanctions against individuals, the "*corporate governance*" approach provides a useful theoretical framework: It is based on the principle that the manager, who is in charge of the daily management of the firm, does not always act solely in the interests of the shareholders. He or she may also pursue personal objectives, such as obtaining rapid career advancement or being awarded a high variable remuneration (such as a bonus) indexed on the firm's short-term performance indicators. This pursuit of personal objectives may lead to a violation of antitrust rules, against the approval of the shareholders or with their consent.

In a first scenario, managers—like a "bad apple" in a healthy firm—will engage shareholders in cartels against their will and without their knowledge (Table 3.13). The managers take advantage of the information asymmetries and the imperfect control of their actions. This scenario is problematic for the shareholders: In case of antitrust proceedings, they cannot exonerate themselves from their liability by invoking the isolated behavior of a manager. Shareholders therefore have an interest in deterring managers from violating antitrust rules, by using internal tools such as the threat of dismissal or the reimbursement of variable compensation in case of an antitrust infringement, the implementation of a compliance program, etc. But in practice, these internal solutions often remain of limited effectiveness (Combe & Monnier, 2020). Conversely, managers may be encouraged by their firms' culture to violate antitrust laws—for example, by being assigned performance targets that cannot be achieved through normal competition ("*toxic corporate culture*").

The most interesting case is the one in which shareholders and managers have a common interest in violating antitrust laws, but for different motives. From the shareholders' point of view, the cartel increases profits, especially if sanctions are low compared to the illicit gain. From the manager's point of view, the cartel allows him or her to obtain a variable remuneration indexed on short-term performances. The alignment of interests between managers and shareholders creates a convergent incentive, which can only be broken by a public intervention, in particular, with criminal sanctions against individuals.

Table 3.14 Behavior of Managers and Shareholders with Regards to Antitrust Rules

	Managers	
Shareholders	*Comply with competition law*	*Engage in a cartel*
Comply with competition law	Convergence of interest to comply with antitrust laws	"Bad apple" divergence of interest
Engage in a cartel	Divergence of interest ("toxic corporate culture")	Convergence of interest to violate antitrust laws

The manager's incentive to violate antitrust rules can be accentuated by behavioral biases such as:

- the reduction in the seriousness of the offense, if the illicit practice receives the consent of his hierarchy; for example, breaking the law could be presented as a "necessary evil" to achieve a lawful result, namely a high profit (Stucke, 2011);
- the underestimation of the objective probability of being caught, given the "*availability*" and "*overconfidence*" bias: Since convicted cartel cases are rare, managers may consider the risk of detection to be nil.

What kind of criminal sanctions?: There are two main types of criminal sanctions: fines and prison sentences. According to the Nobel Prize winner Gary Becker, since a prison sentence can be converted into a monetary equivalent, it is more efficient to impose fines in order to avoid incarceration costs. According to this approach, prison can only be justified once the individuals no longer have the financial ability to pay the full fines: The use of prison appears here as a residual tool. But this approach is questionable:

- in practice, fines against individuals are often capped at low levels compared to the manager's wages. For example, in the United States, over the period spanning 2008-2017, the average fine per person was $84,600. In addition, firms can, on top of it, financially compensate the employee for the personal fine paid;
- it is difficult to determine the optimal amount of a fine in the case of an individual (how to measure the private gain of a cartel?); and, even if we could, this fine may exceed the individual's financial capacity to pay;
- a fine is implicitly based on the idea that all you have to do is to pay a penalty for your offense to be "*laundered.*" This weakens the stigmatizing effect of the sanction.

On the other hand, imposing a prison sentence is a strong deterrent. This type of sanction:

- clearly stigmatizes the individual: Society as a whole judges the offending behavior as being immoral;
- sends a strong signal to the targeted social group (usually "white collars" in the case of cartels) as the prison sentence is widely publicized;
- increases the effectiveness of leniency programs when these are applied to criminal sanctions. Indeed, an individual will more easily agree to cooperate with antitrust authorities if, in return, he obtains full immunity. This is why the United States reformed its leniency program in 1993, guaranteeing legal immunity to the employees of the first firm to denounce the cartel.

If prison appears to be the most dissuasive criminal sanction for individuals, should we opt for long or short sentences? On the one hand, prison imposes a social cost on society: There is the social cost of imprisonment, which includes the direct costs of building, maintaining, operating and staffing prisons. On the other hand, the deterrent and stigmatizing effect depends less on the length of imprisonment than on the fact of going to prison: The marginal gain obtained by increased sentence lengths is low. The combination of an increasing marginal cost of incarceration and a decreasing marginal gain (in terms of deterrence) leads to recommend short prison sentences.

However, criminal sanctions are complex to implement, because many countries do not consider cartel practices to be morally wrong: Sentencing individuals to prison because they were involved in a cartel is not socially acceptable outside the United States. It is therefore useful to consider other forms of less stigmatizing sanctions, such as director disqualification orders: An executive officer who has directly contributed to breaking competition rules, or who has allowed managers to do it for him or her, may be banned from holding executive positions for a certain period of time. This mechanism, adopted, for example, in the United Kingdom through the *Competition Disqualification Orders* system, provides for a maximum disqualification period of 15 years. Disqualification negatively affects the manager's reputation and career prospects, while minimizing costs to society (absence of incarceration); it therefore has a strong deterrent effect. This measure is also more politically and socially acceptable than imprisonment.

§2 The Role of Cartel Damage Claims

Public action and sanctions imposed by antitrust authorities do not exclude victims from suing the cartel members to seek compensation for the harm they've suffered (*see* Chapter 2). Indeed, damage claims come in addition to public sanctions and, therefore, increase the cost of a firm's infringement: Cartels will not only have to pay a fine for violating a public policy ("*public enforcement*"), but they will also have to compensate the cartel's victims ("*private enforcement*") for the higher prices they imposed.

The role of private actions in the United States: While private actions are still underdeveloped in Europe, they play a key role in the U.S. competitive regulatory system. In the United States, the amounts due in compensation can be far greater than the amounts imposed by antitrust authorities, given the efficiency of private class actions and the fact that plaintiffs can claim up to three times the damages they have suffered.

It is therefore important, when comparing the total amount of sanctions between Europe and the United States, to take into account these private compensations. Indeed, if we only consider antitrust sanctions, Europe appears to have been harsher than the United States over the period spanning 1990-2011 (Figure 3.14).

Figure 3.14 Antitrust Sanctions in the United States and Europe (1990-2011)

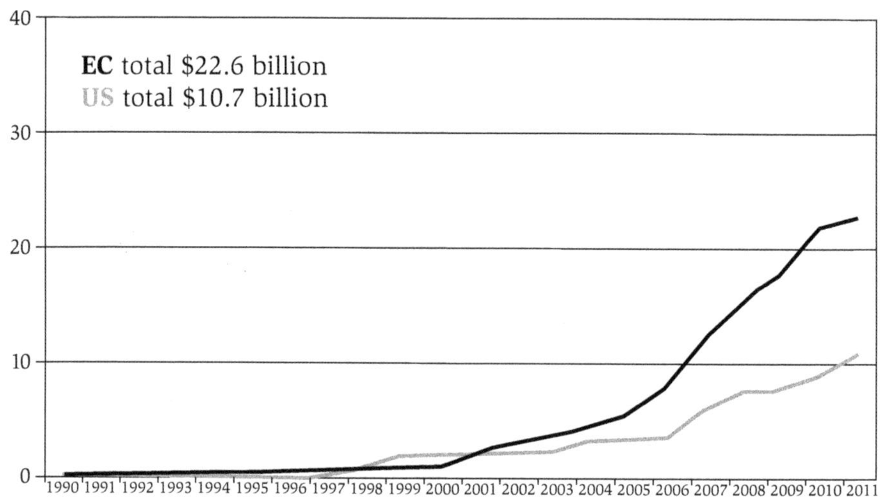

Source: Connor (2012) conference *Competition* "Antitrust Fines: What Is the Right Amount?."

But if we add the estimated amount of private compensations, the American system appears to be far harsher (Figure 3.15). For example, in the Vitamins cartel case, Connor (2012) estimates that the compensations paid amounted to $1.6 billion, or 2.5 times the antitrust sanctions ($676 million). Since the Vitamins cartel was also sanctioned by the Canadian and European antitrust authorities, the total of compensations in the United States can also be compared with the total amount of sanctions imposed worldwide: The U.S. private compensations represent 55% of the $2.9 billion in sanctions paid worldwide.

Figure 3.15 Antitrust Sanctions and Compensations in the United States and Europe

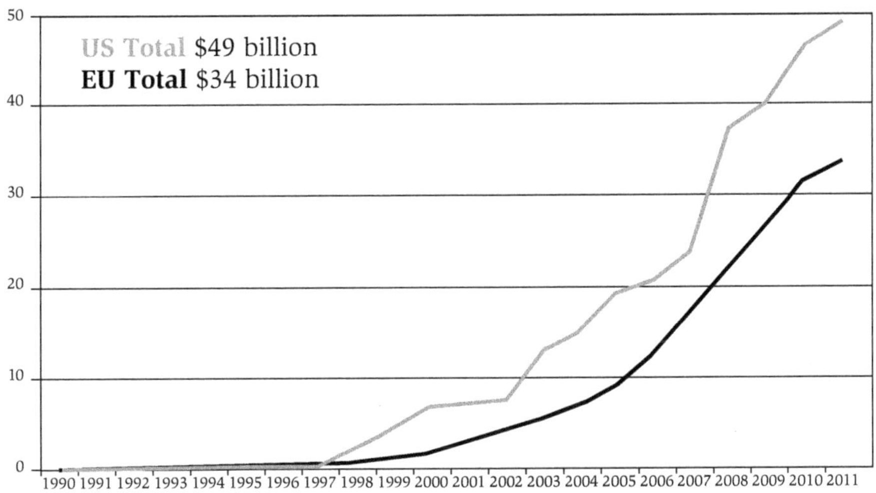

Source: Connor (2012) conference *Competition* "Antitrust Fines: What Is the Right Amount?."

The passing on defense*:* In order to obtain compensation, cartel victims are required to prove three things:

- they must provide evidence of fault, i.e., provide proof of the cartel practice. In most cases, this has already been demonstrated by the fact that the firm has been sanctioned by a competition authority. In Europe, for example, following the Damage Directive (2014), infringement is automatically presumed when a national competition authority or the Commission has sanctioned a firm for being part of a cartel ("*follow-on*" approach);
- they must establish a direct link between the cartel's practices and the harm they have suffered;
- they must quantify the damage suffered. We saw in Chapter 2 that several methods can be used to quantify the damage: "before and after" method, comparative method, etc.

The members of a cartel can contest the amount due in compensation, arguing that victims had passed on the additional costs downstream. This "*pass-on*" effect refers precisely to the ability of a direct victim to transfer the overcharge onto its own customers ("*indirect customers*"). The pass-on rate measures the proportion of the cartel price increase that is passed on to downstream customers:

Pass-on rate = (price increase on the downstream customer)/(price increase suffered upstream)

In Figure 3.16, firms sell an input X at $100 per unit to direct customers, who resell the same product to their final customers at a price of $120, thus achieving a margin of $20 per unit. It is therefore assumed, for simplicity, that direct customers do not incur any costs other than the cost of input X.

Figure 3.16 Vertical Chain with Direct and Indirect Customers

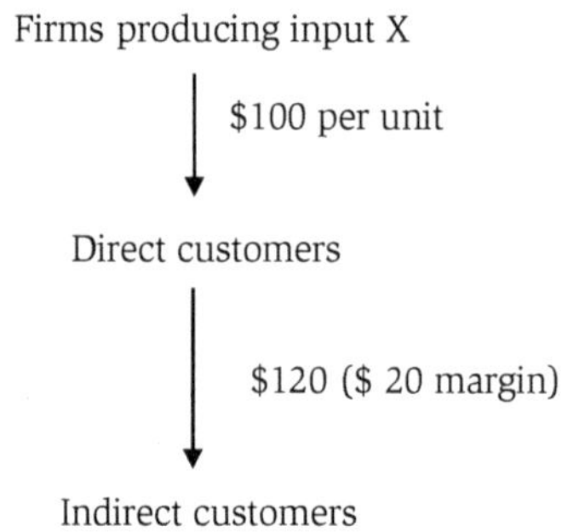

Suppose that the upstream firms decide to form a cartel in order to increase the price from $100 to $110. How will direct customers react? Two diametrically opposed cases can be observed.

In the first case, they do not change their selling price, which remains at $120, and therefore reduce their margin by half (from $20 to $10 per unit). Therefore, direct buyers do not pass anything on to their customers and absorb the total extra cost (Figure 3.17). The pass-on rate is then zero:

Pass-on rate = (+ $0)/(+ $10)

Figure 3.17 Cartel with a Pass-on Rate of 0%

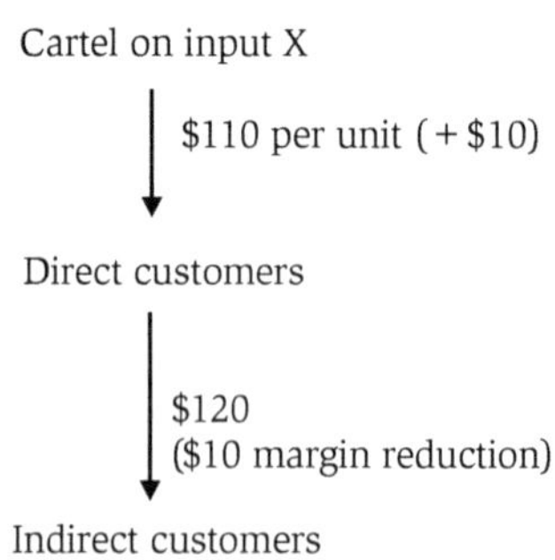

In the second case, direct customers change their downstream price by the amount of the upstream price increase. The price then rises downstream from $120 to

$130. The final customers bear the full additional cost (Figure 3.18) and the pass-on rate is 100%:

$$\text{Pass-on rate} = (+\ \$10)/(+\ \$10)$$

Between these two diametrically opposed cases there are all the intermediary situations, in which only part of the additional price is passed on to the final customer.

Figure 3.18 Cartel with a Pass-on Rate of 100%

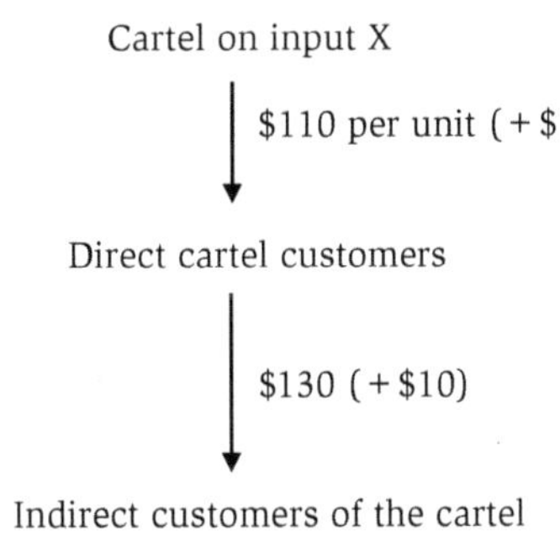

What determines the pass-on rate?: The ability of direct cartel customers to pass on the extra cost downstream depends on several factors:

- the delays in price changes: If prices with final customers are set over a long period, it will be difficult for direct customers to pass on their additional costs quickly. Direct customers will wait for the next contract to increase the price;
- the market structure of the downstream market: If direct customers are in a perfect competitive situation, the resale price is equal to the marginal cost and profits are zero. In our example, before the cartel, direct customers sell their product for $100. If the upstream price increases by $10, direct customers have no choice but to increase the downstream price by the same amount; the pass-on rate is therefore 100%. Conversely, if the customer is in a monopoly situation in the downstream market, the pass-on rate (with linear demand) will be 50%. In a Cournot's oligopoly situation, the pass-on rate depends on the number of firms in the market; as the number of firms in the market increases, so does the amount of extra cost passed on. It can thus be demonstrated that the pass-on rate is equal to N/(1 + N), with N the number of firms. Thus, in a duopoly market, the percentage of the additional cost passed on is equal to 2/3;
- the degree of differentiation of downstream products: If products are highly differentiated, downstream competition is low and the pass-on rate is likely to be limited;
- the price elasticity of demand: If the downstream price elasticity is low, it is likely that a large part of the extra cost will be reflected in the price. Indeed, increasing the price has little effect on the volumes purchased downstream. On

the other hand, if price elasticity is high, it is unlikely that direct customers will pass on the price increase, fearing that downstream customers will stop buying the product;

- asymmetry in the impact on costs: If the cartel affects only a part of direct customers, it is unlikely that the additional price will be passed on downstream. Indeed, in this case, downstream customers would shift their purchases to competitors that were not affected by the extra cost. This situation may arise, for example, when cartel members are vertically integrated and the cartel practice only targets non-integrated competitors;
- the weight of the input in the production cost: In our example, we assumed that input X represented the only cost for direct customers. In practice, the weight of the input in the cost is variable. If it represents a modest share of the total variable cost, passing on 100% of the extra cost will have a small impact on the volume of sales;
- the countervailing power of downstream customers: Where indirect customers are not final consumers, and are, for example, large retail firms, they will leverage their strong bargaining power to avoid any overcharges being passed on.

The total impact of a pass-on strategy*:* When direct customers pass on a part of the additional cost, it is likely that the quantity of downstream sales will decrease (unless the price elasticity is zero); therefore, a pass-on practice will have a negative effect on volumes.

In Figure 3.19, before the cartel was set up, direct customers bought the input at a price c_0 and sold downstream the quantity q_0 at a price p_0. The cartel leads to an increase in price from c_0 to c_1. If direct customers decide to increase the price from p_0 to p_1, part of the additional cost is passed on to downstream customers (area B). However, the increase in price leads indirect customers to reduce their volumes from q_0 to q_1. Direct customers therefore suffer a decrease in profit, equal to the area C.

Figure 3.19 The Effects of a Pass-on Strategy

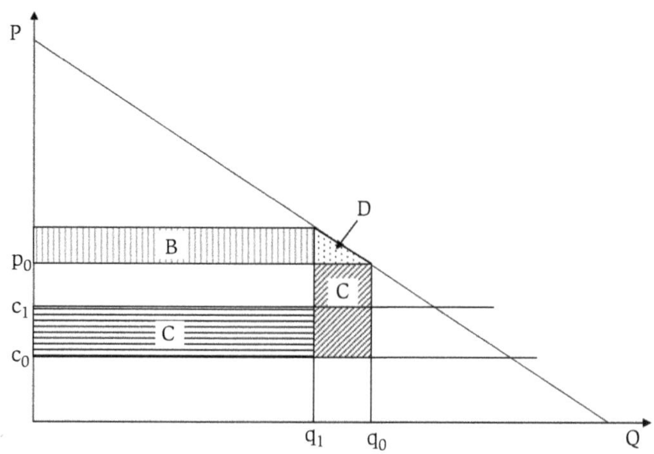

Source: Van Dijk (2010).

The total effect of the cartel on direct customers is the sum of three effects. It is possible that the negative effect on volumes (area C) is even greater than the positive pass-on effect (area B); in this case, the fact that the cartel invokes pass-on practices increases the damage that its direct customers suffer.

The "passing-on defense" in practice: To what extent can a cartel invoke the fact that the claimant passed on the overcharge?

In the United States, the subject is an old one and was initially raised in the 1960s in the Hanover Shoe case (1968). The usual position of the courts is to reject the passing-on defense on the grounds that a cartel must bear all the consequences of its unlawful practice.

In Europe, the case law varies from country to country and does not exclude a defense based on the passing on. Thus, in the Arkopharma case (2006), one of the members of the Vitamins cartel, Hoffmann-La Roche, sought compensation. Hoffmann-La Roche successfully defended itself by arguing that the additional cost had in fact been borne by the final consumers, since Arkopharma had passed on the extra cost downstream. Similarly, in the Doux/Ajinomoto case (2010), in France, the Supreme Court censured the Paris Court of Appeals for failing to investigate whether the alleged victims had "passed on to their customers the additional costs resulting from Ajinomoto's offence, so that the award of damages could have resulted in their unjust enrichment" (free translation).

SECTION 5 CARTEL DETECTION

Because cartels are secret, they are difficult to detect. Competition authorities have to choose between a high probability of detection, which is costly, and a high level of sanction; there is a trade-off between detection and sanction (§1). In order to detect cartels, competition authorities may use corporate leniency programs to encourage cartel members to betray their partners in exchange for a reduction or exemption of fines (§2). We end this section by analyzing the role of "*intellectual reasoning*," when antitrust authorities try to detect cartels: We'll show that this kind of proof is very difficult to use, because antitrust authorities are in an asymmetrical position with firms (§3).

§1 The Trade-Off Between Detection and Sanction

Before sanctioning cartels, antitrust authorities must detect them. As we have seen above, the probability of detection plays an important role, since there is an inverse relationship between the probability of detection and the amount of sanctions imposed:

$$\text{optimal monetary sanction} \geq (\text{illicit gain}/\text{probability of detection})$$

If the probability of detection is low, the optimal sanction must be high for a given illicit gain. For example, if the probability of detection is 50% (i.e., 0.5) and the illicit gain is $80, the optimal sanction should be equal to:

$$\text{optimal monetary sanction} \geq \$80/\ 0.5 = \$160$$

If the probability of detection decreases to 25% (or 0.25), the optimal sanction automatically increases:

$$\text{optimal monetary sanction} \geq \$80/\ 0.25 = \$320.$$

There is no empirical consensus on the probability of detection, although it is certain that it is less than 100%. A first method consists of asking firms themselves or their lawyers about the perception of this probability: The results vary between 30% and 50%. A second, more rigorous method consists of estimating a conditional probability of being caught on the basis of a so-called *"life and death"* model: In a subset of cartels that have been caught, the conditional probability that a cartel will be caught at time t is calculated. Two studies using this methodology produce fairly similar results in the United States and Europe: The probability of detection would be around 15%.

The probability of detection is not exogenous; it depends largely on the choices that antitrust authorities make. In this respect, given that detection is expensive (particularly in terms of human and financial resources), antitrust authorities may arbitrate in favor of a low probability of detection in return for high penalties. However, such a choice would have several limitations:

- it would lead to sanctions being close to infinity, which raises the question of a firm's ability to pay. Moreover, in practice, it is not possible to impose sanctions beyond a certain ceiling for legal reasons: In Europe, the amount of a sanction may not exceed 10% of the worldwide turnover of a firm;
- it is based on the idea that firms that have been caught must pay for those that have not been detected. Such an approach violates the principle of personalization of penalties, because the amount of the sanction depends on a parameter that is not directly related to the behavior of the offending firm;
- if the probability of detection is too low, firms may develop an *"availability bias"*: They will believe that cartels are never detected and this will encourage them to engage in illicit practices. It is therefore necessary for antitrust authorities to maintain a minimum detection rate.

Two detection policies*:* In order to detect cartels, authorities must be able to detect and collect proof on illegal practices. To this end, they carry out *"dawn raids"* within a firm's headquarters or at the private homes of its employees in order to collect evidence (e-mail, planning agendas, etc.). This is a delicate exercise, as cartel members will always try to conceal any incriminating evidence. For example, in the Elevator cartel case (2007), the European Commission noted: "it is clear that firms knew that their behavior was illegal and they were careful to avoid being discovered; their representatives usually met in bars and restaurants, travelled to the countryside or even abroad and used prepaid mobile phone cards to avoid call identification."

Before antitrust authorities can launch investigative operations, they must initially have reasonable grounds that a cartel exists. Incriminating documents or evidence can come from an active policy of detection, from a complaint having been filed by a customer/competitor, or from a regular market "*screening.*" But a cartel can also be detected by a more passive policy, consisting of obtaining insider evidence from a cartel member in exchange for full immunity from prosecution or a reduced penalty. These are "*leniency*" programs.

In practice, the two detection policies appear to be complementary; for example, having an efficient market screening policy may lead to firms applying for leniency.

Screening policies: "*Screening*" consists of identifying the risk of probable cartel behavior in a market before launching a formal investigation. A first method, described as "*structural,*" consists of targeting markets that have characteristics favorable to the developments of cartels, such as high entry barriers, a small number of players, high market concentration, symmetry in production costs, homogeneous products, a stable demand over time, etc. However, this method is rarely used, as such a structural filter is usually too broad: Many markets possess these characteristics without being subject to cartel practices.

A second method, called "*behavioral,*" consists of analyzing price and sales data in order to identify anomalies that are difficult to explain in a competitive context. Several "*markers*" can be used (*see* Table 3.15). For instance, in calls for tenders, the fact that the number of bids is abnormally high and that they are identical between competitors, and the fact that they are won with a perfect rotation between competitors, may raise the suspicion of antitrust authorities.

Table 3.15 Examples of Markers Indicating the Presence of a Cartel

Marker Type	*Possible Interpretation*
An increase in list prices and reduction in price variation between customers.	To be stable, a cartel needs to control the prices charged by each member; the cartel will promote "*price standardization,*" with list prices and rarely give discounts.
A sharp price decrease followed by a sharp price increase in a non-cyclical sector.	A defensive cartel is organized to put an end to a declining demand or a situation of overcapacity by setting prices.
A rise in prices and a concomitant decline in imports.	A price increase that does not lead to an increase in imports may be the sign of a geographical market sharing agreement.
Standardization of the price of the main product and complementary services.	Competition between firms can take place on additional services (delivery costs, for example) and it is therefore likely that a cartel will also coordinate on all prices in order to avoid any cheating behavior.
Low price variances.	Prices tend to vary little in a cartelized market.

Marker Type	*Possible Interpretation*
Stability of market shares over time.	A cartel can lead to a freeze of each player's market shares.
Sudden and brief episodes of price declines in a market usually characterized by price stability.	A sharp and short-lived fall in prices may be a sign of a policy of retaliation by the cartel against deviating firms.

Abrantes-Metz et al. (2006) provide a concrete example of screening by analyzing the evolution of the coefficient of price variation (defined as the ratio of the standard deviation to the average): In a cartel situation, the coefficient of price variation must be lower than in a competitive situation, since a cartel must stabilize prices to prevent and control deviant behaviors. The authors apply this indicator to a cartel that took place in the United States on frozen fish from 1984 to 1988 (Figure 3.20). During the period of the cartel, the average price of frozen fish remained relatively stable, on average at \$3.5, despite variations in the cost of production (i.e., the price of fresh fish). The standard deviation of prices was therefore relatively small (0.078), as was the coefficient of variation (0.022). The cartel ended following the defection of a member in June 1988, which led to a 16% price drop, after an adjustment period spanning July-September 1988.

Figure 3.20 Price and Cost Profile During and after the Cartel

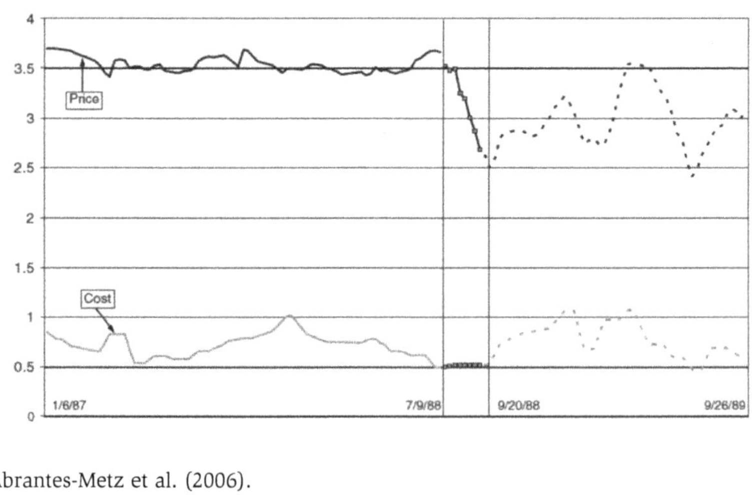

Source: Abrantes-Metz et al. (2006).

The authors found that during the post-cartel period, prices were more volatile: The standard deviation of prices increased by 263% and the coefficient of variation by 332% (Table 3.16). In addition, price movements were more correlated with changes in production costs.

Table 3.16 Average and Standard Deviation of Price and Cost During and after the Cartel

Statistics	*Collusion*	*Competition*	*Differences Across Regimes (%)*
Price			
Mean	3.544	2.97	-16.2
Standard deviation	0.078	0.283	263
CV = standard deviation/ mean	0.022	0.095	332
Cost			
Mean	0.722	0.771	6.8
Standard deviation	0.114	0.173	51.8
CV = standard deviation/ mean	0.158	0.224	41.8

Source: Abrantes-Metz et al. (2006).

§2 The Role of Leniency Policies

In addition to proactive screening policies, competition authorities may use corporate leniency programs to encourage cartel members to denounce their partners in exchange for a reduction or even an exemption of financial penalties. The granting of a leniency reward presupposes that the applicants have ceased participating in the cartel, that they will keep their leniency request secret, and that they will cooperate fully with antitrust authorities throughout the procedure.

Leniency policies have several objectives:

- they enable authorities to detect cartels that would have probably gone undetected, particularly if they are sophisticated cartels;
- they reduce the cost of detection compared to traditional investigative methods and allow cartel cases to be processed more rapidly;
- they create instability within cartels, with each member fearing denouncement by its partners. This is a situation similar to the prisoner's dilemma: While it is collectively advantageous not to denounce the cartel, each firm has an individual incentive to do so to avoid punishment. The "*first in the door*" system creates a form of "*whistleblowing race*" between cartel members;
- they will deter firms from organizing cartels, as firms will fear that the risk of being denounced is too high.

Leniency policies around the world: The United States has had a leniency program since 1978; however, it only really started to work from 1993 onwards, following the introduction of the "first in the door" principle. In the EU, the leniency program, initially launched in 1996 has since been strengthened in 2002 and 2006. In 2019, 60 countries worldwide implemented cartel leniency programs, including emerging countries such as Brazil and China.

In most countries, we can distinguish two types of leniency policies: A first-rank leniency provides total exemption from penalties in exchange for the full cooperation of the first company to provide proof of the cartel. A second-rank leniency allows firms to obtain partial exemption from penalties if they provide evidence that is of significant value compared to the information already available to competition authorities.

Leniency policies have had some success in OECD countries. According to an OECD survey, leniency requests led to 45%-55% of cartels that were detected in countries such as Germany, Canada and South Korea. In the United States, more than 90% of the financial penalties imposed since 1996 have been the result of investigations that were carried out with the cooperation of leniency applicants. In Europe, leniency programs are also central to cartel detection: Over the period spanning 1998-2014, they were applied in 94% of sanction cases, as shown in Figure 3.21. In 70% of cases, the investigations were launched thanks to the leniency program. Out of €24 billion in sanctions imposed during the period spanning 1962-2014, 89% came from the application of a leniency program.

Figure 3.21 Sanctions Against Cartels and the Role of Leniency (Million Euros; 1962-2014)

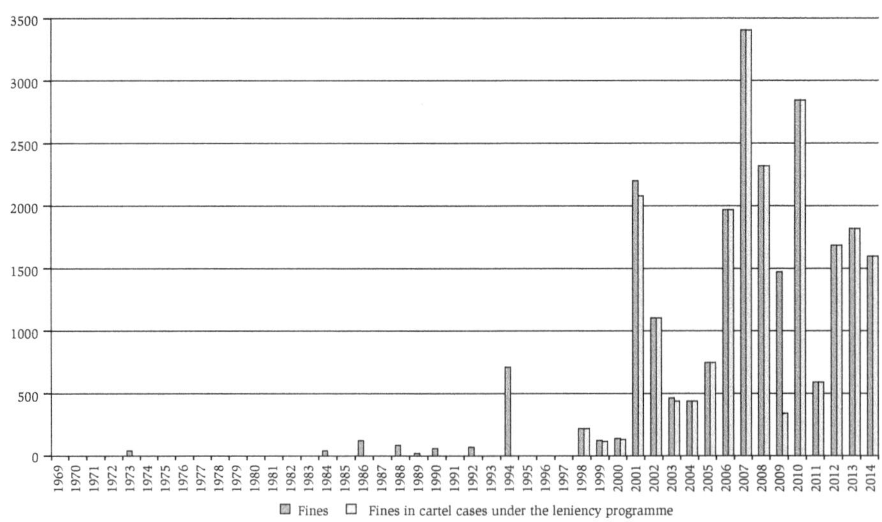

Source: Ordonez-de-Haro et al. (2018).

Ordonez-de-Haro et al. (2018) show that the lifespan of cartels (that have been detected) has decreased significantly over time in Europe, particularly after the strengthening of the leniency program in 2006: In Figure 3.22, we see that the length of each segment, which measures the lifespan of a cartel, decreased during the period spanning 2006-2014.

Figure 3.22 Life Span of Cartels Detected by the Commission

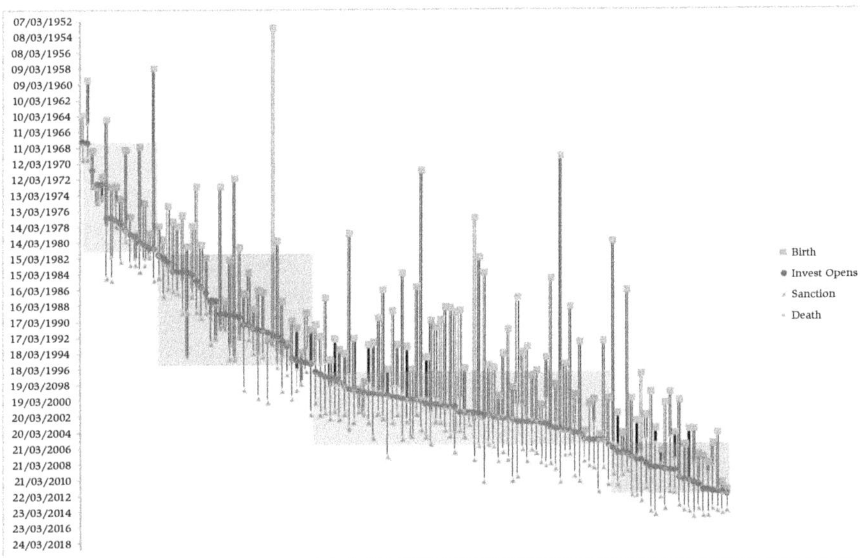

Source: Ordonez-de-Haro et al. (2018).

The effectiveness of a leniency policy*:* The effectiveness of a leniency program depends on several factors:

- the level of fines in the absence of leniency: When antitrust penalties are high, firms have strong incentives to apply first for leniency. Thus, in the United States, it is considered that the leniency program only really worked from 1996, when the antitrust authorities decided to apply severe sanctions in the Lysine cartel case;
- the probability of detection, in the absence of leniency: If the probability of detection is too low, firms have no incentives in denouncing the cartel. It is therefore important that antitrust authorities continue to investigate cartel cases so that firms consider the risk of detection to be credible;
- the scope of the leniency program: Total exemption from fines may be given to the first applicant providing evidence when the antitrust authority does not have sufficient proof to establish the infringement. Similarly, when applying for leniency in Market A, if a firm discovers that it has also participated in a cartel in Market B, it may benefit from a "*leniency plus*" system, wherein immunity is extended to all markets on which it denounces cartel practices. The idea is to encourage firms to investigate and denounce all cartel practices

in which they are involved. On the other hand, if a firm merely applies for leniency in Market A, even though it knows that there is a cartel in Market B, a reverse "*penalty plus*" mechanism is applied;

- the identity of the leniency applicant: As a general rule, no restrictions apply to the identity of the leniency applicant unless the first leniency applicant has forced other firms to participate in the cartel. But the fact that a firm is the instigator of a cartel does not exclude it from the leniency program;
- the credibility and clarity of the leniency program: Firms must be guaranteed sufficient legal certainty, in particular as regards to the order of arrival and the percentage of penalty reduction. As the OECD (2003) points out: "Clarity, certainty, and priority are critical, as firms may be more likely to come forward if the conditions and the likely benefits of doing so are clear. To maximize the incentive for defection and encourage cartels to break down more quickly, it is important not only that the first one to confess receive the 'best deal,' but also that the terms of the deal be as clear as possible at the outset";
- the conditionality of the penalty reduction: The firm reporting the illegal conduct obtains a reduced penalty (or even full immunity) only once the inquiry has been completed in order to encourage it to fully cooperate with antitrust authorities throughout the investigation. Any failure to cooperate results in the withdrawal of immunity;
- the link with criminal proceedings: A firm may hesitate to denounce a cartel in which it participates if it fears there will be criminal proceedings against individuals. It is therefore important to also guarantee criminal immunity to the employees of the firm that denounces, as is already the case in the United States;
- coordination with private actions: A firm may be deterred from reporting a cartel if it believes that it will be easier for victims to obtain compensation. This risk is particularly high in jurisdictions that practice discovery in civil matters, as is the case in the United States. That is why the United States introduced the Antitrust Criminal Penalty Enhancement and Reform Act (2004): It reduces the amount of compensation for the first leniency applicant, who must pay simple damages (and not "*triple damages*") and is no longer jointly and severally liable for the payment of compensation;
- the extent of the reduction in the penalty enjoyed by the first applicant and the difference in the reduction in penalty of the other cartel members (the so-called "*second-rank*" leniency). Indeed, if the reductions in fines are small and uniform between cartel members, they will wait for the launch of an investigation before cooperating with antitrust authorities. This is a situation known as a "*coordination game*": Either no one denounces the cartel or the cartel's members denounce it all at the same time. In Table 3.17, two firms A and B formed a cartel. If they do not denounce the practice, they each make a positive profit of $3, even taking into account detection risk. If both firms denounce the cartel, they are each fined $3. If Firm A is denounced by Firm B, it is fined $6 while Firm B gets a reduced fine of $2. Unlike a prisoner's

dilemma situation, neither firm has an incentive to denounce the cartel if the other does not denounce it; there are two Nash equilibrium in this game.

Table 3.17 Leniency as a Coordination Game

	Firm B	
Firm A	Denounced the cartel	Does not denounce
Denounces the cartel	**(-$3, -$3)**	(-$2, -$6)
Does not report it	(-$6, -$2)	**($3, $3)**

N.B.: In each box, the first figure represents Firm A's gain or loss; the second figure represents Firm B's gain or loss.

Conversely, if the first applicant can obtain a full immunity and the others obtain a small reduction in sanctions (or no reduction at all), the leniency program becomes very attractive. This is a "*leniency race,*" which is like a prisoner's dilemma; each firm has incentive to denounce the cartel, whatever its partner's choice. In Table 3.18, two firms A and B have formed a cartel. If they do not denounce the practice, they each make a positive profit of $3, even taking into account detection risk. If both of them denounce the cartel, they will each be fined $3. If Firm A is denounced by Firm B, it will be fined $6 while Firm B will receive a gain of $4. In this case, each firm will denounce the practice for fear that the other will do the same; there is only one Nash equilibrium in this game, equal to (-$3, -$3).

Table 3.18 Leniency as a Prisoner's Dilemma

	Firm B	
Firm A	Denounces the cartel	Does not report it
Denounces the cartel	**(-$3, -$3)**	($4, -$6)
Does not report it	(-$6, $4)	($3, $3)

N.B.: In each box, the first figure represents Firm A's gain or loss; and the second figure represents Firm B's gain or loss.

The "first in the door" principle, based on full immunity for the first firm, is therefore essential to the success of leniency policies. In most countries, leniency programs provide for a total exemption from penalties for the first applicant. For example, in Europe, in the Truck cartel case, MAN escaped a penalty of €1.2 billion thanks to its cooperation with the European Commission, while other cartel members had to pay €2.9 billion in fines. For other applicants, at the European level, the second firm to denounce the cartel can obtain up to 50% reduction in penalties; the third from 20% to 30%; and the following up to 20%. Some economists believe that this system of decreasing partial reward in Europe reduces incentive to denounce and proposes a system without any reduction for the second claimant, as is the case in the United States.

From leniency to whistleblowing*:* Individuals, whether or not they are employees of the firm participating in a cartel, can also contribute to the detection of these illegal practices by reporting them to antitrust authorities in exchange for a monetary compensation (the so-called "whistleblowing" procedure).

The United States has so far rejected the use of an antitrust report/reward mechanism, although it already exists and works for other types of fraud. For example, the Dodd-Frank Wall Street Reform and Consumer Protection Act (2010) provides a reward mechanism when a whistleblower provides information key to the success of the inquiry of the U.S. Securities and Exchange Commission (SEC). More specifically, since 2012, the SEC has had a reward program for individuals who report a fraud of more than $1 million. The reward can reach between 10% and 30% of the amount collected. It varies according to the relevance of the information provided, the degree of involvement of the whistleblower in the illicit practice, the time he or she took to report it, and whether or not he or she had reported it internally beforehand. Throughout the period spanning 2012-2018, the American agency in charge of this program (the Office of the Whistleblower) allocated $262 million to 53 whistleblowers, including some rewards exceeding $30 million.

With regards to cartels, South Korea was the first country in 2002 to set up a warning mechanism based on the granting of rewards. Throughout the period spanning 2002-2017, it detected 61 cartels in exchange for small amounts of compensation. Since 2008, the United Kingdom has also had a whistleblower remuneration system, with a maximum reward amount of £100,000. However, the reward is not open to people who have taken direct part in the cartel. In 2017, the Competition and Markets Authority (CMA) also set up a digital information campaign to promote this program. As a result of this campaign, the CMA has noted a 30% increase in the number of tip-offs obtained.

In Europe, the Commission has set up a tool that people can use to provide information anonymously. The Commission can communicate with the person who comes forward with information; however, it cannot reveal the person's identity. This system does not provide for any possible remuneration for the whistleblower.

The effectiveness of a whistleblower policy is subject to several conditions:

- authorities prefer to only reward employees not directly involved in the cartel; however, reward mechanisms should not exclude individuals directly involved in the illicit practice insofar as they hold relevant evidence;
- it is necessary to ensure the anonymity of the person who cooperates with antitrust authorities in order to avoid internal reprisals;
- the amount of the reward granted must be sufficient to encourage an individual to take the risk of denouncing the practice. These risks are multiple: the risk of dismissal and a decrease in the individual's future employability, and the impact on the individual's family and social life.

It is true that a whistleblower remuneration policy can have a long-term undesirable effect on business ethics; indeed, the whistleblower is no longer guided by an intrinsic motivation (to not break the law) but by extrinsic motivation, based on the lure of profit. However, it seems from the American experience that extrinsic motivations go hand in hand with intrinsic motivations: Often, whistleblowers initially report the fraud to their employers without success.

§3 Detection and "Intellectual Evidence"

The detection of a cartel practice is based on the collection of material evidence. However, is it possible to rely on purely *"intellectual"* reasoning, consisting of demonstrating that the observed price cannot result from a competitive situation?

This issue refers to the notion of *"parallel behavior,"* whereby firms adopt the same conduct without explicitly coordinating or exchanging information with each other. For example, several firms may, without meeting each other, follow the pricing policy of the leader (most often the dominant firm or the most efficient firm in the market); when the latter increases its price, after having announced it in advance to its competitors, other firms adopt a parallel behavior. This phenomenon results in simultaneous price movements between firms.

The question is whether, on the basis of these price observations alone, without any other material evidence, these parallel behavioral patterns could fall within the scope of antitrust law.

From an economic point of view, a simultaneous and parallel increase in prices can have multiple causes:

- a symmetrical shock on costs. For example, if the price of oil rises sharply, airlines will increase their tickets prices without any collusion existing between them;
- a variation in demand. For example, if demand increases and production capacities are limited, firms have a short-term incentive to increase prices;
- a change in the intensity of competition. For example, in Cournot's oligopoly model, the exit of a firm from the market must lead, all other things being equal, to an increase in price. Similarly, if firms increase product differentiation, competition will decrease and prices will logically increase;
- a collusive strategy, whether tacit or explicit.

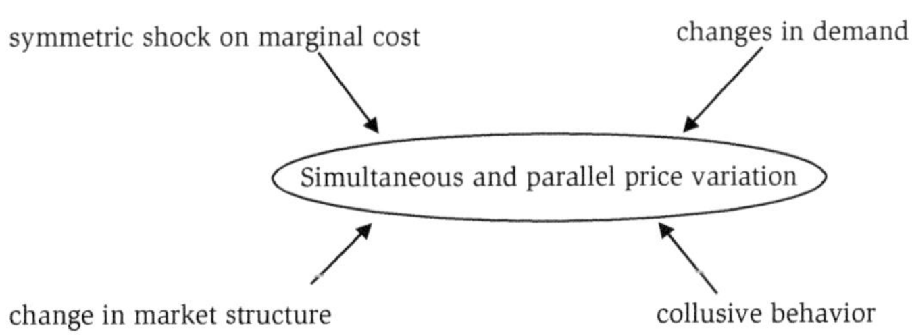

If antitrust authorities want to use intellectual evidence, they must demonstrate that the price increase cannot result solely from changes in costs, in demand, or in the intensity of competition. This demonstration must be based on a comparison between the observed price and a theoretical price, based on market and competition modeling. Such intellectual evidence faces two main shortcomings:

- which model should be used to estimate this theoretical price? In terms of oligopoly, there are many models (Cournot/Bertrand, homogenous/differentiated products, etc.) that do not lead to the same result regarding the equilibrium price;
- how can one estimate the value of the parameters of the demand or cost function? In many cases, competition authorities derive most of their information ... from the firms they investigate. We will develop this second point in more detail below.

The indistinguishability theorem: As soon as antitrust authorities rely on firms to access information regarding demand or costs, firms have incentive to manipulate the value of the parameters in order to make their collusive behavior appear to be a competitive behavior, as shown in the "*indistinguishability theorem*" (Phlips, 1995).

For example, suppose that competition authorities don't know the marginal cost of production c. The firms, which form a cartel, will overestimate their cost so that the observed price appears as a competitive price in a Cournot's situation. Let N firms ($N > 2$), competing in a Cournot model and having the same marginal cost c. The demand function is linear:

$$P = a - bQ \text{ with } b = 1$$

The equilibrium price when N firms adopt a collusive strategy (enabling them to achieve a monopoly profit) is equal to:

$$P^* = (a + c)/2$$

The equilibrium price in Cournot's competition is:

$$P_{cour} = (a + Nc)/(N + 1)$$

To make the collusion equilibrium indistinguishable from the Cournot's equilibrium, firms will overestimate their marginal cost. They will announce a cost C*, such as:

$$(a + c)/2 = (a + NC^*)/(N + 1)$$

$$\Leftrightarrow C^* = (c - a - a + Na + Nc)/2N$$

Let's illustrate the model with a numerical example. If $a = \$10$, $c = \$2$ and $N = 3$, the equilibrium prices in monopoly and Cournot are respectively:

$$P^* = \$6 \text{ and } P_{cour} = \$4$$

If firms form a cartel but want to make the collusion equilibrium appear to be a Cournot's equilibrium, they will overestimate their marginal cost:

$$C^* = 14/3 = \$4.66 > c = \$2$$

The indistinguishability theorem can also be applied to a situation in which two firms located in two distinct markets do not enter their competitor's market. This market situation could be the sign of a collusion between firms, tacit or explicit. But again, it must be demonstrated that other factors cannot explain such a situation: For instance, the lack of mutual market penetration can also result from high transportation costs.

Suppose that two firms are each in two different markets. Their marginal domestic cost is C_L while the cost when they export is C_H with:

$$C_H > C_L$$

The two firms compete in price (à la Bertrand). The demand function in each of the two markets is linear:

$$p = a - bQ \text{ with } b = 1$$

The competitive equilibrium in each market is achieved when the price is equal to the marginal cost when they export:

$$P = C_H$$

If the two firms agree not to enter each other's market, they may apply a monopoly price on their domestic market:

$$P_M = (a + C_L)/2$$

Suppose that competition authorities cannot estimate the marginal cost of exports. In this case, both firms will increase the value of C_H; the collusion equilibrium will be indistinguishable from a competitive equilibrium with high transportation costs, i.e.:

$$C_H = (a + C_L)/2$$

The model can be complexified by assuming that both firms apply a transport cost that varies with the geographical distance between the plant location and the customer's location (Figure 3.23). The segment (0, 1) in Figure 3.23 represents the geographical size of the market, comprising two areas of equal size (market a and market b), with point F corresponding to the border. Firm 1 is located at point $x = 0$, while Firm 2 is at the other end of the segment ($x = 1$). For simplicity, we assume that marginal production costs are zero. The total demand function is linear:

$$P = \alpha - bQ \text{ with } b = 1$$

Figure 3.23 Spatial Competition and Collusion

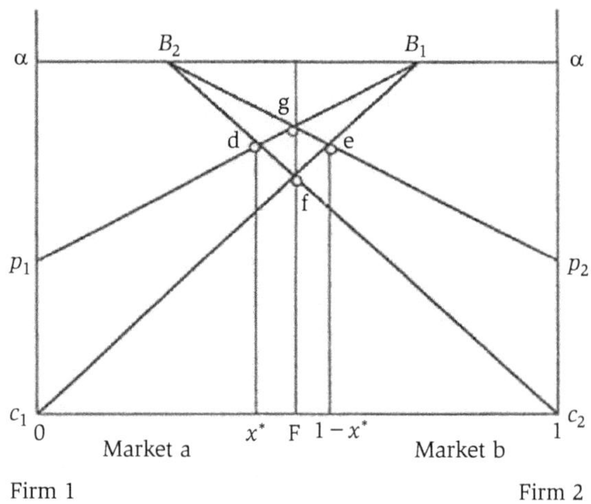

Source: Phlips (1995).

The transportation cost c increases with the distance, from the location of each firm. Firm 1 (left in Figure 3.23) has a transportation cost equal to tx, while Firm 2 has a transportation cost equal to (1 - x)t. The c_1B_1 line represents the transportation cost of Firm 1 according to the location of its customers.

Symmetrically, the c_2B_2 line shows the transportation cost of Firm 2 according to the location of its customers. Given the transportation costs, Firms 1 and 2 do not serve the entire market: Firm 1 does not go beyond point B_1; the same applies to Firm 2 which does not deliver beyond B_2. The line p_1B_1 represents the price profile of Firm 1 according to the location of its customers. We note that Firm 1 is in a natural monopoly situation on a part of the market (between x = 0 and x = x*). It therefore charges a monopoly price on this part of the market, equal to: tx/2. Over the interval between x* and (1 - x*), Firm 1 competes with Firm 2. It therefore cannot charge a monopoly price over this interval and aligns its price with the marginal transport cost of its competitor. In a competitive situation, the price profile is therefore represented by the broken line p_1dfep_2: Near border F, the price of Firm 1 in its domestic market decreases as a result of competition from Firm 2. If the two firms divide the markets, then the price profile is represented by the broken line p_1gp_2: The price increases continuously up to the border F. It could therefore be concluded that the mere observation of price levels around the border F indicates whether or not there is collusion. But if a fixed cost f is added at the border, the price profile in a competitive situation (the broken line p_1dfep_2) is not modified, but the price decrease near the border is now less marked (Figure 3.24).

Figure 3.24 Collusion with Fixed Cost of Transport at the Border

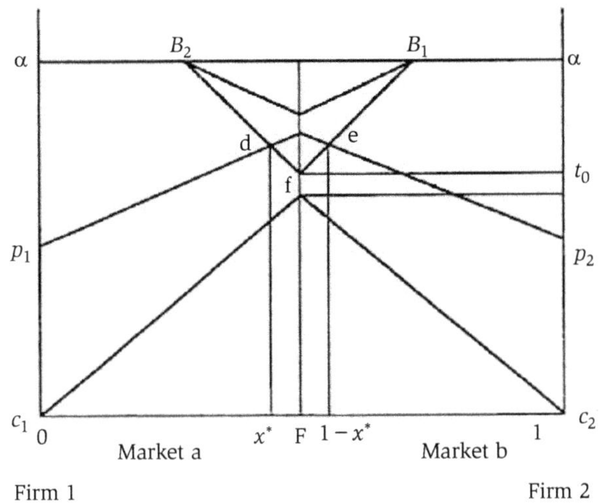

Source: Phlips (1995).

If the two firms conclude a market-sharing agreement, they can make their behavior indistinguishable by overestimating the fixed cost f: They only have to announce a level off so that the competitive price profile is the same as the collusive profile, i.e., p_1gp_2 (Figure 3.25).

Figure 3.25 Overestimation of the Fixed Cost and the Indistinguishability of Collusion

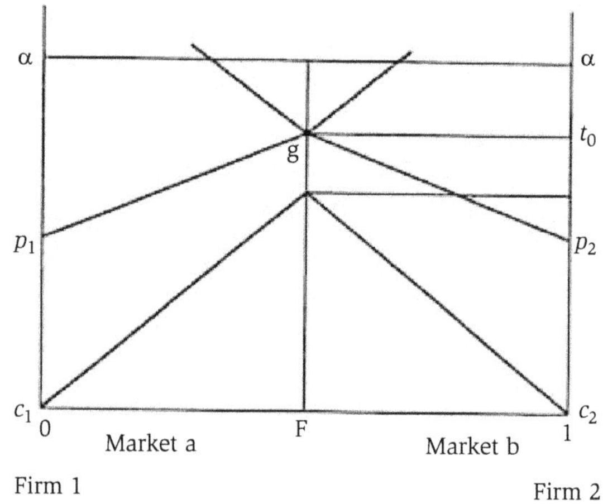

Source: Phlips (1995).

Competition authorities facing parallel behaviors: Given the limits of intellectual evidence, antitrust authorities consider that in the absence of any other evidence, mere parallel behavior is not sufficient to demonstrate an agreement. At best, this intellectual evidence is used as an element to launch an investigation, similar to the screening methods we have mentioned.

In the case of the United States, after considering that it fell within Section 1 of the Sherman Act in American Tobacco case (1946), the American judges considered, in the Pfizer case (1973), that collusion could not be inferred from the observation of a price parallelism. Five pharmaceutical firms (Pfizer, Cyanamid, Bristol, Upjohn, Squibb and Cyanamid) had a similar price of $30.6 in the tetracycline market during the period spanning 1953-1960, even though their production costs were very low (about $3). The U.S. antitrust authorities suspected the existence of a cartel, but were unable to find any physical evidence. The firms justified the high price, arguing that since demand for tetracycline is inelastic, a price decrease would not have had a positive impact on profits. Moreover, the presence of patents prevented the entry of competitors and therefore did not require a limit pricing policy. The judges received this argument favorably and concluded that "the parallel pricing among the tetracycline producers, standing alone, does not indicate price fixing."

In Europe, the ECJ took a similar position in two cases. In the European Sugar Industry case (1973), the European Commission sanctioned firms on the sole basis of parallel behavior; the ECJ then invalidated this decision on the grounds that "the observation of common or parallel conduct by firms cannot, on its own, be sufficient to characterize a concerted practice." Similarly, in the Pulp case (1984), the European Commission sanctioned the firms on the basis of three facts:

- the existence of a quarterly price announcement system with a single currency (in this case, the U.S. dollar);
- the simultaneity of price announcements done by each firm;
- the similar prices and their identical progression at each quarterly announcement.

However, the ECJ held that these three indicators did not constitute sufficient evidence of collusion, since these facts could have also resulted from the competitive activity of the market:

- regarding the quarterly price announcement system, it was introduced after World War II at the initiative of customers, who wanted to have price visibility. As for the use of the dollar as a currency, it is a common practice in the industry that dates back to the 1960s and is requested by customers;
- the simultaneity of price announcements can be explained by the market organization: Each buyer (usually an intermediary) is in contact with several firms, which leads to a rapid dissemination of price information. In addition, information technologies (telex, telephone, etc.) made it possible to inform competitors in real time of a price change initiated by a firm;
- similar price developments can be interpreted as the competitive response of firms to a shock in demand or supply. For example, in 1978, the price increase was due to a strong recovery in demand, in a context of a shortage of production capacity. Concerning the similarity of price levels, the ECJ relies on the argument of the kinked demand curve: Each firm charges the same price as its competitors because it risks losing significant market shares if it increases its own price; if it decreases its own price, firms will gain few new customers.

Review Topics:

What makes a cartel successful?
What factors contribute to the stability of a cartel?
Explain the trade-off between sanctions and detection.
Justify the effectiveness of leniency policies.
How can cartels be detected?

Recommended Readings:

Paolo Buccirossi, *Handbook of Antitrust Economics* (The MIT Press, 2008).
Emmanuel Combe and Constance Monnier, *Fines Against Hard Core Cartels: The Myth of Overenforcement* (Antitrust Bulletin 235-276, 2011).
John Connor and Robert Lande, *Cartels as Rational Business Strategy: Crime Pays* (Cardozo Law Review 455-462, 2012).

Joseph Harrington, *How Do Cartels Operate?* (Foundations and Trends in Microeconomics 1-105, 2006).

Louis Phlips, *Competition Policy: A Game-Theoretic Perspective* (Cambridge University Press, 1995).

CHAPTER 4

Conditional Agreements: Vertical Restraints and Technological Cooperation

In Chapter 3, we analyzed cartels and reviewed how competition authorities are fighting to detect and punish such practices. However, not all anti-competitive agreements, whether horizontal or vertical, should be condemned, especially when they generate efficiency gains that offset the harm done to competition. In Europe, the Guidelines on Horizontal Cooperation Agreements (2011) highlight the ambivalent effects of certain horizontal agreements: "Horizontal cooperation agreements can lead to substantial economic benefits, in particular if they combine complementary activities, skills or assets. Horizontal cooperation can be a means to share risk, save costs, increase investments, pool know-how, enhance product quality and variety, and launch innovation faster. On the other hand, horizontal cooperation agreements may lead to competition problems. This is, for example, the case if the parties agree to fix prices or output or to share markets, or if the cooperation enables the parties to maintain, gain or increase market power and thereby is likely to give rise to negative market effects with respect to prices, output, product quality, product variety or innovation. The Commission, while recognizing the benefits that can be generated by horizontal cooperation agreements, has to ensure that effective competition is maintained."

We'll start by studying vertical agreements, i.e., when a producer and its distributors sign a contract with restrictive clauses. For example, a luxury perfume producer can set up a selective distribution system to ensure that its distributors sell its products in an environment consistent with its luxury brand image. The same reasoning applies when the producer offers a high-tech product that requires resellers to assist consumers or provide them with advice: A producer may select its resellers according to their abilities to offer presale services.

We will review the various forms of vertical restraints (Section 1) and then analyze the motives behind these agreements. We'll explain, by using the transaction cost theory, why a producer chooses vertical restraints rather than having a fully integrated model (Section 2). We'll also explain why a producer does not sell its products to all distributors through a standard contract, which simply specifies a set price and quantity. The choice between a standard contract and a contract with vertical restraints can be explained both by the need to foster economic efficiencies (Section 3) or to strengthen market power (Section 4).

This brings us to the next question: To what extent and under what conditions are these restrictive agreements compatible with competition rules? In this respect, competition policy has evolved significantly—particularly at the European level—towards a greater consideration of efficiency gains, even if the RPM practice is considered differently in the United States and in Europe (Section 5).

We'll finish by studying technological agreements, intended to enable joint R&D or to spread an innovation through a licensing agreement (Section 6): These technological agreements, often concluded between competitors, can, on the one hand, reduce competition but on the other can contribute to economic progress. For example, the launch of a new technological standard may require the pooling of complementary technologies, each owned by different firms; they will pool their patents and then, in return, grant each other licenses to use them. As with vertical restraints, competition authorities take a rather "*liberal*" approach to technological agreements, even when they are concluded between competitors.

SECTION 1 THE ANATOMY OF VERTICAL RESTRAINTS

In a contract between a producer and its distributors, vertical restraints refer to any clause that limits the freedom of either actors, but, in particular, that of the distributor. For example, in the case of a RPM, the producer sets the price at which the distributor will resell its products to customers.

First, we will give a quick overview of the various types of vertical restraints, and then we'll focus on one particular case: franchising. Finally, we'll present the motives behind vertical restraints.

Main forms of vertical restraints*:* Vertical restraints can take different forms, and they can also sometimes be combined with one another. They cover different variables, such as price, quantity, product range, complementary services, geographical scope of sales, etc. Without being exhaustive, we'll review seven key types of restraints:

- territorial exclusivity: the producer grants its distributor exclusive rights to sell within a certain geographical area (a "*catchment area*"). The producer cannot sign a contract with another distributor covering the same territory: The number of resellers of the branded product is therefore restricted and this phenomenon is known as a restriction of intra-brand competition. The distributor may supply customers located outside of its exclusive territory, only if it makes "*passive sales.*" However, the producer may require its distributor not to engage in "*active sales,*" consisting of soliciting customers located outside its territory;

- single branding: The distributor must source from a single producer;
- tied purchases: The producer requires its distributor to buy several products, or even sometimes the entire range of its products, in proportions that may be fixed (e.g., as many products A as products B). It may also require that the products be resold to customers as a package or "*bundle*";
- selective distribution: The producer selects its distributors according to qualitative criteria such as their brand positioning, the homogeneity of the product range in their stores, the quality of the service they offer (in particular before- and after-sales service). Authorized distributors may not supply unauthorized distributors, but may sell to each other. Selective distribution, which is widely used to distribute branded products, reduces the number of authorized distributors in the market;
- exclusive distribution: The producer requires that the distributor sells only its brand's products, excluding those of competitors. An exclusive distribution system is frequently found in the luxury industry;
- quantity commitments: The producer can limit the quantity it sells to the distributor by setting a maximum quota; conversely, it can force a distributor to buy a minimum quantity;
- RPM: the producer can set the resale price (Figure 4.1). A variant of the resale price is the floor price or the ceiling price. The recommended price, which often takes the form of product pre-labeling, is purely indicative and not mandatory. However, when a recommended resale price is monitored by the producer and is widely applied by distributors, it can be considered as a de facto fixed price.

Figure 4.1 The Resale Price Maintenance

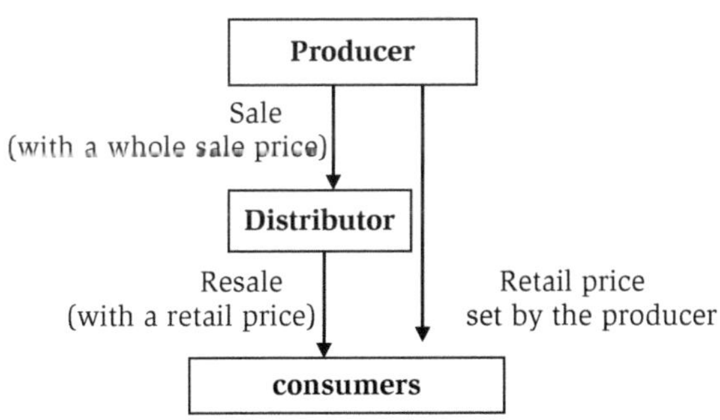

The case of a franchise agreement: Vertical restraints can be illustrated using the case of franchise agreements: A producer, called a "*franchisor,*" grants another firm, called a "*franchisee,*" the right to exploit a set of intellectual property rights (brand, label) in order to produce and/or distribute its products under its name—in exchange for the payment of royalties. The franchise agreement stipulates that the franchisor shall communicate its know-how and provide commercial and technical assistance to the franchisee. The franchisor cannot open another store within a certain geographical distance from the franchisee: There is often a territorial exclusivity clause. The franchise agreement also protects the franchisee against any abusive termination of the contract.

In return, the franchisee bears the specific investments of the franchise; it is generally forced to buy items sold by the franchisor (exclusive supply). Similarly, the franchisee is subject to an exclusive distribution clause, which may be combined with a post-contractual non-competition clause: When the contract has expired, the franchisee may not carry on a commercial activity that directly competes with the franchisor for a certain period. Franchisees are rigorously selected by the franchisor on criteria such as store location, quality of customer service, and so on: The franchise agreement is quite close to a selective distribution system.

In a franchise agreement, fees generally take the form of a two-price tariff. A fixed fee is charged; in addition to this fee, a fee proportional to the turnover ("*royalties*") is applied: The fee rate generally varies between 2% and 10%. The total royalty scheme is therefore equivalent to:

$$\text{Franchise fees} = A + (b \times Q)$$

with A ($A > 0$) the entry fee, b ($0 < b < 1$) the royalty coefficient, Q the quantity sold.

The motives behind vertical restraints: Vertical restraints have given rise to an abundant literature regarding the motivations of firms involved. In Sections 2-4 of this chapter, we will analyze one by one the different cases; but first, here is a general overview. Broadly speaking, there are two main schools of thought (Table 4.1):

- the Chicago School states that vertical restraints are a remedy for market failures; they are a source of economic efficiencies and benefit not only producers and distributors (in the form of higher profits), but also consumers. Below, we will see different arguments that are presented to justify vertical restraints, such as high transaction costs (Section 2), the elimination of double margins, the fight against acts of commercial parasitism, or the protection of the firm's brand value (Section 3);
- a second approach emphasizes that vertical restraints are mainly motivated by the quest for market power, to the detriment of consumers. Along this line of thinking, we find arguments such as the risk of collusion, market foreclosure, or price discrimination (Section 4).

Table 4.1 Why Do Firms Impose Vertical Restraints?

Motives Behind Vertical Agreement	*Explanation*
Reduce transaction costs and protect specific assets (Increase efficiencies)	Vertical restraints avoid a "*hold-up*" behavior by a co-contractor, if the transaction requires investment in specific assets (such as a brand).
Avoid commercial parasitism (Increase efficiencies)	Vertical restraints encourage distributors of the same brand to offer pre-purchase services (such as providing product information, advice, etc.) and avoid "*free riding.*"
Protect advertising investment (increase efficiencies)	Vertical restraints allow a producer to protect its advertising investments from other producers.
Protect the brand against opportunistic distributors (increase efficiencies)	Vertical restraints prevent a distributor from using a producer's brand to develop its own sales.
Facilitate collusion between producers (increase market power)	Vertical restraints facilitate the monitoring of a cartel between producers.
Facilitate collusion between distributors (increase market power)	Vertical restraints allow distributors to set up a downstream collusion.
Exclude an incoming producer (increase market power)	Vertical restraints are used to prevent a competing producer from entering the market by blocking access to distribution.
Facilitate price discrimination between customers (increase market power)	Vertical restraints allow markets to be partitioned and prices to be charged differently.

SECTION 2 VERTICAL RESTRAINTS AND TRANSACTION COSTS

Vertical restraints are often motivated by the costs of using the market, without going as far as doing a vertical integration; this explanation, provided by the transaction cost theory, shows that vertical restraints are an organizational mode that lies between the full integration mode ("*doing it yourself*, "*hierarchy*") and the market mode ("*getting it done,*" "*contracting*" or "*outsourcing*") (§1). Vertical restraints are used in particular when a transaction between two firms requires a specific investment. They are a means of protecting the firm that made the investment against any "*hold up*" behavior of its partner (§2).

§1 Vertical Restraints: Between Market and Hierarchy

Each firm's value chain is part of a larger stream of activities that go from acquiring raw material, to designing and producing a product or service, to delivering it to the end consumers. Most firms rely on the market to provide them with a range of independent suppliers or distributors that they can contract to do the activities that they do not do themselves: They choose a "*market governance*" mode.

Others prefer to have full control of their value chains and integrate all upstream and downstream tasks: They opt for a "*hierarchical governance*" mode. A third option is to sign a contract with vertical restraints: This is a "*hybrid governance*" mode.

Two opposite governance modes: Market and hierarchy: Let's first look at firms that decide to carry out a large part of the value chain themselves rather than relying on the market. For example, a manufacturer of high-quality chocolates may decide to have its own sources of cocoa beans by buying a plantation; it may also open downstream stores to sell its chocolates directly to consumers (Figure 4.2). In this particular case, the chocolate manufacturer has full control over all the activities of its value chain. It chooses an internal governance mode, called "*hierarchy.*"

Figure 4.2 A Hierarchical Governance Mode

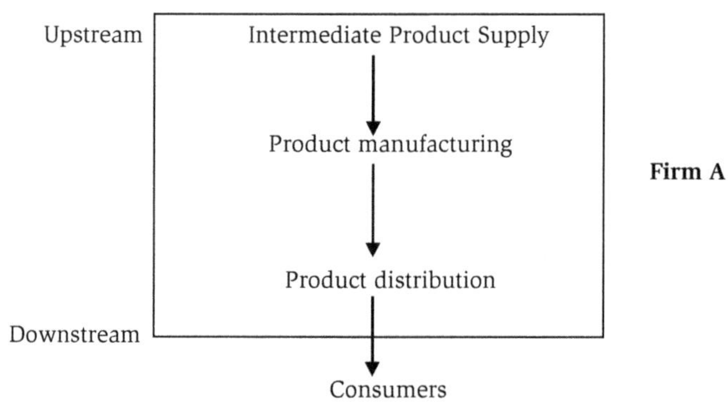

In contrast, a firm can opt for a "*market-governance*" mode: It simply purchases from other firms the goods or services needed to complete its value chain. Thus, a manufacturer which produces low quality chocolates may decide to source cocoa from an external Supplier B and sell its chocolate production through a network of independent distributors (Figure 4.3). Firm A will be less vertically integrated with upstream and downstream tasks outsourced to the market. One can even consider a case in which the chocolate producer outsources the production of its chocolates to a subcontractor in order to concentrate solely on the chocolate design activity. In this case, the chocolate producer chooses a market governance mode.

Figure 4.3 A Market Governance Mode

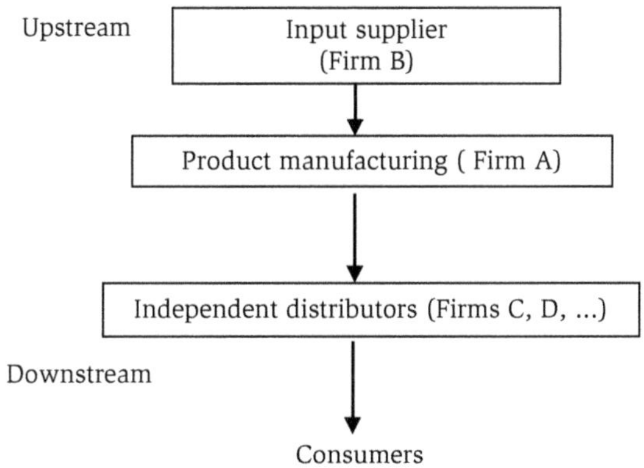

Vertical restraints: A hybrid governance mode: Between the two modes of governance seen above, there is an intermediate mode described as "*hybrid.*" It consists for a firm of outsourcing certain stages of the production process, but on the condition that it maintains close control over the product or service outsourced. This third mode, which is intermediary between opting for full integration and relying on the market, is referred to as a hybrid governance mode. Thus, Firm A may decide to enter into an upstream exclusivity agreement with cocoa Firm B in order to protect itself against supply disruptions without actually buying a cocoa plantation (Figure 4.4). Similarly, at the downstream level, without opening its own shops, Firm A may decide to be very selective when choosing resellers, in order to maintain its brand image, by imposing qualitative criteria or contractual post-contract non-competition clauses. It will then constitute a selective distribution network and will not have a simple reseller contract, solely based on a given price and quantity.

Figure 4.4 A Hybrid Governance Mode

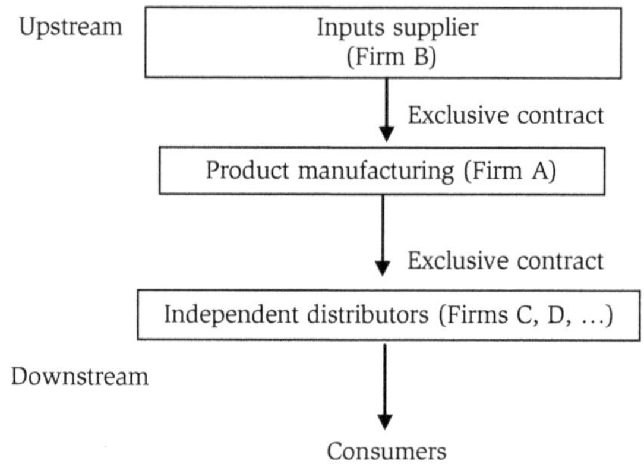

§2 Transaction Costs, Asset Specificity and Vertical Restraints

Transaction costs and choosing a governance mode: The choice of a governance mode—between the market, hierarchical, or hybrid mode—will depend on the magnitude of "*transaction costs*," i.e., the costs of using the market (Coase, 1937; Williamson, 1975). Transaction costs are composed of the costs of seeking information (e.g., to find the right partner) and the costs of negotiating contracts and monitoring their execution. These costs are present both before and after the contract is signed (Table 4.2).

Table 4.2 Types of Transaction Costs

Ex Ante Transaction Costs	*Ex Post Transaction Costs*
Contract writing costs Costs of finding the right partner Costs of negotiating an agreement Costs of developing contractual guarantees Costs of market research	Costs of a poor contract definition Costs of managing and monitoring contracts Costs of renegotiations (Potential) costs of contract termination (penalties, ...)

Source: Saussier and Yvrande-Billon (2007).

Williamson particularly emphasizes the risks of using the market: Since not all events can be predicted ex-ante and firms can behave opportunistically, the successful execution of a contract can lead to high transaction costs. For example, a litigation must be brought before the courts to enforce the terms of the contract. If the cost of using the market is too high, it is better for a firm to produce itself.

However, internalizing all activities within the firm entails higher bureaucratic costs. These bureaucratic costs can be explained by the difficulty of monitoring all activities internally. Therefore, the optimal size of a firm will be determined by comparing market costs to internal bureaucratic costs.

The influence of asset specificity on transaction costs: "*Asset specificity*" is one of the key factors that determines the cost of using the market. An asset is said to be specific if the transaction between the two parties requires an investment that cannot be put to any other use. The risk of doing the transaction increases proportionally with the specificity of the investment; once the specific investment has been made, the firm becomes its partner's hostage. The partner can then take advantage of the situation and renegotiate the contract to its advantage.

For example, suppose that bauxite-selling Firm A negotiates a contract with aluminum Firm B, which uses bauxite as a raw material. Firm B decides to invest in a factory located next to Firm A's bauxite mine, which is the only supplier in the territory (taking into account transportation costs). The value of Firm B's assets therefore depends on Firm A's supply. After having signed the contract, Firm B becomes completely dependent on Firm A. This is referred to in economics as the "*hold-up problem.*" The strong specificity of assets encourages Firm B to carry out a vertical integration in order to avoid the risk of being held up by its partner. On the other hand, if the investment is not specific, it is better to use the market and sign a contract with a supplier.

The choice of a hybrid mode of governance can be explained by the degree of asset specificity. Figure 4.5 shows the three modes of governance for a transaction: the market mode (M), the hierarchical mode (H) and the hybrid mode (X). The cost of governance of each mode depends on the level of asset specificity, noted k. When assets are non-specific, the cheapest governance mode is the market, then the hybrid mode, and finally the hierarchical mode:

$$M\ (k = 0) < X\ (k = 0) < H\ (k = 0) \qquad (1)$$

When asset specificity increases, market costs (transaction costs) increase rapidly, followed by the costs of a hybrid mode and the costs of a hierarchical one:

$$M'(k) > X'(k) > H'(k) \qquad (2)$$

When assets are not very specific ($k < k_1$), the market is the least costly solution; for high levels of asset specificity ($k > k_2$), vertical integration is preferred because it avoids transaction costs. For intermediate levels of asset specificity ($k_1 < k < k_2$), the choice of a hybrid mode minimizes governance costs. In this case, the use of vertical restraints is justified by the intermediate level of assets specificity: A vertical restraint limits the transaction costs of a simple market relationship without requiring a full integration. Vertical restraints are used in particular to protect investments against the threat of a hold up. For example, when a distributor invests in specific assets to resell the products of a producer X, it can protect itself from the risk of a hold up by concluding an exclusive distribution agreement.

Figure 4.5 Asset Specificity and the Choice of Governance Mode

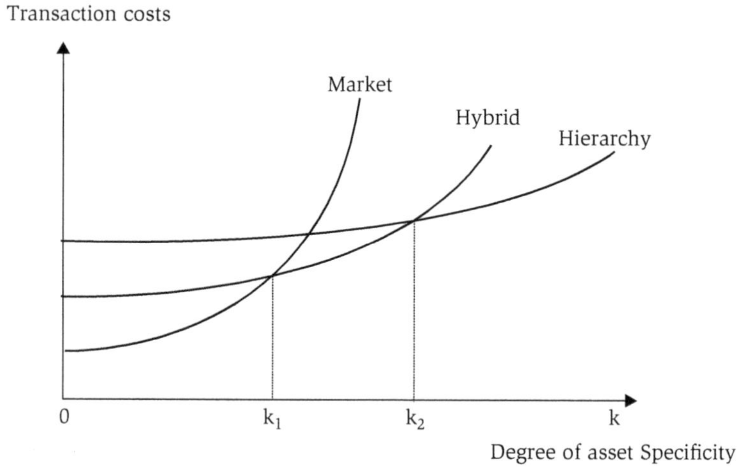

SECTION 3 VERTICAL RESTRAINTS AND EFFICIENCIES

Vertical restraints are not only used to avoid a hold-up situation; they also allow firms to correct certain market failures. Indeed, when firms do not coordinate, a "*negative externality*" can appear. An externality refers to the fact that the action of one firm has an effect, positive or negative, on another firm, without this interaction passing through the price mechanism. An externality is said to be negative when it negatively affects the situation of another firm, without being compensated for this effect. An externality is positive when the action of one firm benefits another firm without any payment.

An externality can be vertical: An upstream supplier will, for example, negatively affect the sales of its downstream distributor by not taking into account the impact of its own behavior on its distributor. It can also be horizontal: For example, two competing firms will lower their profits because they don't take into account the impact of their decisions on their rival's profit. By coordinating themselves through vertical restraints, firms can increase their profits, without having a negative impact on consumers; on the contrary, the consumer surplus will increase, as will profits.

In this section, we'll develop four main arguments illustrating how vertical restrictions can lead to greater efficiency:

- by eliminating double margins, which is a vertical negative externality (§1);
- by pushing distributors to offer presale services, which is a horizontal and positive externality between distributors (§2);
- by protecting advertising investments, which is a horizontal and positive externality between producers (§3);
- by protecting a brand's value, which is a negative and vertical externality (§4).

§1 Eliminating the Double Margin

Suppose that Firm 1 is in a monopoly situation in an upstream market. It produces with a unit cost C and sells its product at price P_1 to Distributor 2, also in a monopoly situation in the downstream market (Figure 4.6). Distributor 2 then resells the product to consumers at price P_2 without incurring any additional cost. Distributor 2 faces a final demand equal to:

$$Q_F(P_2) = a - P_2 \text{ with } a > 0$$

We have a two-step game: Firm 1 sets its price upstream before Distributor 2 sets its price downstream.

Figure 4.6 The Double Marginalization

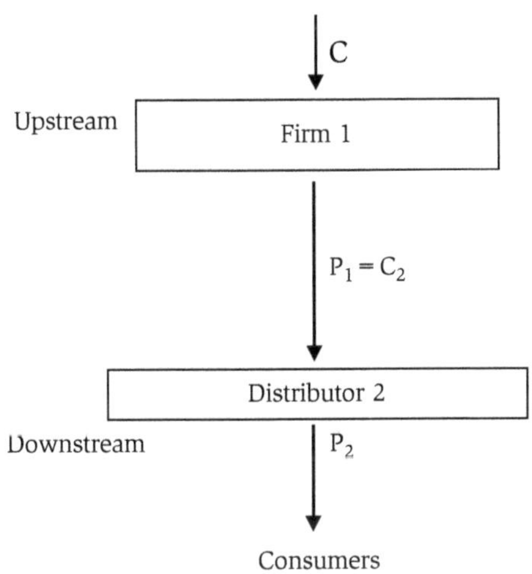

Facing this situation, Firm 1 and Distributor 2 have two choices:

(1) they don't coordinate their behavior: Firm 1 and Distributor 2 earn monopoly profits but their sales are limited due to a double marginalization effect. Consumer welfare will be low;
(2) they coordinate their behavior: Both the producer/distributor surplus and the consumer surplus will increase.

Equilibrium without vertical coordination: Consider the case where each firm maximizes its profit without taking into account the impact of its own behavior on the other firm. At the second stage of the game, Distributor 2 chooses a price P_2 which maximizes its own profit:

$$\Pi_2 = (a - P_2)(P_2 - C_2)$$

$$\Leftrightarrow \Pi_2 = (a - P_2)(P_2 - P_1) \text{ because } C_2 = P_1$$

We obtain the price, quantity and profit of Distributor 2:

$$P^*_2 = (P_1 + a)/2 \quad (1)$$

$$Q^*_F = (a - P_1)/2 \quad (2)$$

$$\Pi^*_2 = (a - P_1)^2/4 \quad (3)$$

At the first stage of the game, Firm 1 maximizes its profit, taking the final quantity Q^*_F as a given. Its maximization program is:

$$Max\, \pi_1 = Max\, \frac{(p_1 - c)(a - p_1)}{2}$$

We obtain the price of Firm 1:

$$P_1^* = \frac{(a + c)}{2}$$

By integrating the price P^*_1 into equation (1), we obtain the price P_2 for Distributor 2:

$$P^*_2 = (c + 3a)/4$$

We can notice that the lack of coordination between the two firms leads to a phenomenon of "*double marginalization.*" Indeed, each firm behaves as a monopoly and therefore charges a price above its own marginal cost:

$$P_2^* = \frac{(c + 3a)}{4} > P_1^* = \frac{(a + c)}{2} > c$$

In terms of profits, Firm 1 makes a higher profit than the Distributor 2:

$$\pi_1^* = \frac{(a - c)^2}{8} > \pi_2^* = \frac{(a - c)^2}{16}$$

Although both firms make a profit, they are mutually victims of a negative externality: The downstream sales of Firm 1 are limited because Distributor 2 sets a monopoly price on the end consumers. Similarly, Distributor 2's sales are limited because it has high costs, equal to the monopoly price of Firm 1. As a result, consumers pay a very high price.

Equilibrium with a vertical coordination: Suppose now that Firm 1 decides to coordinate with Distributor 2 to remedy this symmetrical negative externality. Firm 1 may, for example, require the distributor to resell the product at a price P*, which is the price of a single monopoly. In this case, the profit maximization equation becomes:

$$Max\ \pi = Max(a - p^*)(p^* - c)$$

The price, quantity and profit of the single monopoly are:

$$P^* = \frac{(c + a)}{2}$$

$$Q^* = \frac{(a - c)^2}{2}$$

$$\pi^* = \frac{(a - c)^2}{4}$$

We see that the total profit resulting from a coordination between upstream and downstream monopolies is greater than the sum of the profits of the two uncoordinated monopolies:

$$\Pi^* > \Pi^*_1 + \Pi^*_2$$

This higher total profit is obtained even though the final price has decreased. In other words, a vertical coordination has improved both the producer/distributor surplus and the consumer surplus. Through coordination, the two firms take into account the negative externality and avoid the double margin phenomenon. Consumers, on the other hand, benefit from lower prices.

Solutions to avoid the double margin: To remedy this double margin situation, Firm 1 can use different types of vertical restraints, including:

- contractually impose on Distributor 2 a maximum resale price equal to (c + a)/2. Distributor 2 will then sell the same quantity as the integrated monopoly;
- impose on Distributor 2 a minimum sales quota equal to (a - c)/2. This quota will force Distributor 2 to lower its price to P_1;
- design a contract with fees: For example, Firm 1 may sell its product to Distributor 2 at a marginal cost c. Then, Distributor 2, in a monopoly position, will charge a price P* = (c + a)/2 and sell a quantity Q* = (a - c)/2. Firm 1 will recover the monopoly profit by charging its distributor either a franchise fee equal to the monopoly profit or a commission on each unit sold, equal to the unit margin (P* - c).[29]

29. In reality, the sharing of the total monopoly profit will depend on the bargaining power of the distributor in relation to the producer.

§2 Pushing Distributors to Offer Presale Services

Vertical restraints can also improve the level of service that distributors offer, as Telser (1966) pointed out with the so-called "*presale services*" theory. Again, it is a question of externality: The fear of "*commercial parasitism*" by competitors leads distributors, in the absence of vertical restraints, to underinvest in the presale service.

The presale theory: Main hypothesis: Suppose that the end demand for a good depends on the level of services offered by retailers before the purchase: For example, some individuals will only buy a computer if the seller can provide them with advice and help them during their purchasing process, particularly as to whether the computer's performance matches their needs.[30] In the case of a luxury product, the service may consist of providing a higher quality of service or highlighting the product's image of prestige. Total demand therefore increases with the level of service offered by distributors.

Let us also assume that the consumption of the service and the purchase of the product are two distinct acts: For example, a consumer can ask Distributor 1 for information or advice and then buy the product from Distributor 2. Distributor 1 cannot reap the fruits of its efforts.

Providing customer services is costly for the distributor; it must, for example, invest in staff training or user-friendly product presentations (explanatory brochures, in-store demonstrations, etc.). The efforts to offer a certain level of service (noted s) increases the marginal cost of production C by $\Phi(s)$:

$$C = c + \Phi(s) \text{ with } \Phi' > 0, \Phi'' > 0 \text{ and } \Phi(s = 0) = 0$$

If the market is a perfectly competitive market, the price is equal to the marginal cost and the distributors' profit is nil. In the absence of a service offer ($s = 0$), distributors bear a marginal cost c. Since there is no service, the level of demand is low (the line D' in Figure 4.7). The consumer surplus (which is also the total welfare) is equal to the area (E + F).

If distributors offer a certain level of service s, their marginal costs increase from c to $c + \Phi(s)$, as does the selling price. Thanks to this service, the level of demand also increases: As we *see* in Figure 4.7, the demand increases from D' to D". The total surplus is now represented by the area (F + G). While area G, which represents the increased demand, is larger than area E (which represents the additional cost of providing services), the total welfare has increased. The question is therefore whether distributors will, in the absence of vertical coordination, offer this service to customers.

30. It is therefore assumed that the consumer is able to assess the quality of the advice provided (time spent by the seller, accuracy of explanations, etc.).

Figure 4.7 Pre-sale Service and Demand

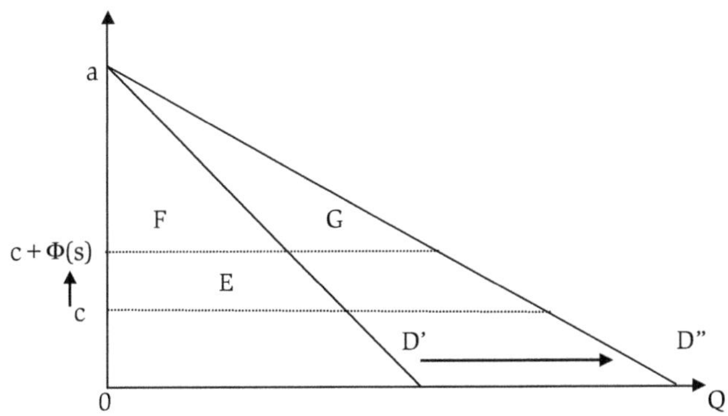

Equilibrium without vertical coordination: In the absence of any coordination between distributors, none of them will offer the service. Indeed, it is in the interest of each distributor not to offer the service, hoping that its competitors will do so: It will lower its prices and attract the customers of the competitors that offer additional services. But since each distributor behaves in the same way, no one offers the service and the demand for the product is low. This situation is harmful both to the producer and to uninformed consumers, who will not buy the product in the absence of any advice.[31]

This situation is similar to a prisoner's dilemma, a well-known situation in the non-cooperative game theory (Table 4.3). Let's take the example of two distributors of the same brand of computers, located in the same territory. Distributor A can offer a service to customers or rely on the service offered by its competitor B (and vice versa). If both distributors offer the service, sales are high because consumers are informed of the product's characteristics and the profit for each distributor is $5. If neither of the two distributors offers the service, the level of sales is low and the profit of each distributor is only $3. Of course, the maximum profit is obtained for a distributor when it does not offer the service and its competitor does: It can "*swallow*" the whole market and then make a profit of $8, while its competitor no longer sells anything (profit of $0). It appears that the best strategy for each distributor is to cheat, which leads to the worst collective situation in terms of individual and collective profits.

31. This scenario actually concerns only a limited number of goods (Scherer & Ross, 1990), since only presales services are concerned. The risk of "*free riding*" is less likely for after-sales services. Second, opportunistic behavior only concerns products of a certain value. Finally, a part of the customers who already know the product is not affected by the low level of service.

Table 4.3 Service Offer and the Prisoner's Dilemma Theory

	Distributor B	
Distributor A	Offers the service	Does not offer the service
Offers the service	(\$5, \$5)	(\$0, \$8)
Does not offer the service	(\$8, \$0)	**(\$3, \$3)**

Equilibrium with vertical coordination: To get out of this suboptimal situation, the producer can put in place vertical restraints to encourage distributors to offer a certain level of service.

A first solution consists of granting each distributor a territorial exclusivity: The distributor is then assured that it will be the only one to benefit from its efforts, since consumers cannot move from one territory to another without bearing a prohibitive transport cost. Matthewson's and Winter's 1985 study confirms, in the case of franchising, the incentive role of territorial restrictions on the franchisee's effort, based on a sample of 25 franchise networks.

A second solution for the producer is to encourage the retailer to provide a service, for example, by setting a minimum resale price: In our example, the producer can require distributors to resell the product at a retail price at least equal to $c + \Phi(s)$ by setting a certain level of service s. In this case, it is in the interest of each distributor to offer the service; if not, the distributor will not be authorized to lower its price. Customers will therefore prefer to purchase the product from a distributor that offers the service.

The use of a selective distribution system is a third solution: The producer selects its distributors by ensuring, for example, that they all have a staff dedicated to providing service.

§3 Protecting Advertising Investments

A reasoning quite similar to the previous one can be applied when producers make advertising investments in order to increase demand. If these investments have generic content (the promotion of a type of product, etc.), they can benefit competing producers: A positive externality appears between producers, which can then lead to a lack of further advertising investment.

Suppose two Producers A and B have similar products that are resold by the same distributor. If Producer A invests in advertising actions to promote its own products, its effort may unintentionally increase Producer B's sales, since the two products are sold in the same outlet and are substitutable.

If both producers invest in advertising, the level of sales is high because consumers are informed of the product's features and the profit for each distributor is \$5 (Table 4.4). If neither of the two producers invests in advertising, the level of sales is low and each producer's profit is only \$3. Of course, a producer obtains maximum profit when it does not advertise while its competitor does: It will "*take*" the whole market and then make a profit of $8, while its competitor no longer sells anything (profit of $0). In the absence of coordination between the two producers, a situation of prisoner's dilemma may arise: Neither of the two producers is willing to invest in advertising.

Table 4.4 Advertising Investment and the Prisoner's Dilemma Theory

	Producer B	
Producer A	Invests in advertising	Does not invest in advertising
Invests in advertising	($5, $5)	($0, $8)
Does not invest in advertising	($8, $0)	**($3, $3)**

To remedy this risk, Producer A that wants to invest in advertising can choose an exclusive distribution system; thus, customers attracted by its advertising campaign will only find the products of Producer A in its exclusive distributor's network.

§4 Protecting the Brand Value

A producer who has heavily invested in order to build its brand image entrusts the distribution of its brand's products to a distributor. What guarantee does the producer have that the distributor will not degrade the brand image and, therefore, its value? This risk is particularly relevant when it comes to luxury goods: The value of a luxury good depends on the context in which it is sold.

For example, in the absence of vertical restraints, a distributor has an incentive to sell luxury products in order to attract customers into its stores: It uses the luxury product as a flagship product. This practice is beneficial for the distributor, but ultimately affects the producer's brand image, and, therefore its sales: Consumers will turn away from the product, which will no longer be considered a luxury product.

A producer with a strong brand image, therefore, will select its distributors on the basis of qualitative criteria, such as the homogeneity of the range of products sold. It can also use an exclusive distribution to ensure that its brand's product will not be used as the distributor's flagship product.

SECTION 4 VERTICAL RESTRAINTS AND REDUCING COMPETITION

The previous approach, in line with the Chicago School's theses, highlighted the efficiency of vertical restraints, which increase both profits and consumer surplus. However, vertical restraints may also be motivated by a market power objective at the expense of consumer's surplus.

We will successively discuss the collusive role of vertical restraints (§1), the use of vertical restraints as an instrument of price discrimination (§2), and the market foreclosure argument (§3).

§1 Vertical Restraints and Collusion

Vertical restraints, and, in particular, a RPM, can facilitate collusion in two ways.

A first scenario is a collusion between producers (manufacturing substitutable goods) on the price P* they charge to their distributors. In order to limit deviant behaviors, producers must ensure that everyone respects the price P*. Suppose that producers do not observe the price of competitors but only the prices P' charged downstream by distributors (with P' > P*). They have to infer from downstream price variations that possible cheating is happening upstream. However, a drop in downstream prices can have two main causes: Either a producer has lowered the upstream price below P*, or the distribution costs have decreased downstream. It's difficult for a producer to distinguish between these two causes. One solution may be for producers to set a resale price P'. Indeed, in this case, no producer has an interest in lowering its upstream price to gain market share over its competitors, since the downstream distributor should apply a resale price P'.

A second scenario is a collusion between a producer and its distributors to act as an integrated monopoly and avoid any competition downstream. For example, a producer may impose a resale price. Producers and distributors then share the outcome resulting from their collusion. In order to ensure that the resale price is respected by all distributors, producers can set up a market monitoring and price policy, with the active support of distributors. Thus, in 2007, the French Competition Council sanctioned several toy producers and three distributors for fixing retail prices. This vertical collusion was coupled with a retaliation policy against deviating distributors, with the involuntary participation of consumers: "The three sanctioned distributors actively participated in these police actions; thus, Carrefour had maintained, for several successive years, an operation called 'Carrefour reimburses 10 times the difference,' encouraging consumers to monitor prices on its behalf. Using feedback on consumer claims, Carrefour systematically intervened with the suppliers concerned to 'solve the problem' of the cheaper product found among its competitors" (free translation).

§2 Vertical Restraints and Price Discrimination

A dominant producer can use vertical restraints to implement a strategy of third-degree price discrimination (according to the Pigou's typology [1920]). This strategy consists of setting different prices on different groups of consumers according to their price elasticity. Consider a producer in a monopoly position; it supplies two different geographic markets (e.g., countries) A and B through local distributors (Figure 4.8). The demand in Country A is less elastic than in Country B: In this case, the monopoly has an incentive to charge a price $P_A > P_B$, in order to increase its total profit.

Figure 4.8 An Example of Price Discrimination Between Two Countries

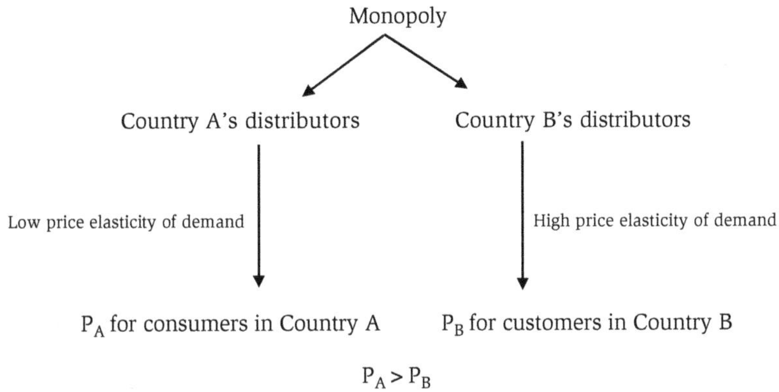

However, this discrimination strategy can succeed only if consumers from Country A (who pay a higher price) cannot buy the product from Country B (Figure 4.9). The role of a vertical restraint is to prevent any arbitration between the two countries.

Figure 4.9 Price Discrimination and the Risk of Arbitration

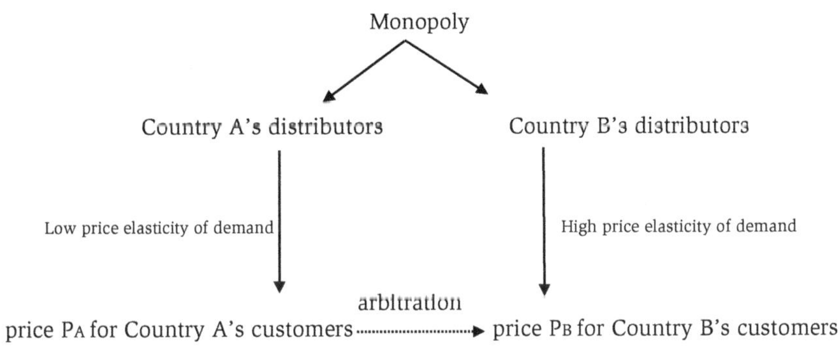

A numerical example with a uniform pricing: Suppose there exists a monopoly in both Countries A and B. The firm sells its products through distributors located in each country. We assume that consumers in Country A and those in Country B do not have the same demand function. The demand function in Country A is:

$$P_A = 36 - 4Q_A$$

$$\Leftrightarrow Q_A = 9 - P/4$$

The demand function in Country B is more elastic:

$$P_B = 24 - 4Q_B$$

$$\Leftrightarrow Q_B = 6 - P/4$$

We assume that the marginal cost of production is constant and equal to \$4. Distribution costs are assumed to be zero.

If the producer does not discriminate between the two markets, it will set the same price in countries A and B. To do this, it will consider the total demand Q*, which corresponds to the addition of the two national demands, i.e.:

$$Q^* = Q_A + Q_B = 9 - P/4 \qquad \text{if } \$24 < P < \$36$$

$$Q^* = Q_A + Q_B = 15 - P/2 \qquad \text{if } P < \$24$$

We see that if the price is higher than \$24, demand only exists in Market A; when the price falls below \$24, there is demand in Markets A and B.

The producer will maximize its profit by equalizing the marginal cost with the marginal revenue:

$$4 = 30 - 4Q$$

$$\Leftrightarrow Q^* = 6.5$$

The monopoly price is then \$17 in Countries A and B and the total profit is:

$$\Pi^* = (17 - 4) \times 6.5 = \$84.5$$

A numerical example with differentiated pricing: The monopoly can obtain a higher profit if it sets a different price on each market. Indeed, in Country A, by equalizing the marginal revenue with the marginal cost, it offers the following quantity:

$$36 - 8Q_A = 4$$

$$\Leftrightarrow Q_A^* = 4$$

It sets a price equal to:

$$P_A^* = \$20$$

and its profit is equal to:

$$\Pi_A^* = (20 - 4) \times 4 = \$64$$

In the more elastic Country B, the monopoly, after equalizing the marginal revenue with the marginal cost, offers a quantity equal to:

$$24 - 4Q_B = 4$$

$$\Leftrightarrow Q_B^* = 2.5$$

It sets a price equal to:

$$P_B^* = \$14$$

and its profit is equal to:

$$\Pi_B^* = (14 - 4) \times 2.5 = \$25$$

We immediately notice that, thanks to a discriminating strategy, the monopoly increases its total profit by \$4.5 compared to a uniform pricing policy:

$$\Pi_A^* + \Pi_B^* = \$89 > \Pi^* = \$84.5$$

This result is due to the fact that the producer takes advantage of its monopoly power in Country A by selling at a higher price (at a price of \$20 instead of \$17). The consumer surplus in Country A decreases. In Country B, the producer reduces its price (from \$17 to \$14) which increases the quantities sold: The consumer surplus in Country B increases. However, we note that the increase in consumer surplus in Country B does not compensate for the decrease in consumer surplus in Country A.

The role of a vertical restraints: The discrimination strategy may, however, be undermined if customers in Country A decide to buy the products from Country B, where the price is lower. The producer must therefore prevent such arbitration—for example, by introducing a clause prohibiting or discouraging distributors in Country B from supplying consumers located in Country A. This clause, which limits "*passive sales*," has been condemned several times in Europe (*see* below), particularly in the automotive industry. For example, in 2005, the European Commission imposed a penalty of €49.5 million on Peugeot for entering into a vertical agreement with its distributors located in the Netherlands with the aim of restricting "*parallel trade*" on its new cars. Indeed, Peugeot set lower prices in the Netherlands than in countries such as France, leading some French consumers to buy in the Netherlands. The vertical agreement mainly took the form of a differentiated bonus: It was only granted to dealers if the cars were registered in the Netherlands. In addition to the Peugeot case, several cases of vertical agreements aimed at limiting parallel trade have been sanctioned in Europe (Table 4.5).

The growth of e-commerce has not put an end to price discrimination strategies: A producer may require its distributors to apply online a "*geographical blocking.*" For example, a European Commission survey (2017) found that only 37% of websites allowed customers from other European countries to complete online purchases. This result is explained by the presence of different obstacles at each stage of the online shopping process: Some websites refuse to deliver in some European countries (51% of cases) or refuse credit card payments when the holder of the card is domiciled abroad (58%). Sometimes, customers are even automatically redirected to the websites of their countries of residence, a practice known as "*rerouting.*"

These strategies of geographical blocking are now the subject of a particular attention by the European Commission because they violate the market integration objective, which is at the heart of the European Economic Union. In December 2018, the European Commission fined Guess (designer and distributor of clothing and fashion accessories) €40 million for preventing its authorized retailers from selling online to customers located outside their allocated territory. According to the European Commission, these agreements have enabled Guess to partition European markets; in particular, by depriving customers in Central and Eastern European countries of the more attractive prices offered in other Western European countries.

Table 4.5 Examples of Vertical Agreements Being Used to Restrict Parallel Trade in Europe

Case	*Type of Discrimination*	*Decision of the Commission*
Volkswagen (1998)	Volkswagen discouraged its Italian dealers from selling certain models to German customers.	€102 million fine, reduced on appeal to €90 million by the ECJ
Opel Nederland (2000)	Opel's Dutch subsidiary prevented its Dutch dealers from exporting new cars.	€41 million
Daimler-Chrysler (2001)	Daimler imposed on its Mercedes dealers a geographical exclusivity.	€72 million
Nintendo (2002)	Nintendo and its distributors had agreed to prevent parallel imports on video games. The price difference for the same console in Europe could reach 75%.	€149 million for Nintendo and €18.8 million for each seven distributors
Peugeot (2005)	Peugeot and its Dutch distributors had agreed to restrict parallel trade in new cars, particularly for the French market.	€49.5 million in fines for Peugeot
Guess (2018)	Guess was preventing its retailers from doing online advertising campaigns and selling products to consumers in other Member States ("*geoblocking*").	€40 million
Nike (2019)	Nike has prohibited its distributors from selling products outside their territory.	€12.5 million
Valve (2021)	Valve, owner of the online PC gaming platform "Steam," and five restricted cross-border sales of certain PC video games on the basis of the geographical location of users.	€7.8 million

§3 Vertical Restraints and Market Foreclosure

Vertical restraints can be used to block downstream access to a newcomer. For example, Producer 1 can force its distributors to sell only its products, excluding those of its competitor, Producer 2 (Figure 4.10). If Producer 1 has a high market share, distributors will accept such a clause, especially if it offers a financial compensation. For Producer 2, the access to the distribution network will be more difficult if the number of distributors is limited by the size of the market or by high fixed costs. The foreclosure effect is more likely if the scope of the exclusivity clause is broad, as its duration, or if the conditions for leaving or renewing the contract are very restrictive (financial penalties for early exit, tacit renewal, etc.).

Figure 4.10 Exclusivity Agreement and Market Foreclosure

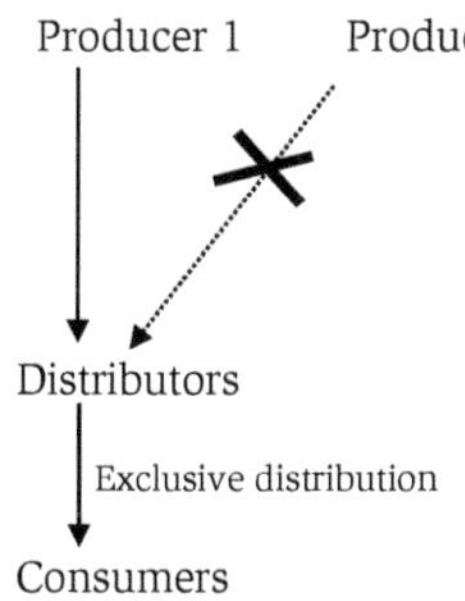

An unlikely foreclosure? The idea that a firm can foreclose the market through an exclusivity clause has been challenged by the Chicago economists (Posner, 1976; Bork, 1993). According to these authors, a producer cannot sign an exclusive contract with its distributors if a more efficient producer can enter the market. This argument can be explained graphically (Figure 4.11).

Suppose Firm 1 is in a monopoly situation. Its marginal cost of production is c_1. Direct customers (i.e., distributors) pay a monopoly price P^M and buy a quantity Q^M. Firm 1 is threatened by the entry of Firm 2, which operates with a marginal cost c_2 lower than c_1. However, Firm 2 is not efficient enough to charge a monopoly price below the marginal cost of Firm 1: $P^M{}_2 > c_1$.

The competition between the two producers is a Bertrand competition: If it enters, Firm 2 will charge a price P* equal to the marginal cost of Firm 1. In a monopoly situation, the surplus of distributors is equal to the aP^MA area. In a Bertrand situation, the surplus of distributors is equivalent to the aDP* area. If Firm 1 wants to prevent the entry of Firm 2, it must conclude an exclusivity agreement with its distributors with a financial compensation equal to the P^MADP^* area. However, the profit of Firm 1 is equal to the P^MABP^* area, which is less than the compensation required: The difference is represented by the gray triangle ABD. Under these conditions, distributors have no incentive to accept an exclusivity contract from Firm 1.

Figure 4.11 An Unlikely Market Foreclosure

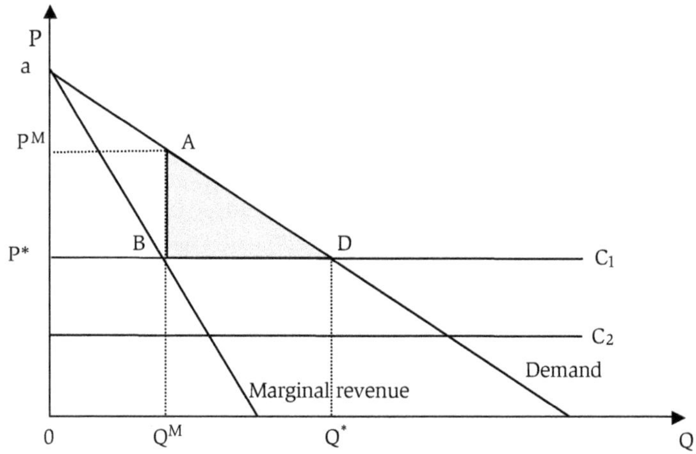

This argument can also be demonstrated algebraically. The demand function is equal to:

$$P = a - Q$$

When Firm 1 is in a monopoly position, its profit maximization program is:

$$\text{Max } \Pi = (a - P)(P - C_1)$$

In a monopoly situation, the price, quantity, profit, and surplus of distributors (which are customers of Firm 1) are equal to:

$$P^M = (a + C_1)/2 \quad Q^M = (a - C_1)/2 \quad \Pi^M = (a - C_1)^2/4 \quad SC^M = (a - C_1)^2/8$$

If Firm 2 enters the market, the price P* decreases to the marginal cost of Firm 1. In this case, the quantity, profit, and surplus of the distributors are equal to:

$$P^* = C_1 \quad Q^* = (a - C_1) \quad \Pi^* = (C_1 - C_2)\,(a - C_1) \quad SC^* = (a - C_1)^2/2$$

Distributors are willing to sign an exclusivity agreement with Firm 1 if it can offer a financial compensation T equal to the reduction in their surplus:

$$T = (a - C_1)^2/2 - (a - C_1)^2/8$$

$$\Leftrightarrow T = 3(a - C_1)^2/8$$

This compensation is higher than the profit made by Firm 1:

$$3(a - C_1)^2/8 > (a - C_1)^2/4$$

The Chicago School's thesis has been challenged in two ways:

(1) if there's uncertainty about the entry of a more efficient competitor, the incumbent can reduce the probability of entry by signing an exclusivity agreement with its customers (Aghion & Bolton, 1987);
(2) in the presence of several customers (and not just one), the incumbent may use the lack of coordination between customers to encourage them to sign an exclusive contract, for fear of paying more (Rasmusen et al., 1991).

Uncertainty about entry and foreclosure: The Aghion and Bolton (1987) model can be presented through a numerical example, based on a two-period game. In period 1, Producer A is in a monopoly position and sells its product to a distributor, which buys at best one unit per period at a maximum price of \$100. The unit cost of production c_A is \$50. In period 2, Producer B can enter the market. Its unit cost of production is unknown by Producer A and the distributor. They only know that c_B is distributed uniformly between \$0 and \$100. If Producer B enters, the two firms are in a Bertrand competition.

In period 2, if c_B > \$50, Producer B does not enter the market: Producer A remains in a monopoly situation and sets a price of \$100. The probability of this scenario is 0.5. If c_B < \$50, Producer B enters the market and charges a price of \$50: It replaces Producer A, which leaves the market. This scenario has a probability of 0.5. In the absence of an exclusive contract with Producer A, the distributor anticipates an expected price of \$75 in period 2:

Expected price in period 2 (without a contract) = (\$50 × 0.5) + (\$100 × 0.5) = \$75

Since the distributor is willing to pay up to \$100 for a unit, it anticipates an expected surplus of (\$100 – \$75) = \$25 in period 2. If it wants to sign an exclusivity agreement with the distributor, Producer A must offer a compensation of at least \$25. Producer A can set a price of \$75 in the second period, with a penalty of \$50 if the customer decides to buy in period 2 from Producer B. This type of contract will have the effect of reducing the probability of entry. Indeed, the distributor will only change if it pays a maximum price of \$25, taking into account the penalty to be paid to Producer A. Producer B cannot therefore charge a price higher than \$25. This assumes that Producer B has a production cost c_2 < \$25. This scenario has a probability of 0.25. The exclusivity contract has reduced the probability of entry from 0.5 to 0.25.

The distributor has an incentive to sign an exclusive contract with Producer A. Indeed, with an exclusive contract, the expected price in period 2 will be:

Expected price in period 2 (with a contract) = (0.75 × \$75) + 0.25 × (\$25 + \$50) = 7\$5

The expected surplus in period 2 is the same as without an exclusive contract: The distributor will sign.

Why will Producer A offer an exclusive contract in period 2? In the absence of an exclusive contract, Producer A's expected profit in period 2 is:

Expected profit of Producer A in period 2 (without a contract):
0.5 × ($100 – $50) = $25

With an exclusive contract, the expected profit in period 2 is:

Expected profit of Producer A in period 2 (with a contract):

0.75 × ($75 – $50) + 0.25 × $50 = $31.25

Producer A's expected profit has therefore increased by: ($31.25 – $25) = $6.25.

Without an exclusive contract, Producer B has a probability of entry equal to 0.5, with a price of $50. If it enters, its unit production cost is on average $25 (since it's distributed uniformly between $0 and $50). Its expected profit is therefore equal to:

Expected profit of Producer B in period 2 (without a contract): 0.5 × ($50 – $25) = $12.5

With an exclusive contract, the probability of entry is 0.25 and Producer B sets a price of $25. Its unit cost being distributed uniformly between $0 and $25, it is on average $12.5. Its expected profit if it enters with an exclusive contract is therefore equal to:

Expected profit of Producer B in period 2 (with a contract): 0.25 × ($25 – $12.5) = $3.13

Producer B's expected profit has fallen by ($12.5 – $3.13), or $9.37, due to the exclusivity agreement.

We see that the exclusive contract has a negative impact on the total welfare. Indeed, the total welfare would have been $62.5 without a contract, while it is $59.38 with an exclusive contract (Table 4.6).

Table 4.6 Surplus and Profits with and Without an Exclusive Contract

	Distributor's Surplus	*Producer A Profit*	*Producer B Profit*	*Total Expected Surplus*
Without an exclusive contract	$25	$25	$12.5	$62.5
With an exclusive contract	$25	$31.25	$3.13	$59.38
Change in surplus	$0	+ $6.25	-$9.37	-$3.12

The exclusive contract reduces the probability of entry of a more efficient competitor. Without a contract, it would have been 0.5. With a contract, it decreases to 0.25. The effect of the contract is to deter the entry of a Producer B whose production cost is between $25 and $50. In other words, if Producer A cannot deter the entry of a very efficient competitor with a unit cost below $25, it can nevertheless deter the entry of a slightly more efficient producer.

Probability of entry with and without exclusivity contract

- Without an exclusive contract:

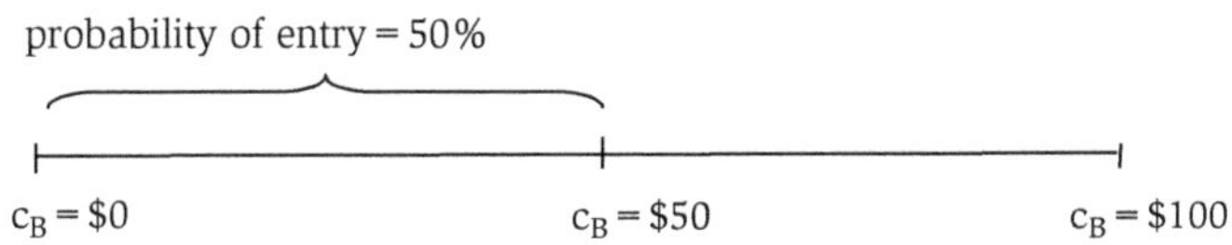

- With an exclusive contract:

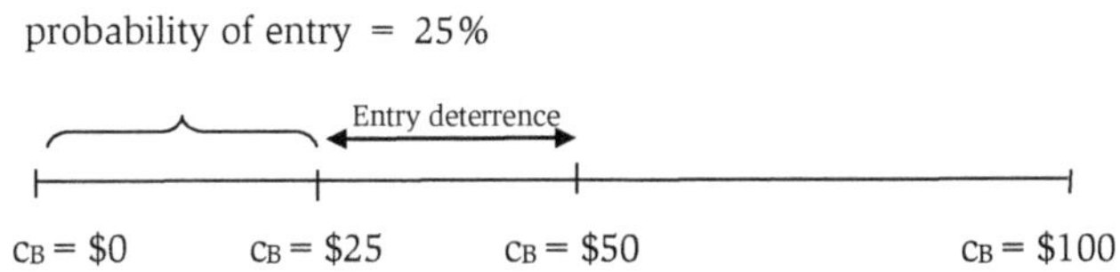

Coordination failure between customers and market foreclosure: The Rasmusen et al. model (1991) shows that an incumbent firm can deter the entry of a more efficient competitor if customers cannot coordinate with each other.

Imagine a two-period game. Producer A has a unit cost c_A equal to $50. In period 2, a new Producer B, more efficient than Producer A, can enter the market with a unit cost of $40. Producer B must also bear a fixed entry cost F (an advertising cost for example) of $60. There are three customers on the market, each willing to pay up to $100 for a unit.

If Producer B wants to make profits, it must have at least two customers. Indeed, with only one customer, the maximum price it can charge is $100, equal to its total cost ($40 + $60). If it has two customers, it must charge a price at least equal to: $40 + $60/2, or $70. If it has three customers, it must charge a price at least equal to: ($40 + $60/3), or $60.

Without an exclusive contract, if Producer A wants to keep customers, it must charge a price of $60 per customer: It has to take into account the entry threat of Producer B. It makes a total profit of (3 × $60) – (3 × $50) = $30.

However, Producer A can offer an exclusive contract at a price of $70 to two of the three customers. Although the price is $10 higher than without an exclusive contract, two customers will sign. Indeed, the one that does not sign will then face a monopoly situation, since Producer B will not enter the market if there's only one customer to serve. The customer that has not signed an exclusivity agreement will therefore have to pay $100. As clients do not coordinate with each other, they have an individual incentive to sign with Producer A at a price of $70, in order to avoid an unfavorable situation.

Exclusivity agreement and market foreclosure: An empirical example: In 2009, the French Competition Council sanctioned France Telecom (now Orange) for having concluded exclusive distribution contracts in Martinique, Guadeloupe and French Guyana with independent distributors selling mobile phone subscriptions and terminals. France Telecom, through its subsidiary Orange Caraïbe, held a local market share of 70%, compared with 20% for its main competitor Bouygues Télécom, which entered the market in 2001, four years after Orange Caraïbe. In order to distribute its products, France Telecom used a network of independent distributors. When it entered the market, Orange Caraïbe selected the best located and most efficient distributors. In addition, in the French West Indies, the number of independent distributors is relatively small.

Once it entered the market, Orange Caribbean signed exclusivity agreements with some 50% of them (110 stores). The scope of the exclusive clauses was broad, since it prohibited independent distributors from accepting the distribution of Orange Caraïbe's competing products and services without its express prior consent. In addition, the duration of the exclusive clauses was particularly long: It applied not only during the period of distribution contracts, but also two years after their termination. Finally, the sanction if an independent distributor breached the contract was severe: it had to pay a compensation equivalent to twelve months' commissions, without prejudice to Orange Caraïbe's right to claim higher damages.

By prohibiting the sales of products competing with its own, Orange Caraïbe considerably reduced Bouygues Télécom Caraïbe's ability to enter the market. Indeed, creating a distribution network requires significant fix and sunk costs (search for commercial leases, training of commercial staff, etc.). Even by offering independent distributors more-attractive commercial terms than those offered by Orange Caraïbe, Bouygues Télécom Caraïbe could not have convinced them to distribute its products and services: Distributors would have had to cease all activity for two years, given the existence of the non-compete clause.

SECTION 5 VERTICAL RESTRAINTS AND COMPETITION POLICY

When competition authorities analyze vertical restraints, they balance the negative effects on competition with the efficiency gains: Vertical restraints are frequently accepted under certain conditions. This balanced approach is in line with the economic analysis, which highlights the ambivalence of vertical restraints on welfare (§1).

However, some vertical restraints are considered to have a sufficiently negative impact on competition that they are considered illegal. This is the case for RPM practices, which are prohibited in most developed countries, even if the situation has evolved in the United States (§2).

We will also see that in the digital age, competition authorities have examined vertical restraints on online sales, as well as some pricing clauses concluded by platforms with their suppliers (§3).

§1 A Conditional Acceptance

Intra- and inter-brand competition: When analyzing the impact of vertical restraints, competition authorities distinguish inter- from intra-brand competition.

Inter-brand competition occurs between producers with different brands. For example, if all producers use an exclusive distribution system, competition between brands will be reduced, as compared to a multi-brand situation: Consumers will have to bear a transaction cost (e.g., in the form of a transportation cost) if they want to compare products of different brands.

Intra-brand competition occurs within the distribution network of the same brand. For example, a system of territorial exclusivity limits competition between distributors of the same brand if consumers are not geographically mobile.

A reduction in intra-brand competition is considered by competition authorities to be less negative for consumers as long as there is a strong inter-brand competition. Indeed, faced with competition from other producers, a producer has no interest in limiting price competition between its own distributors.

The U.S. approach: In the United States, vertical restraints are assessed under Section 1 of the Sherman Act (1890) and Section 3 of the Clayton Act (1914), which deal specifically with exclusive distribution and tying sales. While vertical restraints are now assessed under the rule of reason, this has not always been the case (Table 4.7): For example, until the late 1970s, territorial exclusivity and tying sales were considered as per se violations of the Sherman Act. Case law has evolved since the 1980s towards a greater flexibility. The Schwinn case (1967) is an example in this respect: In 1967, the Supreme Court maintained that territorial exclusivity was prohibited per se. In 1977, the Supreme Court revisited the Schwinn case in the GTE Sylvania case: It was recognized that territorial exclusivity can solve free-riding problems, and, more generally, that vertical restraints not related to price should be assessed according to a rule of reason. Concerning RPM, case law has also evolved in the United States, following the Leegin decision of the Supreme Court in 2007 (*see* below).

Table 4.7 Vertical Restraint Cases in the United States

Case	*Content of the Ruling*
Doctor Miles-John Park & Sons (1911)	The resale price imposed by a producer is reprehensible per se; it expresses a conspiracy between the producer and its distributors.
International Salt (1947)	Tying sales are prohibited if the supplier has a dominant position on the main product.
Standard Oil (1949)	Exclusive distribution is authorized if the producer does not hold a dominant position.
Continental TV-GTE Sylvania (1977)	Territorial restrictions are lawful if they stimulate inter-brand competition.

The European approach: At the European level, vertical restraints may fall under Article 101 §1 TFEU, which forbids agreements that have the effect or object of restricting competition.

In a first step, competition authorities check whether the vertical agreement should be considered as an anti-competitive agreement or whether the restrictions are inherent to the functioning of competition and to product specificities. Thus, since the Metro case (1977), it has been considered in Europe that a selective distribution system does not infringe antitrust law [i.e., Article 101(1) TFEU] and constitutes an appropriate mode of competition, if three cumulative conditions are met:

- the properties of the product justify the use of a selective distribution;
- the criteria for selecting resellers are objective, qualitative, uniform and non-discriminatory;
- the selection criteria are proportionate to the final objective.

This Metro case law has been applied on many occasions in the luxury and high-tech sectors. The ECJ constantly points out that "there are legitimate requirements, such as the maintenance of specialized retailers able to provide specific services for products of high quality and technical sophistication, that justify a reduction in price competition in favor of competition based on factors other than price" (free translation from French). For example, in the luxury industry, Givenchy's (1996) selective distribution network was validated by the ECJ, on the grounds that "it is in the interest of consumers looking for luxury cosmetics that such products are correctly presented at points of sale. In the case of high-quality products whose luxury image is appreciated by consumers, criteria that are designed solely to ensure that they are presented in a way that enhances their value pursue a result which is likely to improve competition by preserving that luxury image and thus counteract the restriction of competition inherent in selective distribution systems" (free translation from French).

If a vertical agreement is considered as anti-competitive (by object or by effect), then competition authorities assess whether it can be exempted under Article 101 TFEU (3):

> The provisions of paragraph 1 may, however, be declared inapplicable in the case of:
>
> - any agreement or category of agreements between undertakings,
> - any decision or category of decisions by associations of undertakings,
> - any concerted practice or category of concerted practices, which contributes to improving the production or distribution of goods or to promoting technical or economic progress, while allowing consumers a fair share of the resulting benefit, and which does not:
>   (a) impose on the undertakings concerned restrictions which are not indispensable to the attainment of these objectives;
>   (b) afford such undertakings the possibility of eliminating competition in respect of a substantial part of the products in question.

Until 2004, in order to benefit from an exemption, vertical agreements had to be notified to the European Commission, but this procedure has been replaced by a "*legal exception*" system: Following the adoption of Regulation 1/2003, firms must now themselves assess the lawfulness of their distribution agreements under the Article 101 TFEU.

In order to clarify the conditions allowing a vertical agreement to escape the prohibition of Article 101 TFEU, the European Commission adopted in 2010 the Regulation 330/2010 and published Guidelines on Vertical Restraints. Broadly speaking, three situations can be distinguished (Figure 4.12).

First, if the market shares of the supplier and the buyer are each below 30% and the agreement does not contain any "*hardcore restriction,*" the vertical agreement is automatically exempted from Article 101 §1 TFEU: This is referred to as a "*block exemption.*" In this case, the European Commission assumes that the agreement improves the distribution of products without significantly altering inter- and intra-brand competition.

Second, if the market shares are less than 30% but the agreement includes a hardcore restriction, the vertical agreement cannot be exempted by category; it must be examined individually. Among the hardcore restrictions, we find in particular:

- the producer has imposed a RPM;
- the authorized distributors are forbidden to sell online;
- the distributors are forbidden to answer any non-solicited sales requests (passive sales);
- the distributors are forbidden to do any cross-selling between themselves;
- restrictions exist on the access to spare parts for repairers and independent service providers.

A hardcore restriction can be "*saved*" if the producer can justify the existence of efficiency gains that outweigh the harm done to competition. For example, a producer that launches a new product may wish to secure the investments of its physical distributors by temporarily limiting online sales. In addition, the restrictions must be indispensable and proportionate to the achievement of this objective; the agreement must not give its members the possibility of eliminating all competition, both intra- and inter-brand competition. The agreement must provide users with a fair share of the resulting benefit.

Figure 4.12 The Assessment of Vertical Agreements under European Law

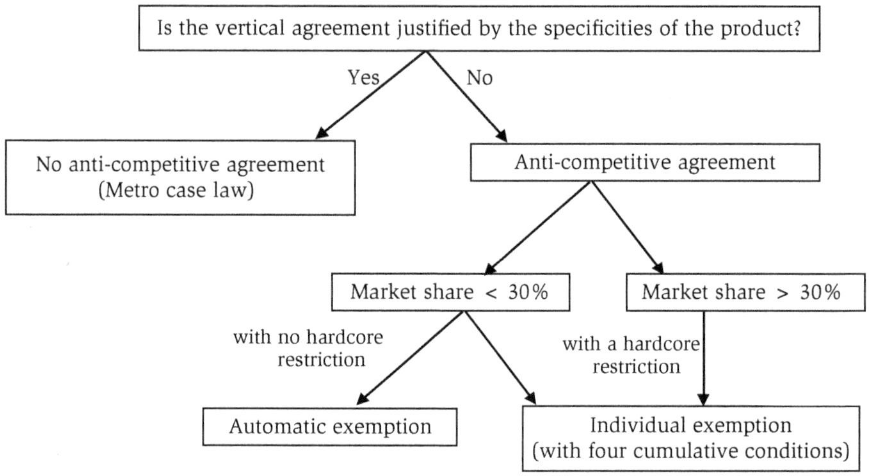

A third situation is the case in which the market shares of the undertakings are above 30%, but without any hardcore restrictions: The vertical agreement cannot be exempted automatically, since it is presumed that it has a negative impact on competition. The vertical agreement is then examined under an individual exemption rule, i.e., on a case-by-case basis. If the vertical agreement significantly reduces competition, firms can claim efficiency gains, which outweigh the harm done to competition. Again, vertical restraints must be necessary and proportionate to the implementation of efficiency gains; the agreement must not give its members the possibility to eliminate all competition, both intra- and inter-brand; the agreement must provide users with a fair share of the resulting benefit.

§2 Banning RPM Agreements

Although economists consider that RPM has ambiguous effects on competition and economic efficiency, most developed countries prohibit such practices per se (or by object in Europe) (OECD, 1998); however, the situation in the United States has evolved following the 1997 Leegin decision.

A recent change in the United States: In the United States, the RPM has long been prohibited: Following the Doctor Miles case (1911), the U.S. Supreme Court found that an RPM constituted an infringement of the Sherman Act. This approach was reaffirmed in 1984 in the case of *Monsanto v. Spray-Rite Service*. The prohibition of RPM was even extended to the maximum resale price in the Albrecht case (1968).

However, the case law has evolved since 1997. In the Kahn case, the Supreme Court stated that setting a maximum resale price was no longer prohibited per se but subject to a rule of reason. The argument was that by setting a maximum price, a producer authorizes its distributors to reduce the price.

This ban on RPM has evolved over time:

- Between 1937 and 1975, the U.S. Congress allowed American states to legalize RPM within their territory in the name of "*fair trade*" and 46 States effectively authorized it. However, in 1975, the U.S. Congress passed the Consumer Goods Pricing Act, which reinstated the per se prohibition: It found that prices were comparatively higher in states where RPM was allowed compared to states where it was prohibited.
- In the Colgate case (1919), the Supreme Court recalled that RPM implied an explicit agreement between a producer and its distributors; a unilateral refusal to sell does not fall under the Sherman Act, since there is no agreement.
- RPM is not prohibited per se in the case of "*consignment sales*"; it consists of a producer entrusting its sales to a distributor, while retaining ownership on the products. The distributor receives a commission on sales and unsold products, after a certain period of time, are returned to the producer. The commercial risk is therefore borne by the producer and not by the distributor. In the General Electric case (1926), the Supreme Court stated that the prohibition of RPM in consignment sales could not apply as long as there is no ownership transfer between the producer and the distributor. The producer is therefore free to set the resale price of its products. In Illinois Corporate Travel/American Airlines case (1989), the Seventh Circuit Court confirmed that a travel agency selling airline tickets was not strictly speaking a reseller because the commercial risk is borne by the airline and not by the travel agency. This exception to RPM has sometimes led some firms to circumvent RPM ban by changing resale contracts into deposit contracts, as was the case in Simpson/Union Oil case (1964).

In 1997, with the Leegin case, the U.S. Supreme Court opened a breach in the—almost century-old—prohibition of the minimum resale price. In this case, Leegin, which was not in a dominant position, applied a minimum resale price policy in order to encourage its distributors to offer service to its customers. Following a complaint filed by a distributor wishing to offer rebates, Leegin was ordered to pay treble damages and this decision was confirmed on appeal. However, the Supreme Court overturned the decision, claiming that the imposition of a minimum resale price could benefit consumers by promoting competition between distributors through the quality of services. The Supreme Court therefore invites competition authorities to treat minimum resale prices with a rule of reason—in particular when the producer does not hold a dominant position—rather than to apply a per se prohibition principle.

A hardcore restriction in Europe*:* At the European level, a RPM is considered to be a hardcore restriction and is excluded from any block exemption. A fixed resale price, or the fixing of a minimum price is prohibited, as are indirect practices, such as setting the distributor's margin or the levels of price rebate it may offer, or imposing delays or suspensions of delivery if the retailer doesn't respect the recommended price. On the other hand, producers can impose a maximum resale price or recommend a selling price as long as there is no constraint on the distributor.

For instance, in France, while fixed resale prices and minimum prices are prohibited under Article L. 420-1 of the French Commercial Code, the practice of the maximum resale price is not. The case of recommended prices is subject to a special treatment: It can be considered under certain conditions to be a fixed resale price. Thus, in Luxury Perfumes (2006), Toys (2007) and Auxiliary Heating Appliances (2016) cases, the French Competition Authority found that the indicative price was in fact a fixed resale price, because the following three conditions were met:

- the explicit mention of a recommended resale price by producers;
- a price monitoring system, so producers could make sure that distributors respected the recommended price. If they cheated, producers would take retaliatory measures;
- a significant number of distributors applied the recommended price.

The French Competition Authority found that the combination of these three conditions—all of which are lawful in isolation—proved that an agreement had been made between producers and distributors designed to set a fixed resale price. This is therefore a presumption. In contrast, in the Nintendo case (2015), in the absence of one of these three conditions (there was no price monitoring), the French Competition Authority dismissed the complaint against Nintendo.

Several cases of fixed resale prices have led to sanctions in Europe and in France (Table 4.8). For example, in May 2001, the European Commission fined Volkswagen €30 million for trying to impose a "*price discipline*" on its German dealers. Volkswagen had required its dealers not to grant a discount when they sold the new Passat in Germany. This requirement removed any intra-brand competition between distributors. In addition, the practice of discounts is common in the automotive industry (around 10%): It is the main tool for dealers to compete against each other.

The prohibition of RPM is justified by the fact that the producer's control over its distributors cannot go so far as to eliminate all price competition. Indeed, as soon as distributors are selected, the objective of maintaining a certain quality or brand image is achieved, without the need to go further. This position is summarized in particular in the Perfumes case (French Competition Council 2006): "Both national and European case law authorizes brands whose images are associated with luxury products to closely monitor the sales outlets distributing their brands and to check the presentation of their products so as to ensure that they are ideally displayed. This is the selective distribution system, which leads to a rigorous choice of the brand's sales outlets. However, this same case law does not allow brands to hinder the freedom of each distributor to set its margin rate and therefore its retail price. This freedom benefits the final consumer, because it enables him to compete between outlets of the same brand and to obtain better prices" (free translation).

Table 4.8 Fixed Resale Price Cases (France and Europe)

Case	*Practice*	*Sanction*
Ray-Ban (2001, France)	Ray-Ban had imposed a minimum resale price on its distributors and had prohibited any discounts. The firm's sales agents had actively monitored distributors.	500,000 French francs
Perfumes (2006, France)	13 firms with luxury perfume and cosmetics brands had agreed with their distributors (including national distribution chains) on setting resale prices.	€45 million to 13 suppliers and 3 perfume distribution chains
Game consoles (2007, France)	Sony had applied a RPM with its resellers, notably on the PS2 console.	€800,000
Toys (2007, France)	Five suppliers had agreed with their distributors on the reselling price of Christmas toys.	€37 million to 5 toy manufacturers and 3 distributors
Kontiki (2011, France)	Kontiki, distributor of Diddl articles in France, had imposed set prices on its retailers between 2003 and 2007.	€1.34 million
Petfood (2012, France)	Three companies specializing in dry dog and cat food had implemented fixed resale prices and territorial restrictions.	€35 million
Wine workshop (2017, France)	Sambri had set the online resale prices of its products.	€3,200
Liquid fertilizers (2018, France)	Liquid fertilizer manufacturers and their wholesale distributors had conspired to set the resale prices of their products.	€355,000
Dammann Frères (2020, France)	The tea producer Dammann Frères, under the pretext of providing its retailers with recommended prices, had, in fact, imposed resale prices.	€226,000
Volkswagen (2001, EU)	Volkswagen had imposed a "price discipline" on its German dealers by prohibiting any discounts in Germany.	€30 million

Case	*Practice*	*Sanction*
Yamaha (2003, EU)	The musical instrument manufacturer Yamaha had imposed resale prices for products such as pianos and guitars in some Member States.	€2.5 million
Guess (2018, EU)	Guess had limited the ability of licensed retailers to independently set the resale price.	€40 million
Consumer electronics manufacturers (2020, EU)	Asus, Pioneer, Denon & Marantz, Philips engaged in RPM by restricting the ability of their online retailers to set their own retail prices for widely used consumer electronics products.	€111 million

A questionable prohibition: The severity of competition authorities in regards to the resale price maintenance is questionable from an economic point of view. Indeed, as we have seen, an RPM may be motivated by anti-competitive reasons—for example, a collusion between producers or between distributors—but it may also generate efficiency gains, beneficial for consumers and their welfare: eliminating a double margin, giving distributors the incentive to offer presale services, etc.

In addition, the argument that the RPM facilitates collusion also applies to other vertical restraints; for example, territorial exclusivity clauses may allow a producer to allocate geographical markets. However, territorial exclusivity clauses are treated differently: They are not subject to a prohibition per se (or by object in Europe), but to a rule of reason.

Finally, most empirical studies conclude that the RPM is frequently efficient and refute the collusive thesis. Thus, on the basis of a sample of claims brought before the American courts, Ippolito (1991) shows that the collusion thesis concerns only 13% of the cases studied, while the theory of presale services explains more than half of the cases.

Lessons from an empirical study: In their study on the Corning Glass case, Ippolito and Overstreet (1996) analyzed the impact of the decision taken by the FTC in 1975 against Corning Glass, a leader in the field of kitchen utensils: The FTC prohibited Corning Glass from setting an RPM, a practice that was tolerated in most American states. The authors investigated whether Corning Glass's RPM was motivated by economic efficiency and coordination problems (particularly in the supply of services by distributors), collusion between distributors, or collusion between Corning Glass and its main competitors. The authors successively used four tests to separate these different explanations.

The first test consisted of observing the characteristics of the firms and the market during the RPM period. The collusion between distributors—whether wholesalers or retailers—seems unlikely, given the heterogeneity of distributors (in terms of size, distribution costs), their large number (30,000 retailers) and the absence of a professional association that could have played the role of coordinator between distributors. Moreover, the fact that Corning applied an RPM for almost 40 years makes it unlikely that there was any collusion between distributors: Changes in market conditions and the rise of new distribution methods such as supermarkets would have broken the collusion. If we now consider the thesis of collusion between producers, the heterogeneity of firms in terms of size and cost and the fact that most of Corning's competitors did not practice RPM does not argue in favor of this explanation. Thus, in the early 1970s, Anchor Hocking, Corning's main competitor, did not use RPM to sell its products.

The second test involved studying the evolution of Corning Glass and its competitors' sales after the ban of RPM in 1975. If the RPM was motivated by economic efficiency—and in particular the supply of presale services—the end of this practice should have led to a decrease in Corning Glass's sales. For Corning Glass's competitors, which did not apply an RPM, the impact should have been positive or zero. Conversely, if the RPM was used by producers or distributors as a collusion tool, the end of the RPM should have resulted in lower prices and therefore increased sales for Corning Glass and its competitors. The authors noted that the end of the RPM resulted in a decrease in Corning Glass sales, even though sales had been on a positive annual trend since 1966. On the basis of these elements, the authors concluded that the RPM was primarily motivated by economic efficiency.

The third test consisted of analyzing the evolution of advertising expenditures after the ban of RPM in 1975. Indeed, if the RPM is a way to encourage distributors to promote a product, its prohibition should have forced Corning Glass to carry out these promotional activities itself. The authors noted a significant increase in Corning Glass' advertising expenditures after 1975, even though they'd been on a declining trend since 1967.

The final test consisted of studying the stock market's reaction to the announcement of the FTC's decision to investigate the RPM, using an "*event studies*" methodology: The aim was to measure the specific impact of this announcement on the stock price of Corning Glass and its competitors, assuming the stock market's efficiency.[32] If the RPM was primarily motivated by economic efficiency, the FTC's announcement should have resulted in a decrease in Corning's future profits, and, therefore, a decrease in its share price, while competitors' prices should have remained unchanged or have been positively affected (Table 4.9). If the RPM had been used as a tool for competing producers to collude, the end of the RPM should have led to a decrease in profits for both Corning and its competitors: The stock price of all firms in the sector should have decreased. Finally, if the RPM had been imposed by distributors on producers, the removal of the RPM should have resulted in an increase in the producers' share price.

32. In a nutshell, the stock market is "efficient" if all the relevant information (past, present and anticipated) is at all times integrated into the share price.

Table 4.9 Impact of the End of the RPM on Firm's Share Prices

Motivation for the RPM	*Corning Glass*	*Anchor Hocking*	*Other Competitors*
Collusion between distributors	+	+	+
Collusion between producers	–	–	–
Economic efficiency	–	0 or +	– if RPM + if no RPM

Source: Ippolito and Overstreet (1996).

The authors estimated the abnormal returns at the announcement of the FTC's decision to open an investigation on October 8, 1971. They showed that the cumulative abnormal return of Corning's share over a five-day window preceding the announcement of the FTC was -12% and -16% over a 10-day window: Corning's share reacted negatively to the event (Figure 4.13), which invalidates the theory of collusion between distributors. As for competitors, Anchor Hocking's share price reacted positively to the announcement: Over a five-day window, the abnormal cumulative return was +3%, and +7% over a one-day window. The other competitors were not significantly affected by the decision. The authors concluded that the event study confirmed the thesis of economic efficiency in the implementation of a fixed resale price.

Figure 4.13 Abnormal Cumulative Returns of Corning Glass

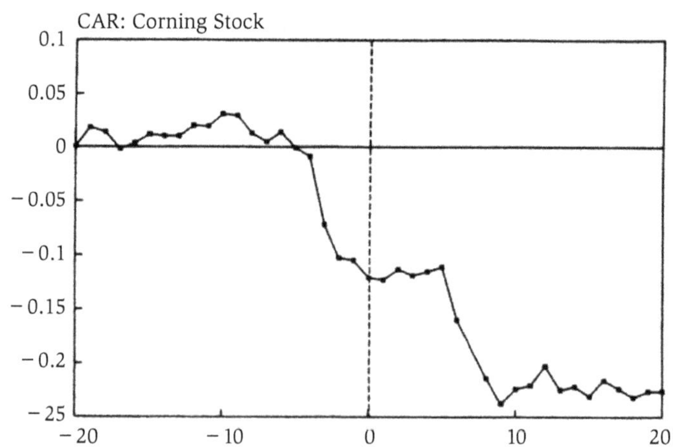

Source: Ippolito and Overstreet (1996).

§3 Vertical Restraints in the Age of e-Commerce

The growth of e-commerce: Since the 2000s, e-commerce has experienced strong growth; in Europe, for example, in 2020, e-commerce represented more than €7.170 billion in revenue and has been growing at an annual rate of 13%, mainly driven by smartphone sales. During the COVID-19 pandemic, e-commerce jumped in Europe and will account for more than 15% of the total retail trade in 2021.

All sectors of activity are now concerned with online sales, including the luxury sector. Most producers have chosen to go beyond a simple "*showcase website*" and sell their products online through several channels (Figure 4.14):

- the launch of e-commerce websites under their own brand names;
- the launch of e-commerce websites by their physical distributors;
- sales on general or specialized marketplaces;
- sales on websites of "*pure players*," which are only present on the internet (like Amazon).

Figure 4.14 The Different Online Sales Channels

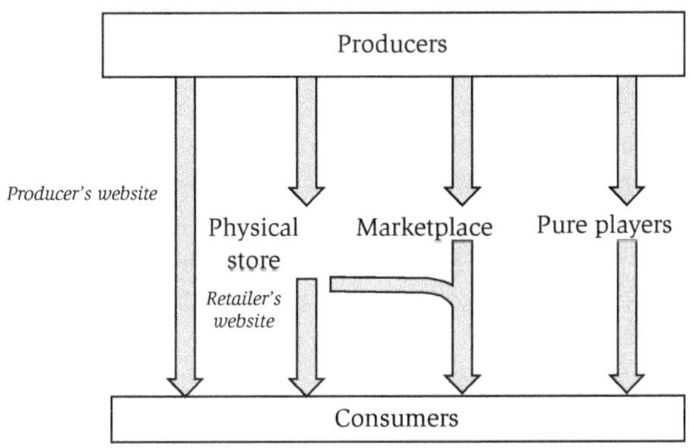

For consumers, e-commerce offers many advantages:

- larger markets, with geographical distance being overcome and new territories being opened up;
- ease of use (especially regarding opening days and hours, compared to a physical store);
- depth of products mixed with a wider variety of products.

On the producer side, the growth of online commerce is more questionable: On the one hand, e commerce allows them to expand their market size, to conquer new customers and to regain a direct access to the client without having to go through a distributor. However, on the other hand, it strengthens inter- and intra-brand competition, as it facilitates price comparisons and increases the number of players (producers and distributors) in the market.

Vertical restraints in online sales: The general principle in Europe is that any authorized distributor has the right to sell on the internet: A producer cannot reserve this distribution channel for its own benefit.

However, the producer may transpose to online sales the qualitative criteria it imposes on its distributors for sales in physical stores, in particular concerning the website's presentation or online customer support. A general principle of equivalence then applies: The conditions imposed for online sales may not be more restrictive than those imposed for physical sales. More generally, a producer may not require the online reseller to comply with conditions that would not pursue the same objectives as those required for in-store sales.

The producer can refuse online sales to a distributor that only operates on the internet (pure players or market places) and does not have any physical sales outlets; this position is explained by the fear of some European producers—and, in particular, the luxury industry—that the sales of pure players will destabilize the network of physical stores. In the Coty case (2017), the ECJ ruled that a producer can refuse its authorized distributors the right to sell on marketplaces as long as there are other sales channels on the internet, in particular, through the websites of authorized distributors.

As for physical stores, some restrictions on online sales are considered as hardcore restrictions in Europe; for example, a producer cannot prevent passive sales by requiring the customer to buy on the website of a distributor located in the same physical territory. Similarly, a producer cannot limit the distributor's internet sales, by, for example, imposing a proportion of online sales in relation to sales in physical stores: It can simply impose a minimum turnover in physical sales outlets. Another example: A producer may not set a higher price for products sold online rather than in physical stores ("*dual pricing*"). As for physical sales, a producer may not impose a RPM on the online sales of its distributors.

An extreme case of hardcore restriction is when a producer refuses its authorized distributors the right to sell online. In France, the Pierre Fabre case (2008) clarified the debate on this subject. The dermo-cosmetic producer prohibited its own selective distribution network from selling its skincare creams online. The French Competition Council found that such a prohibition was not proportionate to the objective of product quality, raised by Pierre Fabre: A reworking of the criteria imposed on physical stores to online sales was sufficient to achieve this objective. In 2011, the ECJ confirmed that the clause prohibiting any sale on the internet of cosmetic and personal hygiene products does constitute a hardcore restriction and cannot be exempted. Following the Pierre Fabre case, the French Competition Authority sanctioned several cases of prohibition of online sales by authorized distributors (Table 4.10).

Table 4.10 Cases of Vertical Restraints in e-Commerce

Case	*Practice*	*Sanction*
Pierre Fabre (2008)	Pierre Fabre had banned its authorized distributors from selling its brand's products on the internet.	€17,000 and an injunction to modify contracts
Bang & Olufsen (2012)	Bang & Olufsen had banned its distributors from selling its brand's products on the internet from 2001 to 2012. The entire selective distribution network, composed of 48 distributors, was concerned by this commercial policy.	€900,000 (reduced on appeal to €10,000)
Atelier du Vin (2017)	From 2011 to 2016, Sambri had set the resale price of items marketed under the brand name "L'Atelier du Vin."	€3,200
Guess (2018, EU)	Guess had limited the ability of licensed retailers to independently set the resale price.	€40 million
Stihl (2018)	Between 2006 and 2017, Stihl had forbidden online sales of certain products, such as chainsaws, on the websites of its authorized distributors.	€7 million
Liquid fertilizers (2018, France)	Liquid fertilizer manufacturers and their wholesale distributors conspired to set the resale prices of their products.	€355 000
Dammann Frères (2020, France)	Tea producer Dammann Frères, under the pretext of providing its retailers with recommended prices, had in fact, imposed resale prices.	€226 000
Consumer electronics manufacturers (2020, EU)	Asus, Denon & Marantz, Philips Asus, Pioneer engaged in RPM by restricting the ability of their online retailers to set their own retail prices for widely used consumer electronics products.	€111 million

The rise of intermediation platforms: On the internet, the role of digital platforms is to act as an intermediary between suppliers and customers. For example, an online hotel booking site connects customers (demand) with hotel operators (supply). As a general rule, intermediation platforms make money through a commission system: Suppliers pay them a commission for each transaction made (Figure 4.15). On the other hand, the platform access is free of charge for customers. This is typically a so-called "*two-sided*" market: One side of the market (customers) does not pay the platform directly, while the second side of the market (suppliers) pays a commission to the platform. The platform development is governed by powerful cross-network effects: The more visitors there are on a platform, the more suppliers want to also be present on it. Symmetrically, the more suppliers there are on a platform, the more attractive it becomes for customers. The market platform market is therefore conducive to strong market share concentration, to the benefit of a dominant player.

Figure 4.15 How Intermediation Platforms Work

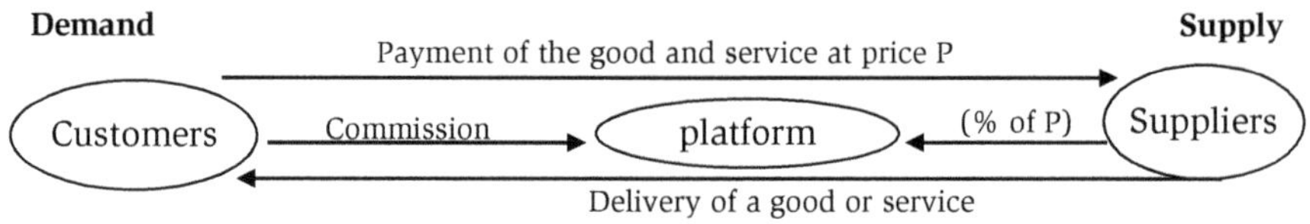

The case of the Across Platform Parity Agreement (APPA)*:* A dominant platform may introduce a vertical restraint, referred to as an APPA: The supplier must set a price that is always equal to or lower than the price it offers on a competing platform. In Figure 4.16, Platform 1 (an online hotel reservation site, for example) requires that the supplier (a hotel, for example) sets a price P_1 less than or equal to the one it charges on Platform 2. While the supplier is free to set its price and change it (it is therefore not a fixed resale price) it cannot, however, differentiate it at the expense of Platform 1.

APPAs can be explained by the need to protect investments. Indeed, a platform invests in the quality of its website in order to attract customers. Once the product has been found on the platform (e.g., a hotel room), customers may be tempted to book on a competing platform that offers a lower price because it didn't invest in the same quality of service. The APPA aims at avoiding commercial parasitism between competing platforms.

However, APPAs can also be used by a dominant platform to reduce competition in the market:

- The entry and development of a new platform is more difficult, as it cannot charge a lower price to attract its first customers.
- APPAs reduce the intensity of competition between existing platforms. Indeed, platforms also compete with each other through the commission rates charged to suppliers: Without an APPA, a new incoming Platform 2 can decide to reduce its commission rates, which will result in a price reduction for the customer (if the supplier passes on the reduction in commission in the selling price). Conversely, with an APPA, if Platform 2 reduces its commission rate, the supplier should pass on the price reduction to Platform 1 as well. The incentive of Platform 2 to lower commission rates is therefore reduced.
- In case of a collusion between platforms on commissions, the incentive to cheat and lower the price disappears, since any price decrease must be passed on to the competing platform.

Figure 4.16 How an APPA Works

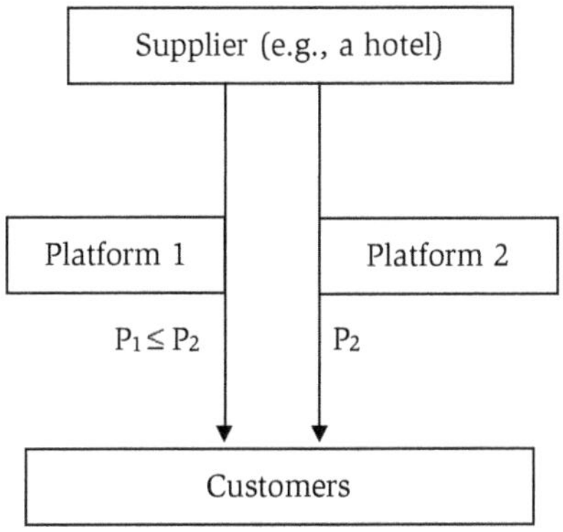

Several price parity agreements on platforms have led antitrust authorities in both the United States and Europe to open investigations, most often concluded with a settlement. Thus, in France, Hotel Reservation Platforms (called "OTAs" for Online Tourism Agency)—and, in particular, the European leader Booking.com—included in their contracts with hotels a so-called "*extended parity clause.*" With this clause, they required hoteliers to offer a rate, number of nights, and other conditions (booking conditions, inclusion or not of a breakfast, etc.) at least as favorable as those offered on competing platforms, as well as on all other distribution channels (online and offline), including the hotels' own distribution networks (website, telephone, e-mail, hotel counter, etc.). Following the investigations of the French Competition Authority, Booking.com made several commitments in 2015, in particular, to remove any obligation to offer the same price on the different OTAs: Hotels can now offer to other online booking platforms lower rates than those posted on Booking.com.

SECTION 6 THE CASE OF TECHNOLOGICAL AGREEMENTS

After having studied vertical agreements in the distribution sector, we'll turn our attention to technological agreements, which also receive a balanced treatment by competition authorities. Indeed, the launch of new products or production processes generally has a positive impact on welfare by enabling the cutting of costs and price and the improvement of product quality. However, the launch of innovations faces many obstacles, in particular, the lack of incentives for firms to invest in Research and Development (R&D), given the specificities of the innovative activity.

In order to remedy this market failure, one solution, in addition to strengthening intellectual property rights, is to authorize under certain conditions R&D cooperation between firms. We will see that R&D agreements are common practice in high-tech industries: For example, in June 2019, Airbus and Comat signed a 10-year R&D partnership to jointly develop mechanisms for satellites (§1).

Regarding R&D agreements, competition authorities adopt a liberal approach based on a rule of reason: They balance the efficiency gains of such agreements with their negative impacts on competition, particularly when agreements concern competing technologies (§2). A firm's incentive to innovate also depends on the opportunities to spread its innovation: The anticipation of a licensing agreement or a patent pool can encourage a firm to invest in R&D (§3). Once again, competition authorities consider technology transfer agreements favorably, even if certain risks must be prevented, particularly in terms of collusion. In this respect, competition authorities differentiate between license transfers of complementary technologies, which lead to efficiency gains, and license transfers of substitutable technologies, which present greater risks for competition. Finally, in the case of a standardization process, competition authorities welcome patent pools when they concern "*essential*" technologies (§4).

§1 Incentive to Innovate, and R&D Agreements

Technological innovation is the result of an investment in research and development (R&D), with the aim of discovering or improving a new product or process. This activity has several specific characteristics, which may lead to an underinvestment in R&D compared to the best situation for the society as a whole ("*social optimum*"). R&D agreements, including those between competing firms, can remedy this lack of incentive: They're most often guided by economic efficiencies (Table 4.11). We will review below the main arguments in favor of an R&D cooperation between competing firms.

Table 4.11 What Motivates Firms to Enter R&D Agreements?

The Motives Behind an R&D Agreement	*Explanation*
Pooling of complementary skills (increase efficiencies)	Each firm controls only a part of the innovation process and must have access to the skills of other firms.
Sharing the risk of innovation (increase efficiencies)	Given the risk of failure, firms may diversify their R&D portfolio by cooperating with other firms.
Sharing of R&D costs (increase efficiencies)	The R&D investment can be high and undivided, which encourages firms to share costs. R&D cost sharing avoids also the risk of duplication when firms explore the same research avenues.
Internalizing the technological externality (increase efficiencies)	Firms do not want to search alone, fearing they will then be copied by their competitors.

The Motives Behind an R&D Agreement	*Explanation*
Collusion in R&D (increase efficiencies)	The patent race can lead to an excessive R&D effort (compared to the social optimum). Competitors coordinate their efforts in order to slow down the pace of innovation.

Pooling complementarity skills: The launch of a new product or the development of a new process may require the combination of different R&D skills. Developing these missing skills internally takes time. Similarly, buying other firms to access new skills can be very expensive. The third option available to firms is to cooperate with others to pool complementary R&D resources, i.e., use R&D agreements.

Sharing the risk of innovation: Investing in R&D, compared to other types of investments, is risky, because the research effort may not lead to usable results. For example, in the pharmaceutical sector, the launch of a new drug is a long process, with a high attrition rate at each stage: Out of 10,000 molecules analyzed in the first exploratory step, only 100 are selected for preclinical tests and only 10 drugs will pass all the three stages of clinical tests (called "phase I, II, III"). Among these 10 drugs, only one will be launched on the market. In addition, unsuccessful R&D investments are often sunk costs: It is unlikely that an investment in a particular therapeutic area can be "re-used" for other therapies. An investment in R&D is different from an investment in a physical asset, which has a residual resale value: For example, an airline that invests in an aircraft can always resell it on the second-hand market.

From this perspective, R&D cooperation allows firms to diversify their investments over several projects and thus reduce risk. Let's take a firm that has a total budget of $1 billion to carry out R&D. If it invests this amount in a single R&D project, it risks losing everything if the research project does not succeed. On the other hand, the firm can choose to mitigate risks and invest $200 million with other firms on five different projects, making up a total amount of $1 billion. Thus, R&D agreements are an efficient way of mitigating risk.

Sharing research costs: Innovating often requires a high *"entry ticket."* For example, the development of a new drug in the pharmaceutical industry requires an investment of $800 million to $1 billion over a period of 10-12 years. This investment is not divisible, i.e., it does not vary with respect to volume. It is similar to a fixed cost, with a minimum sum that must be invested.

For example, if the discovery of a new drug requires an investment of $1 billion, spending $100 million does not mean that the firm will find one-tenth of the new therapy. An R&D agreement between competitors then increases the probability of discovering something new. Suppose that two firms have $500 million each; the research project requires a ticket of $1 billion. If each firm invests separately, the probability of discovery is equal to zero; conversely, by pooling their two R&D budgets, firms can ensure that the minimum threshold is reached and that they have a good chance of succeeding.

Furthermore, if two or more firms are following the same lines of research, they will have duplicated their efforts if, in the end, they all make the same discovery. Cost sharing through R&D agreements avoids the risk of making redundant investments.

Appropriating the returns from innovation*:* The innovative activity can be assimilated to the discovery of information (Arrow, 1962): A piece of information is a "*non-excludable public good.*" This means that once found, it is difficult for its inventor to claim the innovation as being his or hers, and competitors can benefit from it "*free of charge.*"

The innovation creates a "*positive externality,*" i.e., there is a benefit that spills over from the innovator to the imitators. For instance, a firm that discovers a new molecule in the pharmaceutical sector can easily be imitated because a new molecule is a chemical formula. This externality goes through multiple channels, as highlighted in the empirical study of Levin et al. (1987):

- technical publications within a legal framework (an article in a scientific review for instance) or industrial spying;
- conversations with the employees of the innovative firm;
- an inter-firm mobility of staff, through the recruitment of engineers from the innovative firm (which can justify non-competition clauses in labor contracts);
- reverse engineering: The copier dismantles the innovative product and then reproduces it.

The consequence of a positive externality is a lack of incentive to innovate: Fearing imitation, firms will underinvest in R&D compared to the social optimum. In such a context, allowing competing firms to cooperate in R&D can restore this incentive.

The incentive role of an R&D agreement can be analyzed with a Cournot's duopoly model (Jacquemin & d'Aspremont, 1988). The competition process is carried out in two stages. In the first stage, Firms 1 and 2 determine their R&D investments, and then, in a second stage, they set their production (Figure 4.17). In the first step, each firm can invest in R&D in order to reduce its production cost (it is therefore a process innovation) by making an effort x. We assume that each firm benefits in part from the R&D effort of its competitor:

$$C_i\ (q_i, x_i, x_j) = (A - x_i - \beta x_j)q_i \qquad (1)$$

with: $0 < \beta < 1$; $A > (x_i - \beta x_j)$

We note that the production cost of a Firm i (i = 1.2) depends not only on its own production q_i and its own research and development effort $x_{i,}$ but also on the R&D effort x_j of its competitor j.

The coefficient β (with $0 < \beta < 1$) measures the magnitude of this R&D externality: When β is close to 1, the effort of Firm j strongly benefits Firm i; conversely, when β is close to 0, Firm j completely appropriates its R&D effort.

The cost of R&D investment is represented by a quadratic function (which means that R&D returns are decreasing):

$$\gamma x_i^2/2$$

At the second stage of the game, the demand function is linear:

$P = (a - bQ)$ with: $Q = q_1 + q_2$, $a, b > 0$; $p > A > 0$; $Q < a/b$

Figure 4.17 The Jacquemin and d'Aspremont Model

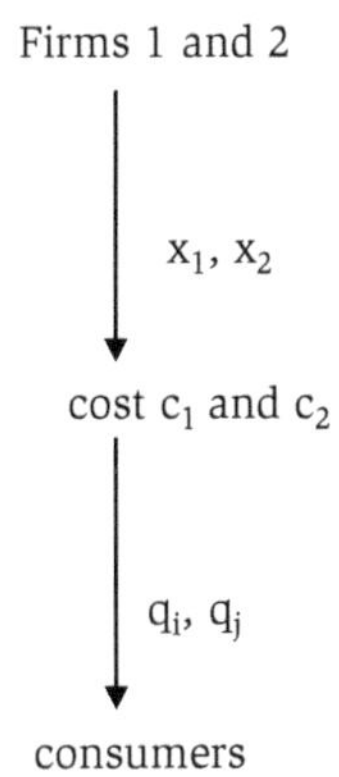

Different market configurations can be compared:

- full competition: The two firms compete at both stages of the game;
- upstream "*semi-collusion*": The two firms cooperate in R&D but compete downstream;
- full collusion: The two firms cooperate in R&D and set the downstream production together. This is a situation of integrated monopoly;
- social planner: The social planner is a decision maker who aims at maximizing collective welfare. This case allows us to compare the three first solutions with the one that would be socially optimal.

When the level of externality is high (formally, when $\beta > 0.5$), the ranking of R&D efforts is as follows:

$$x^W > x^{***} > x^{**} > x^{*} \qquad (2)$$

with:
x^w, the R&D effort of a social planner.
x^*, the R&D effort of each firm when firms compete at both stages.
x^{**}, the R&D effort of each firm in a semi-collusion situation.
x^{***}, the R&D effort of each firm in a situation of full collusion.

The inequality (2) means that partial or total cooperation results in a higher level of R&D compared to a competitive situation, when the technological externality is high. This result is not surprising: In a competitive situation with a high level of externality, firms underinvest in R&D because their effort benefits competitors. Cooperation allows firms to internalize the externality and therefore leads to an increase in R&D investments.

Second, the R&D effort appears to be higher in a situation of full collusion compared to a situation of semi-collusion. Indeed, when firms collude downstream, they capture a larger share of the R&D effort through a monopoly profit, which leads to an increase in their R&D effort.

Finally, we note that an R&D cooperation allows firms to get closer to the social optimum, even if the R&D effort in a cooperative situation remains lower.

If we compare the levels of downstream production, we obtain the following result:

$$Q^W > Q^{**} > Q^{*} > Q^{***} \quad (3)$$

with:
Q^W, the production of a planner (which maximizes the welfare).
Q^*, the production when firms compete at both stages.
Q^{**}, the production in a semi-collusion situation.
Q^{***}, the total production in a situation of full collusion.

First, we observe that semi-collusion always implies a higher level of production than with full collusion: In a situation of full collusion, the increase in R&D effort (and the resulting reduction in production costs) is not sufficient to compensate for the "*Malthusian*" behavior of a monopoly. Second, the quantity produced in a situation of semi-collusion is lower than the quantity offered by a social planner, but higher than the quantity offered when firms compete at both stages.

Moreover, while semi-collusion (i.e., an R&D cooperation) can remedy this lack of incentives, it does not mean that it is the only public tool to stimulate innovation: Public authorities could also strengthen intellectual property rights (patent, trademark, design) by guaranteeing innovators an effective exclusivity on the commercial uses of their innovations.

Avoiding overinvesting in R&D: The main lesson of the above model is that, in the presence of high R&D externalities, R&D cooperation increases the level of R&D effort and the quantities produced. However, this result supposes that technological externalities are sufficiently high. Otherwise, firms will invest heavily in R&D in order to stay ahead of their competitors. Thus, in a technological race situation where several firms compete to win a "*trophy*" (in the form of a patent for example), the technological externality effect can be offset by a competitive externality effect if the trophy is unique and excludes the followers: Each firm, fearing elimination from the market, overinvests in R&D, which can even lead to an overall R&D effort higher than the social optimum (Reinganum, 1989). In such a situation, an R&D agreement would lead to a reduction in R&D effort.

Why do firms cooperate in R&D? An empirical study: Why would a firm want to share its R&D investment with competitors? Based on a sample of 798 R&D joint ventures, Hernan et al. (2003) tried to answer this question by analyzing the key determining factors that push firms to participate in Research Joint Ventures (RJVs).

Their econometric approach (probit test) required a control group, composed of a sample of 53,812 firms that had not formed an RJV.

The authors showed that the probability of forming an RJV depends on multiple factors, including:

- the R&D intensity of the industry (measured by the ratio of R&D expenditure to total sales): A positive and significant relationship was observed. An RJV enables firms to share their R&D costs among themselves;
- the magnitude of technological externalities: A first proxy variable is the speed at which competitors in the same industry copy an innovation. If the time needed to copy the innovation is long, firms can reap the benefits of their R&D efforts before they are copied: The incentive to form an RJV is therefore reduced in this case. The authors obtained a negative and significant relationship between the time needed to copy an innovation and the probability of forming an RJV. A second proxy variable is the degree of protection granted by a patent in an industry, as measured by Levin et al. (1987): If the patent is effective against imitations, the incentive to form an RJV is limited. The authors observed an inverse and significant relationship between the degree of the innovation's protection and the probability to form an RJV.

§2 Antitrust Policy and R&D Agreements

The European case: At the European level, while the first two paragraphs of Article 101 TFEU forbid anti-competitive agreements, the paragraph 3 allows to exempt an agreement if it contributes "to promoting technical or economic progress."

Until 2004, to be able to benefit from an exemption, the European Commission had to be notified of R&D agreements; but this procedure was replaced by a "*legal exception*" system: Since Regulation 1/2003, firms have had to themselves assess the lawfulness of their R&D agreements under Article 101 TFEU. The Regulation 121/2010 and the Guidelines on Horizontal Cooperation Agreements (2011) provide useful guides for assessing the compliance of R&D agreements with antitrust law. Broadly speaking, three cases can be distinguished.

First, if an R&D agreement is concluded between firms that are not direct competitors for existing products or technologies, it benefits a priori from the block exemption, whatever the market shares of the undertakings. In particular, the Guidelines on Horizontal Cooperation Agreements state that an R&D agreement concluded at a "fairly early stage, very far from the exploitation of possible results" is unlikely to infringe on Article 101 TFEU;

Second, if firms cooperate in R&D but compete in the market for existing products and technologies, or in the innovation market, it is necessary to assess their market shares. If the undertakings combined market share does not exceed 25%, the R&D agreement is automatically exempted from Article 101 TFEU, because it does not significantly affect competition. If the undertakings market share exceeds 25%, the R&D agreement cannot benefit from an automatic exemption, and must be assessed individually. In this case, the undertakings must ensure themselves that their agreement does not adversely affect competition. If so, they must prove that the gains from the R&D cooperation offset the detrimental consequences on competition, with four cumulative conditions:

- the R&D agreement will foster innovation;
- the R&D agreement is necessary to the technical or economic progress: Undertakings must demonstrate that no less restrictive alternatives exist;
- the economic benefits resulting from the R&D agreement must be shared with consumers, in the form of lower prices, shorter innovation times or improved product quality;
- the R&D agreement must not have the effect of eliminating all competition on the market.

Third, irrespective of the market share, an R&D agreement cannot benefit from an automatic exemption if it contains a hardcore restriction. For example, an R&D agreement that restricts the freedom to pursue R&D activities independently in areas other than that covered by the agreement cannot be exempted. The same logic applies to an R&D agreement that would limit the production as a result of the R&D cooperation, or that would lead to prices being set jointly.

The example of the Engine Alliance: In order to illustrate the European Commission's approach to R&D agreements, it is interesting to review its implementation before the Regulation 1/2003: Before 2004, for firms to benefit from an exemption, the European Commission had to be notified of firms' R&D agreements and then issue formal decisions.

Thus, in 1996, two of the three aircraft engine manufacturers decided to cooperate in R&D by creating Engine Alliance, a joint venture (JV) owned by General Electric Aircraft Engines (GEAE) and Pratt & Whitney (P&W). The purpose of this JV was to design, produce and sell a new engine (GP 7000) for large commercial aircrafts, such as the Airbus A380. In the market for wide-body engines, none of the three operators (Rolls-Royce, GEAE and P&W) offered such an engine. GEAE and P&W notified the Commission of their agreement.

In a first step, the European Commission delimited the relevant market: It found that the relevant market included all engines that can power an Airbus A380. Engines already in use in existing aircrafts were not considered as substitutable for this new engine. However, the European Commission found that in the long term, the new engine could be adapted to equip other wide-body aircraft engines already in service: The market for wide-body aircraft engines is therefore a neighboring market to the market for engines developed for the A380. With regard to the relevant geographic market, the European Commission considered a worldwide market.

After delimiting the relevant market, the European Commission assessed the market shares of the firms. As the market for A380 reactors did not yet exist, it was impossible to give market share estimates: The European Commission therefore relied on data on the market of reactors for large aircrafts already in service. During the period spanning 1996-1999, the market shares were as follows:

- GEAE: 34%.
- P&W: 29%.
- CFMI (JV between GEAE and Snecma): 20%.
- Rolls-Royce: 16%.

Thus, it appears that GEAE and P&W had a very high combined market share of 63%. The European Commission then examined the supply and demand conditions on the future market for large aircraft reactors:

- on the demand side, potential customers were Boeing and Airbus, which offered an "aircraft plus engines" bundle to airlines. Airlines had strong bargaining power vis-à-vis aircraft and engine manufacturers;
- on the supply side, there were high entry barriers, due to high R&D costs. Only three firms could offer this type of engine (P&W, GEAE and Rolls-Royce) and no new entrant was expected in the near future. Consequently, the European Commission found that "the creation and operation of the Engine Alliance appreciably restricts competition for the new engine by reducing the choice of suppliers from three potential suppliers to two" (free translation).

However, the European Commission granted an exemption to Engine Alliance, considering that the JV fulfilled the four conditions of Article 81(3) (now 101 TFEU):

- The R&D agreement makes a clear contribution to technical progress by putting on the market a new engine *"cheaper in terms of maintenance costs and cost per passenger and per kilometer traveled, and producing fewer exhaust and noise emissions than engines already developed by the undertakings. No in-use engine fulfills these criteria"* (free translation).
- The R&D agreement is beneficial to consumers: The new engine will lower operating costs for airlines, which should benefit passengers (by price reductions) because competition between airlines is strong.
- Engine Alliance enables the new engine to be developed more quickly and will therefore increase competition. Indeed, if the three firms have the capabilities to build a new engine, only Rolls-Royce can quickly offer an engine derived from one of its existing models (the Trend 600). In the absence of Engine Alliance, Rolls-Royce would have a monopoly position: As the European Commission points out, "cooperation is therefore necessary in order to have a competing engine on the market earlier than would otherwise be possible" (free translation). Airbus was itself in favor of Engine Alliance, because it will have the choice between two engine suppliers for its A380.
- The R&D agreement does not eliminate any competition: Rolls-Royce will also offer its new engine (the Trent 900) for the A380.

However, the exemption was subject to conditions and obligations. In particular, the Engine Alliance's activity has to be limited to the development, marketing and maintenance of the new engine for transport aircraft with more than 450 passengers. Indeed, "if the joint venture were also allowed to market and sell the engines developed by the parties, this could result in a restriction of competition between the parties with respect to their existing engine programs" (free translation).

The U.S. registration system: In the United States, R&D agreements fall under Section 1 of the Sherman Act. Two cases can be distinguished:

- the R&D agreement is, in fact, a practice designed to jointly set quantities, prices or market allocations. In this case, the agreement is subject to a per se prohibition, in the same way as a cartel;
- the R&D agreement restricts competition but provides efficiency gains: The U.S. antitrust authorities then apply a rule of reason by checking that the efficiency gains offset the negative impact on competition. The Antitrust Guidelines for Collaborations Among Competitors (2000) stresses in particular that R&D agreements between competitors can lead to a slower pace of innovation. The anti-competitive risk of an R&D agreement can be assessed not only in the market for existing products and technologies but also in the "*innovation market*." In the latter case, the U.S. Guidelines consider that if at least three independent R&D projects compete with the R&D agreement, the latter is not likely to affect substantially competition in the innovation market.

In parallel with Section 1 of the Sherman Act, the United States established an administrative procedure to facilitate R&D cooperation by adopting the National Cooperative Research Act (NCRA) in 1984. The NCRA was replaced in 1993 by the National Cooperative Research and Production Act (NCRPA). This initiative was taken in a particular context, marked by the rise of Japan as a technological leader, particularly in electronic products. The U.S. government identified that the strong propensity of Japanese firms to cooperate in R&D was one of the key factors explaining Japan's success.

The NCRA established a procedure for registering R&D agreements: Firms had to declare their R&D project to the U.S. DOJ. In return for this registration, firms were assured, if their agreement was challenged by a third party, their project would be evaluated under a rule of reason and not with a per se approach. Following the adoption of the NCRA, the number of projects registered grew steadily until 1995 and then declined somewhat: Over the period spanning 1985-1998, 741 RJVs were registered at the U.S. DOJ.

Compared to the NCRA, which focuses on joint R&D activities, the NCRPA allows members of an RJV to extend their cooperation beyond the R&D phase and to jointly exploit the results of their research, under certain conditions.

§3 The Spreading of Innovation and Licensing Agreements

The anatomy of a licensing agreement: Technological agreements do not only aim to jointly develop new products or production processes. They also consist of transferring patented technologies through a licensing agreement: The patent holder (referred to as the "*licensor*") grants the right to use its innovation to another firm (referred to as the "*licensee*") in exchange for the payment of royalties.

Licensing transfers are a frequent practice: On the basis of a sample of different types of agreements between firms (JVs, R&D agreements, licenses, marketing agreements, production agreements) during the period spanning 1990-1993 in the United States, Anand and Khanna (2000) estimate that licensing agreements represented on average 26% of the total sample, and this figure even exceeds 38% in the chemical industry. In the case of large firms, licensing revenues can reach significant amounts; for example, Qualcomm received in 2018 more than $6 billion annually from its mobile communications technology licenses.

A licensing agreement may cover the development of a technology or the production/ distribution of a product protected by a patent. The licensor may give an exclusive license or use a multiple license system. The licensing agreement includes a transfer of know-how from the licensor to the licensee, and, in return, confidentiality obligations by the licensee. For example, grant back clauses require that the licensee informs the licensor of any improvements it has made on the patented technology. More generally, licensing agreements include restrictive clauses (temporal, geographical, product related), which limit the licensee's use of the technology.

Licensing fees take the form of a two-part tariff, composed of a fixed part A and a variable part (at rate r), which depends on the licensee's level of production:

$$\text{Licensing fees} = A + (r \times Q).$$

It is common to distinguish between a unilateral license, whereby Firm A transfers the use of its technology to Firm B, and cross licensing: In the latter case, Firms A and B exchange with each other their technologies. A cross-licensing agreement may sometimes also include the payment of royalties.

In some cases, firms share their patents in a "*patent pool*": Each member obtains a single license on all shared technologies in exchange for the payment of a common fee. Thus, in the case of the MPEG2 video compression standard, a pool of more than 730 patents, belonging to 25 firms, has been set up. Patent pooling can be done through a dedicated entity, such as a JV owned by all pool members.

Licensing agreements and economic efficiencies*:* A licensing agreement is generally motivated by economic efficiencies (Table 4.12).

First, licensing agreements can have a positive effect on the incentive to innovate: The anticipation of an innovation transfer to a third party may encourage small firms to invest in R&D. This is particularly true for firms specialized in R&D, such as pharmaceutical start-ups: If they discover a new molecule, they will grant a unilateral license to a major lab for the development and the distribution of the drug.

Second, a unilateral license allows a firm to have access to an efficient technology. Let us consider two Firms 1 and 2, competing in a Cournot's duopoly. Firm 1 holds a process patent on a non-drastic innovation; its marginal cost is therefore lower:

$$0 < c_1 < c_2$$

Without a licensing agreement, Firm 1 makes a higher profit than its competitor Firm 2. If Firm 1 transfers a license to Firm 2 in exchange for the payment of a royalty

Φ on each product sold ("*per unit fee*"), it will set a royalty equal to the cost reduction achieved by Firm 2, i.e.:

$$\Phi = (c_2 - c_1) - \varepsilon$$

As a result, the production cost of Firm 2 and its profit are the same as before. Similarly, the consumer surplus stays unchanged. On the other hand, the profit of Firm 1 has increased since it now includes a license fee:

$$\pi_1 = \pi_1^{cour} + \Phi\, q_2^{cour}$$

Cross-licensing and patent pools can also be guided by economic efficiency:

- they avoid disputes over intellectual property rights, particularly in sectors where technological change is rapid and complex: "In these sectors, for example in the semiconductor industry, the inventor is not sure to maintain his or her R&D lead. Others are in positions to make improvements to the innovation. On the other hand, it is difficult for the inventor to foresee future infringements of property rights. Some are related to innovations that have not been developed, others concern patents that have not yet been examined. By agreeing to cross-license future technology and improvements not yet patented, innovators protect themselves against the risk of not being able to exploit their inventions and being sued in court" (free translation) (Leveque & Meniere, 2003);
- if the validity of a patent is challenged, firms may decide to settle their dispute through a cross-licensing agreement, rather than engaging in a long and costly litigation. This practice is common in industries where patents provide little protection against imitation: According to Anand and Khanna (2000), this explains the high proportion of cross-licensing agreements in the electronics industry (20% of total licenses in this sector) compared to the chemical industry (10% of total licenses);
- patent poolings or technology exchanges avoid the mutual payment of royalties, which would increase production costs. In particular, when firms offer complementary technologies, each sets a high price, since it has a monopoly on its own product. This situation of multiple margins leads to a "*royalty stacking*" situation that is collectively suboptimal: If everyone has to pay licenses to other firms, the production cost will increase, thereby reducing demand. The decline in demand will affect not only final customers but also producers. A solution would be to merge, which is unlikely when there are a large number of firms on the market. A patent pool allows firms to overcome the multiple margins problem;
- through a "*one-stop shop*" process, a patent pool limits the negotiation costs of licensing agreements, especially when the launch of a new product requires multiple patents from different firms to be combined. This situation, known as

the "*patent thicket*," is found in industries such as semiconductors or smartphones;
- license exchanges or pools are used to overcome blocking patent situations: Each firm owns only a part of the technology necessary to produce the final good; it must access the technology of another firm to produce the entire product. Without a license transfer, no firm can launch the product on the market;
- patent pools can promote the development of a technological standard between competitors by pooling technologies. For example, the MPEG1 (Motion Picture Expert Group) is the result of the pooling of 27 patents from eight firms. Some patents are now recognized as "*Standard Essential Patents*," (SEPs) particularly when they encourage a process of standardization.

Table 4.12 Efficiencies from Licensing Agreements and Patent Pools

Type of Efficiencies	*Explanation*
Incentive to innovate (unilateral license)	The anticipation of a licensing agreement encourages specialized or small firms to invest in R&D.
Access to an efficient technology (unilateral license)	A licensing agreement allows firms to access a more-efficient technologies.
Intellectual Property Dispute Resolution (cross licensing)	A cross-licensing agreement can close an intellectual property litigation that could be long and costly.
Limitation of transaction costs (cross licensing)	A cross-licensing agreement avoids negotiation costs on the royalties.
Elimination of double margins (cross licensing)	A cross-licensing agreement prevents each firm from charging its partner a license fee; this "*royalty stacking*" would lead to a price increase of the final product.
Access to a blocking patent (unilateral or cross licensing)	A licensing agreement provides access to an otherwise unobtainable technology needed to produce a final good.
Development of a technological standard (cross licensing)	A cross-licensing agreement allows each member to access common resources in order to develop a standard.

Licensing agreements and collusion: While generally motivated by economic efficiency, licensing agreements can also restrict competition, in particular by promoting collusion. For instance, the first patents pools in the aircraft industry (1917) and sewing machine production industry (1856) were formed to set prices: They were similar to a cartel. This risk of collusion is particularly strong if the pooled technologies are substitutable.

First, a cross-licensing agreement may allow a collusive equilibrium to be achieved. Suppose that two Firms 1 and 2 each have a technology complementary to the other: The production of X requires a combination of the two technologies. Firms 1 and 2 will therefore grant each other a license and compete on the product X. Without license fees, Firms 1 and 2 are in a Cournot's duopoly situation. They may decide to give a license to each other, setting a variable royalty rate high enough to achieve a monopoly profit.

Second, a unilateral license can promote the stability of a collusive agreement, when firms have different production costs. Suppose, for example, that Firms 1 and 2 are competing in a Bertrand's duopoly on an infinite horizon. Firm 1 has a lower marginal cost than its competitor Firm 2: $c_1 < c_2$. In a competitive situation, the price will therefore be equal to c_2. If the two firms decide to form a cartel, the collusion is likely to be unstable because the threats of punishment are asymmetrical: Indeed, if Firm 1 cheats, Firm 2 can punish it by charging a price equal to its marginal cost c_2. In this case, Firm 1 will still make a positive profit. On the other hand, if Firm 2 cheats, Firm 1 can punish it by returning to the competitive price $P = c_2$. Firm 2 will then have a zero profit. Firm 1 has a high incentive to cheat as the difference in production costs increases. In order to stabilize the collusion, Firm 1 can grant a license to Firm 2, which then can produce at c_1: The punishment, in case of cheating, becomes more severe and symmetrical, which discourages Firm 1 from cheating. Paradoxically, by granting a license, Firm 1 gives its competitor a "*stick to be beaten with*," which stabilizes the collusion.

Third, a licensing agreement may be granted to a competitor if it renounces the right to launch its own product. This type of license has been observed in the pharmaceutical sector in the United States and Europe (also *see* Chapter 3): Faced with the expiry of their patents, some firms have "*paid for delaying*" the entry of generics. This mechanism can be explained through a simple example: A monopoly A makes a profit of $50 per period; in case of entry of Firm B, the market structure will become a Cournot duopoly—the total profits will decrease to $30. Therefore, Firm A is willing to pay between $15 and $35 to Firm B in order to avoid its entry. For example, if Firm A offers Firm B payment of $20, this agreement is mutually advantageous: Firm B obtains a higher profit than the profit obtained if it enters the market ($15). Whereas Firm A, keeps a profit of $50 – $20 (or $30), which is higher than the profit obtained if Firm B enters the market. This type of agreement can take the form of a license transfer from Firm A to Firm B; in exchange, Firm B delays the launch of its own product. This pay-for-delay practice has given rise to several antitrust cases in the pharmaceutical sector. In 2014, for example, the European Commission fined Servier (also for an abuse of a dominant position) and five generic manufacturers €427 million for delaying the launch of a cheaper version of a cardiovascular drug in exchange for payments and license transfers.

Finally, a cross-licensing agreement can sometimes support a cartel: Cartel members exchange licenses in order to increase the stability of collusion. Indeed, as long as no members cheat, each participant uses its own technology, even though it has access to the technology of its competitors: The competitors' licenses are therefore not used and are "*sleeping licenses.*" On the other hand, if a member cheats, the other cartel participants can retaliate by using the license of the deviating firm. A cross-licensing agreement is like a "*stick*" that cartel members give each other in order to prevent (and punish) any attempt to cheat.

§4 Antitrust and Licensing Agreements

With regard to licensing agreements, competition authorities adopt a pragmatic approach, balancing the economic benefits of these agreements with their potential anti-competitive impact. We will successively analyze the American and the European cases.

The American case: In the United States, the antitrust view on licensing agreements has evolved over time.

In the Bement (1902) and General Electric (1926) cases, the U.S. Supreme Court held that a licensor with a monopoly on a technology could introduce restrictive clauses such as an RPM or a sales quota; in support of its decision, the Supreme Court argued that General Electric could achieve a similar result by setting a variable license fee equal to the monopoly margin.

A first shift occurred from the 1970s onwards: The antitrust "*goodwill*" has given way to a more formal approach that focuses on unlawful clauses in licensing agreements. These include restrictions on the licensee's commercial activity (when this activity concerns products other than the patented product), tying sales, the licensee's obligation to grant back future improvements to the licensor, and the setting of a minimum resale price or sales quotas. For example, in 1994, the U.S. antitrust authorities challenged the "*per processor*" licensing agreement between Microsoft and computer manufacturers. This contract provided for a fixed fee on each computer produced, whatever the operating system installed by the manufacturer. In the late 1980s, Nintendo was also under an antitrust investigation, due to the exclusivity clauses it imposed on licensed game programmers.

A second shift occurred starting in the 1990s, leading antitrust authorities to move away from an exclusive focus on restrictive clauses to a global analysis of the licensing agreement impact. For example, the Antitrust Guidelines for Licensing of Intellectual Property (2017) emphasize that licensing agreements must be evaluated under a rule of reason by balancing competitive impact and efficiency gains. Licensing agreements are considered to be lawful if the undertakings have a market share of less than 20% and if they are not manifestly anti-competitive by their terms.

Regarding patent pools, the U.S. authorities also adopt a balanced approach. When they only concern "*essential*" or complementary patents, patent pools are viewed favorably, because they can generate efficiency gains. In particular, complementary patent pools can promote a technological standard. Antitrust authorities check that the conditions of access to the pool for members and third parties are determined in a fair, reasonable and non-discriminatory way; we talk about "FRAND" ("Fair,

Reasonable, and Non-Discriminatory") licenses. Thus, in 2008, the RFID (Radio Frequency Identification) consortium obtained the green light from the U.S. authorities, because it concerned essential and complementary patents in the field of RFID tags.

On the other hand, when patent pools mainly concern substitutable technologies, they raise the vigilance of antitrust authorities, particularly with regard to collusive risks. Thus, at the beginning of the 20th century, in the National Harrow case (1902), antitrust authorities condemned harrow producers, who'd formed a holding company called National Harrow, to which they pooled their competing patents. Each producer could use the patented technology of its competitors by applying for a license from the holding. In practice, each producer only used its own technology: The licenses acted as "*sleeping licenses*," allowing, in cases of cheating, to severely punish the deviant firm by selling its technology.

Another example of collusion through a patent pool can be found in the Hartford Empire case (1944). During the 1930s, Hartford, a firm that produces glass containers, formed a cartel with its competitors and a pool of more than 600 patents. The creation of the pool was a credible means to deter any deviating behavior inside the cartel.

More recently, in 1998, the FTC accused Summit Technology and VISX of pooling their patents in order to reduce competition. Both firms are active in the market for laser eye surgery devices and have been in conflict over intellectual property rights. In order to settle their dispute, Summit and VISX decided in 1992 to transfer their patents to a pool called Pillar Point Partners (PPP): This pool therefore included both substitutable and non-complementary technologies. The PPP pool charged a license fee of $250 each time a laser-equipped machine was used by an ophthalmologist. The royalties were then allocated between the two firms according to a predetermined formula. According to the FTC, "the effect of this per-procedure fee was that neither firm had an incentive to charge doctors less than $250 per procedure. The other effect of the pool was that the firms no longer had any incentive or ability to compete in the licensing of PRK technology—neither firm could license its own technology without the approval of the other."

The exemption system in Europe: As with R&D agreements, licensing agreements in Europe fall under Article 101 TFEU and its paragraph 3, which grants the benefit of a conditional exemption to agreements that "contribute to improving [...] technical or economic progress." The Guidelines on Technology Transfer Agreements (2014) recall that these agreements are treated rather favorably: "Most license agreements do not restrict competition and create pro-competitive efficiencies. Indeed, licensing as such is pro-competitive as it leads to the dissemination of technology and promotes innovation by the licensor and licensee(s). In addition, even license agreements that do restrict competition may often give rise to pro-competitive efficiencies, which must be considered under Article 101(3) and balanced against the negative effects on competition. The great majority of license agreements are therefore compatible with Article 101."

Until 2004, in order to benefit from an exemption, licensing agreements had to be notified to the European Commission, but this procedure gave way to a "*legal exception*" system: Since Regulation 1/2003, firms have had to themselves assess the lawfulness of their licensing agreements.

In 2014, the European Commission adopted the Block Exemption Regulation 316/2014, which sets out the conditions for an automatic exemption of a technology transfer agreement. This Regulation is accompanied by the Guidelines on Technology Transfer Agreements, published in the same year. Broadly speaking, two situations can be distinguished:

- the licensing agreement is automatically exempted from Article 101 TFEU if the combined market share of undertakings does not exceed a 20% threshold and if the agreement does not contain any hardcore restriction. When firms are not competitors, the agreement is exempted if the market share of each undertaking does not exceed 30%;
- in other cases, a licensing agreement may benefit from an "*individual exemption,*" either because it has no anti-competitive impact, or because its impact on competition is offset by efficiencies, in particular in terms of innovation. Firms must therefore assess first whether their licensing agreement could, by its object or its effects, restrict competition. If the licensing agreement adversely affects competition, firms must prove that it is necessary and proportionate to achieve these efficiencies, that it does not lead to the elimination of competition on the market, and that it reserves for consumers a fair share of the efficiency gains.

If the licensing agreement contains hardcore restrictions, it cannot be exempted and must be examined individually, whatever the market shares of the undertakings. For instance, a license agreement must not restrict a party's ability to set a price to third parties or limit the licensee's "*passive sales.*" Similarly, a cross-licensing agreement cannot lead to a common setting of prices or to divide markets. In this respect, a cross-licensing agreement stipulating an unreasonably high level of royalties between the parties may be an indicator of collusion, as highlighted in the Guidelines on Technology Transfer Agreements: "When royalties are calculated on the basis of individual product sales, the amount of the royalty has a direct impact on the marginal cost of the product and thus a direct impact on product prices. Competitors can therefore use cross licensing with reciprocal running royalties as a means of coordinating and/or increasing prices on downstream product markets. However, the Commission will only treat cross licenses with reciprocal running royalties as price fixing where the agreement is devoid of any pro-competitive purpose and therefore does not constitute a bona fide licensing arrangement. In such cases where the agreement does not create any value and therefore has no valid business justification, the arrangement is a sham and amounts to a cartel" (paragraph 100).

Moreover, a licensing agreement must not restrict a party's ability to perform its own R&D or to launch its own products; it cannot require that improvements made to the licensed technology will be reserved exclusively to the patent holder ("*grant back*" clause).

Concerning patent pools, when technologies are complementary, the Commission considers that these agreements can limit transaction costs or avoid double margin problems. When technologies are considered as "*essential*," the European Commission verifies that the access to the pool is determined in a fair, reasonable and non-discriminatory way (FRAND licenses). When a patent pool concerns competing technologies, the European Commission pays particular attention to the risks of collusive behavior, as indicated in the Guidelines on Technology Transfer Agreements: "Technology pools may also be restrictive of competition. The creation of a technology pool necessarily implies joint selling of the pooled technologies, which in the case of pools composed solely or predominantly of substitute technologies amounts to a price fixing cartel. Moreover, in addition to reducing competition between the parties, technology pools may also, in particular when they support an industry standard or establish a de facto industry standard, result in a reduction of innovation by foreclosing alternative technologies. The existence of the standard and a related technology pool may make it more difficult for new and improved technologies to enter the market" (paragraph 246).

Review Topics:

Explain the transaction costs theory and its impact on the choice of vertical restraints.
Justify the European competition policy towards vertical restraints.
Should the practice of RPM be banned?
What is the impact of R&D agreements on the incentive to innovate?
How do competition authorities consider R&D agreements?
What are the reasons that justify a licensing agreement?
How do competition authorities analyze licensing agreements?

Recommended Readings:

Bharat Anand and Tarun Khanna, *The Structure of Licensing Contracts* (Journal of Industrial Economics 103-133, 2000).

Richard Gilbert and Carl Shapiro, *Antitrust Issues in the Licensing of Intellectual Property: The Nine No-No's Meet the Nineties* (BPEA Microeconomics 283-336, 1997).

OECD, *Vertical Restraints for Online Sales* (Paris 276, 2013).

CHAPTER 5

The Abuse of Dominant Position

In July 2019, the European Commission fined Qualcomm €242 million for abusing its dominant position in the market of mobile phone chips ("*baseband chipsets*"): Qualcomm sold its chips at below-costs price in order to exclude its main competitor, Icera, from the market. If competition can lead to inefficient firms exiting the market, the demise of a competitor raises a question: Was it a "natural" consequence of the intrinsic superiority of a dominant firm that was, for instance, more innovative? Or was it the result of a deliberate strategy to exclude an as-efficient competitor?

Antitrust authorities are in charge of deterring unilateral conduct that results from an "abuse of dominant position." This task is delicate because having a dominant position is not prohibited per se: Antitrust authorities should only condemn conduct when it is considered "*abusive.*" As the European Court of First Instance pointed out in the Michelin decision (2003): "Whilst the finding that a dominant position exists does not in itself imply any reproach to the undertaking concerned, it has a special responsibility, irrespective of the causes of that position, not to allow its conduct to impair genuine undistorted competition on the common market. Similarly, whilst the fact that an undertaking is in a dominant position cannot deprive it of its entitlement to protect its own commercial interests when they are attacked, and whilst such an undertaking must be allowed the right to take such reasonable steps as it deems appropriate to protect those interests, such behavior cannot be allowed if its purpose is to strengthen that dominant position and thereby abuse it."

The objective of competition policy is, therefore, not to protect particular competitors, even small ones, but to preserve the competitive process, which can sometimes lead to the exit of inefficient firms. As the ECJ pointed out in its Intel decision (2017): "Not every exclusionary effect is necessarily detrimental to competition," and, "competition on the merits may, by definition, lead to the departure from the market or the marginalization of competitors that are less efficient and so less attractive to consumers from the point of view of, among other things, price, choice, quality or innovation."

Moreover, a dominant firm may argue that, although dominant, it has the right to protect its own interests when attacked head on by its competitors; the question is to what extent its response goes beyond the defense of its legitimate interests and adversely affects both competition and consumers.

We will first review the current legal and institutional framework in the United States and Europe (Section 1). Then, we will analyze the different steps used by antitrust authorities to demonstrate an abuse of dominant position.

The first step is to delimit the relevant market and to assess the firm's dominant position (Section 2). The second step aims at characterizing the abuse (the "*theory of harm*") and its potential or actual effects on the market. We'll present the main forms of abuse, as observed by competition authorities: We'll differentiate exclusionary abuses from exploitative abuses (Section 3). We'll focus on a particular case of exclusionary abuse, called "*predatory pricing*," which has triggered long and heated debates among economists (Section 4).

Beyond these ex-post strategies, consisting of a firm marginalizing an existing competitor from the market, we will finish this chapter by studying "*deterrence strategies*": They consist of preventing the entry of a new competitor into the market, even if proving the existence of such a strategy remains a difficult task (Section 5).

SECTION 1 THE LEGAL AND INSTITUTIONAL FRAMEWORK

We present in this first section the legal and institutional framework in place in the United States and EU.

The American case: In the United States, Section 2 of the Sherman Act states: "Every person who shall monopolize, or attempt to monopolize, or combine or conspire with any other person or persons, to monopolize any part of the trade or commerce among the several States, or with foreign nations, shall be deemed guilty of a felony, and, on conviction thereof, shall be punished by fine not exceeding $10,000,000 if a corporation, or, if any other person, $350,000, or by imprisonment not exceeding three years, or by both said punishments, in the discretion of the court."

We can note that in addition to making market "*monopolization*" illegal, Section 2 also applies to any "*attempt to monopolize.*" However, the case law requires that the attempt should be characterized by a "*dangerous probability of success*" (Swift and Co case in 1905) in order to be prosecuted. Section 2 has been applied cyclically in the United States since 1890.

At the beginning of the 20th century, the U.S. DOJ initiated a first wave of actions against major firms such as Standard Oil, General Electric, DuPont, American Tobacco, International Harvester and U.S. Steel. Some of these investigations ended in radical decisions: For example, Standard Oil Company, accused of predatory pricing, was dismantled in 1911 and divided into 33 separate companies.

The antitrust activism declined after the 1920s, particularly following the 1920 United Steel decision: The case was dismissed due to insufficient proof of market monopolization. The New Deal (1933-1939) years were marked by a low antitrust activity until the beginning of World War II.

A second wave of proceedings based on Section 2 of the Sherman Act was initiated in the period spanning 1945-1970s: Following the 1945 Alcoa decision, a broad understanding of the notion of market monopolization was adopted. Major investigations were launched against large companies such as IBM, AT&T, Rank Xerox, Firestone, Goodyear and Kellogg's. These lawsuits led to the 1982 dismantling of AT&T into seven companies, called "*Baby Bell.*" On the other hand, after 13 years of investigation, the charges against IBM were dismissed, as was the case against Kellogg's (accused of "*product proliferation*").

After a lull in antitrust activities during the 1980s, the 1990s marked the beginning of a third wave of antitrust investigations: Companies such as Microsoft, Intel and Dentsply were prosecuted. In particular, Microsoft was accused of monopolizing the emerging internet browser market by preinstalling Internet Explorer on its Windows' operating systems, which was used by most personal computers at the time. The Microsoft case took a critical turn when Judge Thomas Penfield Jackson proposed in 2000 to dismantle Microsoft into two separate entities: one dedicated to the Windows operating system, and the other focused on applications software. The Microsoft case was closed in 2002 with a settlement with the U.S. DOJ: Microsoft was not dismantled but had to commit to giving third-party developers greater access to its Windows operating system.

Since the 2000s, few antitrust cases have been initiated under Section 2, even though U.S. activity has remained strong in the fight against cartels. However, there are a few cases involving patent abuse (such as the Rambus case) or practices aimed at limiting the entry of generic competitors into the pharmaceutical market. In June 2019, the U.S. FTC and the DOJ opened investigations against digital giants such as Google and Amazon.

The European case: In Europe, Article 102 TFEU condemns the abuse of dominant position and lists, in a non-exhaustive manner, certain prohibited practices: "Any abuse by one or more undertakings of a dominant position within the internal market or in a substantial part of it shall be prohibited as incompatible with the internal market in so far as it may affect trade between Member States.

Such abuse may, in particular, consist of:

(a) directly or indirectly imposing unfair purchase or selling prices or other unfair trading conditions;
(b) limiting production, markets or technical development to the prejudice of consumers;
(c) applying dissimilar conditions to equivalent transactions with other trading parties, thereby placing them at a competitive disadvantage;
(d) making the conclusion of contracts subject to acceptance by the other parties of supplementary obligations which, by their nature or according to commercial usage, have no connection with the subject of such contracts."

While Article 102 TFEU lists various types of abusive practices, it does not define the notion of "dominant position." It was in the Hoffmann-La Roche decision (1979) that the ECJ clarified the meaning of this concept, emphasizing the capability of a firm behaving independently: "The dominant position this referred to relates to a position of economic strength enjoyed by an undertaking which enables it to prevent effective competition being maintained on the relevant market by affording it the power to behave to an appreciable extent independently of its competitors, its customers and ultimately of the consumers."

It should be noted that the abuse of dominant position is an objective notion, without the need to prove an intent, as recalled by the ECJ in the Hoffmann-La Roche decision (1979): "The concept of abuse is an objective concept relating to the behavior of an undertaking in a dominant position which is such as to influence the structure of a market where, as a result of the very presence of the undertaking in question, the degree of competition is weakened and which, through recourses to methods different from those which condition normal competition in products or services on the basis of the transactions of commercial operators, has the effect of hindering the maintenance of the degree of competition still existing in the market or the growth of that competition."

In contrast with Article 101 TFEU, there is no explicit and two-step mechanism in Article 102 TFEU: An abusive behavior cannot be "*exempted*," after its anti-competitive effect has been proven. In reality, two arguments are open to the defendant in order to avoid being accused of behaving abusively:

- the defendant can prove that its behavior is "*objectively necessary*," for example, for reasons relating to safety or public health, as recalled in the Hilti decision of the ECJ (1991);
- the practice leads to efficiency gains. The defendant has to demonstrate that four conditions are cumulatively met: The efficiency gains do indeed result from the practice; there are no practices less damaging to competition to obtain these gains; the efficiency gains are sufficient to offset the harm done to consumers; they do not lead to the elimination of all competition on the market.

A major shift in the application of Article 102 TFEU occurred after the publication of the Commission's Communication on Exclusionary Practices (2009). This Communication calls for:

- a move from a formal approach—focusing on predefined categories of abuses—to a more concrete approach orientated towards the effects of the abuse. However, it is not necessary to demonstrate that the abuse of dominant position has had a concrete anti-competitive effect on the markets, but only that it tends to restrict competition or is likely to have such an effect (Tomra decision, ECJ, 2012);
- an "*as efficient competitor (AEC)*" test. It means that the competitor excluded from the market should be as efficient as the dominant undertaking. This test avoids protecting competitors that are not victims of an abuse but of their own

inefficiency. This approach has been used on several occasions by the ECJ, notably in the Post Denmark (2011) and TeliaSonera (2011) decisions.

The European Commission has dealt with many cases of abuse of a dominant position since the 1960s, including Hoffmann-La Roche (1979), Michelin (2003), British Airways/Virgin (1999), Microsoft (2004, 2013) and Intel (2009). Since 2015, there have been many cases in the field of the Digital Economy and New Technologies (Table 5.1). For instance, in June 2019, the Commission opened an investigation against Amazon.

Table 5.1 Examples of Abuse of Dominant Position (2017-2019) Sanctioned by the European Commission

Case	*Nature of the Abuse*	*Fine*
Google shopping (2017)	Google had abused its dominant position on the search engine market by giving an illegal advantage to its price comparison service.	€2.42 billion
Google Android (2018)	Google had imposed illegal restrictions on Android device manufacturers and mobile network operators in order to consolidate its dominant position on the internet search market.	€4.34 billion
Qualcomm (2018)	In the Long Term Evolution (LTE) baseband chipsets market, Qualcomm had prevented its competitors from expanding by paying a major customer in exchange for an exclusive supply contract.	€997 million
Qualcomm (2019)	On the 3G baseband chipsets market, Qualcomm sold its chips at below-cost prices in order to exclude its competitor Icera.	€242 million

Case	*Nature of the Abuse*	*Fine*
Google (2019)	Google had imposed a number of restrictive clauses in its contracts with third-party websites, preventing its competitors from setting their contextual ads on these websites.	€1.49 billion

SECTION 2 IDENTIFYING A DOMINANT POSITION

Before a behavior can be qualified as abusive, competition authorities must first demonstrate the existence of a dominant position: A behavior can only be qualified as abusive if the undertaking is able, by its conduct, to significantly affect competition. Therefore, competition authorities must start by delineating the relevant market (§1) and then assessing if a firm has a dominant position or not on this relevant market (§2).

§1 Delineating the Relevant Market[33]

Unlike merger control, the relevant market delineation is based on a retrospective and not a prospective approach. As Philippe (1998) points out, "it is a question of determining ex post all the products that have, during a given period of the past, constituted the market. We must reconstruct the past and imagine what it could have been without the possible abuse of dominant position" (free translation).

Opting for a broad or narrow delineation? The delineation of the relevant market is often controversial: The offending firm will usually declare a broad relevant market in order to "*dilute*" its market share, while competition authorities may adopt a more restrictive approach (Table 5.2). Thus, in the United States, in the Kodak case (1992), Kodak argued that the components of its photocopiers belonged to the wider market for photocopier components, regardless of the brand. However, the U.S. Supreme Court held that the relevant market was the market for components specific to Kodak photocopiers. Kodak, therefore, had a quasi-monopoly position, even though its overall market share in photocopiers was less than 25%.

Similarly, in 2014, the European Commission sanctioned the Servier laboratory for an abuse of dominant position, taking as the relevant market the molecule of perindopril (and its generic versions). In 2018, the European Union Court of Justice overturned the decision on the grounds that the relevant market also included other molecules that could be substituted for perindopril: Since the Servier laboratory was no longer in a dominant position, no abuse of dominant position could be established.

33. The indices and methods for delimiting the relevant market are developed in Chapter 6.

Table 5.2 Controversies over the Relevant Market Delineation

Case	*Relevant Market According to the Defendant*	*Relevant Market According to the Competition Authorities*
Alcoa (1945; USA)	All aluminum ingots including scrap metal Market share: 33%.	Only fresh aluminum ingots Market share: 90%.
DuPont (1956; USA)	All packaging materials Market share: 16%-20%.	Cellophane paper Market share: 75%-100%.
Xerox (1975; USA)	All copiers Market share: 65%.	Copiers on plain paper Market share: 90%.
Kodak (1992; USA)	Components for photocopiers Market share: 15%/25%.	Components and maintenance services for Kodak photocopiers Market share: 90%.
British Airways/Virgin (1999; EU)	Air transport market	U.K. market for travel agency services
Michelin (2001; EU)	National markets for new truck tires	World market for new truck tires

The "cellophane fallacy": When delineating the relevant market, antitrust authorities use a test called the "*hypothetical monopolist test.*" This test, which is explained in detail in Chapter 6, consists of analyzing the impact of a 5%-10% price increase on the profit of the dominant firm. If the price increase is profitable, then the relevant market is limited to the dominant firm's products only. If this is not the case, the scope of the relevant market is extended.

The hypothetical monopolist test can lead to a reasoning error, as illustrated by the DuPont case (1956). DuPont was in a monopoly situation on the cellophane paper market; it was therefore likely that DuPont was charging a monopoly price. By definition, it was not profitable for DuPont to increase its price above the monopoly price, as its profit would have decreased.

Hence, in this situation, the monopoly test would have led to a fallacy: A firm that is already in a monopoly position will not be considered a monopoly, because an increase of its price would not be profitable.

Let's illustrate this fallacy with an algebraic example. Consider the following linear demand function:

$$P = 100 - Q$$

The marginal cost of production is assumed to be constant and equal to \$20. In order to maximize its profit, the monopoly equals the marginal revenue with its marginal cost:

$$P^* = \$60$$

$$Q^* = 40$$

$$\Pi^* = (\$60 - \$20) \times 40 = \$1{,}600$$

It is not profitable for the monopoly to increase its price above the monopoly price. For example, a 10% price increase (from $60 to $66) leads to a decrease in profit, as the positive effect on the margin does not offset the decrease in quantities:

$$P = \$66$$

$$Q = 34$$

$$\Pi^* = (\$66 - \$20) \times 34 = \$1564 < \$1{,}600$$

Indeed, for a price of $60, the price elasticity of demand (for a price increase of 10%) is equal to:

$$\begin{aligned}(dQ/Q)/(dP/P) &= (-6/40)/(6/60) \\ &= (-0.15)/(0.1) \\ &= -1.5\end{aligned}$$

with (dQ/Q), the relative change in quantities and (dP/P) the relative change in price.

Since the price elasticity is greater than one (in absolute value), it is not profitable to increase the price. However, it will be false to conclude that the firm is not a monopoly.

To avoid such a mistake, it's necessary to delineate the relevant market by starting from a competitive price and not from the price charged by the dominant firm.

§2 Assessing a Dominant Position

From an economic point of view, the notion of dominant position is very close to that of market power: It refers to the ability of a firm to sustainably maintain its prices above its marginal cost. Margin rates (i.e., the difference between price and costs, relative to price) increase as the firm's market power increases. In practice, in order to assess a dominant position, antitrust authorities use a set of indicators, but structural indicators are the most widely used.

Multiple criteria: Three types of criteria are used to assess a dominant position (Table 5.3): the market structure, the firm's behavior, and its financial performances. In practice, antitrust authorities make little use of performance criteria. Thus, in Europe, the ECJ has rejected several times the argument that a firm's low profitability proves the absence of a dominant position. For example, in the United Brands case (1978), the ECJ recalled that "a low profit margin or even temporary losses are not incompatible with a dominant position just as high profits may be compatible with a situation of effective competition."

Table 5.3 Indicators of a Dominant Position

Types of Indicator	*Examples*
Performance indicators	- price levels compared to costs - high profit margin
Behavioral indicators	- restrictive clauses imposed on clients - "limit pricing" policies - loyalty discount practices
Structural indicators	- market share of the offending firm - distribution of market shares between firms - entry barriers (patent, brand image, range extension, etc.) - counterpower of customers

On the other hand, behavioral criteria have been used sometimes to characterize a dominant position. Thus, in the United States, in the Alcoa case (1945), Judge Learned Hand inferred a dominant position because Alcoa succeeded in convincing its electrical energy suppliers not to supply its competitors. Similarly, in Europe, in the Michelin case (1981), the European Commission pointed out that "the finding of a dominant position is also based on evidence of its abusive exploitation because a manufacturer selling a product with such a market position can impose conditions on resellers that do not necessarily correspond to those that would prevail in a market where competition is effective" (free translation). The European Commission based its decision on two factors: The practice of large-scale loyalty discounts, and the distributors' dependence on Michelin. Indeed, Michelin appeared as an "*essential partner*": Any dealer that did not offer Michelin tires was considered less attractive than those that did.

The predominance of structural indicators: The market share is the first and main structural indicator used, either to delimit a "*safety zone*" or to presume a dominant position.

In practice, an undertaking with a small market share will generally not be considered to be in a dominant position. Thus, in the United Brands decision (1978), the ECJ declared that "A trader can only be in a dominant position on the market for a product if he has succeeded in winning a large part of this market."

Similarly, in the Metro decision (1977), the ECJ pointed out that market shares between 5% and 10% generally exclude the existence of a dominant position. In its 2009 "Communication on the Enforcement Priorities in Applying Article 82 of the EC Treaty to Abusive Exclusionary Conduct by Dominant Undertakings," the European Commission thus delineated a safety zone: "The Commission considers that low market shares are generally a good proxy for the absence of substantial market power. The Commission's experience suggests that dominance is not likely if the undertaking's market share is below 40% in the relevant market."

Conversely, a dominant position is presumed if the firm's market share is more than 50%, as the ECJ pointed out in the Akzo, Hoffmann-La Roche, and Michelin decisions.

Calculating market shares is not always easy:

- when market shares are volatile over time, they must be assessed over a time period of several years;
- while market shares are generally calculated on the basis of the turnover, antitrust authorities sometimes use volume-based indicators: For example, in the raw materials sector, market share can be estimated by taking into account the reserves available to each company. Similarly, market shares can be calculated on the basis of production capacities in order to estimate the distribution of excess capacities between firms.

A second structural indicator is the distribution of market shares between firms; the presumption of a dominant position is reinforced if the offending firm has a high market share, while its competitors have small ones. Thus, in the Michelin decision (1983), the ECJ held that Michelin's market share (between 57% and 65%) compared to that of its competitors (between 4% and 8% each) constituted an additional indicator of its dominant position. A similar analysis was carried out in the Hoffmann-La Roche case (1979), with the ECJ emphasizing that "Since the relevant market thus has the particular features of a narrow oligopolistic market, in which the degree of competition by its very nature has already been weakened, Roche's share, which is equal to the aggregate of the shares of its two next largest competitors, proves that it is entirely free to decide what attitude to adopt when confronted by competition."

A third structural indicator consists of analyzing the magnitude of entry barriers (*see* Chapter 6 for a list of entry barriers). While having a significant market share is a necessary condition for holding a dominant position, it is not a sufficient one: The offending firm must not be threatened by the entry of new competitors. Thus, in the Alcoa decision (1945), Judge Hand stressed the importance of the potential competition resulting from the opening of the American market to imports: "[...] it was the threat of greater foreign imports which kept 'Alcoa's' prices where they were, and prevented it from exploiting its advantage as sole domestic producer; indeed, it is hard to resist the conclusion that potential imports did put a 'ceiling' upon those prices."

In contrast, in the United Shoe case (1953), American antitrust authorities concluded that the offending firm was in a monopoly situation not on the basis of its market share, but because entry barriers (resulting from patents) were high. In Europe, in the Michelin case (2001), the European Commission used Michelin's technological lead as an indicator of its dominant position, as well as the prestige of the brand, the firm's strong presence in adjacent markets, and the importance of Michelin's commercial service through its Euromaster integrated distribution network.

A fourth structural indicator consists of analyzing the countervailing power of customers. Indeed, a high market share of the offending firm does not necessarily allow it to be dominant if customers are themselves powerful. In particular, customers may escape the dominant position of their suppliers, for example, by threatening to adopt a vertical integration strategy.

The case of aftermarkets: Suppose a firm offers both a main product on the primary market and spare parts on the aftermarket. In this particular case, the question is: Are the two markets distinct? Or should they be considered as one when assessing the firm's market share? And, therefore, can a firm be considered as being in a dominant position on its own spare parts market, even though it is not dominant on the primary market?

The reasoning of competition authorities consists of first assessing whether there is competition on the aftermarket. If there are several suppliers of spare parts on the aftermarket, the anti-competitive risk is low. If there is no competition on the aftermarket, then antitrust authorities analyze the competition intensity on the primary market; they also consider whether customers, when choosing the main product on the primary market, take into account the price of spare parts on the aftermarket.

Thus, in the Pelikan/Kyocera decision (1995), the European Commission found that Kyocera did not hold a dominant position on the secondary market of cartridges for its printers in view of the main characteristics of the primary market (i.e., printers). In particular, the European Commission found that customers took into account the price of cartridges when purchasing a printer: The "*total cost per page*" is the most common criteria used by customers to make their choices. Similarly, in the Xerox case (2016), the French Competition Authority estimated that customers made their choices by taking into account the price of both the copier and the maintenance. The price of a printer's maintenance throughout its entire lifespan, as compared to its purchasing price, is high (between 1.5 and 1.8 times), and maintenance is systematically offered at the time of the printer's purchase. It also found that the number of potential customers on the primary market was large and fluid enough to regulate the aftermarket. When a price increase occurred on the aftermarket, customers would switch to another supplier on the primary market.

SECTION 3 MAIN CASES OF EXCLUSIONARY AND EXPLOITATIVE ABUSES

After defining the relevant market and proving the dominant position, the next step for competition authorities is to establish the existence of abusive behavior. Competition authorities need to build a scenario demonstrating that the undertaking has maintained or extended its dominant position, and thereby has behaved abusively. This abusive behavior should have a negative—real or potential—effect on competition.

While there is no exhaustive and pre-established list of abuses of dominant position, several practices that competition authorities have sanctioned can be identified and classified into two different categories:

- exclusionary abuses: Excluding or marginalizing an as-efficient competitor through pricing or non-pricing strategies;

- exploitative abuses: When a dominant firm imposes unjustified conditions on its customers, particularly in terms of price, or treats them in a discriminatory way.

As illustrated in Figure 5.1, abuses of dominant position sanctioned by competition authorities fall mainly under the first category of exclusionary abuses.

Figure 5.1 Main Abuses of Dominant Position Sanctioned by the European Commission (2000-2017)

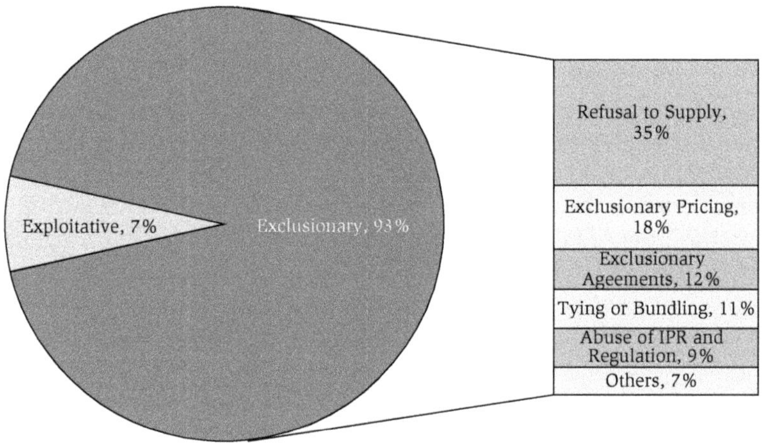

Source: OECD (2018).

We will first study some exclusionary abuses that are non-pricing related, such as tying practices or exclusivity agreements (§1). We'll continue by analyzing three main forms of price-based exclusionary abuses (§2). We'll finish by describing some exploitative abuses, such as price discrimination and excessive pricing (§3).

§1 EXCLUSIONARY NON-PRICING ABUSES

Without being exhaustive, we can identify five non-price exclusionary practices that we'll review one by one:

- tying practices;
- exclusivity agreements
- refusal to access an essential infrastructure;
- commercial disparagement (defamation) of a competitor;
- abusive interference with a public authority.

Tying practices: A tying strategy consists of offering different products in the same package: For example, a firm selling disposable razors will simultaneously sell its razors with a can of shaving cream. Tying sales can be *"pure"*—the two goods are never sold separately—or *"mixed,"* i.e., the customer has the choice between a separate or a bulk purchase.

Tying is a common business practice and is generally driven by economic efficiency:

- tying strategies reduce transaction costs when the components in the package are complementary. For example, when customers buy computers, they obtain packages that include a screen, a central unit, a keyboard and connection sockets. Without this bundled offer, customers would have to purchase all these components separately and create their own comprehensive sets;
- tying sales solve problems of asymmetric information about the quality of products. Indeed, a product's proper functioning may depend on the quality of the complementary goods used with. Thus, IBM was accused in the 1960s of abusing of its dominant position through tying sales and defended itself by invoking the need to protect the quality of its computers: IBM computers could only function optimally with IBM-branded punch cards; the use of punch cards from other brands could lead to breakdowns, which, in turn would damage the reputation of IBM computers;
- tying strategies increase the size of the market by encouraging customers to buy the good for which they have a low willingness to pay. Consider the case of a monopoly that offers two products A and B (Table 5.4) to two consumers (1 and 2). We assume that the production cost is nil and that the monopoly is fully aware of the two consumers' willingness to pay. Consumers have opposing preferences. Indeed, Consumer 1 prefers A to B: His willingness to pay is equal to $12 for A and only $5 for B. Consumer 2 prefers B: His willingness to pay is $12 for B and only $5 for A. If the firm sells the two products separately, it will charge a price of $12 for A and $12 for B. Consumer 1 will buy A and not B. Conversely, Consumer 2 will buy B and not A. The firm's total profit will be $24. The firm has no interest in charging a price of $5: The size of the market would increase (since it would sell both products to consumers A and B), but its total profit would decrease from $24 to $20.

If the firm practices product tying, it can offer a package (A + B) at a price of $17: It will sell two packages and make a total profit of $34. The profit increase is due to the fact that tying induces both consumers to buy the product for which they have a low willingness to pay. Through tying, Consumer 1 buys product B and Consumer 2 buys product A. It should be noted that the total consumer surplus remains unchanged and therefore is not negatively affected by the tying practice.

Table 5.4 Pure Tying and Willingness to Pay (with Negatively Correlated Preferences)

	Willingness to Pay: Consumer 1	*Willingness to Pay: Consumer 2*
Product A	$12	$5
Product B	$5	$12
Package (A + B)	$17	$17

More generally, it is profitable for a firm to practice tying if consumer preferences are negatively correlated. If this is not the case, tying does not increase profits.

Consider the case of a monopoly that offers two products A and B (Table 5.5) to two consumers (1 and 2). We assume again that the production cost is nil and that the firm is fully aware of the two consumers' willingness to pay. Consumers 1 and 2 prefer A to B, even if they do not have the same willingness to pay. If the firm sells the two products separately, it will charge $12 for A and $8 for B. Consumer 1 will buy both products and consumer 2 will not buy anything. The total profit will therefore be $20. The firm has no interest in selling A for $5 and B for $2: Its profit would be equal to (2 × $5) + (2 × $2), or $14. If the firm practices a pure tying, it will offer a package (A + B) at a price of $20: It will sell a single package to Consumer 1 and make a total profit of $20. Tying does not allow for an increase in profits because consumer preferences are positively correlated.

Table 5.5 Pure Tying and Willingness to Pay (with Identical Preferences)

	Willingness to Pay: Consumer 1	*Willingness to Pay: Consumer 2*
Product A	$12	$5
Product B	$8	$2
Package (A + B)	$20	$7

Tying and exclusion of an as-efficient competitor: Tying may also be used by a dominant firm to marginalize an equally efficient competitor when the latter is only present in one of the two markets (Whinston, 1990; Nalebuff, 2004).

Let us consider two complementary products A and B. Firm 1 is in a monopoly situation in the market of Product A, while it is threatened by the entry of Firm 2 in the market of Product B. In order to exclude Firm 2 from the market, Firm 1 can offer a bundle, with Product A as the tying product and Product B as the tied product.

Such a tying policy allows Firm 1 to leverage its monopoly profits made in Market A to subsidize its product in Market B. Indeed, by bundling the two products and selling the bundle on both markets, the production cost of Product B is implicitly reduced by the margin realized in Market A. The competition in Market B is therefore tougher when Firm 1 offers a package, compared to the situation where the two products are sold separately. This reduction in profits in Market B may discourage Firm 2 from entering the market if the anticipated profit does not recover its fixed entry cost.

However, the success of such an exclusion strategy is subject to two conditions:

- consumers must not exhibit a strong preference for Product B offered by Firm 2. If they do exhibit such a preference, consumers will give up buying the package, especially if they consider Product A of little value;
- to be credible, the tying commitment must be irreversible: It must take the form, for example, of a technological integration of different products. For example, in the Microsoft case (2000), the District of Columbia Court found that the integration of Internet Explorer into Windows was difficult to reverse: In particular, Internet Explorer could not be removed from Windows 1998. Conversely, if the package is based solely on a marketing or packaging aspect, the tying commitment is easily reversible and therefore not credible.

Under competition law, a tying policy is not prohibited per se for a dominant firm, but it may be considered an abuse of dominant position in certain circumstances (Table 5.6), as highlighted in Europe with the Hoffman-La Roche (1979) and Microsoft (2007) cases. In the latter case, the European Commission concluded that Microsoft had abused its dominant position on the Operating Systems (OS) market by linking the sale of Windows with the sale of Media Player: The purpose and effect of tying was to reduce competition on the multimedia software market.

In practice, when assessing the abuse resulting from a tying strategy, competition authorities take into account the market share of the dominant firm; if the firm is in a monopoly position on the tying product, the foreclosure effect is almost automatic. In 2003, the French Competition Authority sanctioned Sandoz for having linked the sale of certain pharmaceutical drugs. This bundle enables the firm to sell cyclosporine (a molecule necessary for the treatment of patients having had a transplant), for which it held a monopoly, with other drugs, over which there was a high level of competition.

More generally, antitrust authorities consider that tying can constitute an abuse of dominant position when several conditions are cumulatively met:

- there are two separate relevant markets for each product;
- the firm implementing the tying policy is in a dominant position in the market of one of the tied products;
- the firm leaves no choice to consumers regarding the combination of the different products. The characteristics of tying sales are therefore considered: A pure tying offer is more harmful for competition than is a mixed tying offer;
- the tying practice restricts competition on the market of the tied product, without sufficient efficiencies to compensate for the competitive infringement;
- there is no objective justification for tying.

Table 5.6 Examples of Tying Practices Considered as Abusive

Case	*Purpose of the Abuse*	*Decision*
Kodak (1992, USA)	Photocopier maintenance companies accused Kodak of monopolizing the Kodak photocopier maintenance-and-repair-service market by linking the sale of spare parts with its after-sales service offer.	The Court ordered Kodak to sell its spare parts to independent maintenance firms at a non-discriminatory price.
Microsoft (2001, USA)	The District of Columbia court (2000) accused Microsoft of monopolizing the internet-browsing software market by integrating its Internet Explorer software with Windows.	The Court of Appeals (2001) held that the integration of Internet Explorer into Windows should be analyzed under a rule of reason. In the final agreement with the U.S. government, Microsoft committed to giving computer manufacturers the choice of their Windows configuration.
Microsoft (2004, EU)	The Commission accused Microsoft of eliminating competition in the market for media broadcasters by linking its Media Player product with its Windows operating system.	Penalty of €497 million (also for an abuse of the server operating system market); Microsoft obliged to offer a version of Windows without Media Player.
Google Android (2018, EU)	The Commission concluded that Google engaged in two instances of illegal tying: (1) Google ensured that its Google Search app is preinstalled on almost all Android devices. (2) Google ensured that its mobile browser Chrome is preinstalled on almost all Android devices.	Penalty of €4.34 billion

Case	*Purpose of the Abuse*	*Decision*
Sandoz (2003, France)	Sandoz, benefiting from in a dominant position on two drugs (Sandimmun and Néoral), set up a tying system where it offered a discount to French hospitals if they agreed to purchase Sandimmum and Néoral with other products in the bundle. This enabled Sandoz to bypass competition for the other drugs in its bundle.	Penalty of €7.8 million

Exclusivity agreements and economic efficiencies: A dominant firm may conclude an agreement with its customers stipulating that it will be the only firm to supply them. The aim of this strategy could be to exclude an equally efficient competitor.

According to the Chicago School, such a practice cannot succeed if the competitor is efficient. Indeed, suppose that Firm 1, in a dominant position, is threatened by the entry of a more efficient competitor Firm 2 (i.e., with a lower marginal cost of production). In order to deter Firm 2 from entering the market, Firm 1 will offer its customers an exclusivity agreement. However, customers will only agree to sign such an agreement if they can obtain a surplus at least as high as the one they would obtain by contracting with Firm 2. However, the maximum financial compensation that Firm 1 can offer, equal to its monopoly profit, is less than the surplus obtained by consumers if they choose to source from Firm 2: It is therefore impossible for Firm 1 to deter the entry of a more efficient competitor with an exclusivity agreement.

This argument can be illustrated graphically (Figure 5.2). Let us consider the case of a producer, Firm 1, in a monopoly situation, with a marginal cost of production c_1: The customers pay a monopoly price P^M and buy a quantity Q^M. Firm 1 is threatened by the entry of a Firm 2 which operates with a marginal cost of production $c_2 < c_1$. However, Firm 2 is not efficient enough to charge a monopoly price below the marginal cost of Firm 1. The competition between the two producers is a Bertrand competition: If it enters, Firm 2 will charge a price P^* equal to the marginal cost of Firm 1. In a monopoly situation, the consumer's surplus is equal to the area aP^MA. In a Bertrand competition, their surplus is equivalent to the area aDP^*. If Firm 1 wants to prevent the entry of Firm 2, it must conclude an exclusivity agreement with its distributors, offering them a compensation equal to the area P^MADP^*. However, the profit of Firm 1 is equal to the area P^MABP^*, which is lower: The difference is represented by the gray triangle ABD. Under these conditions, Firm 1 will not be able to offer a sufficient compensation to consumers.

Figure 5.2 Entry Deterrence and Exclusive Agreement

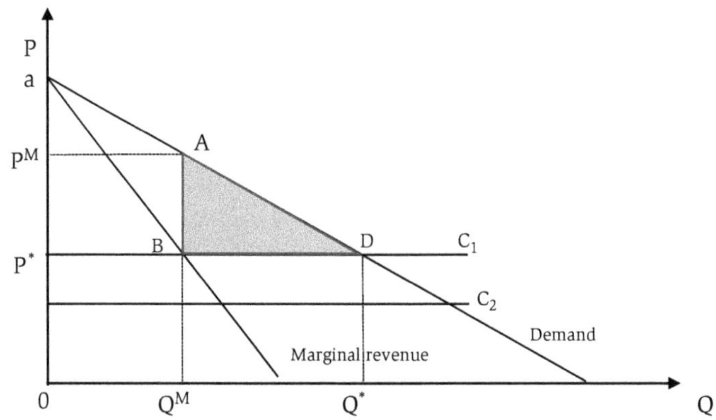

This means that, according to the Chicago School, an exclusivity agreement is only motivated by efficiency gains. For example, an exclusivity agreement over a long period of time will enable the firm to secure large and risky investments, particularly when they are specific to a commercial relationship: The investor fears opportunistic behavior on the part of its client, and requires that it signs an exclusivity contract.

Exclusivity agreements and exclusion: Under certain conditions, an exclusivity agreement, even if beneficial to both parties, may exclude from the market an equally efficient firm:

- if Firm 1 is active in several markets while the newcomer Firm 2 can only enter one market, Firm 1 can use profits from other markets to provide sufficient compensation to customers so that they agree to contract with it;
- if there is an uncertainty about the entry of a more efficient competitor, the incumbent can reduce the probability of entry by concluding an exclusivity agreement with the customers (Aghion & Bolton, 1987). This point is developed in Chapter 4 on vertical agreements;
- when there are many customers and the entrant, Firm 2, has to reach a minimum threshold of customers to cover its fixed costs, Firm 1 can use exclusivity contracts to deter entry; because there is a large number of customers, they cannot coordinate with one another. Each customer will sign an exclusivity agreement with Firm 1, depriving the entrant of a sufficient market share. The foreclosure effect will be likely if the number of customers and the fixed entry costs are high. This point is also developed in Chapter 4 on vertical agreements;
- the dominant firm may be unavoidable regarding a significant part of the demand—called the "*non-contestable demand*"—for example because it has most of the production capacities. In this case, it may conclude an exclusivity agreement with its customers in the "*contestable*" part of demand, in which competition could exist.

While exclusivity agreements are not prohibited in principle, even for a dominant firm, competition authorities may consider that they can constitute an abuse of dominant position in certain cases: A case-by-case approach is adopted. In order to assess the effects of such agreements, competition authorities take into account factors such as the share of non-contestable demand, the duration of the exclusivity contract, the terms of the contract renewal, its scope compared to the size of the market, the conditions for the contract termination (particularly in terms of penalties) and the demand dispersion. Regarding this topic, European case law dates back to the Hoffmann-La Roche decision (1979), which highlights two interesting points:

- the fact that customers accept the exclusivity agreement is not a sufficient argument: "It is an abuse of a dominant position for an undertaking in a dominant position on a market to bind purchasers—even at their request—by an obligation or promise to obtain all or a considerable part of their requirements exclusively from that undertaking";
- the exclusivity does not necessarily result from an explicit obligation in the contract but may also result from a system of loyalty discounts, leading customers to buy a significant part of their needs from the dominant firm.

In a recent decision (2019), the European Commission fined Google €1.49 billion because Google abused its market dominance by imposing a number of restrictive clauses in contracts with third-party websites, which prevented Google's rivals from placing their search ads on these websites. Websites such as newspaper websites, blogs, or travel-site aggregators often have a search function embedded. When a user searches using this search function, the website delivers both search results and search ads, which appear alongside the search result. Through AdSense for Search, Google provides these search ads to owners of "publisher" websites. Therefore, AdSense for Search works as an online search advertising intermediation platform between advertisers and website owners. Starting in 2006, Google included exclusivity clauses in its contracts. This meant that publishers were prohibited from placing any search ads from competitors on their search results pages. As of March 2009, Google gradually began replacing the exclusivity clauses with so-called "Premium Placement" clauses. These required publishers to reserve the most-profitable space on their search results pages for Google's ads, and request a minimum number of Google ads. As a result, Google's competitors were prevented from placing their search ads in the most visible and clicked on parts of the websites' search results pages. Therefore, Google first imposed an exclusive supply obligation, which prevented competitors from placing any search ads on the most commercially significant websites. Then, Google introduced what it called its "relaxed exclusivity" strategy, aimed at reserving for its own search ads the most-valuable positions, and at controlling competing ads' performance.

Refusal of access to an essential facility: When a firm is present at several stages of an industry's value chain (i.e., vertically integrated) and has an upstream infrastructure essential to operate downstream, it can handicap its downstream competitors by denying them access to its upstream infrastructure.

This abusive behavior has been formalized through the doctrine of "*essential facilities*," which emerged in the United States at the end of the 19th century following the Terminal Railroad case. In this case, an association of rail transport companies had acquired the control of all the infrastructure necessary to load freight and to drop off passengers in the city of St. Louis, Missouri. In response to a complaint by competitors, the U.S. Supreme Court required the association to provide access to other railways at a reasonable and non-discriminatory price.

In Europe, the Commission has used on several cases the notion of essential facilities but under certain conditions:

- the facility should be necessary to enter the market. Thus, in the IMS Health case (2001), the European Commission found that the structuring of IMS's medical database, although protected by a copyright, was essential because it had become the reference standard in the geographical classification of pharmaceutical data;
- the facility is difficult to duplicate, for technical or cost reasons. This means that there are no economic and/or technical alternatives that can be used as substitutes. It should be noted that the essential nature of the resource is subject to an objective analysis, which does not take into account the specific characteristics of the firm requesting the access. Thus, in the Bronner decision (1998), the ECJ held that the refusal of a dominant firm (MediaPrint) to integrate the distribution of a competing daily newspaper into its own home delivery system did not fall within the principle of essential facilities. Indeed, there were other systems for the distribution of daily newspapers, such as the postal service or newsstands sales. In addition, the ECJ found that there were no technical or economic barriers that would prevent Bronner from creating its own home delivery system. The fact that Bronner was unable to create its own distribution network was not, in itself, a sufficient condition to force MediaPrint to open up the access to its network;
- the firm that owns the facility is in a dominant position and access refusal will eliminate all competition on the market;
- there is no justification for access refusal (capacity constraint, etc.) by the dominant firm.

While the principle of essential facilities has been used on several occasions, it has its limitations. First, fear of an access obligation may discourage firms from investing in radical innovations or new large-scale infrastructures: If they are successful, innovative firms will have to provide competitors with access to their new facilities or services.

Second, the obligation of access is by essence an infringement of property rights, particularly in the field of intellectual property; in this respect, American case law has evolved towards a very cautious approach concerning "*compulsory licenses*," as in the U.S. Supreme Court's decision in the Trinko case (2004).

Competitors' access to essential resources is nowadays an issue in the debates regarding technological norms and standards. Indeed, a firm may hold an essential patent on a technical standard; therefore, to manufacture products that comply with the standard, all other firms must have access to this patent through a license. As a general rule, firms holding essential patents ("Standard Essential Patents" or *SEPs*) should grant licenses voluntarily to other firms in a Fair, Reasonable, And Non-Discriminatory way ("*FRAND*" licensing terms).

A firm that holds an essential patent and participates in a standardizing process can charge higher royalties once its standard has been adopted; this hold-up behavior is called "*patent ambush.*" Once its technology has become the standard, the patent holder will try to obtain from its competitors more advantageous conditions than those provided under a FRAND license. For example, Samsung launched complaints against Apple in 2011 for patent infringement, even though Samsung had agreed to transfer FRAND licenses to Apple. The European Commission opened proceedings against Samsung, which ended in 2014 with commitments. The commitments provided a "*safe harbor*" for all potential licensees of the Samsung SEP: They are protected against SEP-based injunctions by Samsung.

In the United States, in the Rambus case, the U.S. FTC accused the firm (Rambus) holding patents on DRAMs (Dynamic Random-Access Memory) of a patent "*ambush*" practice; Rambus became a member of Jedec (Joint Electron Device Engineering Council) as they were defining an industry standard for DRAMs. Rambus participated in setting the standard; however, it didn't disclose the fact that it held several essential patents related to the standard. Once the standard was adopted, Rambus revealed its patents and requested royalties from those using the standard. The FTC condemned Rambus's ambush practices, but the decision was overturned on appeal in 2008: The Court of Appeals held that the causal link between Rambus's strategy and the restriction of competition was insufficient.

Disparaging a competitor: Disparagement consists of discrediting a competitor by disseminating erroneous information about its products. A disparagement strategy differs from a simple criticism: It comes from a competitor that seeks to gain a competitive advantage from the dissemination of false information. The practice of disparagement can be particularly effective when the dominant firm benefits from a strong reputation or trust, for example, due to its status as a former public monopoly. Similarly, in sectors such as the pharmaceutical industry where risk aversion is very high, disparagement may discourage prescribers (i.e., doctors and pharmacists) from turning to the new entrant's product. In France, several decisions have concerned disparaging practices (Table 5.7).

Table 5.7 Examples of Abuse of Dominant Position by Disparagement (France)

Case	*Form of Disparagement*	*Decision*
France Telecom (2007)	Solutel—a France Telecom competitor in the market for engineering, consulting and control of private telephone installations—was repeatedly denigrated by a regional unit of France Telecom, which questioned Solutel's ability to provide reliable services to customers.	Injunction to cease all disparaging practices against Solutel
Plavix (2013)	Sanofi-Aventis had implemented a strategy to denigrate Plavix generics among healthcare professionals (doctors and pharmacists) in order to limit their market entry and promote its own products.	Sanction of €40.6 million
Subutex (2013)	In 2006, when generics of Subutex entered the market, Schering-Plough, the patent holder of the Subutex drug, issued an alarmist and unfounded speech to doctors and pharmacists about the risks involved in prescribing the generic.	Sanction of €15.3 million
Durogesic (2017)	Janssen-Cilag, owner of a patent on Durogesic, delayed the launch of Durogesic generics, in particular by spreading misleading messages to health professionals about the efficiency and safety of generics.	Sanction of €25 million

Case	*Form of Disparagement*	*Decision*
Age-Related Macular Degeneration (2020)	Novartis sought to discredit the decisions made by some ophthalmologists who prescribed Avastin off-label instead of its original drug Lucentis. Three firms have been also sanctioned for engaging in misleading discourse regarding the risks related to the use of Avastin to treat age-related *macular degeneration*	Sanction of €444 million

For instance, in the Subutex case, the French Competition Authority demonstrated that the commercial speech held by the dominant firm was not based on objective findings, and that it was "likely to raise an objective doubt as to the merits of competing generic specialties" (free translation). This slanderous communication regarding generics, which can be broadcasted in one click, has had a lasting effect on the market structure: The generics market share has been durably lower than expected as compared with that of similar drugs with expired patents that were in competition with generics.

Abusive interference in the work of a public authority: A particular form of non-price abuse is the interference with public authorities in an unjustified manner or on an erroneous basis, with the aim of delaying a competitor's entry.

In France, for example, in 2017, the French Competition Authority sanctioned Janssen-Cilag for unduly interfering in the national procedure designed to grant a market authorization to a generic drug, with the objective of delaying the entry of generics on the market. In particular, the laboratory had inappropriately highlighted the risks to public health resulting from a drug substitution. Similarly, at the European level, pharmaceutical firm AstraZeneca was sentenced to €60 million in 2006 for misusing the patent system and pharmaceutical marketing procedures to delay the entry of generic competitors. In particular, AstraZeneca had provided misleading information to several national patent offices in order to obtain a longer term of patent protection for its medicine.

§2 EXCLUSIONARY PRICE-BASED ABUSES

There are three main forms of price-based exclusionary abuses: rebates, margin squeeze and predatory pricing. The first two practices have the effect of excluding a competitor from the market, but they do not necessarily imply that the dominant firm makes temporary losses, unlike in the case of predatory pricing. It is therefore necessary to assess, on a case-by-case basis, whether, in the absence of these practices, an equally effective competitor would have stayed in the market. We will first study the role of rebate before analyzing the practice of "*margin squeeze.*" Concerning predatory pricing, because this strategy presents strong specificities, we develop it in a dedicated section of this chapter (Section 4).

Rebates and exclusion of an equally efficient competitor: A rebate consists of a firm offering a price reduction according to criteria such as the quantity of goods purchased (quantity rebate), the degree of client loyalty (loyalty rebate), or the range of products they purchase (range rebates). These practices are quite common in today's everyday business life and, in most cases, are motivated by economic efficiencies.

For example, it is quite normal for a customer to benefit from a quantity discount: A higher volume of sales enables the supplier to achieve economies of scale, and, thus, to lower its production cost. Similarly, loyalty discounts can encourage customers to buy more to benefit from the discount. Similarly, the simultaneous sales of different products enable the supplier to pool costs (economies of scope), for example, in terms of distribution.

In particular cases, a dominant firm may grant discounts in order to exclude an equally efficient competitor from the market. The most interesting case is when a discount is granted if the purchase exceeds a certain market share. In this case, several parameters should be taken into account:

- the "*captive*" market share of the dominant firm in the absence of any discount: If this market share is high, competitors have access to only a small part of the market (called the "*contestable*" market share) and the exclusionary risk is strong;
- the threshold above which the discount is applied and the amount of the discount: The exclusionary effect increases as the threshold and the discount increase. Indeed, in this case, the competitor will have to offer the customer an even higher discount;
- the type of discount: It is necessary to distinguish between an incremental discount, which is only applied to sales volumes above a certain threshold, and retroactive discount, which covers all volumes as soon as a threshold is exceeded. A retroactive discount has a greater potential exclusionary effect than an incremental discount. We develop this point below.

Incremental versus retroactive discounts: The differentiated effects of these two types of discounts can be illustrated with a simple numerical example.

Suppose a computer manufacturer A needs to order 10 million chips each year. It can get them from two suppliers X and Y competing in a Cournot duopoly with differentiated products. Firm X can produce up to 10 million chips per year, while its small competitor Firm Y has only a production capacity of 2 million chips. In this case, it will be considered that the "*contestable part*" of the demand is 2 million chips per year. Firm X is therefore certain to sell at least 8 million chips to A. The marginal cost of production of Firm X is $8. It sells its chips for $10 each. Firm Y is more efficient than Firm X: Its marginal cost is only $7. It sells its chips for $8.

In the absence of any discount, the computer manufacturer A will buy 80% of its needs from X and 20% from Firm Y, which is cheaper. It will spend in total:

$$(\$10 \times 8 \text{ million}) + (\$8 \times 2 \text{ million}) = \$96 \text{ million.}$$

Suppose that Firm X offers an incremental discount to A: If A buys more than 8 million chips, it will receive a discount of $2 per chip. In this case, A can buy the entirety of its chips from Firm X for a total cost of $96 million. But Firm Y, which is more efficient than Firm X, can react by lowering its price from $8 to $7.9. In this case, the customer will refuse the discount offered by Firm X and will purchase 20% of its needs from Firm Y. Its total expenditure will now be equal to:

$$(\$10 \times 8 \text{ million}) + (\$7.9 \times 2 \text{ million}) = \$95.8 \text{ million.}$$

The incremental discount did not allow Firm X to marginalize its competitor. It even had the opposite effect of increasing competition, allowing the customer to benefit from a better price.

Suppose now that Firm X offers a retroactive discount of $1 per chip if A buys all its chips from it. In this case, A will accept, since it will spend a total of $90 million (10 million chips at $9 per chip). Firm Y cannot counter this offer: Even if Firm Y sells its chips at $7, it is not profitable for A to buy 2 million chips from Firm Y. Indeed, its total expenditure would be:

$$(\$10 \times 8 \text{ million}) + (\$7 \times 2 \text{ million}) = \$94 \text{ million.}$$

If Firm Y wants to stay on the market, it has to charge a price below its marginal cost. Indeed, in order for A to buy 2 million chips from it, Firm Y must charge a price per chip P* so that the customer's total expenditure is equal to $90 million:

$$(\$10 \times 8 \text{ million}) + (P^* \times 2 \text{ million}) = \$90 \text{ million.}$$

$$\Leftrightarrow P^* = \$5 < \text{marginal cost of Y}$$

As we can see in this case study, a price rebate offered by a dominant supplier can increase competition by pushing prices down, but it can also sometimes eliminate an as-efficient competitor, especially when the discount is retroactive.

Antitrust and discounts: While discounts are not prohibited as such, even for a dominant firm, competition authorities may nevertheless consider them abusive: A case-by-case approach is always adopted. Competition authorities balance the direct effects of a discount—i.e., a price reduction (favorable to customers)—against the indirect effects of excluding an equally efficient competitor.

Discount practices are classified into three main categories:

- quantitative discounts are in principle permissible;
- exclusivity discounts are prima facie abusive when the undertaking is in a dominant position;
- discounts that have a loyalty effect, by encouraging the customer to achieve a certain sales threshold, are assessed according to their effects on competition.

At the European level, several decisions of the Court of Justice have marked the case law (Table 5.8): Hoffmann-La Roche (1979), Michelin 1 (1983), Michelin 2 (2003), British Airways (2007), Tomra (2012), Post Danmark (2015) and Intel (2017). For example, in the Post Danmark case, the Court of Justice held that the discounts granted by the Danish Post should be regarded as abusive, since they were retroactive, significant in their rates (from 6% to 16%), and covered a relatively long period. Moreover, the captive (i.e., non-contestable) market share of the Danish Post exceeded 70%.

Table 5.8 Examples of Abuse of Dominant Position Through Rebates (Europe)

Case	*Purpose of the Rebate*	*Decision*
British Airways (1999)	British Airways (BA) signed agreements with British travel agencies that included incremental and retroactive bonuses if they achieved a certain threshold of BA tickets sales.	In 1999, the Commission fined BA €6.8 million. The European Court of Justice confirmed the Commission's decision in 2007.
Tomra (2006)	Tomra, the European market leader in automatic reclaimers for used and empty packaging, concluded exclusivity agreements with supermarket chains that included an individualized quantitative target and an individualized retroactive rebate scheme.	In 2006, the Commission imposed a penalty of €24 million on Tomra; the Court confirmed the decision in 2012.
Intel (2009)	Intel attempted to exclude its competitor AMD from the x86 CPU market by granting a discount to four major computer producers if they purchased all or almost all of their x86 CPUs from Intel.	The Commission imposed a penalty of €1.06 billion In 2017, the Court overturned the Tribunal's decision, which confirmed the Commission's decision and referred the case back, on the grounds that the Tribunal had not sufficiently analyzed Intel's arguments on the effects of the discount on the market.

Margin squeeze: Another form of price-based exclusionary abuse is the practice of "*margin squeeze.*" In Europe, margin squeeze is defined as the fact that a dominant company "may charge a price for the product on the upstream market which, compared to the price it charges on the downstream market, does not allow even an equally efficient competitor to trade profitably in the downstream market on a lasting basis" (Commission notice on Article 82).

Consider the case of vertically integrated Firm X: It is the only one to offer an input necessary to operate downstream. Firm X produces at a marginal cost C. It competes downstream with Firm Y, which must access the input of Firm X (Figure 5.3). A margin squeeze practice consists for Firm X of charging a price P_c (for access to its upstream input) higher than the retail price P_X it charges downstream to its consumers:

$$P_C \geq P_X$$

It is therefore impossible for Firm Y to operate on the downstream market: The price P_C, which corresponds to its marginal cost of production, is higher than the retail price at which Firm X sells downstream.

Figure 5.3 The Margin Squeeze

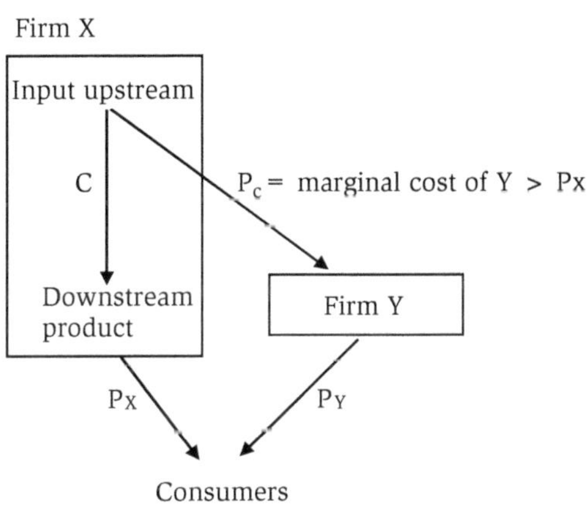

In Europe, in order to consider a margin squeeze as abusive, competition authorities examine several cumulative conditions:

- the access to the input held by the dominant firm must be necessary to operate downstream: There must be no equivalent alternative inputs enabling a non-integrated firm to operate downstream;
- the integrated firm must be dominant on the upstream wholesale market. It is not necessary to demonstrate a dominant position on the downstream market;

- the practice must have an anti-competitive effect: A potential competitor as efficient as the vertically integrated firm will incur losses if it enters the downstream market.

To measure margin squeeze, competition authorities carry out the so-called "*margin squeeze test*." This test is "designed to establish whether a competitor having the same cost structure as that of the downstream activity of the vertically integrated undertaking is able to be profitable on the downstream market given the wholesale and retail prices charged by that undertaking" (Telefonica, 2012).

Antitrust authorities compare the dominant firm revenues on the downstream market and the costs it incurs on the downstream market with the wholesale price it applies to its competitors.

The margin squeeze test normally involves only the price and the costs of the dominant firm, as recalled by the European Court of Justice in the Deutsche Telekom case (2012). The use of costs of the dominant firm is justified by a principle of legal certainty: It ensures that the dominant firm has all the necessary elements to check the lawfulness of its conduct. However, there are sometimes exceptions to this general principle, as stated by the European Court of Justice in the Teliasonera case (2011): For example, if the cost structure of the dominant firm is not precisely identifiable for objective reasons, the cost structure of competitors in the same market could be used.

Network industries such as telecoms, gas and electricity are particularly exposed to the risk of a margin squeeze; indeed, they are characterized by infrastructures that are difficult to reproduce and are owned by a historical company, which operates upstream and downstream. For example, in the Deutsche Telekom (2003) and Telefonica (2007) cases, the European Commission found that the difference between the wholesale price charged by incumbents for access to their local loops and downstream prices in the internet subscription market did not enable an equally efficient competitor to enter the market. The margin squeeze test was based on the costs of the vertically integrated dominant firm in order to assess the legality of its behavior; the test consists of showing that if the dominant firm has to acquire the intermediate good at the price at which it invoices its competitors, it would experience losses on the downstream market.

In France, the French Competition Authority sanctioned a margin squeeze practice in the TDF case (2015): TDF abused its dominant position by setting an upstream price on the Eiffel Tower site, which did not allow its rivals to compete on the downstream market.

§3 EXPLOITATIVE ABUSES

There are three main exploitative abuses:

- price discrimination;
- non-price discrimination: This consists of a dominant firm applying different commercial conditions that are not objective, transparent and uniform according to customers. We will not analyze this practice in this chapter;

- excessive pricing practices.

In this subsection, we'll describe two of these different exploitative abuses: price discrimination and excessive pricing.

Price discrimination: "*Price discrimination*" means that a firm applies different prices from different consumers for the same good or service, even though the production cost is the same. Suppose two consumers 1 and 2 are supplied by the same Firm X, respectively at price P_1 and P_2. Firm X bears a marginal cost c_1 for Consumer 1 and a marginal cost c_2 for Consumer 2. There is price discrimination between the two consumers if the ratio of price to marginal cost is not identical:

$$P_1/c_1 \neq P_2/c_2$$

On the other hand, if supplying Consumer 2 costs three times more, it is not discriminatory to charge the Consumer 2 three times more. For example, the fact that the same product is sold at a different price depending on the location doesn't necessarily imply that there's a price discrimination: The difference can also result from a difference in transportation costs.

A price discrimination strategy is based on demand factors: The aim of the firm is to take back a part of the consumer surplus. It is common to distinguish three forms of price discrimination:

- First-degree discrimination consists of charging a different price for each unit sold; if we assume that each customer has a different willingness to pay, this means that the firm sets a different price for each customer.
- Second-degree discrimination consists of fixing a different price according to the quantity purchased, whether in the form of a package, tying sales, or a dual price (fixed fee + price based on the consumption).
- Third-degree discrimination consists of segmenting the demand into different groups, each with its own price elasticity, and setting a price for each group. For example, a firm may charge different prices according to the age of individuals, offering a lower price for young people or retirees. It may also set different prices according to the geographical location of the customer ("*spatial discrimination*") or over time ("*dynamic pricing*").

We discuss below the first- and third-degree discrimination cases.

Let's start with the first-degree discrimination. Suppose Firm A is in a monopoly situation, with a marginal cost of production c_A, equal to \$2 (Figure 5.4). Firm A knows the willingness to pay of each of its ten customers, numbered from 1 to 10: For Customer 10 it is equal to \$10, while for Customer 1 it is equal to \$1.

If Firm A sets a uniform price, it sets a monopoly price P^M of \$6 and sells 5 units. Its total profit is then equal to: (5 × \$6) – (5 × \$2), or \$20. Consumers 1-5 do not buy the product, while customers 6-10 buy it.

Figure 5.4 Uniform Pricing of a Monopoly

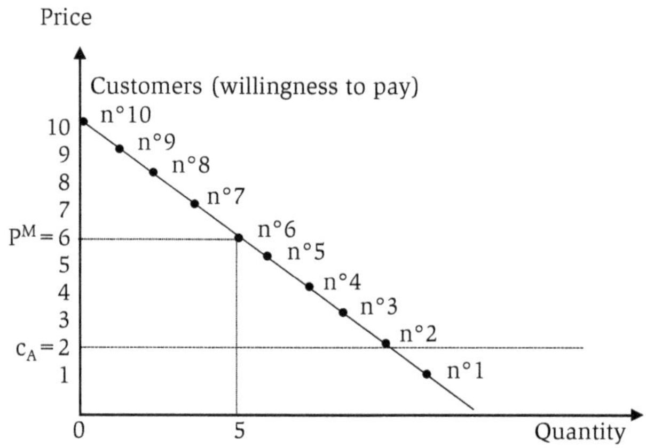

Firm A can, however, increase its profit by applying a first-degree pricing strategy: It will set a price equal to each consumer's willingness to pay (Figure 5.5).

Firm A will set a price of $10 for customer 10, $9 for customer 9, and so on, down to $2. Of course, this strategy can only succeed if all arbitration between consumers is prevented.

The total profit of Firm A will be equal to the shaded area in Figure 5.5:

$$\Pi = (\$10 - \$2) + (\$9 - \$2) + (\$8 - \$2) + (\$7 - \$2) + (\$6 - \$2) + (\$5 - \$2) + (\$4 - \$2) + (\$3 - \$2)$$

$$\Leftrightarrow \Pi = \$36$$

Figure 5.5 Pricing with First-Degree Discrimination

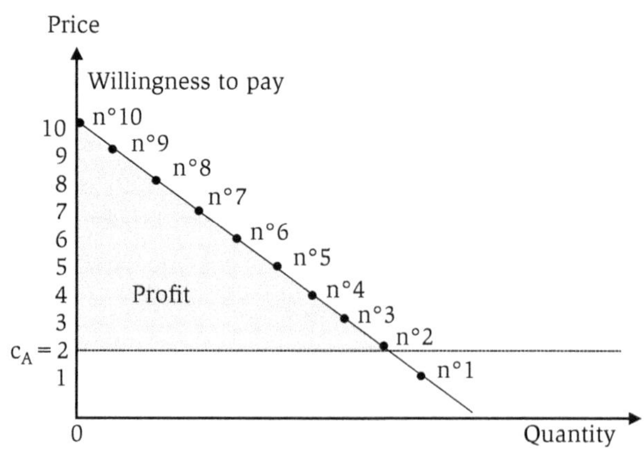

We note that the first-degree discrimination leads to a profit increase for two reasons:

- consumers who highly value the product pay a higher price: The margin per unit increases. In Figure 5.5, this is the case for consumers 7-10;
- some consumers who did not buy the product when the price was uniform buy it now with a personalized price. The firm increases its profit by selling more.

A first-degree discrimination strategy not only increases the profit of Firm A; it is also beneficial for consumers 2-5, who can now access the market. However, it also reduces the surplus of consumers 7-10, who now pay more for the same product. The total effect on welfare is ambiguous: First-degree discrimination increases the firm's profit, reduces the surplus of some consumers, and opens up the market to new consumers.

A similar reasoning can be applied in the case of a third-degree discrimination strategy, consisting of classifying consumers into different groups, and applying to each of them different prices.

Let us take again the previous example. We assume now that consumers 1-5 are students (Figure 5.6). Firm A can then set two prices: a price for non-students (customers 6-10) and a price for students. Of course, Firm A needs to ensure that only students can benefit from the lower price, for example, by requiring their student card. In this case, Firm A will set a price P*of $6 for non-student consumers and a price P** of $4 for students. Its profit, compared to a uniform price of $6, will increase: It is now equal to ($20 + $4), or $24. Discrimination has also allowed the firm to sell to a larger market: Consumers 4 and 5 now buy the product, whereas they didn't beforehand.

Figure 5.6 Third-Degree Discrimination

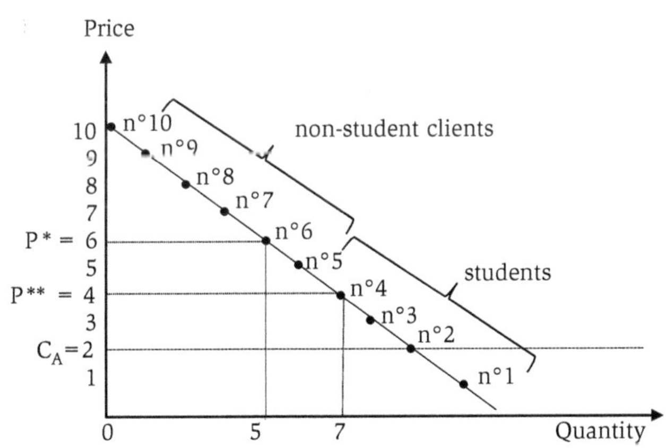

We see that price discrimination strategy can be beneficial to consumers, even if it increases the profits. This occurs when the discrimination significantly increases the market size. It is therefore necessary to analyze the impact that a price discrimination strategy has on volumes on a case-by-case basis before concluding that it has had an abusive effect (Table 5.9).

Table 5.9 Price Discrimination and Market Size

	Increase in Demand	*Unchanged Demand*
Price increase for certain clients	The price discrimination benefits new clients but hurts existing consumers.	The price discrimination hurts all clients.
No price increase	The price discrimination benefits all clients.	-

Price discrimination: Antitrust authorities remain prudent: In the United States and Europe, differentiating prices for the same product according to consumers may constitute an abuse of dominant position if these differences are not objectively justified, in particular, by differences in production costs.

For example, in the United States, Section 2 of the Clayton Act prohibits discrimination when it has the effect of restricting competition "*substantially.*" Similarly, the Robinson-Patman Act forbids sellers from offering for the same product different prices to purchasers: "It shall be unlawful for any person engaged in commerce, in the course of such commerce, either directly or indirectly, to discriminate in price between different purchasers of commodities of like grade and quality, where either or any of the purchases involved in such discrimination are in commerce, where such commodities are sold for use, consumption, or resale within the United States [...] and where the effect of such discrimination may be substantially to lessen competition or tend to create a monopoly in any line of commerce, or to injure, destroy, or prevent competition with any person who either grants or knowingly receives the benefit of such discrimination, or with customers of either of them."

The law allows different prices to be charged only if the lowest price (a) is offered to all buyers; (b) is explained by different costs according to the buyers; (c) corresponds to a competitor's price (but is not higher); or (d) reflects market evolution or the quality of the products. In practice, however, these provisions are rarely applied in the United States; over the past 25 years, the competition authorities have only dealt with one case.

In Europe, Article 102 TFEU states that the fact of applying "dissimilar conditions to equivalent transactions with other trading parties, thereby placing them at a competitive disadvantage" may constitute an abuse of a dominant position. In practice, cases are rare: In the Aeroport de Paris case (1998), the European Commission found that ADP had abused its dominant position by charging different fees to different customers without these differences being objectively justified. These differentiated charges were likely to affect competition downstream by disadvantaging one competitor over the other.

A problematic concept: Excessive prices: In Europe, Article 102 TFEU considers "directly or indirectly imposing unfair purchase or selling prices or other unfair trading conditions" to be a form of abuse of dominant position. This provision not only prohibits low prices such as predatory prices, but also prohibits excessive prices.

Such a provision is also found in U.S. antitrust law in a more indirect way. Indeed, Section 5 of the FTC Act prohibits unfair and deceptive practices such as excessive prices: "Unfair methods of competition in or affecting commerce, and unfair or deceptive acts or practices in or affecting commerce, are hereby declared unlawful."

The notion of excessive price is, however, problematic from an economic point of view, because a high price is not always due to an abuse and should not always be considered illegal.

First, when a firm enjoys some market power, it sets a price above its marginal cost. This price can even be significantly high compared to its marginal cost. Let us consider Firm A in a situation of monopoly. Its marginal cost is assumed to be constant and equal to $1. The demand function is linear:

$$P = 100 - Q$$

In order to maximize its profit, Firm A has to equalize the marginal revenue with its marginal cost; we obtain the following monopoly price, quantity and profit:

$$P^* = \$50.5$$

$$Q^* = 49.5$$

$$\Pi^* = (\$50.5 - \$1) \times 49.5 = \$2450$$

We find that Firm A will set a price equal to more than 50 times its marginal cost. However, it is difficult to talk about an excessive price: Since the monopoly position is not prohibited in itself, the difference between price and cost simply results from the structural parameters of the market.

Second, if a price is abnormally high and there's no legal entry barrier, this situation can only be temporary; the high price will encourage new operators to enter the market and the price will decrease. The market itself will solve any excessive price issues.

Third, when the firm is not in a situation of monopoly, it is difficult to assess the excessive nature of a price, given the number of parameters that determine a price: A price's level does not depend only on marginal costs and the price elasticity of demand (Figure 5.7). Take the case of a firm that charges a price considered to be excessive. This high price can be explained by the fact that the market structure is a Cournot's duopoly with a very inelastic demand, high entry barriers, a low countervailing power of consumers, highly differentiated products and a high level of demand.

Figure 5.7 The Main Determinants of an Oligopoly Price

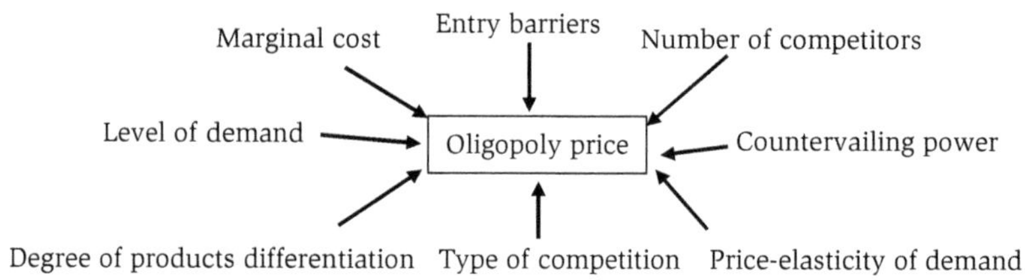

Fourth, if a price is considered excessive—in particular, for reasons of social justice—other instruments besides antitrust laws can be used to regulate prices: For example, public authorities can cap prices; they can also use their bargaining power to negotiate a "*fair*" price with the supplier. This is the case in the pharmaceutical industry in some countries: In France, for instance, the price of a new drug eligible for a refund is negotiated between the pharmaceutical firm and the public health agency.

Finally, a prohibition against excessive prices amounts to a prohibition against monopoly pricing. This would mean that the prohibition of excessive prices would penalize the mere fact that a firm holds a dominant position; however, this contradicts competition law, which does not prohibit dominant positions per se, but only their abuse.

There is therefore a risk of disincentive to invest, as a firm fears that it will be prosecuted ex-post because it sets an excessive price.

Excessive price: Competition authorities remain prudent: Given the vagueness of the concept of excessive price, competition authorities are very cautious.

In the United States, while the notion of excessive price has been invoked on several occasions, there have been no successful antitrust cases.

In Europe, cases of excessive price convictions remain rare: There are a few cases such as General Motors (1976), United Brands (1978) or British Leyland (1986). In the United Brands case (1978), the ECJ held that a price "that is excessive because it has no reasonable relation to the economic value of the product supplied would be such an abuse."

To demonstrate an excessive price, a two-step test is performed:

- one needs to check whether the production cost and the price charged are clearly disproportionate;
- in case of an obvious disproportion, one must examine whether the price is "*unfair*" either in absolute terms or in comparison with competing products.

A variant of charging excessive prices consists of suddenly raising a price sharply: This scenario is different from the previous one, because the issue is no longer to assess a price level but a price variation. An abuse of dominant position may be found if there is no objective justification for the price increase (Table 5.10). In France, this concept has been used in several cases: Electricité de Strasbourg (2005), Assurance Responsabilité Civile Médicale (2006), and Presse Gratuite (2006). But the French Competition

Authority concluded in each case that the price increases were the result of a "*price catch-up*" phenomenon. However, in 2018, for the first time, the French competition authority condemned Sanicorse for having abruptly, significantly, persistently and unjustifiably increased the charges applied to Corsican hospitals and clinics to dispose of their healthcare waste. However, the decision was overturned by the Court of Appeals of Paris.

Table 5.10 Some Cases of Excessive Price Increases

Cases	*Purpose of the Abuse*	*Sanctioning*
Aspen (2016, Italy)	Aspen had increased the price of its anti-cancer drug Cosmis by up to 1,500% after threatening to stop the distribution in Italy. The Italian Competition Authority found that the rate of return was excessive and that the increase was not justified.	Sanction of €5 million.
Pfizer (2017, United Kingdom)	Pfizer and its distributor Flynn had increased the price of Epanutin to 2600%. The U.K. Competition Authority (CMA) found that the price increase was unfair, particularly in view of the abnormally high rate of return.	Sanction of £90 million. The Court of Appeals overturned the decision, because the CMA did not compare the price of the product with that of other comparable products.
Sanicorse (2018, France)	Sanicorse had abused its dominant position through excessive pricing: It had sharply and significantly increased the price applied to Corsican hospitals and clinics for the disposal of their healthcare waste.	Sanction of €199,000; decision overturned by the Court of Appeals of Paris.

Cases	*Purpose of the Abuse*	*Sanctioning*
Aspen (2021, EU)	In 2017, the Commission announced a formal investigation into Aspen's pricing practices regarding six critical off-patent cancer medicines. After acquiring the cancer medicines from another company, Aspen started in 2012 to progressively increase its prices, often by several hundred percent. Aspen sought to address the Commission's concerns by proposing a set of commitments.	Aspen's commitments provide that it will reduce its prices across Europe for the six cancer medicines by 73 % over the coming 10 years.

SECTION 4 THE CASE OF PREDATORY PRICING

A "*predatory pricing*" strategy is a particular form of price-based exclusionary practice: A dominant firm (the "*predator*") sets a low price in order to exclude from the market an equally efficient competitor (the "*prey*"). This strategy consists of sacrificing short-term profits for long-term gains: It is profitable only if the competitor exits the market, which then allows the dominant firm to raise its price. A predatory pricing strategy is based on an inter-temporal trade-off between decreasing short-term profits and high (expected) long-term profits. Thus, in the Wanadoo case (2004), the French Competition Authority pointed out this aspect: "Predatory pricing is a practice whereby a dominant operator sells below its production costs with the aim of eliminating, weakening or disciplining its competitors, subject to the possibility of recovering in the long-term and in any form whatsoever the losses deliberately accumulated" (free translation).

Take two firms A and B that have the same marginal cost c. The two firms are in a Bertrand's competition. At equilibrium, the two firms set a price P_C, equal to the marginal cost c, and make a profit Π^C equal to zero (Figures 5.8 and 5.9). Firm A decides in t' to lower its price to P_W below the marginal cost: It makes losses (i.e., a negative profit, equal to Π^W) until t*, the date when its competitor B leaves the market. After t*, Firm A finds itself in a situation of monopoly, and can then increase its price to P^M and obtains a monopoly profit Π^M.

Figure 5.8 The Dynamics of Predatory Pricing

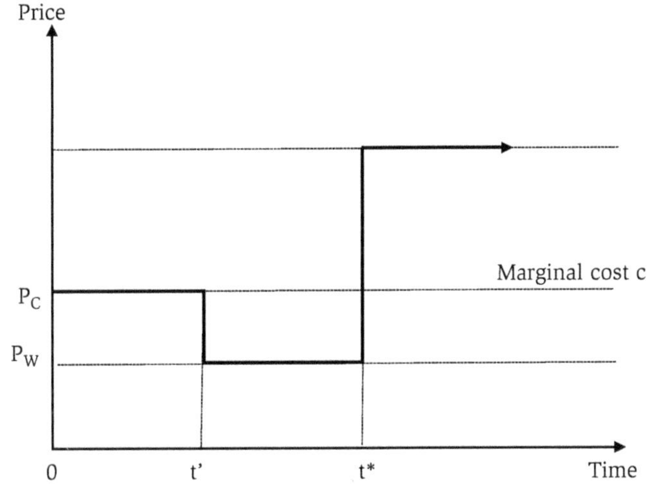

The predatory pricing strategy is only profitable if the (discounted) losses incurred between t' and t* (represented by the light gray area on the Figure 5.9) are less than the (discounted) monopoly profits after t* (represented by the gray area).

Figure 5.9 Predatory Pricing and Profit Dynamics

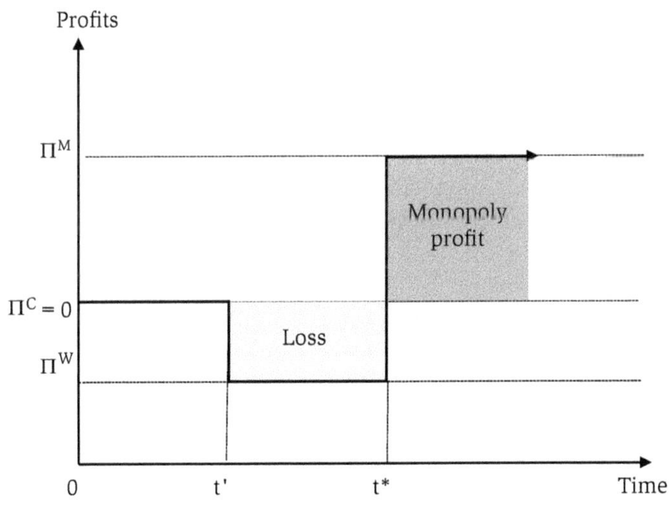

Π^C: competitive profit; Π^W: predatory profit; Π^M: monopoly profit

How long can a dominant firm apply a predatory pricing? It depends on several factors, including:

- the predator's aggressiveness: The predator must choose between the level of losses per period and the number of periods necessary to eliminate its competitor. The more aggressive the pricing strategy, the higher the losses per period, leading to a fast demise of the rival;
- the degree of the prey's resistance: In particular, if the investments made by the victim are sunk costs, the victim will be more resistant.

Even though predatory pricing strategies are quite simple to understand, the Chicago School has caused a lot of turmoil among economists by refuting its existence: Predatory pricing is a "*myth*" (§1). But in certain cases, and under certain conditions, predatory pricing can be a very efficient way to increase profits, as demonstrated by the Structuralist School (§2). Finally, we will review the American and European competition authorities' stands on predatory pricing and the various tools they use to detect such practices, such as the price/cost test (§3).

§1 PREDATORY PRICING: A "MYTH"

The idea that a firm can temporarily lower its price in order to eliminate an equally efficient competitor is not unanimously accepted by economists and has sparked considerable debate since the 1960s. In particular, Chicago economists give little credence to predatory pricing, affirming it to be, to use Koller's expression (1971), a "*myth.*" Predation would be an irrational strategy, because it is risky, unprofitable and non-credible. In addition, predatory pricing strategies are reported to be uncommon in practice, although big firms are sometimes accused of such practices.

A risky and unprofitable strategy: In a review of the Standard Oil case (a trust dismantled in 1911), McGee (1958, 1980), Easterbrook (1981) and Bork (1993) questioned the relevance of a predatory pricing policy, using five main arguments:

- during the price war, the predator bears huge losses. Let's take two symmetrical firms A and B in a Bertrand's competition with homogeneous products. At equilibrium, the two firms charge a price P^C equal to the marginal cost C and make no profit (Figure 5.10). The total production is Q^C and each firm produces $Q^C/2$. Firm A decides to lower its price to P^W. The demand increases from Q^C to Q^W. The best response of Firm B is to keep its price unchanged: All losses (measured by the gray rectangle on Figure 5.10) are borne by the predator;
- once the price war is over, the price increase encourages the prey (or a newcomer) to return to the market. Entry/return is all the more likely as the production capacity of the prey can be bought back. The profits of the predator are, therefore, short-term gains at best;
- there are other strategies to obtain a monopoly position that are less costly than predatory pricing: For example, a merger and acquisition (M&A) can

durably strengthen the firm's market power. However, this argument is questionable, since M&As are now overseen by competition authorities, and can be blocked when they have the effect of monopolizing the market;

- predatory pricing cannot succeed if the victim knows that it is a temporary strategy. In this case, it only needs to borrow some money to get through the rough times. From the lender's point of view, a commitment to help its client is low risk: The mere promise of a loan deters the predator from launching a price war and the loan is therefore not used. As Bork (1993) points out: "If the potential victim would find resistance to predation a profitable use for his liquid asset, a lender should find it equally profitable to lend the required capital. In fact, in any case in which the predator must use a technique that inflicts proportionally equal or greater losses upon himself, the victim would merely have to show the predator his new line of credit to dissuade the predator from attacking";
- customers (especially in the case of firms) have an incentive to support the prey if they're afraid of facing a monopoly. For example, the prey may conclude a long-term agreement with its customers at a price higher than the predator's price. As Posner (1976) notes, however, this argument presupposes that customers are informed of the predatory pricing practice and do not take advantage of it individually by acting as "*free riders*." Indeed, defending the prey benefits all: Each customer has an incentive to purchase from the predator, relying on other customers to stay loyal to the victim.

Figure 5.10 Predatory Pricing: The Predator's Losses per Period

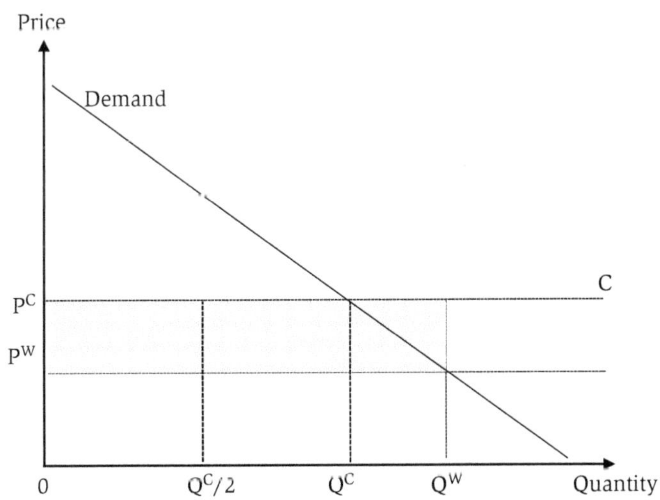

A non-credible strategy: The Chicago School's arguments about predatory pricing have found an interesting echo in the non-cooperative game theory, with Selten's (1978) famous "*chain store paradox.*"

Let's take Firm A, which is in a monopoly situation in 20 different local markets. Consider the following sequential game repeated over 20 periods (Figure 5.11): At each period, a new competitor B can enter one of the 20 markets. The best solution for Firm A is that Firm B does not enter: It remains in a monopoly position on each market and makes a profit of $10 for each period. If Firm B enters, Firm A must choose between an entry accommodating strategy (i.e., it accepts a duopoly situation) and a predatory strategy. The first strategy consists of adapting: Each firm then makes a duopoly profit of $4. In case of predatory pricing, Firm B will incur a loss of $5 and Firm A's profit will be nil. We thus obtain the following sequential game, repeated 20 times.

Figure 5.11 The Credibility of Predation

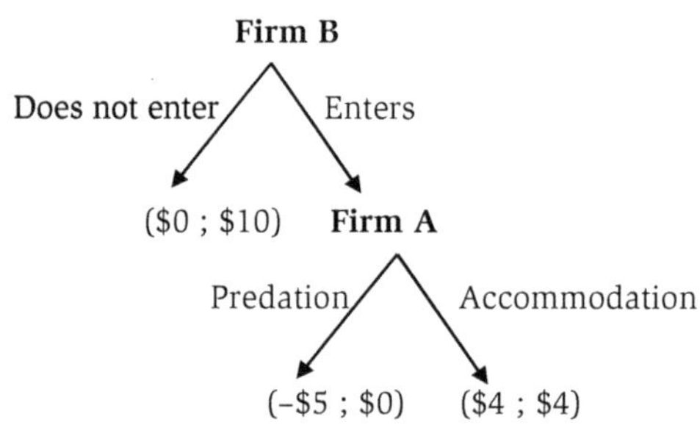

We can solve this repeated game by applying the backward induction method. In the last period of the game (the 20th), the best strategy for Firm A is to be accommodating: The accommodating profit is higher than the predatory profit ($4 > $0). By backward induction, Firm A prefers to adapt at each period of the game. The predation threat is not credible and the solution of this game (called "*perfect subgame equilibrium*") is ($4, $4) at each period: Firm B enters at each period and the two firms will be in competition in all 20 markets.

Predatory pricing: an argument used by inefficient firms?: Chicago economists consider predatory pricing to be a rare practice, even though antitrust cases have been brought up on this ground. The main predatory pricing cases brought before the American courts were thus re-examined: Reviewing 123 cases in the United States between 1890 and 1970, Koller (1971) shows that predatory pricing charges are not supported by any solid arguments. The antitrust policy was in fact subject to an intense lobbying activity, initiated by inefficient firms. They filed complaints against efficient firms in order to deter them from lowering prices. Paradoxically, competition authorities were defying their purpose by protecting inefficient competitors at the expense of more-efficient firms.

Moreover, according to the Chicago School, predatory pricing accusations are based on a misunderstanding of what competition is: It is a dynamic process of selecting the most-efficient firms. Low price strategies also allow firms to launch new products and win over the first consumers. Similarly, when a firm launches a new product, a low starting price results in large quantities and thus reduces the cost of future production through a learning-curve effect.

§2 WHEN CAN A PREDATORY PRICING STRATEGY BE PROFITABLE?

The Chicago School's arguments are based on strong assumptions that can be challenged. In this subsection we'll present different cases when a predatory pricing strategy becomes not only possible, but also profitable:

- when firms have unequal access to the financial market;
- when there is a "*learning curve*";
- when there are "*network effects*";
- when there is uncertainty regarding the nature of firms on the market.

The "deep pockets" thesis: In the Chicago School's argument, it is assumed that firms have equal access to the financial market. If there are asymmetries in access to borrowing, a predatory pricing policy can become successful. This thesis, initiated in the 1960s by Telser (1966) and often referred to as the "*deep pocket story*," has given rise to numerous models.

Thus, in the Fudenberg and Tirole model (1986), two firms A and B compete over several periods. At the end of the first period, they must invest to stay in the market in subsequent periods. It is assumed that Firm A faces no financial constraints, while Firm B has no initial wealth and must therefore borrow, at the end of the first period, all or part of the required investment. Since the bank has little information regarding the financial health of Firm B, the total cost of the loan will increase, as large sums are required.

With these assumptions, the authors demonstrate that Firm A may charge a low price in the first period; at the end of the first period, Firm B will have low profits and should borrow a large amount. The extra cost of borrowing may become so high that Firm B will not invest and will exit the market, leaving A in a monopoly situation.

The role of financial variables in predatory pricing strategies can be illustrated through a simple model, inspired by Benoît (1984). Consider a Firm A, already on the market, and a Firm B that wants to enter (Figure 5.12). The game between Firm A and Firm B takes place over (T + K) periods, with $K \geq 1$. In the first period, Firm B chooses to enter or not. In case of entry, Firm A may be accommodating or aggressive; in subsequent periods, if it has already entered the market, Firm B must choose between leaving or staying in the market, taking into account that Firm A may react with accommodating or aggressive behavior. In case of predation, both firms make a negative profit equal to Π^W. If Firm B enters the market and Firm A is accommodating, each firm makes a positive profit Π^C. If Firm B doesn't enter the market, Firm A makes a monopoly profit Π^M. We therefore have the following inequality:

$$\Pi^M > \Pi^C > 0 > \Pi^W$$

Suppose Firm B has fewer assets S_B than Firm A (which has assets S_A). Firm B can survive for a maximum of T periods in case of predation:

$$S_B = -T\,\Pi^W < S_A$$

Let's consider the simplest case in which $T = K = 1$: The game therefore is a two-period game (Figure 5.12). In case of predation in the first period, Firm B cannot survive in period two. If Firm B enters the first period and Firm A reacts by being accommodating, the best response for B is to stay in the second period. Indeed, Firm A will react by being accommodating again, insofar as $\Pi^C > \Pi^W$. In the game's first period, Firm A must therefore choose between being accommodating or aggressive in case of entry. It will choose a predatory strategy if:

$$\Pi^W + \delta\Pi^M > \Pi^C(1 + \delta) \text{ with } \delta \text{ the discount factor.}$$

If this condition is met, the best strategy for Firm B is not to enter in the first period: Firm A will make a total profit equal to $(\Pi^W + \delta\Pi^M)$.

Figure 5.12 Predation and Financial Constraint

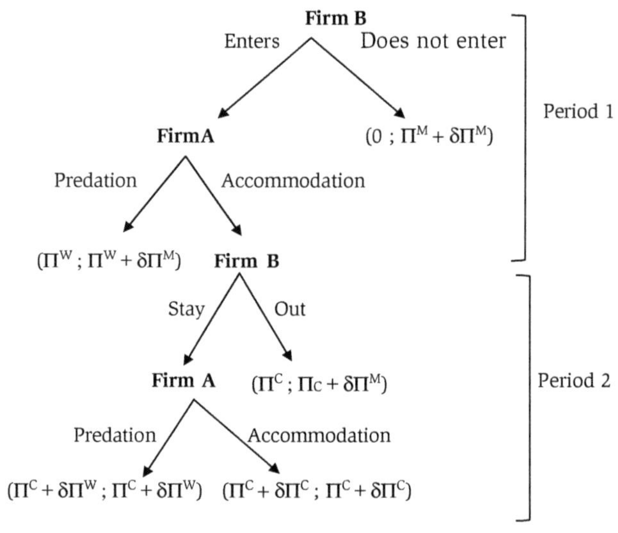

Predatory pricing and the learning curve*:* The Chicago School's argument is based on the assumption that the temporary exit of the prey does not affect its cost function: The level of cost is the same tomorrow as it is today. This cost reversibility hypothesis can be discussed when there is a "*learning curve.*"

A learning curve appears when the average cost of production decreases with the cumulative quantity produced: The longer a firm has been producing, the more experience it has acquired, which lowers its average cost. Suppose that the experience curve is 90%: Each time the firm's cumulative production doubles, the unit cost decreases by 10%, thanks to the experience acquired.

Suppose two firms A and B compete with the same production capacities. Each firm can produce one unit in each period. Firm A decides to adopt a predatory pricing strategy when it enters the market, for four periods. Therefore, it will have produced four units after four periods: With an experience curve at 90%, its unit production cost will be equal to $(0.9)^2$, or 0.81 of the first unit cost. As Firm B stayed out of the market during the first four periods, it suffers a production cost disadvantage compared to A when it enters the market in the fifth period: It has not yet accumulated experience and starts with a production cost disadvantage of 19%.

Predatory pricing and network effects: A network effect can encourage a firm to charge a predatory price when it enters the market. A positive network effect (or "*network externality*") occurs when the utility that an individual receives from the use of a product increases with the number of individuals who use it. For example, the utility that a person obtains from being in a social network increases with the number of people who are present in that same network. In the presence of network effects, it's crucial for a firm to make a "*good start*" in order to trigger a snowball effect.

Suppose that two competing firms A and B launch a new technology. Each technology is assumed to be incompatible with that of the competitor: Consumers must therefore choose between Firm A's or Firm B's technology (Table 5.11). The utility resulting from a technology is an increasing function of the number of users of the same technology and a decreasing function of the price. Consumers arrive in cohorts of 1,000 during each period and all have the same utility function. Initially, Firm A's technology is inherently superior to the technology of Firm B: It provides a utility of 10 for the first 1,000 consumers as compared to a utility of 9 provided by the technology of Firm B. Firms A and B have the same marginal cost.

The first cohort of consumers should therefore opt for technology A since it provides greater utility. The second cohort of consumers will do the same; they will choose the technology of Firm A, which now provides a utility of 12, rather than the technology of Firm B, which has not yet started and provides a utility of 9. In the absence of any predatory practice, Firm A's technology should therefore become the standard of the market.

Table 5.11 A Standardization Race with Network Effects

Consumer Cohorts	*0-1,000*	*1,000-2,000*	*2,000-3,000*	*3,000-4,000*	*4,000-5,000*
Utility of A	10	12	14	16	17
Utility of B	9	11	13	14	15

But Firm B can change the outcome of the standardization race by adopting a predatory pricing strategy. Suppose that Firm B offers its technology to the first 1,000 customers: Since utility also depends on the price paid, the first consumers will opt for the technology of Firm B. The second cohort of consumers will also adopt the technology of Firm B: The latter benefits from a network effect and provides a utility of 11, higher than that of the technology of Firm A, which has not yet started the race (11 > 10). Subsequent cohorts of consumers will also opt for the technology of Firm B. A snowball effect takes place, which leads to the Firm B's victory. Through a predatory pricing behavior at the beginning of the race, Firm B has changed the outcome of the race by excluding Firm A from the market.

Predatory pricing and reputation: A dominant firm can engage in a predatory pricing strategy in order to acquire the reputation of being a strong firm in the first market and deter subsequent entry into other markets, as noted by Scherer and Ross (1990): "If, in the face of measures taken in market A by a seller operating in several markets, competitors come to fear that their entry or expansion into markets B and C will lead to significant price decreases or other crowding-out reactions, they may be deterred from taking aggressive action in those markets. Thus, in addition to the benefit expected by the conglomerate from its foreclosure practices in market A, the discounted value of the anti-competitive effects that its example has in markets B and C will be added."

This strategy is based on an informational asymmetry between firms A and B: Firm B does not know if A is strong (i.e., if its production cost is low) or weak (i.e., its production cost is high). Let us consider again the sequential game of Selten, repeated over 20 periods: At each period, Firm A is confronted with the entry of Firm B into one of the 20 markets. Firm A can be of two types (Kreps & Wilson, 1982):

- a weak firm: If Firm B enters the market, the accommodating strategy provides a greater profit than the predatory pricing strategy (Figure 5.13). In a situation of perfect information, Firm A would therefore always accommodate Firm B's entry;

Figure 5.13 Sequential Game with a Weak Firm

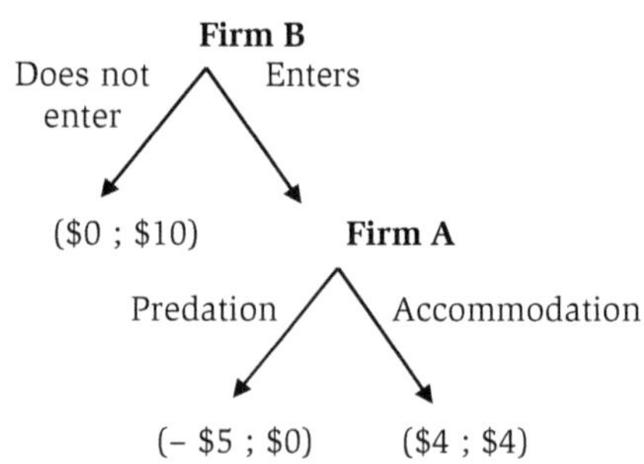

- a strong firm: In case of Firm B's entry, the accommodation strategy results in a loss of $1 for Firm A, greater than the predatory pricing strategy (Figure 5.14). In a situation of perfect information, Firm A will therefore apply a predatory pricing strategy if Firm B enters the market.

Figure 5.14 Sequential Game with a Strong Firm

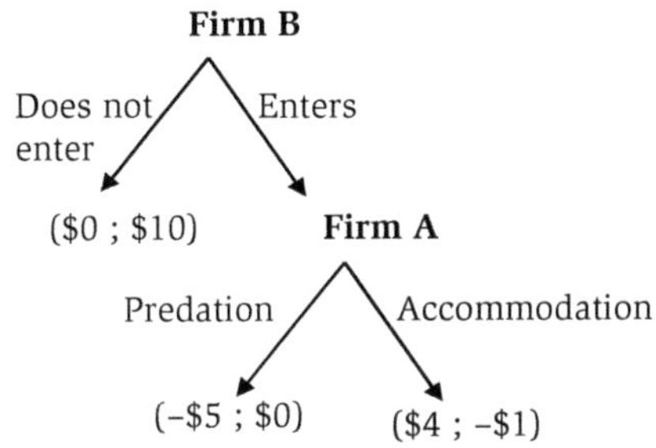

When the information is perfect, Firm B always enters the market if Firm A is weak: It knows that the predatory threat is not credible. Conversely, if Firm A is strong, Firm B never enters the market.

In a situation of imperfect information, Firm B does not know what type of competitor it faces: Is Firm A weak or strong? Firm B assigns an a priori probability at the beginning of the game and revises its beliefs throughout the 20 periods after having observed the behavior of Firm A during the previous period. For example, if Firm A is accommodating from the beginning of the game, Firm B can infer that the probability of a weak competitor A is high.

The game in its extensive form (for one period) can be represented as in Figure 5.15.

Figure 5.15 Sequential Game with Incomplete Information

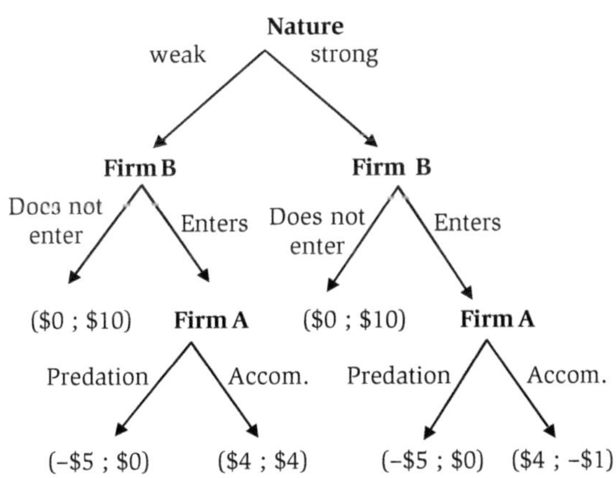

Suppose that Firm A is weak. At the beginning of the game, it may implement a predatory strategy in order to suggest that it is a strong firm. Firm A will sacrifice profits, since it will give up $4 if its competitor B enters the market. But Firm A will acquire a reputation of being a strong competitor, which may lead Firm B not to enter during the subsequent periods in order to avoid a loss of $5. Firm A will be in a monopoly situation and will make a profit of $10 per period.

Let's illustrate this mechanism with a numerical example. If Firm A is accommodating from the beginning of the game, it reveals its true nature of being a weak firm. Firm B then enters the market during each period: The total gain for Firm A is (20 × $4), or $80. If Firm A is aggressive from the beginning of the game, Firm B will be convinced that A is strong and will renounce entering the market. For example, suppose that after six predatory periods, Firm B renounces entering the market. In this case, the total gain of Firm A is:

$$(- \$5 \times 6) + (\$10 \times 14) = \$110.$$

The reputation, acquired through a predatory pricing strategy, is more profitable ($110 > $80) than a "*naïve*" strategy, consisting of revealing its true nature of being a weak firm.

Jung et al. (1994) have empirically tested the Kreps and Wilson reputation model on a sample of individuals. The game protocol is as follows: Firm A, in a monopoly situation, is faced with the arrival of a new competitor B over eight periods. Firms A and B play simultaneously over the eight periods. Firm B has the choice of entering or not entering. If it does not enter, Firm A stays in a monopoly situation and makes a profit of $300, whatever its type. Firm B gets a profit of $95 if it stays out of the market. Firm A, on the other hand, can choose between a soft strategy and a predatory strategy ("*war*"). The profit depends on what type Firm A is: If Firm A is strong (i.e., if Firm A has a low production cost), its best strategy is to make war ($160 > $70). If Firm A is weak (i.e., if Firm A has a high production cost), it will be accommodating ($160 > $70). If Firm B is certain that Firm A is strong, it stays out of the market. Conversely, if Firm B is certain that Firm A is weak, it enters because it anticipates that Firm A will be accommodating. Individuals participating in this experience are informed in advance of the overall structure of the game and the payments associated with each choice (Figure 5.16).

Figure 5.16 The Payment Matrix

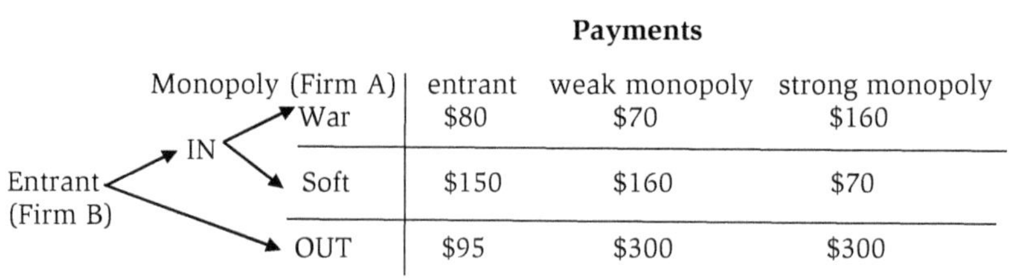

Source: Jung et al. (1994).

Suppose there's an informational asymmetry between A and B: Firm A is weak but Firm B does not know it. Firm B will therefore set an a priori probability on the nature of Firm A and it will revise its belief, after having observed the past behavior of

Firm A. The probability of facing a strong firm is set at the start of the game at 0.33. The simultaneous and repeated game (a session of eight periods) is played 72 times. The experimental protocol distinguishes between inexperienced individuals, who have not yet participated in a game session, and experienced individuals.

The Kreps and Wilson model predicts that even when it is weak, Firm A will be aggressive at the start of the game in order to acquire a reputation of being a strong firm. Given the payments chosen in the experiment, the model predicts that a weak monopoly should never be accommodating during the first three periods of the game, and should then be more accommodating from the fourth period onwards; in the eighth (and last) period, the weak monopoly should always choose to be accommodating (Table 5.12).

The experiment conducted by Jung et al. confirms the prediction of the model:

- during a full game (eight periods), players A are never accommodating during the first periods and are then less aggressive (Table 5.12, columns 2 and 3);
- the occurrence of aggressive behavior at the start of a game increases with experience: Players who've already played 30 sessions and who still play 42 sessions play harder in order to build a reputation of being a strong monopoly.

Table 5.12 Expected and Observed Frequency of Accommodating Behavior (in the Case of a Weak Monopoly)

Stage of the Game	*Predicted Frequency*	*Observed Frequency (First 30 Games)*	*Observed Frequency (Games 31-72)*
1	0.000	0.150	0.000
2	0.000	0.000	0.000
3	0.000	0.000	0.000
4	0.188	0.000	0.000
5	0.346	0.111	0.000
6	0.416	0.083	0.182
7	0.560	0.269	0.425
8	1.000	1.000	0.926

Source: Jung et al. (1994).

§3 DETECTING AND SANCTIONING PREDATORY PRICING

In the United States, the dismantling of Standard Oil Company in 1911 was the first—and probably the most famous—decision regarding predatory pricing. The Rockefeller brothers were accused of having built their oil empire by using predatory prices against small petrol distributors. The sanction was to cut Standard Oil Company into 33 separate companies. Until the late 1970s, American courts considered predatory pricing to be a common practice and, as such, the proof presented by plaintiffs was relatively weak: The simple fact that a firm had been hurt by a competitor's price decrease was sufficient condition to launch an investigation.

From the 1980s onwards, under the influence of the Chicago School's theses and with the development of tests to measure predatory prices, American case law became more cautious, raising the level of proof to a very high level. In 2000, for example, the complaint against American Airlines, which had significantly lowered prices following the entry of the low-cost airline Vanguard, fell through because the Court maintained that the American Airlines strategy only expressed a competitive response. In Europe, the case law is also limited to a few major cases (Table 5.13).

Table 5.13 Main Predatory Pricing Cases (United States and Europe)

The Case	*Description of the Practice*	*Decision*
Standard Oil (1911, United States)	Standard Oil had selectively lowered the price of petroleum products to exclude local competitors.	Sanctioned for violation of the Sherman Act. Standard Oil was dismantled in 1911
Utah Pie (1967, United States)	Pet Milk, the U.S. leader in frozen food, had tried to eliminate Utah Pie from the frozen pie market in Utah by charging a predatory price in this state.	Sanctioned for violation of the Sherman Act, but the decision was overturned on appeal
Zenith/ Matsushita (1986, United States)	Zenith accused 21 Japanese companies of predatory pricing in the U.S. television market.	Complaint rejected by the U.S. Supreme Court
Brooke (1993, United States)	Brown & Williamson was accused of selling branded cigarettes below-cost to counter the generic cigarette sales of Brooke's subsidiary Liggett.	Sanctioned for violation of the Sherman Act, but the decision was overturned by the U.S. Supreme Court, on the grounds that Brown and Williamson could not recoup the losses
American Airlines (2000; United States)	American Airlines had lowered ticket prices and increased capacity on flights from Kansas City to Dallas to counter the entry of low-cost Vanguard.	Complaint rejected, because the American Airlines strategy was an aggressive but non-predatory pricing practice

The Case	*Description of the Practice*	*Decision*
Akzo (1985, EU)	Akzo, which was active on the European chemical additives market, had selectively lowered its prices in the English market to counter the entry of a competitor on the continental European market.	Sanctioned €10 million
Tetra Pak (1991, EU)	Tetra Pak, the European leader in the aseptic packaging market, had sold its non-aseptic packs below-cost in the Italian market in order to eliminate its local competitor Elopak.	Sanctioned €75 million
Wanadoo (2003, EU)	Wanadoo had implemented a predatory pricing strategy in the high-speed internet access market, selling below its average variable cost.	Sanctioned €10 million
Qualcomm (2019, EU)	In the 3G baseband chipsets market, Qualcomm had sold its chips at below-cost prices in order to foreclose its competitor Icera.	Sanctioned €242 million

Detecting a predatory price is difficult: Competition authorities need to distinguish between an abuse of dominant position and a price reduction resulting from a normal but competitive process. Indeed, a price reduction often has other origins than a predatory intent:

- when the demand decreases, the price must adjust downward if the supply cannot decrease in the short term or if products are difficult to stock;
- a decrease in the marginal cost of production (as a result of an organizational innovation, for example) results in a decrease in price;
- a firm trying to establish itself in a market can attract the first consumers by offering promotional prices. Similarly, a firm may temporarily sell its products at low prices in order to benefit from a strong learning curve effect: A low price today results in large quantities, which will reduce tomorrow's production costs;
- a temporary price decrease may result from the entry of new competitors into the market, which implies in the short term an overcapacity. Under these conditions, firms will reduce their prices before a restructuring of the sector occurs (factory closures, mergers, etc.).

The price/cost test: To detect predatory pricing, antitrust authorities use a cost test (also called the "*Areeda and Turner test*" or the "*Akzo test*"), based on a comparison of the cost structure of the dominant firm with the observed price. The reference to the costs of the dominant firm allows authorities to check that the victim is at least as efficient. Moreover, it allows a dominant firm to check that its behavior is in line with current rules and regulations.

Areeda and Turner's original rule (1975) states that if the price is below the short-term marginal cost, there is a presumption of predatory behavior. Indeed, it is not rational for a firm to sell a unit at a price below its additional cost. Since it is difficult to assess the marginal cost, Areeda and Turner propose using the average short-term variable cost as a proxy.

Remember that the total cost (TC) is divided into a variable cost (VC) and a fixed cost (FC):

$$\text{Total Cost} = \text{Variable Cost} + \text{Fixed Cost}$$

The variable cost includes all costs that vary according to the quantities produced, such as the purchase of raw materials. The fixed cost, like the construction of a factory or the purchase of an aircraft, does not depend on the level of current production. The average total cost is therefore equal to the sum of the average variable cost and the average fixed cost:

$$\text{Average Total Cost (ATC)} = \text{Average Variable Cost (AVC)} + \text{Average Fixed Cost (AFC)}$$

Three situations arise when we compare the set price with the cost structure (Figure 5.17):

- if the price is above the average total cost (ATC), the firm makes a positive profit. Predatory pricing behavior is excluded ("*white zone*");
- if the price is between the average variable cost (AVC) and the average total cost (ATC), the firm makes losses because the price does not cover its ATC. However, since the price is higher than the AVC, it may be rational in the short-term to produce, as long as the price covers the variable cost and a part of the fixed costs. In this case, described as a "*gray zone*," it is necessary to have other indicators to presume we're in the presence of a predatory pricing practice: Competition authorities must establish an anti-competitive scenario;
- if the price is lower than the AVC, it is not rational for a firm to produce, since the price does not even cover the AVC (purchase of raw materials, supplies, services, etc.). In this case, a predatory pricing behavior is presumed ("*red zone*"), without the need to go further in the analysis.

Figure 5.17 The Price/Cost Test

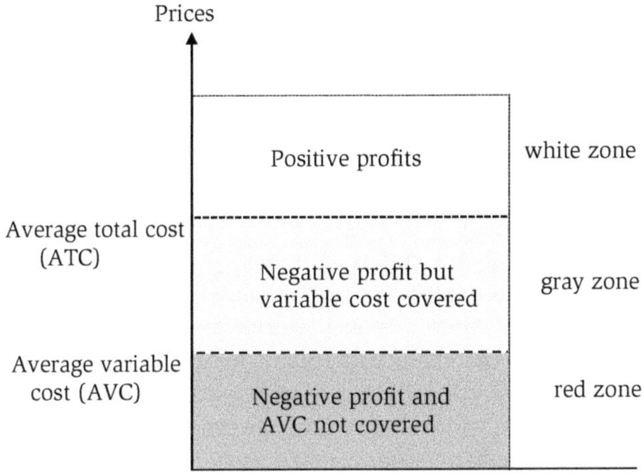

A numerical example can be used to explain the rational of the price/cost test. Suppose that an airline has a total cost function consisting of renting an aircraft (with a fixed cost of $10,000) and a variable cost, such as the cost of fuel per passenger ($80 per passenger). Its total cost function is therefore written:

$$\text{Total cost} = (\$80 \times Q) + \$10{,}000$$

Suppose that the airline carries 120 passengers per flight. The total cost of a flight is therefore equal to:

$$\text{Total cost} = (\$80 \times 120) + \$10{,}000$$
$$= \$19{,}600$$

And the average total cost is equal to:

$$\text{Average total cost} = (\$80 \times 120)/120 + \$10{,}000/120$$
$$= \$80 + \$83.3$$
$$= \$163.3$$

If the airline charges a ticket price higher than $163.3, the presumption of a predatory pricing is ruled out because the airline makes a positive profit. If it sells its tickets between $80 and $163.3, it makes a loss, but it is not sufficient to infer that a predatory price was applied: It may be rational to sell below-cost, because the ticket price covers a part of the fixed cost. For example, if the airline sells its tickets at $100, it covers its average variable cost of $80 and has $20 per ticket to cover a part of the plane's rental. Its loss is equal to ($10,000 – $20 × 120), or $7,600. If it had not flown, the loss would have been higher, since the airline would have had to bear the cost of renting the plane, i.e., \$10,000. If the airline sells its tickets under \$80, predatory behavior is presumed: Indeed, the airline incurs higher losses than it would have to bear if it stopped flying. For example, if it sells the tickets at \$70, it incurs a total loss of (\$10,000 + \$30 × 120), or \$13,600: This loss is higher than the loss resulting from a passive strategy, consisting of not flying its plane (\$10,000).

Using the price/cost test: In Europe, following the Akzo decision of the European Court of Justice (1991), the price/cost test has become a standard when proving predatory behavior. In the Akzo case, the Court stated: "Prices below average variable costs (that is to say, those which vary depending on the quantities produced) by means of which a dominant undertaking seeks to eliminate a competitor must be regarded as abusive. A dominant undertaking has no interest in applying such prices except that of eliminating competitors so as to enable it subsequently to raise its prices by taking advantage of its monopolistic position, since each sale generates a loss, namely the total amount of the fixed costs (that is to say, those which remain constant regardless of the quantities produced) and, at least, part of the variable costs relating to the unit produced. Moreover, prices below average total costs, that is to say, fixed costs plus variable costs, but above average variable costs, must be regarded as abusive if they are determined as part of a plan for eliminating a competitor. Such prices can drive from the market undertakings which are perhaps as efficient as the dominant undertaking but which, because of their smaller financial resources, are incapable of withstanding the competition waged against them."

A predatory price is alleged if the price is lower than the AVC ("*red zone*") but the defendant can refute this presumption. On the other hand, when prices are lower than the ATC, but higher than the AVC ("*gray area*"), antitrust authorities need to demonstrate that the low price is part of a plan aimed at eliminating an as-efficient competitor.

After the publication of the Guidelines on the Application of Article 82 (2009), the European Commission extended the price/cost test to situations where the dominant firm is a multi-product firm or operates additional production capacities. The notion of marginal cost has then been replaced by the average avoidable cost (AAC): It is the average of the costs that could have been avoided if the firm had not produced the additional quantity suspected of being predatory (Figure 5.18). In practice, this means verifying that the income from the additional sales covers the additional costs.

Similarly, the average total cost is replaced by the long-term incremental cost (LTIC): This cost refers to the average of all costs, fixed as well as variable, which the firm bears. We obtain:

Average Total Cost (ATC) = Average Avoidable Cost (AAC) + Long-Term Average Incremental Cost (LTAIC)

Figure 5.18 The Generalization of the Price/Cost Test

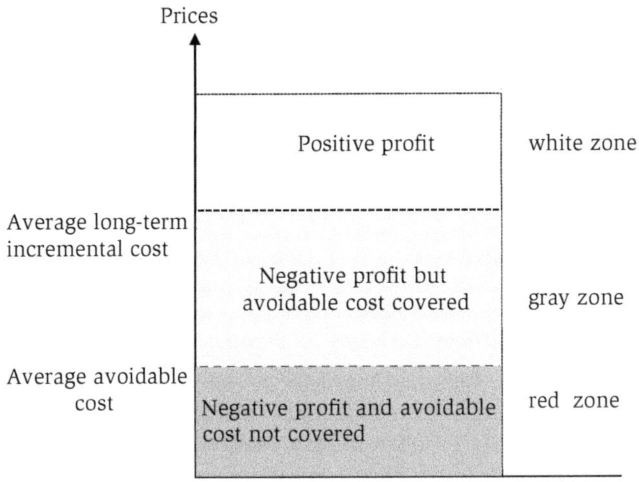

Beyond the price/cost test*:* If the dominant firm does not charge a price below its avoidable cost, antitrust authorities must demonstrate a predatory pricing intent. Several elements can be used:

- high entry barriers encourage predatory pricing, because the dominant firm can increase its price after the competitor has left the market. The reasoning consists of estimating the probability that the predator can recoup its losses. In the Cargill/Monfort of Colorado (1984) and Matsushita/Zenith (1986) cases, American antitrust authorities rejected the predatory scenario because the absence of entry barriers made a price increase unlikely. More recently, in the Brooke case (1993), the charge against Brown & Williamson was dismissed by antitrust authorities: It could not be proven that the firm would have been able to recover the losses after the price war. This thesis of "*recoupment*" of losses is now widely accepted by the American courts, but it's not a necessary element in Europe to demonstrate a predatory price. Indeed, in the Tetra Pak case (1979) the ECJ found that it was "not appropriate to require as additional evidence that Tetra Pak had a real chance of recovering its losses."
- one possible policy to prevent predatory pricing would be to force firms that have lowered their prices to maintain them at the same level once competitors have left the market (Baumol, 1979). In the same vein, Williamson (1977) suggests that a company that increases its production should maintain this level of production once competitors have left the market;
- the selective nature of the price reduction: A firm can charge different prices for the same product according to the markets. It will charge a low price in some areas in order to deter the entry of competitors. For example, in the Utah Pie case (1967), the U.S. Supreme Court found that Pet Milk was engaging in

a predatory pricing strategy, because it was lowering its prices in the Utah region where it faced a small competitor, and not throughout the United States;
- asymmetries between firms: For example, a multi-product or multi-market firm (considered here as a multinational firm) that enjoys market power can more easily implement a price war when its competitor is a single-product or single-market company. The strategy implemented by Tetra Pak, a world leader in the cardboard packaging of liquid food products, is interesting in this respect. Tetra Pak had a quasi-monopoly position in the aseptic packaging segment and generated significant margins in this activity, representing more than 90% of its total profits. In the non-aseptic packaging segment, however, Tetra Pak competed with other specialized suppliers, such as the Italian producer Elopak. According to the European Commission, Tetra Pak used its financial strength in the aseptic packaging market to implement a predatory pricing strategy in the non-aseptic packaging segment. On the Italian market, Tetra Pak sold its Rex cardboard for seven years at a price below its direct variable costs (between -30% and -35%). Present only on non-aseptic markets, the Elopak group could not reply by lowering its price;
- direct evidence of an eviction strategy, such as action plans to eliminate an as-efficient competitor by temporarily lowering prices.

Detection of predatory prices and asymmetric information: The use of a cost test requires that competition authorities have access to full information on the dominant firm's costs. If this is not the case, the firm accused of predatory pricing can manipulate information about its true cost in such a way that its behavior becomes indistinguishable from a Cournot behavior (Phlips, 1995).

Consider a Cournot's duopoly with incumbent Firm i and newcomer e. The demand function is linear:

$$P = a - b(q_i + q_e)$$

The two firms produce respectively at a marginal cost c_i and c_e and each bears a fixed cost K_i and K_e. The profit functions are therefore:

$$\Pi_i = (a - b(q_i + q_e) - c_i)q_i - K_i \quad (1)$$

$$\Pi_e = (a - b(q_i + q_e) - c_e)q_e - K_e \quad (2)$$

At Cournot's equilibrium, each firm's production and price are equal to:

$$q^*_i = (a - 2c_i + c_e)/3b \quad (3)$$

$$q^*_e = (a - 2c_e + c_i)/3b \quad (4)$$

$$p^* = (a + c_i + c_e)/3 \quad (5)$$

Suppose that Firm i adopts a predatory pricing strategy: It offers a quantity q^W such that the profit of newcomer Firm e becomes nil. The reaction function of Firm e is:

$$R_e = (a - bq_i^W - c_e)/2b \quad (6)$$

When Firm i adopts a predatory pricing strategy, the profit of Firm e is zero:

$$\Pi_e = [(a - bq_i^W - c_e)/2]^2\, 1/b - K_e = 0 \qquad (7)$$

From equation (7), we obtain the predation quantity q_i^W:

$$q_i^W = (a - c_e)/b - 2\sqrt{\frac{Ke}{b}} \qquad (8)$$

We deduce the predatory price p^W and the quantity q_e^W corresponding to a profit equal to zero for Firm e:

$$P^W = \sqrt{(K_e\, b)} + c_e \qquad (9)$$

$$q_e^W = \sqrt{\frac{Ke}{b}} \qquad (10)$$

Suppose that antitrust authorities do not know the marginal cost of the incumbent: Firm i will make its predatory behavior look like a Cournot's behavior. In other words, the predator will announce a very low marginal cost, in which case, the best response of Firm e is to stay out of the market. Firm i will announce a value of c_i such that the predation quantity is equal to that which is obtained in a Cournot's situation, or:

$$(a - c_e)/b - 2\sqrt{\frac{Ke}{b}} = (a - 2ci + c_e)/3b \qquad (11)$$

We deduce from (11) that the announced value of c_i, noted c** is:

$$c^{**} = 3\sqrt{\frac{Ke}{b}} + 2\,c_e - a \qquad (12)$$

Let's illustrate this behavior through a numerical example by assigning the following values to the different parameters:

$$a = 10\ ;\ b = 1\ ;\ c_i = c_e = 3\ ;\ K_i = K_e = 4$$

In a Cournot's competition, the equilibrium quantity and price for Firm i is:

$$q_i^* = (a - 2c_i + c_e)/3b$$

$$\Leftrightarrow q_i^* = (10 - 6 + 3)/3$$

$$\Leftrightarrow q_i^* = 2.33$$

$$p^* = (a + c_i + c_e)/3$$

$$\Leftrightarrow p^* = (10 + 3 + 3)/\ 3$$

$$\Leftrightarrow p^* = 5.3$$

In order to reduce the newcomer's profit to zero, Firm i will increase its production level:

$$q_i^W = (a - c_e)/b - 2\sqrt{\frac{Ke}{b}}$$

$$\Leftrightarrow q_i^W = (10 - 3)/1 - 2\sqrt{\frac{4}{1}}$$

$$\Leftrightarrow q_i^W = 3 > q_i^* = 2.33$$

This increase in production leads to a decrease in price:

$$p^W = \sqrt{(K_e\, b)} + c_e$$

$$\Leftrightarrow p^W = \sqrt{4} + 3$$

$$\Leftrightarrow p^W = 5 < p^* = 5{,}33$$

If antitrust authorities do not know the marginal cost of Firm i, it will announce a marginal cost c**, lower than its true marginal cost:

$$c^{**} = 3\sqrt{\frac{ke}{b}} + 2\,c_e - a$$

$$\Leftrightarrow c^{**} = 3\sqrt{4} + (2\times 3) - 10$$

$$\Leftrightarrow c^{**} = 2 < c_i = 3$$

Suppose now that antitrust authorities do not know the parameters of the demand function (respectively, the value of parameters a and b). Once again, Firm i will make its predatory behavior look like a Cournot's behavior. To do this, Firm i will change the values of parameters a and b. It will announce the values a* and b* such that the observed price is equivalent to the Cournot's price:

$$P^W = a^* - b^*(q_i^W + q_e^W)$$

$$\Leftrightarrow \sqrt{(K_e\, b)} + c_e = a^* - b^*\left[(a - c_e)/b - 2\sqrt{\frac{Ke}{b}} + \sqrt{\frac{Ke}{b}}\,\right]$$

$$\Leftrightarrow a^* = \sqrt{(K_e\, b)} + c_e + b^*\left[(a - c_e)/b - \sqrt{\frac{Ke}{b}}\,\right] \qquad (13)$$

For the predation quantity to appear as a Cournot's quantity, the equation (8) must be equal to the equation (3):

$$(a - c_e)/b - 2\sqrt{\frac{Ke}{b}} = (a^* - 2c_i + c_e)/3b^*$$

Using the value of a* given by the equation (13), we immediately find the value of b*:

$$b^* = b[\sqrt{(K_e\, b)} + 2(c_e - c_i)]/[2(a - c_e) - 5\sqrt{(K_e\, b)}] \qquad (14)$$

Let's illustrate this behavior with the former numerical example. The antitrust authority can observe the following values:

$$q_i^W = 3\ ;\ q_e^W = 2\ ;\ p^W = 5$$

If Firm i announces that $a^* = 7.5$ and $b^* = 0.5$, the quantity q_i^W becomes identical to the quantity obtained in a Cournot's situation: By underestimating the level of demand, Firm i makes its predatory behavior look like a Cournot's behavior.

SECTION 5 BEYOND EXCLUSIONARY STRATEGIES: ENTRY DETERRENCE

Until now, we have studied abusive behaviors which tend to push existing competitors out of the market. But the economic theory goes further and considers that the purpose of an abuse of dominant position can also be to deter the entry of a new competitor: This strategy will occur before any entry. An abundant economic literature has developed since the 1960s on this topic; it analyzes the behavior of a monopoly, facing the entry of an equally efficient competitor.

Suppose Firm A is in a monopoly situation; it makes a profit in each period of \$100 (Figure 5.19). If competitor B enters the market, the two firms are in a Cournot's situation: The total profit decreases to \$60 and is shared between firms A and B. Firm A has an incentive to spend up to \$70 in order to deter Firm B from entering the market: Without any entry threat, Firm A would not have implemented such a deterrence strategy.

Figure 5.19 The Incentive to Deter Entry

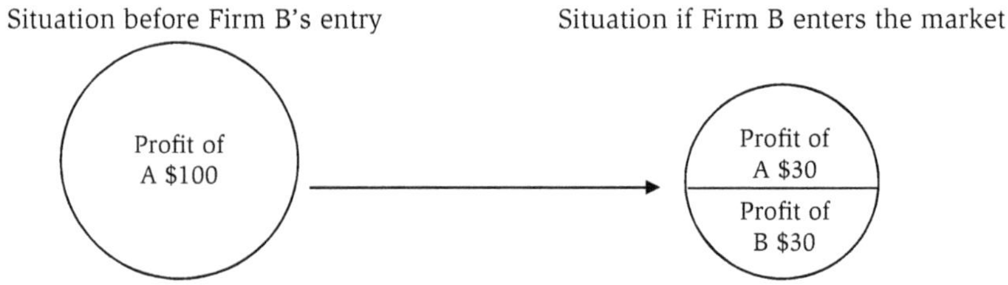

We analyze below under which conditions a deterrence strategy is both credible and profitable for a dominant firm (§1) before presenting a full numerical model of deterrence (§2).

§1 WHAT ARE THE CONDITIONS NECESSARY TO DETER ENTRY?

To implement a deterrence strategy requires several conditions to be met:

- the number of incumbents must be small. If not, each firm will behave as a free rider because a firm that does not participate in the deterrence action can still benefit from it. That is why deterrence is carried out by a dominant firm or even a monopoly;
- the deterrence strategy should not be too costly: If the cost of deterrence is prohibitive, the dominant firm will let the newcomer enter the market;
- there must be a temporal asymmetry between firms: The incumbent must act first, before the newcomer enters the market;
- to be effective, a deterrence strategy must be credible: The newcomer should be convinced that the incumbent will carry out its threat if it enters the market.

The subsections below will be dedicated to developing these last two conditions.

The need for the dominant firm to act before entry: In order to deter the entry of a competitor B, Firm A must act before it enters. This principle can be illustrated with the following sequential game (Figure 5.20): Firm B decides at the first stage whether or not to enter; in the second step, Firm A can choose, if Firm B enters the market, between making war or being accommodating. If Firm B does not enter, its profit is $0, while Firm A stays in a monopoly situation and makes a profit of $100. If Firms B enters and Firm A reacts by being accommodating, the two firms are in a Cournot competition and each makes a profit of $30. If Firm A decides to start a price war, each firm suffers a loss of $10.

Figure 5.20 A Deterrence Game

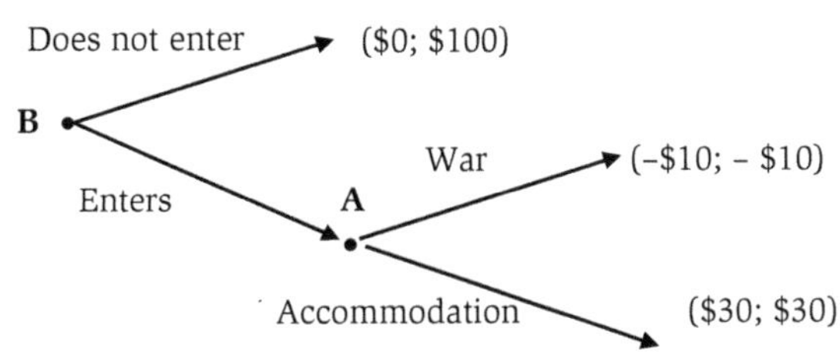

NB: At the end of the game, the first number represents the profit of the player who plays first (here B) and the second number the profit of the player who plays next (here A).

To solve this sequential game, the method consists of proceeding by backward induction, i.e., from the end of the game and going back to the previous steps. In this example, in the second step of the game, Firm A must choose between a war strategy that would mean losing money (- $10) and an accommodating strategy, which would generate a profit of $30. Firm A will therefore choose to be accommodating. In the first period, Firm B knows that if it enters, Firm A will never start a war (Figure 5.21).

Figure 5.21 The Game's Resolution

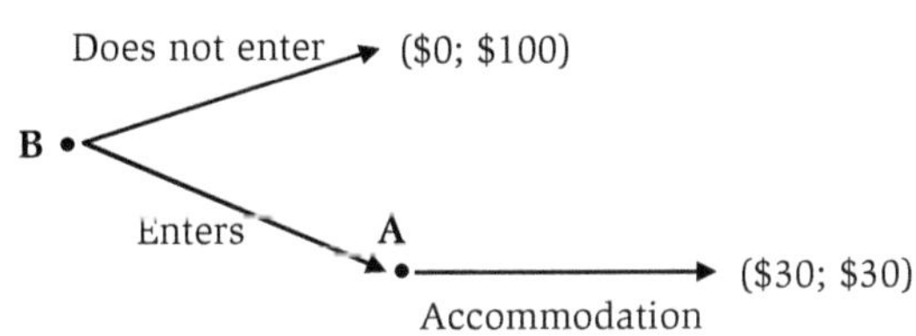

NB: In the payments, the first number represents the profit of the player who plays first (here B) and the second number represents the profit of the player who plays next (here A).

Firm B has the choice between *"do not enter,"* which enables it to obtain a profit of $0, and *"enter,"* which enables it to make a profit of $30: Firm B will always enter. This result is due to the fact that Firm A does not play first.

Now suppose that Firm A can act in the first period by starting a price war before Firm B's decision to enter. In the second period of the game, having observed Firm A's choice, Firm B will decide whether or not to enter the market (Figure 5.22). If we start from the second period of the game, Firm B does not enter if Firm A chooses to start a price war in the first period. Firm B enters if Firm A chooses to be accommodating in the first period. Knowing these two possible outcomes, Firm A must choose in the first period between going to war or being accommodating: The war strategy gives it a higher profit ($100 > $30). To deter a competitor from entering, the incumbent needs to act first.

Figure 5.22 A Deterrence Game with a First-Mover Advantage

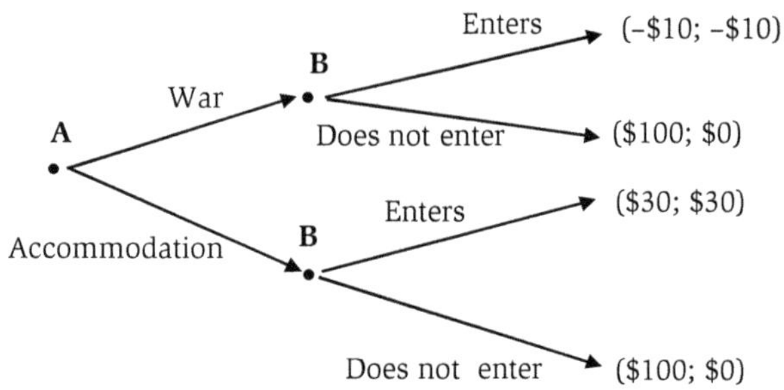

NB: In the payments, the first number represents the profit of the player who plays the first (here A) and the second number the profit of the player who plays next (here B)

The credibility of a deterrence strategy*:* To deter entry, the threat of going to war must be perceived as being credible by the newcomer: The newcomer must be convinced that if it enters the market, the incumbent will carry out its threat.

The question of credibility of a threat was debated in the late 1950s with the famous "*limit-pricing*" model (Modigliani, 1958; Sylos-Labini, 1962). According to this model, a firm in a monopoly situation can deter the entry of a competitor by increasing its production level (and thus lowering its price) in such a way that entry is no longer profitable. By lowering the price today, the incumbent makes a lower profit but avoids the subsequent entry of its competitor and remains tomorrow in a monopoly position. The limit pricing model is based on several assumptions:[34]

- two periods: The pre-entry ($t = 1$) and the post-entry ($t = 2$). Entry can only take place at $t = 2$;
- an incumbent Firm A faces a potential entrant B; if Firm B enters, the two firms are in a Cournot duopoly;
- the two firms have the same cost function and offer identical products;
- the demand does not change during the two periods;
- in period $t = 1$, Firm A produces a quantity Q_A and commits to maintaining it at $t = 2$, whatever the level of production of Firm B.

By definition, Firm B only enters the market if its profits are positive. Firm A will try to dissuade it from entering the market by intentionally setting the production Q_L such that Firm B's best response will be: $Q_B = 0$. The level of Q_L is higher than the monopoly production and forces Firm A to lower its price: The Q_L production is associated with a "*limit price*" P_L.

This limit production Q_L can be determined graphically (Figure 5.23). The CM_A curve represents the average cost function of A; that of Firm B, CM_B, is identical but shifted to the right, taking into account that Firm B maximizes its profit on the residual

34. We adopt the presentation made by Gilbert (1996).

demand, equivalent to $D(P) - Q_L$. We see that for a Q_L production, Firm B can never obtain a positive profit: The residual demand line is tangent to its average cost curve. By applying a quantity limit and a limit price, Firm A discourages Firm B of entering and remains in a monopoly position in period t = 2 with a production level Q_L.

Figure 5.23 The Limit Pricing Model

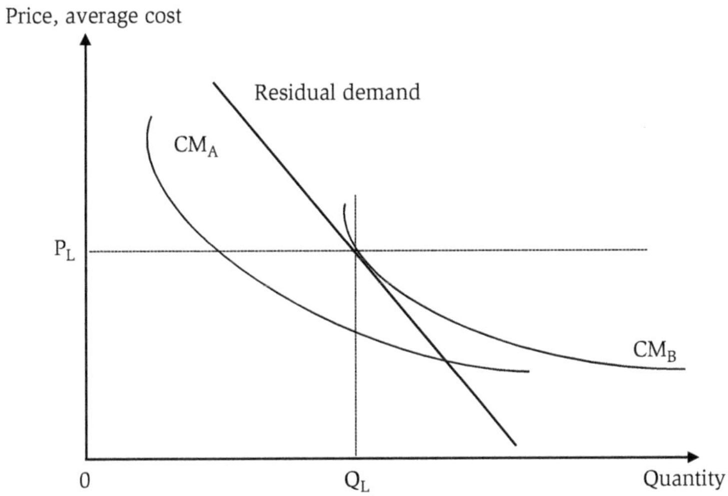

In the limit pricing model, it is assumed that Firm A will not adjust its production level if Firm B enters the market. But in reality, this commitment is not credible: Indeed, if Firm B enters, Firm A's best response would be to adjust its production to the Cournot level and not to maintain Q_L. Anticipating this adjustment, Firm B's best response would be to enter in t = 2. Firm A, knowing that Firm B will always enter, must choose between a limit profit Π_L and a monopoly profit Π_M in the first period: Its best choice is to take advantage of its (temporary) monopoly position in t = 1. We see that, contrary to the initial result, the best strategy for Firm A is to set a monopoly price at t = 1 and let the competitor enter at t = 2.[35]

Why is maintaining a limited quantity Q_L not considered to be a credible threat by Firm B? A threat is perceived as credible if it is irreversible: The entrant must be convinced that if it enters, the incumbent will have no choice but to carry out its threat. However, a limit pricing strategy is not credible because a commitment to maintain the same price and the same quantity if the entrant enters is not irreversible. Indeed, it is rapid and easy for Firm 1 to change its price instantly if Firm B enters the market.

35. The limit pricing strategy can be rehabilitated if there is an information asymmetry between firms. For example, suppose that Firm B does not know with certainty Firm A's cost of production; in this case, a limit pricing strategy can credibly indicate the cost of production of the incumbent firm (Milgrom & Roberts, 1982A).

Here we find a classical teaching of the military theory, which states that to coerce an adversary one must convince him that there is no choice but to execute the threat if he resists. Thus, in his book *Art of War*, the Chinese strategist Sun Tzu illustrated this principle in a vivid way: "At the critical moment, the leader of an army acts like one who has climbed up a height and then kicks away the ladder behind him. He carries his men deep into hostile territory before he shows his hand."

Only an irrevocable commitment can make a threat credible; the essence of a deterrence strategy therefore lies in the voluntary and irreversible sacrifice of its freedom of choice. As Schelling points out in *The Strategy of Conflict* (1960), credible strategies are based on the following paradox: the power to compel an opponent depends on the power to compel oneself irrevocably; no one can bind unless he is bound himself or gives the appearance of being bound.

§2 A CREDIBLE AND COST-EFFECTIVE DETERRENCE MODEL

The credibility principle can be illustrated through a simple sequential game, which also highlights another important condition: the profitability of deterrence.

The hypotheses of the model: Firm A, in a monopoly situation, is threatened by the entry of newcomer B (Dixit, 1982). In the absence of entry, Firm A retains a monopoly profit Π^M, equal to \$100. In case of entry, Firm A must choose between:

- launching a price war: This choice results in a negative profit Π^W for both firms, equal to -\$10;
- letting Firm B enter the market and accepting a duopoly situation. In this case, each firm receives a positive profit Π^D, equal to \$30;

By definition, we have:

$$\Pi^M > \Pi^D > 0 > \Pi^W$$

As we have seen above, in the absence of any action of Firm A before Firm B's entry, Firm B will always enter since it anticipates that Firm A's best response is to accept a duopoly situation: $\Pi^D > \Pi^W$.

Now suppose that Firm A can, in the first period of the game, make an irreversible investment K before Firm B decides to enter (Figure 5.24). This investment cannot be recovered by being resold: For instance, it is an advertising or R&D investment. The aim of this investment is to give credibility to the threat of war if Firm B enters the market. It therefore does not affect the (negative) profit of Firm A if it decides to go to war. On the other hand, this investment affects the profit of Firm A if it does not use it, either because Firm B decides not to enter or because Firm A accepts the duopoly situation. In the first case, the profit of Firm A is:

$$(\Pi^M - K)$$

$$\Leftrightarrow (\$100 - K)$$

In the second case, the duopoly profit for Firm A is reduced by investment K:

$$(\Pi^D - K)$$

$$\Leftrightarrow (\$30 - K)$$

The three-step sequential game can be represented as follows:

Figure 5.24 A Credible Deterrence Model

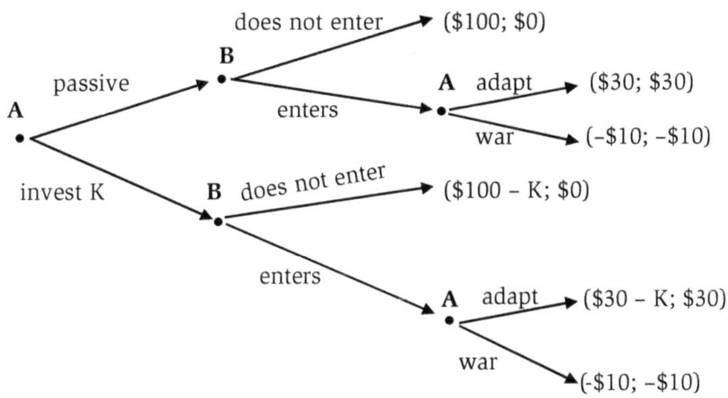

NB: In the payments, the first number represents the profit of the player who plays the first (here Firm A) and the second number, the profit of the player who plays next (here Firm B).

The two conditions for deterrence: The implementation of a credible deterrence strategy requires two conditions to be met simultaneously:

- a credibility condition: K must be high enough to deter Firm B from entering the market. To do this, Firm A, in case of Firm B's entry, must suffer lower losses if it opts for war, than if it chooses to adapt:

$$\Pi^W > (\Pi^D - K) \qquad (1)$$

$$\Leftrightarrow K > \$40$$

Indeed, if Firm A invests, for example, $41, it suffers a loss of $11 if it does not start a price war, instead of a loss of $10 if it does go to war;

- a profitability condition: K should not be too high. The profit of Firm A when it discourages Firm B's entry should be higher than the profit it would obtain if it had stayed passive. This second condition implies:

$$(\Pi^M - K) > \Pi^D \qquad (2)$$

$$\Leftrightarrow (\$100 - K) > \$30$$

$$\Leftrightarrow K < \$70$$

The deterrence strategy will be effective and profitable if conditions (1) and (2) are simultaneously verified. It means that the value of K must be within the following inequality:

$$(\Pi^M - \Pi^D) > K > (\Pi^D - \Pi^W)$$

$$\Leftrightarrow \$70 > K > \$40$$

If we represent the investment K on a horizontal axis, we have three cases (Figure 5.25):

- if the investment is less than \$40, the strategy is profitable but not credible, because the level of investment is insufficient;
- if the investment is more than \$70, the deterrence strategy is credible but not profitable for Firm A. This is the case, for example, if the entrant is very efficient: Discouraging the entry would be too expensive for Firm A;
- for an investment between \$40 and \$70, Firm A can deter the entry in a credible and profitable way.

Figure 5.25 Level of Investment and Deterrence

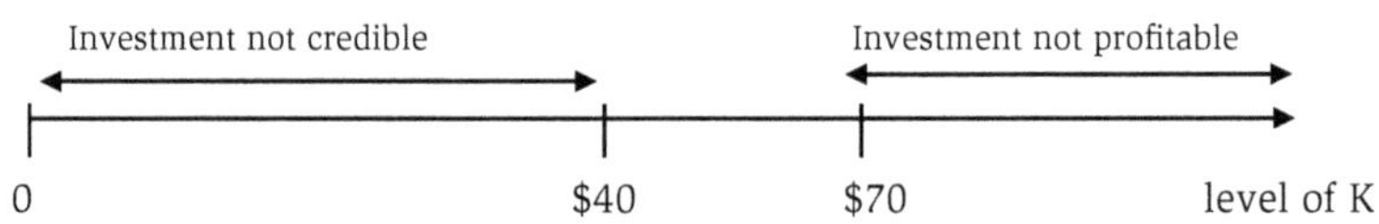

Figure 5.26 A Credible Deterrence Model

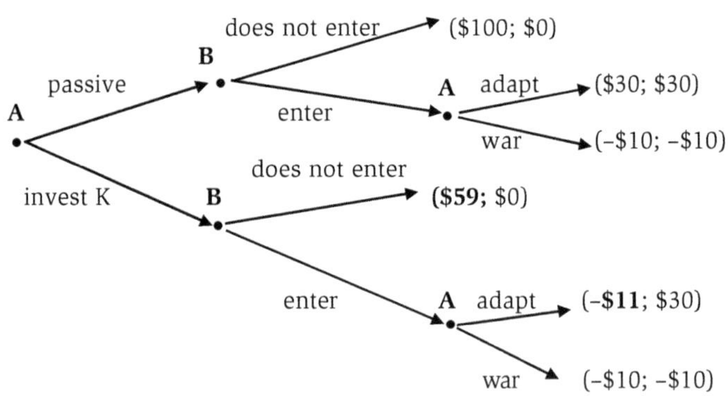

NB: In the payments, the first number represents the profit of the player who plays the first (here Firm A) and the second number, the profit of the player who plays next (here Firm B).

If we use integers, Firm A should invest \$41 in order to deter Firm B from entering the market; it would stay in a monopoly position and would obtain a profit of \$59, instead of \$30 if it had remained passive (Figure 5.26).

Some examples of irreversible investments*:* An irreversible investment can take many forms that can be classified into two categories, depending on whether it concerns production costs or the demand function (Neven, 1989).

Concerning cost-based deterrence, the incumbent can implement different strategies:

- invest in excess production capacity: The incumbent will increase its production capacity beyond the level it would have chosen in the absence of entry threat (Spence, 1977; Dixit, 1980). It thus modifies its marginal cost function, which influences its reaction function. This commitment is only credible if the investment in production capacity is irreversible; this is the case, for example, if the investment is specific with a low resale value on the second-hand market;
- increase rivals' cost of production: Rather than acting on its own cost of production, the incumbent can increase the entrant's cost of production. Consider the case of an incumbent firm that uses a relatively capital-intensive production process, while the newcomer uses a relatively labor-intensive production process (Williamson, 1968; Salop & Scheffman, 1983). Let us also assume that the industry in which both firms operate includes a workers' union. The wage bargaining process takes the following form: The union first negotiates with the incumbent firm. The entrant has no choice but to align itself with the wage conditions already negotiated. It may be advantageous for the incumbent firm to give a wage increase to the worker's union; this choice will negatively affect its marginal production cost, but will further handicap the new entrant, given the high labor intensity of its production process;[36]
- accelerate the technological pace: The dominant firm may prevent the entry of competitors by filing news patents (Gilbert & Newbery, 1982) without using them. The firm Rank Xerox implemented this so-called *"sleeping patent"* strategy in the photocopier market during 1970s.

Concerning demand-based strategies, two main strategies can be implemented:

- a product proliferation strategy: An incumbent firm with a product X can launch a new product Y with the sole purpose of preventing the entry of a competitor on product Y in competition with its product X. The incentive for a monopoly is similar to that described in the case of technological preemption:

36. The reasoning can be extended to variables other than wages; for example, a discriminatory tax such as a customs tariff imposed on imports which, by definition, does not affect domestic enterprises.

The total profit of the incumbent when it produces both X and Y is higher than the total profit when a competitor introduces a product Y. It is important to note that the incumbent would not have launched the product Y if there had not been a threat of entry. Moreover, this strategy is only credible if the launch of the product Y is irreversible (e.g., with high exit costs). The case of breakfast cereals is a well-known case of "*product proliferation*" (Schmalensee, 1978): In 1981, the U.S. FTC opened an investigation against the three American breakfast cereal leaders because they introduced more than 150 new products to the market during the period spanning 1950-1970, with the aim of deterring the entry of new competitors. According to the FTC, new firms were discouraged from entering the market given both fixed costs (production and marketing) and the space saturation of product characteristics;[37]

- the use of advertising expenses: Since advertising expenses are a fixed and sunk cost, the incumbent can increase its level of investment in order to deter entry. This strategy reduces the profitability of entry: The newcomer needs to make heavy advertising investments or significantly reduce its price to attract its first consumers. However, the effectiveness of an advertising deterrence strategy raises doubts: As Schmalensee (1983) notes, this strategy can expand the market size and thus make it more attractive for a new firm.

These different deterrence strategies, while theoretically possible, remain very difficult to demonstrate empirically, because the potential competitor has not entered the market; many reasons other than an abuse of dominant position may explain why a newcomer ultimately decides not to enter the market. The standard of proof of an ex-ante abuse of dominant position would necessarily be very high, making it difficult for antitrust authorities to detect and prove.

Review Topics:

Under what conditions can an entry deterrence strategy be successful?
What are the main forms of exclusionary abuses?
What are the main forms of exploitative abuses?
How can one assess a firm's dominant position?
What is the scope and limitations of the "essential facilities" theory?
What are the conditions necessary for predatory pricing to be profitable?
What are the scope and limitations of the Chicago School's predatory pricing arguments?
How can one detect predatory pricing?

Recommended Readings:

Avinash Dixit, *The Role of Investment in Entry Deterrence* (Economic Journal 95-106, 1980).
Avinash Dixit, *Recent Developments in Oligopoly Theory* (American Economic Review 12-17, 1982).

37. The case was dismissed.

Richard Gilbert, *Mobility Barriers and the Value of Incumbency,* in *Handbook of Industrial Organization* [R. Schmalensee and R. Willig (eds.) Chapter 8, North Holland, 1996].

Damien Neven, *Strategic Entry Deterrence: Recent Developments in the Economics of Industry* (Journal of Economic Surveys 213-233, 1989).

John McGee, *Predatory Pricing Revisited* (Journal of Law and Economics 289-300, 1980).

Paul Milgrom and John Roberts, *New Theories of Predatory Pricing,* in *Industrial Structure in the New Industrial Economics* [G. Bonanno and D. Brandolini (eds.) 112-136, Clarendon Press, 1990].

Louis Phlips, *Competition Policy: A Game-Theoretic Perspective* (Cambridge University Press, 1995).

CHAPTER 6

Merger Control

The life of a market is continuously driven by external growth operations, through which firms develop by merging with other firms. There have been several consecutive waves of mergers and acquisitions (M&A) since the end of the 19th century.

The first wave occurred between 1897 and 1907, mainly in the United States. This movement concerned sectors born during the second industrial revolution, such as railways, the oil and mining industry, and food distribution, and took the form of takeovers of competitors. It led to quasi-monopolistic market structures, prompting the U.S. DOJ to prosecute big firms for violating the Sherman Act.

A second wave took place in the United States during the 1916-1929 period, even though the government had adopted the Clayton Act in 1914, which contains provisions on anti-competitive mergers. During this second wave, there were vertical and oligopolistic mergers, particularly in the banking, chemicals and agri-food industries.

A third wave occurred in the United States and in Europe between 1965 and 1969. In the case of America, conglomerate mergers were developed: firms, driven by a strong economic growth, built up diversified business portfolios.

Between 1984 and 1989, a fourth wave coincided with an era of deregulation and privatization. During this period, hostile takeover bids developed (consisting of buying a firm against the consent of its managers), as well as takeovers financed by a massive debt.

A fifth wave took place during the 1990s and was marked by a refocusing of firms on their core business, in contrast to the diversification strategies that prevailed during the 1960s. We also saw "*mega deals*," bringing together leaders in their sector, such as in the media (Time Warner/AOL, Vivendi/Seagram, and so on) or in telecoms (France Telecom/Orange). Cross-border mergers and acquisitions multiplied (in particular, transatlantic M&As), reflecting the globalization of markets in several sectors: traditional mature activities (steel, automobile), but also sectors facing digitalization (communications and media) or new technological challenges such as the pharmaceutical industry, with the development of biotechnologies and many blockbuster patents expiring.

A sixth wave took place between 2003 and 2007, before the 2008 financial crisis that led to a sharp decline in the number of mergers.

Since 2013, M&A activity has been re-emerging worldwide, with the development of mega deals worth more than $10 billion: For instance, the merger between American operators Sprint and T-Mobile US resulted in a stock market valuation of $26.8 billion.

Why do firms merge?: Mergers are motivated by different factors. Most often, they are presented (by managers, investment funds, bankers, etc.) as a way to create market value for shareholders. The famous "*1 + 1 = 3*" thesis claims that the value of the new firm after the merger will be higher than the sum of the values of the two separate firms. This promise to create market value explains why a merger results in the payment of a premium to shareholders of the targeted firm. This premium is on average 15%.

Efficiencies are the first cause of value creation; thanks to the merger, merging firms will reduce their production costs, create revenue synergies and acquire new technologies or skills. However, a merger can also create market value in another way: By reducing competition, it will raise prices. A simple example illustrates this second effect.

Suppose that two firms A and B with identical marginal costs compete in a Cournot duopoly (Figure 6.1). Each firm makes a profit of $15. Firm A decides to takeover Firm B, in order to reduce its marginal cost (through a scale effect). This efficiency leads to a price decrease. But the merger between the two firms also leads to a monopoly situation. The new entity (A + B) will therefore reduce quantities and increase the price. Through the merger, Firm A will not only recover the market share and profits of Firm B (i.e., $15), it will also increase its profit by $20. The increase in profit for Firm A is therefore ($15 + $20), i.e., $35. Despite the gain in efficiencies, the merger will lead to higher prices, which reduces the consumer surplus (although it may increase the overall surplus by increasing the profit of the new entity).

Figure 6.1 The Competitive Impact of a Merger: A Duopoly Example

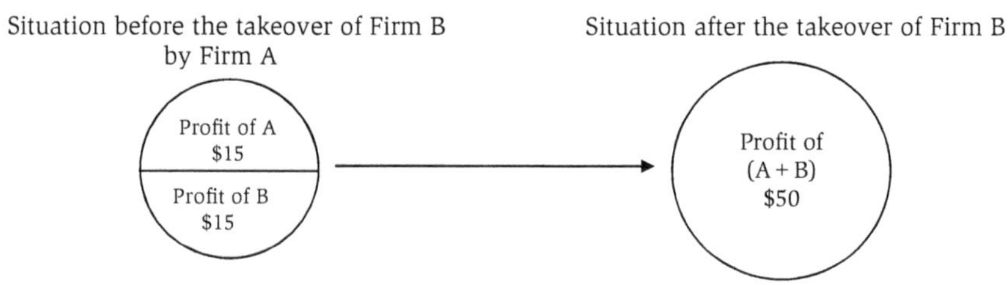

The role of competition authorities: Because mergers have an ambivalent effect on welfare, many countries have set up a system of merger control: Before merging, firms must first notify the competition authorities of their merger project in order to obtain approval beforehand.

For example, during the period spanning 2010-2020, the EU received between 300 and 400 merger notifications per year, while the U.S. authorities were notified of 1,000-2,000 projects per year (Figure 6.2).

Figure 6.2 Merger Notifications in Europe and the United States

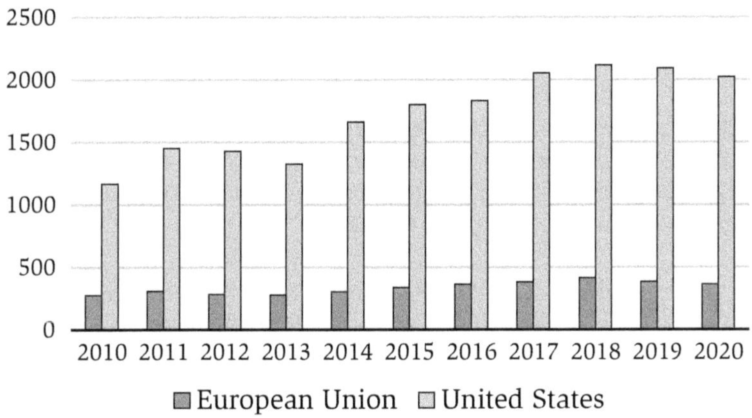

Source: Made by the author using data from the European Commission and the FTC.

In this chapter, we will first analyze the merger control process, which can lead to several outcomes (Section 1).

We'll then review the first step of the merger control process, which consists of defining the relevant markets (Section 2), and then focus on how market shares evolve before and after the merger (Section 3).

Once it has been established that the merger will strongly increase market concentration, competition authorities must analyze whether the project is likely to thwart competition or not. This is done by developing a "*theory of harm*" (Section 4). On the other hand, merging firms can try to defend their project by arguing that, even if the merger may have some anti-competitive effects, it will also produce efficiencies that will offset the competition infringements (Section 5).

SECTION 1 THE MERGER CONTROL PROCEDURE

In this first section, we'll review the legal framework in the United States and in Europe, before analyzing the way in which competition authorities control mergers. We'll show that the control takes place before the merger project occurs and is a selective process, with some thresholds (§1). We will then present the process of control and its different outcomes, from unconditional approval to prohibition (§2).

The legal framework in the United States and Europe: In the United States, Section 7 of the Clayton Act (1914) states that a M&A may be prohibited if it has the effect of significantly reducing competition or creating a monopoly. The scope of this text, initially limited to the acquisition of securities, was extended to the acquisition of assets with the adoption of the Celler-Kefauver Act in 1950 and the Hart-Scott-Rodino Act in 1978.

Merger notifications are reviewed by the FTC and the Antitrust Division of the DOJ. Depending on their sectorial expertise, the FTC and the DOJ share the file review: For example, the DOJ generally deals with files in the Air Transport industry, while the FTC has an expertise in the oil industry. In order to help firms assess the competitive impact of their merger, U.S. authorities have published Horizontal Merger Guidelines (2010) for mergers between competitors and Non-Horizontal Merger Guidelines (2020) for vertical and conglomerate projects.

In the EU, the merger control was not included in the Treaty of Rome (1957); it was introduced in 1990 through the Merger Regulation 139/2004, and was accompanied by the publication of various guidelines (on the relevant market, horizontal mergers, non-horizontal mergers and remedies).

Table 6.1 Merger Control Texts and Guidelines

Country	*Legal Texts*	*Guidelines*
United States	- Clayton Act, Section 7 (1914) - Celler-Kefauver Act (1950) - Hart-Scott-Rodino Act (1976)	- Non-Horizontal Merger Guidelines (2020) - Horizontal Merger Guidelines (2010)
European Union	- Merger Regulation 139/2004	- Communication regarding the relevant market (1997) - Communication regarding acceptable remedies (2008) - Non-Horizontal Merger Guidelines (2008) - Horizontal Merger Guidelines (2004)

§1 A Prior and Conditional Control

Unlike antitrust activities, which assesses anti-competitive behaviors a posteriori, merger control takes place before the merger project occurs (i.e., an ex-ante control). This control is mandatory as soon as the merger exceeds certain thresholds in terms of turnover. It covers any transaction that leads one firm to exercise a "*decisive influence*" over another firm, and is not limited to mergers and acquisitions.

Merger notification: Principles and specificities: Merger control is based on a "*prior notification*" system: Firms must obtain approval before carrying out their projects. The prior notification process prevents competition authorities from challenging a merger after it's been completed. It is based on the adage "*prevention is better* *than cure*"; because detecting anti-competitive behavior is difficult, it is better to monitor market structures.

However, this a priori method means that the effects of a merger should be assessed before its implementation. The risk is therefore twofold for competition authorities: First, prohibiting a merger that would in reality have been pro-competitive ("*type 1 error*"); second, allowing a merger that will be harmful to competition to go forward ("*type 2 error*").

The notification system presents several specific features:

- it is mandatory, as long as the project fulfills certain conditions. Failure to notify, whether through negligence or intentional infringement, may be sanctioned. For example, in France, the French Competition Authority fined Colruyt €392,000 in 2012 for carrying out a merger without any prior notification;
- the project is temporarily stopped: The merger can only be effectively implemented once competition authorities have given approval. Carrying out a merger before obtaining this approval—a practice known as "*gun jumping*"—may be sanctioned. Thus, in 2016, the French Competition Authority sanctioned Altice with a fine of €80 million for having carried out two mergers (the acquisition of SFR and Virgin Mobile) before obtaining clearance. Similarly, in 2018, the European Commission fined Altice €124.5 million for having exercised its control over PT Portugal before the Commission's approval;
- it is carried out within strict deadlines, in Europe. In the United States, however, there is no official deadline for notification, but a merger cannot be effectively completed until American competition authorities have been notified and have approved;
- all undertakings are concerned, whatever their nationality: For example, if two American firms, that sell in Europe, decide to merge, they should not only notify U.S. authorities of their project, but equally authorities in Europe. This situation leads to multi-notifications in the case of mega deals, which entails significant legal costs for the undertakings. Given the variety of evaluation criteria used in the various countries and the different competitive impact of the same merger across countries, the merger assessment is not always the same between countries: In the General Electric/Honeywell case (2001), the project was authorized in the United States but blocked by the European Commission, leading the two firms to abandon their merger;
- it commits firms to provide accurate information: Any omission or inaccurate statement may result in financial penalties. For example, in 2017, the European Commission imposed a penalty of €110 million on Facebook for providing incorrect and misleading information about Facebook's acquisition of WhatsApp;
- there is a certain legal formalism: In Europe, for example, firms should file a form and send it to the Competition Directorate. This form is composed of different sections, including information on the merger, the relevant markets,

the affected markets, the structure of supply and demand, and the entry barriers;
- the notification system may take the form of a "*simplified procedure*" when the merger is not likely to raise competitive concerns; this is the case, for example, if the undertakings are not present in the same or related markets;
- in Europe, the notification system is based on a "*one-stop shop*" principle: If the merger is controlled by the European Commission, it is not controlled by one of the Member States.[38]

The definition of a merger*:* The notion of merger goes beyond the mere case of a full merger or acquisition. Thus, at European level, the Merger Regulation 139/2004 refers to any transaction involving a change of corporate control:

> 1. A concentration shall be deemed to arise where a change of control on a lasting basis results from:
>   (a) the merger of two or more previously independent undertakings or parts of undertakings, or
>   (b) the acquisition, by one or more persons already controlling at least one undertaking, or by one or more undertakings, whether by purchase of securities or assets, by contract or by any other means, of direct or indirect control of the whole or parts of one or more other undertakings.
> 2. Control shall be constituted by rights, contracts or any other means which, either separately or in combination and having regard to the considerations of fact or law involved, confer the possibility of exercising decisive influence on an undertaking, in particular by:
>   (a) ownership or the right to use all or part of the assets of an undertaking;
>   (b) rights or contracts which confer decisive influence on the composition, voting or decisions of the organs of an undertaking.
> 3. Control is acquired by persons or undertakings which:
>   (a) are holders of the rights or entitled to rights under the contracts concerned; or
>   (b) while not being holders of such rights or entitled to rights under such contracts, have the power to exercise the rights deriving therefrom.
> 4. The creation of a joint venture performing on a lasting basis all the functions of an autonomous economic entity shall constitute a concentration within the meaning of paragraph 1(b) (Article 3).

For example, the acquisition of a minority shareholding, when shareholders are dispersed and the new shareholder has a decision-making power, could be considered as a merger. Similarly, the possibility for the new shareholder to increase its stake at a later stage (e.g., by holding securities convertible into shares), or other elements such as the capability to influence the strategic decisions, are taken into account when estimating the "*decisive influence*" that one firm has on another. The Merger Regulation also applies to JVs if the latter is jointly controlled by its founders and if it performs all the functions of an autonomous economic entity. To be considered as a "*full function*" JV, "a joint venture must operate on a market, performing the functions normally carried out by undertakings operating on the same market. In order to do so

38. However, there is a possibility of partial referral to a Member State.

the joint venture must have a management dedicated to its day-to-day operations and access to sufficient resources including finance, staff, and assets (tangible and intangible) in order to conduct on a lasting basis its business activities within the area provided for in the joint-venture agreement" (point 12).[39]

Notification thresholds: The prior notification system is selective; the aim is to assess a merger that may affect competition on a market. Given the large number of mergers concluded each year and the limited resources of antitrust authorities, a systematic audit of all mergers would not only be unnecessary but also impossible.

Which criteria and what thresholds do competition authorities use? The most common criterion is based on the undertaking's turnover. The turnover criterion has the advantage of being simple, as firms and competition authorities can quickly know whether the thresholds have been reached. However, such a criterion may lead to exclude from the control small and innovative firms with a low turnover but whose acquisition could have a strong impact on competition, for example, because of their growth perspectives.

At the European level, the Merger Regulation 139/2004 applies to mergers with a European dimension. The definition of thresholds is fundamental because it determines the allocation of cases between the European Commission and national authorities. The thresholds are defined in terms of turnover on the basis of three cumulative thresholds:

- the main threshold: The total worldwide turnover of all undertakings exceeds €5 billion;
- the "*de minimis*" threshold: The total turnover achieved individually in the EU by at least two of the undertakings exceeds €250 million. We can see that while the global turnover threshold is high, the one for Europe is low: A merger between two large non-European firms that have most of their turnover outside Europe may fall under European regulations;
- the transnationality threshold: Each of the undertaking firms does not achieve more than two-thirds of its total turnover in a single Member State. Otherwise, the European Commission's competence gives way to that of a national authority.

A merger that does not reach the above thresholds is nevertheless of a European dimension if:

- the total worldwide turnover of all the undertakings exceeds €2.5 billion;
- in each of at least three EU countries, the total turnover of all undertakings exceeds €100 million;
- in each of at least three EU countries, the total individual turnover of at least two undertakings exceeds €25 million;

39. Commission Communication of March 2, 1998 on the concept of a full-function joint venture.

- the aggregate EU-wide turnover of at least two undertakings individually exceeds €100 million, unless each undertaking achieves more than two-thirds of its EU-wide turnover within a single country.

It may be noted that the European Commission may, in particular cases, refer some mergers with a European dimension to a national competition authority. At the same time, the European Commission may examine a transaction with a national dimension at the request of the undertakings or a national competition authority.

§2 Merger Control: Process and Outcome

Two phases of investigation*:* A two-stage procedure is applied in most countries. The first stage, "*phase 1*," is quite brief (25 working days in Europe) and constitutes a necessary step for any merger: If the case does not raise competition issues or if these issues are resolved by appropriate commitments, the merger control is ended and an authorization is given, with or without commitments.

If the competition authority considers that there are serious doubts about the competitive impact, it may then decide to open a "*phase 2*" (or an "*in-depth investigation phase*"). This second phase is longer (around two to three months, depending on whether there are commitments or not) and binding for undertakings. In the European case, Phase 2 implies that undertakings will receive a "*statement of objections*" and the procedure is quite similar to that of an antitrust case: The Commission may collect all the necessary information and carry out any checks, in particular by interviewing third parties. The undertakings must provide the information requested by the Commission in a complete, accurate and timely manner; if not, they may be subject to sanctions. In the United States, if the DOJ or the FTC wish to investigate further, they send undertakings a request for additional information.

At the European level as well as in the United States, we can see that Phase 2 is rarely initiated: During the 2010-2020 period, it concerned between 2% and 4% of cases (Figure 6.3). This is therefore a rare procedure, although it sometimes attracts large media attention given the size of the mergers and the financial stakes.

Figure 6.3 Percentage of Phase 2 in the United States and the EU

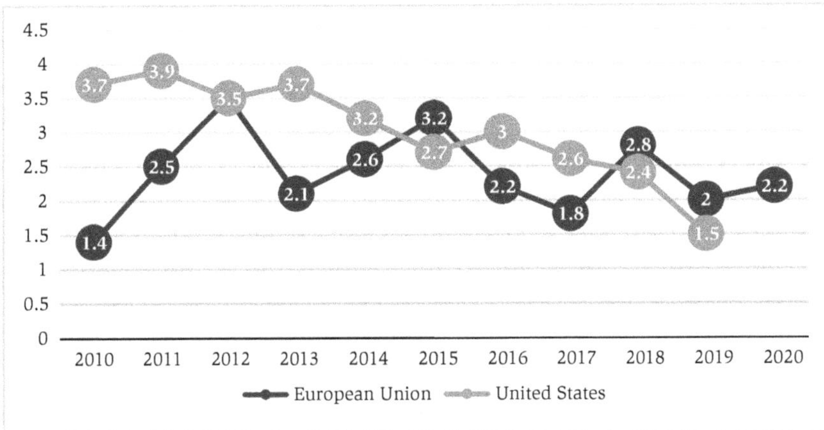

Source: European Commission and FTC (2021).

The results of the investigation*:* At the end of the investigation process, three types of decisions can be made:

- unconditional approval. At the European level, most projects are cleared (Figure 6.4): During the period spanning 2010-2020, 91% of a total of 3679 notifications were cleared unconditionally (in phase 1 or 2);
- approval with commitments or injunctions: Competition authorities accept the merger, but undertakings must propose remedies or accept injunctions to solve competition concerns. These remedies can be proposed in Phase 1 as well as in Phase 2. At the European level, during the period spanning 2010-2020, 186 operations were accepted with corrective measures, representing 5% of the total number of notified cases. If we consider only notifications that went through Phase 2, during the period spanning 2010-2020, 46 mergers were authorized with commitments, representing an intervention rate of 51%;
- prohibition: The merger is blocked by the competition authorities. Prohibition decisions remain rare, although they are usually subject to a lot of media coverage. At the European level, from 2010 to 2020, 10 mergers were blocked, representing less than 1% of notified cases (Figure 6.4). If we compare the bans with the number of Phase 2 investigations, the risk of prohibition is 11%. For example, in February 2019, the European Commission blocked the merger between Alstom and Siemens because the project would have been harmful to competition in the markets for rail-signaling systems and very high-speed trains in Europe.

Figure 6.4 Outcomes of Merger Control in the EU

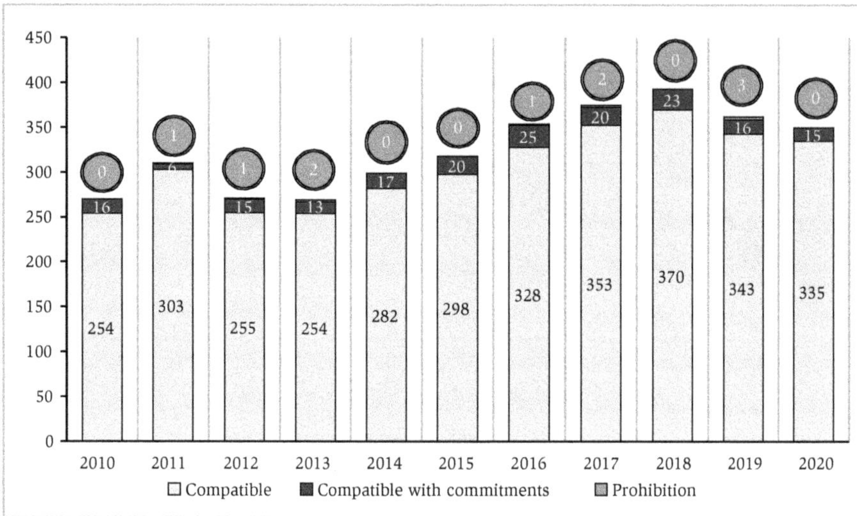

Source: European Commission (2021).

Undertakings can contest a competition authority's decision: In the United States, before a Federal Court of Appeals and then the U.S. Supreme Court; in the EU, before the Court of First Instance and then the ECJ. Thus, in 2002, the Court of First Instance cancelled the European Commission's decision to block three mergers:

- in the Airtours/First Choice case, the Court found that the European Commission did not provide sufficient evidence in support of its claim regarding the risk of a "*coordinated effect*" (*see* below);
- in the Schneider/Legrand case, the Court found that the European Commission's economic analysis was tainted by errors and omissions. In addition, the European Commission infringed the undertaking's defense rights by not basing its decision on the same grounds as those indicated in the statement of objections;
- in the Tetra Laval/Sidel case, the Court concluded that the European Commission overestimated the anti-competitive effects of the merger: The risk of extending Tetra Laval's dominant position from the cardboard packaging market to the plastic bottle market remained hypothetical.

The role of remedies: When a merger raises competitive concerns, the undertakings may propose remedies in both Phases 1 and 2. There are two types of remedies:

- structural remedies: Undertakings sell a part of their assets to third parties, most often competitors. For example, in 2017, the European Commission approved the merger between Dow and DuPont but required the divestiture of

a significant part of DuPont's global pesticide business, including its global R&D entity. Similarly, in 2018, when Bayer acquired Monsanto, the European Commission cleared the merger, conditional on the divestiture of a wide range of activities to address overlaps in the seeds, pesticides, and digital agriculture sectors. In particular, all of Bayer's seed R&D activity was sold to a competitor, BASF;
- behavioral remedies: Firms commit to adapt their behavior to third parties, especially in the use of their property rights. Behavioral measures are frequent when the merger has a vertical aspect, with a risk of market foreclosure: Merging firms should renounce exclusive contracts, facilitate competitors' access to essential infrastructures, or accept to give a license to competitors.

In practice, remedies can address both structural and behavioral commitments. For example, in 2001, the European Commission approved EDF's entry in the stock of the German electricity firm EnBW but required several counterparts: EDF had to terminate its commercial relations with Compagnie Nationale du Rhône and divest itself of its voting rights; EDF also had to promote the opening of the French market to competition, by auctioning *"drawing rights,"* allowing competitors to have a virtual capacity of 6,000 megawatts.

In order to guide undertakings in designing acceptable remedies, antitrust authorities publish Guidelines on Remedies. For example, in the United States, the FTC publishes an information notice on the implementation of remedies,[40] and several key features are worth noting:

- the asset divested should be used independently, which may require a broader transfer of assets. Conversely, if the undertakings propose to divest only part of an activity, they must show that the buyer has the additional skills to carry out the activity normally;
- the potential buyer must be a financially viable competitor, able to restore competition on the market. The FTC generally requires that the transfer must be completed before the end of the control ("*up-front buyer*" method);
- the transfers must be carried out within strict deadlines. Some consent decrees also include so-called "*crown jewels*" clauses: If the undertakings do not complete the transfer within the prescribed time limits, new assets must be sold;
- the divestiture agreement may include obligations to assist the buyer if the asset is particularly complex to transfer. In particular, when the undertakings sell intangible assets such as patents or know-how, they must ensure that the transfer will be effective.

Similarly, at the European level, the implementation of corrective measures gave rise in 2008 to a Commission Communication, which emphasizes several key points:

40. *Statement of the FTC's Bureau of Competition on Negotiating Merger Remedies* (2003); *see also*: Parker & Balto (2000).

- the undertakings should demonstrate that the proposed commitments, once implemented, will remove competition concerns raised by the European Commission;
- the business transferred must be viable: It should be operated independently. Thus, the European Commission may include assets related to markets in which it has not identified competition concerns. In addition, the viability of a business also depends on the identity of the acquirer: "the purchaser must possess the financial resources, proven relevant expertise and have the incentive and ability to maintain and develop the divested business as a viable and active competitive force in competition with the parties and other competitors";
- the proposed remedy must be sufficiently precise to be assessed by the European Commission;
- it must be possible to implement the commitments effectively and in a timely manner;
- a trustee is appointed and has to check the right implementation of corrective measures. This trustee has a wide scope of action, including the right to propose and, when appropriate, to impose measures to comply with the commitments.

Structural or behavioral remedies?: Compared to behavioral commitments, structural remedies have the advantage of not requiring an ex-post supervision: This explains why they are generally preferred by competition authorities. Thus, in its Communication on Remedies (2008), the Commission recalls that: "commitments which are structural in nature, such as the commitment to sell a business unit, are, as a rule, preferable from the point of view of the Merger Regulation's objective, inasmuch as such commitments prevent, durably, the competition concerns which would be raised by the merger as notified, and do not, moreover, require medium or long-term monitoring measures. Nevertheless, the possibility cannot automatically be ruled out that other types of commitments may also be capable of preventing the significant impediment of effective competition" (paragraph 15).

However, structural remedies can raise several difficulties:

- they are riskier for antitrust authorities, as they are largely irreversible. If assets divested are sold to a firm that later proves to be an inefficient firm, it is not possible to go back;
- with economies of scope, the structural remedy requires the sale of a wide portfolio of products, including those not directly affected by the merger;
- undertakings may voluntarily depreciate the value of the divested assets (staff transfers, etc.) or select a buyer that is unable to stimulate competition on the market. To avoid these pitfalls, the potential purchaser must be approved by competition authorities (the so-called "*up-front buyer*" procedure). Similarly, in order to limit asset impairment behavior, competition authorities may impose strict time limits for reselling: If the deadlines are not respected, the

scope of the divested assets is increased (the so-called "crown jewels" procedure);
- structural remedies are not always possible: There is not necessarily a viable competitor able to buy the divested assets, as in the Boeing/McDonnell Douglas case. Similarly, a merger may lead the undertaking to control an "*essential infrastructure*," which is not divisible: In this case, the undertakings must commit to guarantee competitors access to their infrastructure.

The competitive analysis of a merger: Once the notification file has been submitted, competition authorities analyze the merger, adopting a multi-step approach.

The first step consists of delineating the markets in which the undertakings operate in order to identify possible market overlaps: This step of delineating the relevant markets is a prerequisite for any analysis.[41]

Once relevant markets have been delineated, competition authorities move on to a second stage: They analyze the market after the merger by considering the evolution of market shares. If the market concentration after the merger is low enough, the analysis stops at this second step and the merger is approved.

On the other hand, if the undertaking's market shares will be high after the merger, a third step is open. It consists of evaluating the risk that the merger will be harmful for competition by developing a "*theory of harm*" scenario. Indeed, the relationship between market share and market power is not automatic and justifies a case-by-case analysis.

If the risks are likely, competition authorities analyze if the merger generates sufficient efficiencies to offset the harm done to competition, or, if the target, in the absence of the merger, would have gone bankrupt. This last argument, known as the "*failing firm exception*," is explicitly taken into account in the United States in Section 11 of the Horizontal Mergers Guidelines (2010): "(...) a merger is not likely to enhance market power if imminent failure of one of the merging firms would cause the assets of that firm to exit the relevant market."

Similarly, in Europe, the argument of the failing firm can be used if three cumulative conditions are met, as the ECJ pointed out in its 1998 Kali + Salz case:

- the undertakings must demonstrate that, in the absence of the takeover, the target firm would have disappeared from the market in the short term. The aim here is to distinguish a real risk of bankruptcy from a transitional situation of financial losses;
- there are no alternative solutions that are less damaging to competition;
- the acquiring firm would have taken the market share of the target if the latter had disappeared from the market.

41. On rare occasions, an analysis based directly on the effects of the transaction is carried out without explicitly fulfilling the preliminary step of defining the relevant markets.

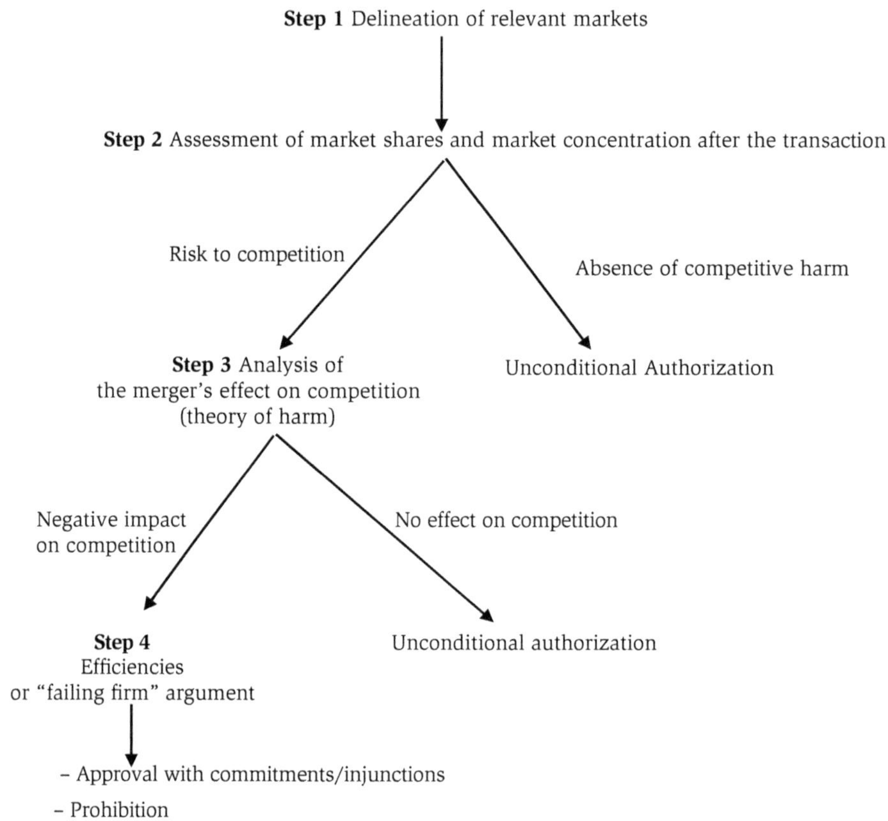

SECTION 2 DELINEATING THE RELEVANT MARKET

Before assessing the competitive impact of a merger, competition authorities must first identify the markets in which the merger takes place: Which product and geographic markets are likely to be affected by the merger? This is a delicate exercise based on a prospective analysis (and not retrospective, as in an abuse of dominant position or a cartel) and a set of both qualitative and quantitative indicators.

It is not surprising that the market delineation step gives rise to divergent assessments between competition authorities and undertakings, the latter being prone to adopt a broader market delineation. Thus, when the FTC challenged the acquisition of Dr. Pepper by Coca-Cola in 1986, the latter argued that the relevant market was the beverage market in general, because there was a close substitution between Coca-Cola's products and other beverages (such as fruit juices). The FTC responded that Coca-Cola's relevant market was a narrower market, given the strong brand image of Coca-Cola.

We'll start by presenting the notion of "relevant market" and the key role played by demand substitutability (§1). We'll continue by analyzing the main qualitative indicators used to delineate the relevant products market (§2). We'll then list the main qualitative indicators used to delineate the geographical relevant market (§3). We'll finish by exploring some quantitative methods that may be used by competition authorities to delineate the relevant market (§4).

§1 What is a Relevant Market?

The key role of demand substitutability: From an economic point of view, a market can be defined as a set of products that are highly substitutable with each other, both in terms of demand and supply within a geographical area. Demand-side substitutability means that different products are considered interchangeable by consumers within a given geographical area. In Europe, for instance, the Guidelines on the Definition of the Relevant Market (1997) state: "A relevant product market comprises all those products and/or services which are regarded as interchangeable or substitutable by the consumer, by reason of the products' characteristics, their prices and their intended use."

Concerning the geographic market, it "comprises the area in which the undertakings concerned are involved in the supply and demand of products or services, in which the conditions of competition are sufficiently homogeneous and which can be distinguished from neighbouring areas because the conditions of competition are appreciably different in those area."

Supply-side substitutability, on the other hand, means that new producers (already present on the market or able to enter quickly) can offer a product similar to those already on the market within a very short timeframe. Product B is considered a substitute for Product A if, in response to an increase in price of Product A, Product B suppliers can quickly modify their production to produce Product A.

In practice, competition authorities generally focus on demand-side substitutability to delineate the relevant market, with supply-side substitutability being analyzed during the assessment of the merger impact on competition (entry barriers, etc.).

The SSNIP test: A way to measure a relevant market: In theory, one way to delineate the relevant market is to ask whether the undertakings could increase their prices profitably by 5% to 10% after the merger.

If this is the case, then the relevant market is limited to the products of the merging firms. If this is not the case, the test is repeated with a wider range of products—the products of the undertakings plus relevant substitutes. This process is repeated over and over again, each time adding on other relevant substitutes until the price increase becomes profitable. This test is known as the "*hypothetical monopolist test*" or the "*SSNIP*" test (Small but Significant Non-Transitory Increase in Price).

The SSNIP test is used in the United States, as mentioned in the Mergers Guidelines (2010):

> The hypothetical monopolist test requires that a product market contain enough substitute products so that it could be subject to post-merger exercise of market power significantly exceeding that existing absent the merger. Specifically, the test requires that a hypothetical profit-maximizing firm, not subject to price regulation, that was the only present and future seller of those products ("hypothetical

> monopolist") likely would impose at least a small but significant and non-transitory increase in price ("SSNIP") on at least one product in the market, including at least one product sold by one of the merging firms.

The SSNIP test can be explained through a numerical example: Firms A and B produce Product A and Product B respectively. The marginal cost of each product is $60 and each firm sells 1,200 units at a price of $100. The profit of each firm is therefore equal to:

Pre-merger profit of Firm A: (100 – 60) × 1,200 = $48,000

Pre-merger profit of Firm B: (100 – 60) × 1,200 = $48,000

Firms A and B decide to merge and the market becomes a monopoly. After the merger, the new firm (A + B) will increase the price of Product A by 10%: The price therefore increases to $110. Suppose that Firm A, for every 1% increase in its price, loses 20 units in favor of firms other than Firm B, and 10 units in favor of Firm B. The reasoning is symmetrical for Firm B if it increases its price by 10%.

The question is then whether a 10% increase in price of Product A is profitable for the new entity: Does the additional margin on each unit sold compensate for the reduction in the number of customers? By increasing the price by 10%, Firm A loses 200 units in favor of firms other than Firm B, and 100 units in favor of Firm B. The profits of Firm A and Firm B are now equal to:

Post-merger profit of Firm A: [(1,200 – 200)](110 – 60) = $50,000

Post-merger profit of Firm B: [1,200 + 100](100 – 60) = $52,000

The price increase of Product A is therefore profitable for the new entity since the total profit of Firm (A + B) has increased from $96,000 to $102,000. It can therefore be found that the relevant market is limited to products A and B.

On the other hand, suppose that a 10% increase in the price of Product A leads to a two-thirds shift in sales to firms other than Firm B and only 10% to Firm B. The profits of Firms A and B are now equal to:

Post-merger profit of Firm A: [(1,200 – 800)](110 – 60) = $20,000

Post-merger profit of Firm B: [1,200 + 120](100 – 60) = $52,800

In this case, the 10% increase in the price of Product A is no longer profitable for the new entity (A + B): The total profit after the merger ($72,800) is less than the sum of the profits before the merger ($96,000). The new entity (A + B) cannot act as a monopolist after the merger. The market must be extended by including products from third parties. The SSNIP test is repeated until the price increase—each time including a new product/new firm—becomes profitable.

The risk of making a mistake when defining the relevant market: The cellophane fallacy: To be valid, the SSNIP test should be applied by starting from a competitive price; if not, the result could lead to a misinterpretation known as the "*cellophane fallacy.*" In the DuPont case (1956), DuPont was suspected of abusing its dominant position in the cellophane paper market. The U.S. antitrust authorities concluded that DuPont did not have a dominant position: At the price at which cellophane was sold, it was not profitable for DuPont to increase its prices because consumers would have switched to substitutable products. This reasoning is in fact misleading; if DuPont had been alone in the cellophane market, it would have already charged a monopoly price and therefore it would never have been profitable for it to increase its price by 5% above the monopoly price. This SSNIP test can therefore lead to a fallacy: A firm that charges a monopoly price will not be considered as a monopoly because a price increase would not be profitable. To avoid such pitfalls, it's necessary to delineate the relevant market for prices close to competitive prices.

In real life, as it is difficult to have sufficient empirical data to carry out the SSNIP test, competition authorities use a set of indicators consisting of qualitative and quantitative criteria to assess the contours of the relevant market. Without claiming to be exhaustive, we will now list the main criteria used, separating those used to define product market from those used to delineate the geographical market. We will present quantitative criteria in §3.

§2 Product Market Definition: Main Indicators

From a practical point of view, in order to define the contours of products markets, antitrust authorities use different qualitative indicators, such as: price differences, physical characteristics of products and their use, consumer behavior, distribution channels, the role of brands, and marketing strategies (Table 6.2). We will review each of them below.

Table 6.2 Relevant Product Market: The Main Qualitative Indicators

Indicator	*Interpretation*
Price differences	Significant and lasting price differences reflect a low substitutability between products.
Product characteristics	Similar products do not always have the same use; physically different products may satisfy the same use.
Consumer's behavior	Different types of clients can be identified according to consumption habits, etc.
Distribution channels	Different distribution channels for similar products reduce the substitutability of demand.
Role of brands	The presence of brands creates vertical differentiation and a market segmentation according to quality levels.
Marketing strategy	The targeting of marketing policies on certain products reveals a market segmentation.

Price differences: Significant and lasting price differences between two products can be the sign of a low substitutability.

Suppose that the price of Product X is twice as high as that of Product Y within the same geographical area. If the two products belong to the same market, this price difference is not sustainable: Consumers will shift to Product Y, which would lead to a decrease in the price of Product X.

Thus, when Nestlé acquired Perrier in 1992, the European Commission found that spring water was not substitutable with soft drinks (lemonades, etc.), given the wide price differential between these two types of product. Similarly, in the VUP/Lagardère case (2004), the European Commission questioned the segmentation of the book market, particularly by format. In particular, it distinguished between hardback books and paperback books, on the grounds that the distribution of price was very different between the two types of books.

The physical and usage characteristics of the products: Physically different goods often do not belong to the same relevant market. Thus, in the SEB/Moulinex case (2002), the European Commission distinguished 13 product markets within small electrical appliances. For example, a mini-oven market was identified: It included "ovens weighing around 20 kg and with a capacity varying from 10 to 35 liters used to cook all types of food within their capacity." These mini ovens must be distinguished from free-range ovens and built-in ovens, taking into account the difference in capacity and the range of technical functions.

In some cases, different goods may belong to the same market if they have the same uses. Thus, in the Kimberly-Clark/Scott (1996) case, the European Commission found that boxed tissues belonged to the same market as prepackaged pocket tissues, despite the difference in packaging, insofar as they satisfy the same end use. Similarly, in the SeaFrance/Eurotunnel case (2012), the French Competition Authority found that for leisure travel, trains were in the same market as ferry transports.

However, similar goods do not always belong to the same market if they do not satisfy the same needs. Thus, in the Entremont/Sodial case (2010), the French Competition Authority found that raclette cheese belongs to a market separate from other uncooked pressed pastes because of its specific use.

Consumer's behavior: Demand analysis aims to identify consumer preferences, and, in particular, to identify different groups of customers or products. This analysis can be based:

- on questionnaire surveys of clients (usually households);
- on econometric tests to characterize the demand function;
- on indirect methods, such as the study of suppliers' business strategies. For example, advertising campaigns or the layout of different products on supermarket shelves provides information on the segmentation of demand.

Thus, when examining the Coca-Cola/Amalgamated Beverage case (1999), the European Commission distinguished carbonated soft drinks (CSDs) from other types of beverages (fruit juices, dairy products, water, etc.), in particular because of consumption patterns: "The pattern of consumption seems to vary considerably from one type of drink to another. Mineral waters and fruit juices, for example, are consumed mainly at mealtimes at home and, in the case of fruit juices, at breakfast. CSDs are often consumed on other occasions, such as in fast food restaurants or at friendly meetings … ."

Similarly, different categories of consumers can be distinguished in some cases, despite the functional substitutability of the products:

- the market is not the same for individual consumers and for industrial clients. For example, in the Eridania/ISI case (1991), the European Commission divided the refined sugar sector into two: In the first market, sugar is sold in large quantities to agri-food firms; in the second market, sugar is sold in 1 kg bags to consumers and transport costs are high;
- the market is different when the buyers are public or private entities. Thus, in the Aerospatials/MBB (1991) case, the European Commission found that the market for civil helicopters should be distinguished from the market for military helicopters;
- the market is different depending on whether buyers are traveling for leisure or business purposes. Business travelers are looking for speed, comfort and frequency, while those on leisure trips consider price to be important.

Distribution channels: Technically similar products may nevertheless be perceived by consumers as being different if they are sold through different distribution channels. For example, in the Sara Lee/Benckiser case (2000), the French Competition Authority found that there were two distinct distribution channels for shoe care products: supermarkets and specialized stores (shoe shops, etc.). Indeed, several elements led to differentiate these two distribution channels:

- the price in the specialized circuit was two to three times higher than in supermarkets;
- firms selling shoe wax in both channels had different brands for each distribution mode;
- sales methods were not identical between the two channels.

Similarly, in the Coca-Cola/Orangina case (1999), the French Competition Authority considered two distribution channels for non-alcoholic soft drinks: the mass distribution channel and the out-of-home catering channel (hotels, cafés, restaurants).

Conversely, different distribution channels can nevertheless be considered as substitutable: This is the case of online operators, which may be in the same market as offline stores. Thus, analyzing a merger in the retail sector of games and toys in 2019, the French Competition Authority concluded:

> The substitutability of the two channels was confirmed by the majority of respondents to the market test conducted by the inspectors. They consider that online sales and in-store sales now fall within the same market for toy retail distribution. In addition, respondents to the market test widely indicated that, in case of a 5% to 10% increase in toy prices by the merged entity after the transaction, a majority of consumers would go to online sales sites. In the present case, the substitutability of distribution channels is also apparent from a series of precise and consistent indicators relating to: the penetration of online toy sales, the

> development of a commercial strategy taking into account online sales specialists, the analogy of product ranges and services offered in stores and online, the increasing price standardization within the various distribution channels, and the development of an "omnichannel" distribution model (free translation).

The role of brands: Differentiation by quality—and particularly by brand image—can be taken into account when defining the relevant market.

Thus, in the Guinness/Grand Metropolitan case (1997), the European Commission found that there were different market segments in spirits, because of the predominant role of brands:

> The importance of branding, and its application to individual spirit types, is a key characteristic of competition in the spirits industry, and is not consistent with a product market wider than that for each main spirit type. Product development, advertising and promotion expenditure are normally focused on the brand rather than the category or company, especially at the consumer level. Thus, for example, advertisements are typically for Johnnie Walker's whisky rather than for Guinness's range of whiskies or for their spirit products collectively. It is also of interest in this connection that, in general, brands do not appear to be easily transferable between spirit types; for example, there is no Johnnie Walker gin or Gordon's whisky. This behavior is consistent with product markets based on each spirit type, since it implies that manufacturers have adopted a strategy of branding for, and within, each spirit type in order to satisfy specific consumer demands in terms of taste, price and image.

The question of brands is particularly problematic when both branded and non-branded products are sold: To what extent should the two types of products be considered substitutable? In this respect, competition authorities proceed on a case-by-case basis. For example, when Marie Brizard was acquired in 2019, the French Competition Authority adopted a single market for branded and non-branded products excluding high-end and entry-level products for vodka and whisky.

Marketing strategies*:* The analysis of a firm's marketing policy helps to define the relevant market. For example, in the Schneider/Legrand case (2001), the European Commission found that electrical equipment manufacturers carried out a large number of special offers on some individual components rather than on all the components required to produce an electrical panel. The importance of these deals and their targeting of a single type of component indicates that competition is focused on each type of component, rather than between electrical panels.

§3 Geographic Market Definition: Main Indicators

Having delineated the products markets, we need to consider the geographical market because distance limits substitutability between two products. According to the French Competition Authority (2007), the relevant geographic market corresponds to the "geographical area in which monopoly power could actually be exercised, without being exposed to competition from other suppliers located in other geographical areas or from other goods and services" (free translation).

In order to define the contours of geographic markets, antitrust authorities use different qualitative indicators, such as: price differences, travel time and transportation costs, national regulations, international trade flows, or consumer preferences (Table 6.3). We will review each of them below.

Table 6.3 Geographic Relevant Market: Main Qualitative Indicators

Indicator	*Interpretation*
Price differences	Significant and lasting price differences for the same product reflect the low substitutability in the area chosen.
Transport costs, travel time	High transport costs and travel time limit the geographical substitutability of products.
National regulations	National regulations, particularly in terms of products standards (safety, etc.), limit trade-offs between countries.
International trade flows	Low international trade flows, when prices are different and transport costs limited, reflect the existence of different preferences between countries.
Customer preferences	Different customer preferences between regions or countries may indicate low substitutability between products.

Price differences: As with product market delineation, the persistence of a price differential between two areas for the same product implies that they are not in the same geographic market. Indeed, if the price of Product X is higher in area A than in area B, the arbitrage process should lead to a price convergence between the two geographical areas. If not, we can consider that the two areas are not part of the same market.

For example, in the Kimberly-Clark/Scott (1996) case, the European Commission found that there were substantial and lasting price differences between Great Britain and continental Europe in the toilet paper sector: The price of toilet paper that British consumers paid was more than 40% higher than that applied in Germany, Italy and Spain. In the case of handkerchiefs, the price difference was more than 100%, without any arbitrage between countries. The European Commission concluded that there were two relevant geographic markets: The United Kingdom and continental Europe. It should be noted that the comparison of a price differential between two countries with different currencies requires the use of an exchange rate: The choice of the latter may partly influence the result.

Travel time and transportation cost: Geographic distance implies a transportation cost or a travel time, which limits spatial arbitrage. In particular, when transportation costs are high compared to the product value, the relevant geographic market may be relatively small. This is particularly true for heavy and low-value products, such as building materials (cement, concrete, etc.). When consumers shop in physical stores, the travel time constraint also plays an important role.

Thus, in the Carrefour/Promodès case (2000), the European Commission determined a locally downstream market, based on consumers' shopping areas, products characteristics (perishable nature of the food, etc.), transport infrastructure, and existing commercial structures. In France, different catchment areas are determined in the case law in food retail distribution—particularly according to the size of the store and its location in the French territory.[42] For example, in the case of a hypermarket outside Paris, the catchment area includes customers located less than 30 minutes away by car.

In contrast, in the Hitachi/NEC case (2000), the European Commission found that the relevant market for dynamic memories (DRAMs) included all EU countries, given the low transport costs compared to the price of a DRAM, the similarity of preferences for this type of product, and the absence of import barriers. Similarly, in the GE/Honeywell case (2001), the European Commission concluded that there was a relevant worldwide market in all three aircraft engine markets (respectively: large commercial aircraft engines, regional aircraft engines, corporate jet engines) given the low transport costs.

National regulations*:* National regulations can fragment geographic markets, particularly when different official standards or rules exist between countries.

Thus, in the Astra/Zeneca case (1999), the European Commission found that the requirement for a national market approval, the conditions for reimbursing drugs, and the disparity of medical "cultures" led to define the markets on a national basis. Similarly, in the Schneider/Legrand case (2001), the European Commission found that the electrical equipment markets were national, because of the normative barriers between Member States:

- installation rules vary from country to country, particularly with regard to safety. These standards lead to using different components in low-voltage electricity distribution boards. For example, circuit breakers sold in Germany are single pole while they must be double pole in France and Italy;
- in addition to the mandatory CE marking,[43] it is often necessary to obtain the stamp of approval awarded by the national administration in order to sell a product in a Member State.

International trade flows: Import and export flows are sometimes used to delineate a market's geographic contours.

In the Kimberly-Clark/Scott case (1996), the European Commission found that the low level of trade flows in toilet paper between the United Kingdom and continental Europe indicated that relevant markets were national, despite some price differences:

42. In the particular case of Paris, the extent of the catchment areas is limited to a radius of 300-500 meters, taking into account travel constraints and store characteristics.
43. The letters "CE" appear on products traded on the extended Single Market in the European Economic Area (EEA). They signify that products sold in the EEA have been assessed to meet high safety, health, and environmental protection requirements.

"Its geographic location combined with the substantial cost for the transport of finished goods is a further indicator of the separation of the UK from Continental Europe. At a late stage of the proceedings, the parties have provided data indicating lower transport costs (of the order of [0-10%] (14) from France to the UK). Nevertheless, price differences still appear to remain significant, for example the price difference between the UK and Germany for toilet tissue would more than compensate for the additional transport expenses, so that exporting from Germany to the UK would appear very profitable. It could be argued that this price difference is explained by superior product quality in the UK compared to Germany. Nevertheless, even in the case of France, the price difference is such that there would appear to be sufficient scope for profitable export from France to the UK."

Consumer preferences: The European Commission has used in several cases the consumer habits to delimit the geographic market.

In the Kimberly-Clark/Scott case (1996), it found different habits in the purchase of paper tissues in Europe: In continental European countries, the consumption of pocket tissues was very high, while it was very low in Ireland and the United Kingdom. On the other hand, this situation was reversed for the consumption of boxed tissues.

Similarly, in the Pernod Ricard/Diageo/Seagram case (2001), the European Commission defined the relevant markets on a national basis, taking into account local specificities in the consumption of alcoholic beverages: For example, Pastis is an aperitif that is mainly consumed in France.

§4 The Use of Quantitative Tests

In addition to these qualitative indicators, antitrust authorities may use quantitative tests in order to delineate both geographic and product markets. We will review below the use of the price elasticity test, cross-price elasticity test, price correlation test, stationarity test, SSNIP (Small but Significant and Non-transitory Increase in Price) test and crash test (Table 6.4).

Table 6.4 Quantitative Tests to Delineate the Relevant Market

Quantitative Test	*Criteria for Delineating the Relevant Market*
Price elasticity	High price elasticity.
Cross-price elasticity	High cross-price elasticity between two goods.
Price correlation test	Strong positive correlation between price changes of two goods (once the series have been restated to eliminate common influences).
Stationarity test	High stationarity of the price ratio between two goods.
SSNIP Test	Profitability of a non-transitory price increase from 5% to 10%.

Quantitative Test	*Criteria for Delineating the Relevant Market*
Crash test	A sharp and unexpected shock affecting the price of Product X has an opposite impact on the market for Product Y.

The price elasticity test: The price elasticity of demand for Product X, noted ε_X, is defined as the relative variation in the demand for Product X, after a small relative variation in its price (all other things being equal):

$$\varepsilon_X = (dQx/Qx)/(dPx/Px)$$

with (dQx/Qx) the relative variation in quantity of X and (dPx/Px) the relative variation in price of X.

The value of the price elasticity is between 0 (when demand is inelastic) and $-\infty$ (when demand varies very strongly after price change).

The price elasticity is normally negative (or zero), because the relationship between demand and price is decreasing: When the price increases, demand decreases, all other things being equal. If the price elasticity is low (i.e., close to 0), this means that after a price increase, customers do not shift to another product. This suggests that the product has few substitutes. Conversely, if the price elasticity is high (greater than –1) when the price increases, it means either that some customers have stopped consuming the product, or that they've shifted to a substitutable product.

However, there are methodological limits with the use of a price elasticity value:

- the value depends on the starting price. Indeed, on a demand function, the (absolute) value of price elasticity decreases with price. It is therefore necessary to specify the starting price on the basis of which the price increase is calculated;
- it is necessary to ensure that the condition "*all other things being equal*" is well verified; many factors other than price can affect demand;
- the time period used to determine the value of price elasticity is important. For example, in the cement industry, price elasticity is probably lower in the short term than in the long term. Indeed, in the long term, cement users such as real estate developers can arbitrate with other materials, such as glass or steel.

The cross-price elasticity test: The cross-price elasticity is defined as the relative variation in demand for Product Y after a small relative variation in the price of Product X (all other things being equal):

$$\varepsilon_{Y,\,X} = (dQy/Qy)/(dPx/Px)$$

with (dQ_y/Q_y) the relative variation in quantity of Y and (dPx/Px) the relative variation in price of X.

Three situations should be identified:

- if $\varepsilon_{Y,X} < 0$, the two goods are complementary: A variation in the price of Product X leads to an opposite variation in the quantity of Product Y. For example, if the price of gasoline increases sharply, it is likely that demand for cars will decrease;
- if $\varepsilon_{Y,X} = 0$, the two products are independent: A change in the price of Product X does not change the demand for Product Y;
- if $\varepsilon_{Y,X} > 0$, the two goods are substitutable. When $\varepsilon > 1$, the goods are closely substitutable: An increase in the price of Product X leads to a strong variation in the demand for Product Y. It can therefore be found that both products belong to the same market.

For example, in the CVC/Lenzing *(2001)* case, the European Commission calculated the impact that a price increase of viscose fibers had on cotton, polyester and polypropylene fiber volumes. As shown in Table 6.5, the values of cross-price elasticity are close to zero; the price increase of viscose does not lead to a significant increase in the sales of cotton, polyester, or polypropylene, suggesting that viscose is not in the same relevant market as other fibers.

Table 6.5 Cross-Price Elasticity of Viscose Compared to Other Textile Fibers

VSF/Cotton	**VSF/Polyester**	**VSF/Polypropylene**
[0.05 - 0.10]	[0.04 - 0.15]	[0.03 - 0.10]

Source: European Commission (2001).

Given the difficulties involved in collecting data, the estimation of cross-price elasticities is rarely carried out and, if done, the results are difficult to interpret:

- at what value of cross-price elasticity should products be considered closely substitutable? In particular, in a horizontally or vertically differentiated product market, there is a continuum in the value of cross-price elasticities;
- the value of the cross-price elasticity depends on the starting price used and is therefore generally not constant;[44]
- the change in the demand for Product Y after a price increase of Product X is not always instantaneous: Two products may be substitutable in the long term although they are not in the short term. What time period should be taken into account when measuring cross-price elasticity?
- in a competitive market, the value of cross-price elasticity is paradoxically low, because the demand is distributed throughout a large number of firms. Take the example of 100 firms competing in the same market. If a firm increases its price, consumers will shift their demand to the other 99 producers, which will

44. Unless special cases are considered, such as the Cobb-Douglas function, whose elasticity is constant and equal to the unit.

each earn 1/99 of this additional demand. By calculating the cross-price elasticity, we will find a value close to 0;
- there may be threshold effects. If changes in consumption are relatively linear for everyday consumers goods (food, for example), this is not always the case, especially for intermediate products: If the price of an input increases by 5%, a firm does not change its technology; but for a 10% increase, it may become profitable to adopt another technology.

The price correlation test: The correlation coefficient r measures the degree of linear dependence between two variables X and Y. It is equal to the ratio of covariance to the product of the standard deviations of X and Y:

$$r(x, y) = cov(x, y)/\sigma_X \sigma_Y)$$

with: cov(x, y), the covariance between x and y; σ_X the standard deviation of X; σ_Y, the standard deviation of Y.

The correlation coefficient is between [-1; 1]:

- when it tends towards 1, the two variables move in the same direction and in the same proportions;
- when it tends towards –1, the two variables move in the opposite direction and in the same proportions;
- when it tends towards zero, the two variables evolve independently.

The correlation coefficient can be applied to two products A and B, whose prices are P_A and P_B respectively. A strong positive correlation (close to 1) over time between P_A and P_B may indicate a strong substitutability between Product A and Product B, even if prices are different in level.

For example, if the price of a high-speed train between Paris and Marseille increases by 10%, some customers will switch to air travel, thereby pushing airline ticket prices up (Figure 6.5). On the other hand, if train fares fall sharply, customers will switch from plane to train, reducing the price of plane tickets.

Figure 6.5 High Positive Correlation of Prices

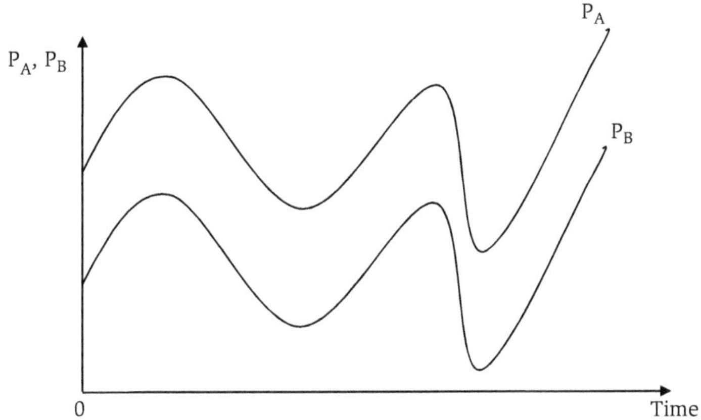

In the Nestlé/Perrier case (1992), the European Commission found that bottled spring water did not belong to the same market as soft drinks because the prices of these two products were not correlated over time: While the price of spring water had risen sharply, that of soft drinks had declined. On the other hand, the analysis of price correlations between still mineral waters and sparkling mineral waters revealed a strong price correlation between these two types of mineral waters.

Similarly, in the Lenzing/CVC case (2001), the European Commission defined the relevant market by using a price correlation analysis. The issue was whether viscose fibers belonged to the same market as cotton, polyester and polypropylene: As shown in Table 6.6, the correlation coefficients are close to zero and the highest is only 0.44. The Commission concluded that viscose fiber does not belong to the same relevant market as other textile materials.

Table 6.6 Correlation Between Prices for Viscose-Based Fibers and Other Textile Materials

	Cotton[60]	**Polyester LP**[61]	**Polyester HP**[61]	**Polypropylene LP**[61]	**Polypropylene HP**[61]
VSF62	0.04	0.39	0.44	0.06	0.24

Source: European Commission (2001).

The correlation test can also be applied to the evolution of sales volumes. Thus, in the Schneider/Legrand case (2001), the undertakings found that the high correlation of volumes between the different components used to produce an electrical panel demonstrated the existence of a single market for components.

However, there are several difficulties in calculating and interpreting a correlation coefficient:

- a correlation coefficient can be artificially high if the prices of both statistical series are influenced by common factors. For example, prices of some petroleum products can be highly correlated with each other, simply because the cost of oil varies widely and constitutes a significant input. Similarly, price seasonality can artificially increase the correlation of prices over time. Thus, in the Schneider/Legrand case (2001), the European Commission criticized the correlation test used by undertakings (and the consulting firm NERA) by stressing the need to de-seasonalize the series: "NERA's correlation calculation takes no account of the seasonal nature of the business. Seasonal variations can, however, occasionally be very wide, in particular during August, when sales volumes can fall by more than 75% from July levels. By failing to separate out these factors, the data supplied by NERA therefore significantly overestimate the real correlation of sales volumes. To measure the real correlation, the Commission has performed its own calculations on the basis of the data supplied by the parties. These calculations show that, if seasonal sales variations are separated out, the correlation drops significantly to ranges (in the region of 0.7) that do not allow precise conclusions to be drawn." High inflation in a country can also lead to an overestimation of correlation between products. It is therefore necessary to restate the raw price data to eliminate common influences (e.g., by de-seasonalizing price series);
- the delays in adjusting demand can reduce the correlation between two products. Indeed, if the price of Product X increases, it is possible that consumers shift to Product Y with a certain time lag: They must detect this price difference and change their consumption habits before making an arbitrage in favor of Product Y. It may be necessary to include a time lag in the analysis of the two statistical series;
- in order to eliminate outliers in a series, it may be useful to conduct the correlation analysis in logarithms;
- it is difficult to determine the threshold at which a correlation level is high enough to indicate that the two products belong to the same market. One possible solution is to take as a reference the value of the correlation coefficient of two goods that obviously belong to the same market. Thus, in the Nestlé/Perrier case, the correlation coefficient of five brands of still mineral water in the same geographical market was used by the European Commission as a reference to estimate the degree of correlation between still and sparkling mineral waters. The correlation coefficient between the five brands of mineral water was 0.89: If the correlation coefficient between sparkling and mineral waters was greater than or equal to this value, the two types of products could have been considered to be substitutable. In this case, the value of the correlation coefficient between sparkling and mineral waters was 0.90;

- in a volume correlation analysis, a high correlation coefficient may signify that the products are complementary and not substitutable. This risk is highlighted by the European Commission in the Schneider/Legrand case (2001), where the undertakings found a strong correlation of volumes between the components of an electrical panel: "It is clear that there will always be some relationship between sales of the different types of component, since final sales relate to finished switchboards and these are obtained by assembling the components in question. The Commission nevertheless takes the view that the existence of this relationship does not make it possible to conclude that all the components belong to a single product market. When transposed to another sector, the line of argument developed by NERA would be tantamount to considering that, since there is (probably) a relationship between sales of car tires and engines (sales of both these components being linked to car sales), tires and engines belong to the same product market. Such a conclusion would be absurd given the total lack of substitutability between the two products (on both the demand and the supply side) and fundamental differences in the structure of competition between the two sectors (presence of integrated manufacturers, level of concentration, etc.)";
- the value of the correlation coefficient may depend on the length of the series considered. For example, in the Coca-Cola/Orangina case (2000), the French Competition Authority showed that the correlation coefficient between the price of the Coca-Cola drink and that of Pepsi-Cola during the period spanning 1995-1998 was 0.68, but that this coefficient decreased to 0.54 or even 0.30 if the analysis period was reduced by a few months.

The stationarity test: The use of a stationarity test (also called "*unit root test*") partially avoids the difficulties raised by price correlation tests. A time series is considered stationary if it returns to a constant value, which means that the impact of a shock is temporary.

For instance, if two products X and Y belong to the same market, the relative price P_X/P_Y must be stationary: Indeed, if the price of Product X falls, the modification of the relative price P_X/P_Y will imply a substitution in favor of the most expensive product (on the supply side) or towards the cheapest product (on the demand side). Through this substitution mechanism, the relative price must quickly return to its initial level.

This type of test has two advantages:

- it eliminates common influences that affect the price of both goods, since only the price ratio is taken into account;
- reaction times in price adjustment can be evaluated: With a stationarity test it is possible to assess how quickly the relative price returns to a constant value.

In 2006, the British Competition Authority (OFT) used a stationarity test in the Nutreco/Hydro Seafood case. The aim was to delineate the salmon market, both in terms of products and geography. Concerning the product market, the question was whether the Norwegian salmon belonged to the same market as the Scottish salmon. The test showed that the relative price of these two products (calculated over a period of three years and on the basis of weekly surveys) was stationary: The relative price, following temporary deviations, returned to a constant value, which was a sign of strong substitutability between the two categories of salmon (Figure 6.6).

Figure 6.6 Evolution of the Relative Price of Norwegian and Scottish Salmon

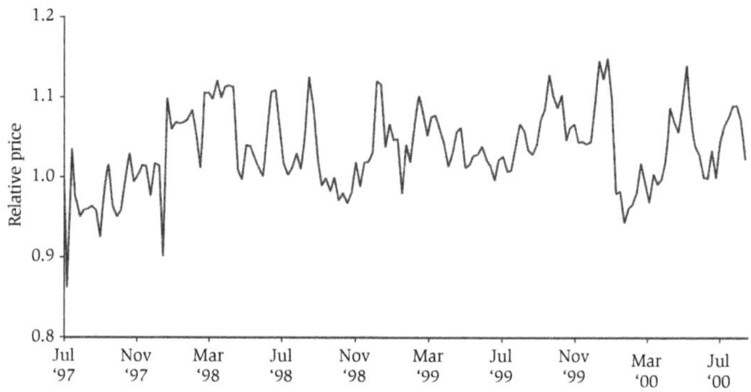

Source: Lexecon, *An Introduction to Quantitative Techniques in Competition Analysis* (2001), http://judgestraining.eu/wp-content/uploads/2017/10/kokkoris-quantitative_techniques-mergers-lexecon.pdf.

Concerning the geographical delineation, the question was whether the market should be defined on a national or regional basis. The price of Scottish salmon in France and Europe relative to the price of Scottish salmon in England also appeared to be stationary, leading the OFT to adopt a market delineation on a regional rather than national basis (Figure 6.7).

Figure 6.7 Changes in the Relative Price of Scottish Salmon in France and in the United Kingdom

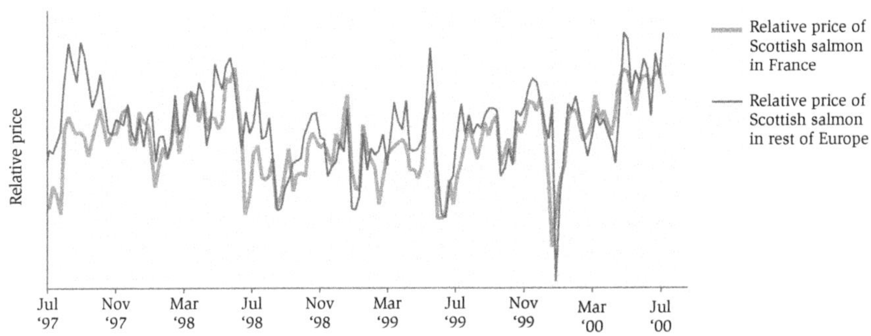

Source: Lexecon, *An Introduction to Quantitative Techniques in Competition Analysis* (2001), http://judgestraining.eu/wp-content/uploads/2017/10/kokkoris-quantitative_techniques-mergers-lexecon.pdf.

The SSNIP test: The SSNIP test, presented at the beginning of this chapter, can be subject to a quantitative approach if relevant data on margin, direct price elasticity, and cross-price elasticity are available.

Suppose there are two firms A and B which produce respectively Product A and Product B. Before the merger, the profit of each firm is equal to:

$$\Pi_A = (P_A - C_A)\, Q_A$$

with P_A the price of Product A, C_A the marginal cost, and Q_A the quantity of Product A.

$$\Pi_B = (P_B - C_B)\, Q_B$$

with P_B the price of Product B, C_B the marginal cost, and Q_B the quantity of Product B.

The total profit pre-merger is therefore equal to the sum of the two profits:

$$\Pi_{A+B} = (P_A - C_A)\, Q_A + (P_B - C_B)\, Q_B$$

Firms A and B decide to merge and Firm A increases its price from P_A to $(P_A + \Delta P_A)$.

The profit of (A + B) post-merger is equal to:

$$\Pi'_{A+B} = (P_A + \Delta P_A - C_A)\, (Q_A - \Delta Q_A) + (P_B - C_B)\, (Q_B + \Delta Q_B)$$

The change in total profit after the merger is therefore equal to:

$$\Delta\Pi'_{A+B} = \Delta P_A Q_A - (P_A - C_A)\, \Delta Q_A + (P_B - C_B)\, \Delta Q_B$$

We see immediately that the evolution of total profit depends on three factors:

- the increase in the margin of Product A (i.e., $\Delta P_A Q_A$);
- the decrease in sales of Product A (i.e., $- [P_A - C_A]\ \Delta Q_A$);
- the shift in sales from Product A to Product B (i.e., $[P_B - C_B]\ \Delta Q_B$).

The change in profit after the merger is positive if:

$$\Delta P_A Q_A - (P_A - C_A)\ \Delta Q_A + (P_B - C_B)\ \Delta Q_B > 0$$

$$\Leftrightarrow 1 + [(P_A - C_A)/P_A]\ (- \varepsilon_{A/A}) + [(P_B - C_B)/P_B]\ [(P_B\ Q_B)/(P_A Q_A)]\ \varepsilon_{B/A}$$

$$\Leftrightarrow 1 - m_A\ |\ \varepsilon_{A/A}| + m_B\ [(P_B\ Q_B)/(P_A Q_A)]\ \varepsilon_{B/A} > 0$$

with: m_A, the margin on Product A; m_B, the margin on Product B; $|\ \varepsilon_{A/A}\ |$, the absolute value of the price elasticity of the demand for Product A; $\varepsilon_{B/A}$, the cross-price elasticity of Product A to Product B.

In the symmetrical case (same margin and therefore same turnover for firms A and B), the price increase is profitable for the new entity if:

$$m\ (|\ \varepsilon_{A/A}\ | - \varepsilon_{B/A}) < 1$$

If the change in total profit is positive after the merger, products A and B can be considered to belong to the same relevant market. If this is not the case, the test must be repeated by extending it to a third Product C; it requires empirical data on the margin of Product C, the direct price elasticity of Product C, and the cross-price elasticities between products A and C and between products B and C.

The crash test: The crash test methodology consists of analyzing the impact of an unexpected shock to the supply or demand of a Product X. For example, if the price of Product X suddenly increases, will customers quickly switch to other substitutes? The shocks studied may be of different kinds: technological change, exchange rate changes (following a devaluation), social movements, sudden increases in production costs, etc.

For instance, in the United Kingdom, branded light yoghurts were promoted in the form of a "*three packs for two purchased*" offer during the period spanning February-March 2003. What was the impact of this special offer on the sales of ordinary yoghurts? Figure 6.8 shows a sharp decrease in sales of regular yoghurts during the period when the price of low-fat yoghurts fell, which could be an indication of substitutability between the two products.

In the Schneider/Legrand case (2001), the European Commission qualitatively used a crash test to counter the undertaking's argument that there was a substitutability between components of an electrical panel: "The data supplied by the parties also suggest that these special offers have a very substantial impact on sales of the items concerned by the offer, but only limited effects on sales of the other components designed to be combined with the item concerned in order to form 'solutions.' [...]. This suggests that sales promotions on components do not have a uniform effect on all the components necessary for building an electrical switchboard, which again confirms the existence of a second level of competition at component level."

Figure 6.8 Impact of a Special Offer on the Sales of a Competing Product

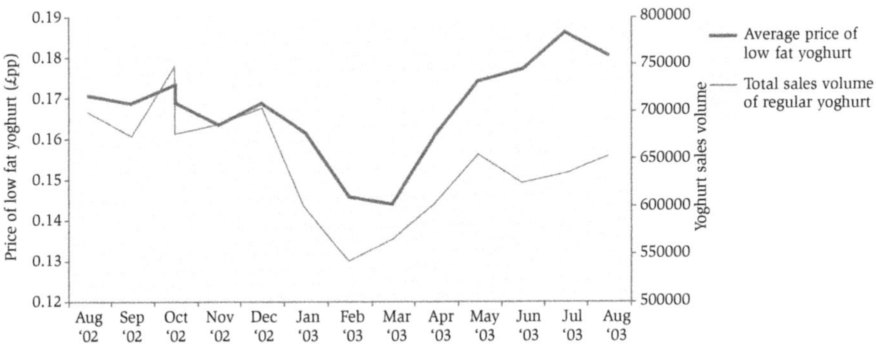

Source: Lexecon, *An Introduction to Quantitative Techniques in Competition Analysis* (2001), http://judgestraining.eu/wp-content/uploads/2017/10/kokkoris-quantitative_techniques-mergers-lexecon.pdf.

SECTION 3 MEASURING MARKET CONCENTRATION

Once the product and geographical markets have been delineated, the second step is to measure the market concentration before and after the merger. In addition to simply calculating market shares, antitrust authorities use a concentration index: the Herfindahl-Hirschman Index (HHI).

The underlying assumption is that there is a likely relationship between market shares or market concentration and market power, as proven in the Cournot's model (*see* Chapter 1):

Increase in market share of the undertakings → Possible increase in market power

Increase in market concentration after the merger → Possible increase in market power

The sum of market shares: A first method is to add the market shares of the merging firms. For example, if Firms 1 and 2 represent 18% and 20% of the market share respectively before the merger, it can be assumed that the market share of the new entity will be 38%, without taking into account any efficiencies. Once the market share of the new entity has been calculated, two thresholds can be determined:

- a threshold below which it appears unlikely that the merger will raise competition concerns. Thus, in practice, the European Commission finds there is a "*safety zone*" in terms of market shares if the market share of the new entity is less than 25% in the case of a horizontal merger or 30% in the case of

a vertical (or conglomerate) merger. Above these thresholds, it cannot be assumed that the merger will not have an impact on competition;
- a threshold above which there is a presumption that the merger will negatively affect competition: In Europe, a post-merger market share of more than 50% suggests the existence of a significant market power, even if this presumption is refutable.

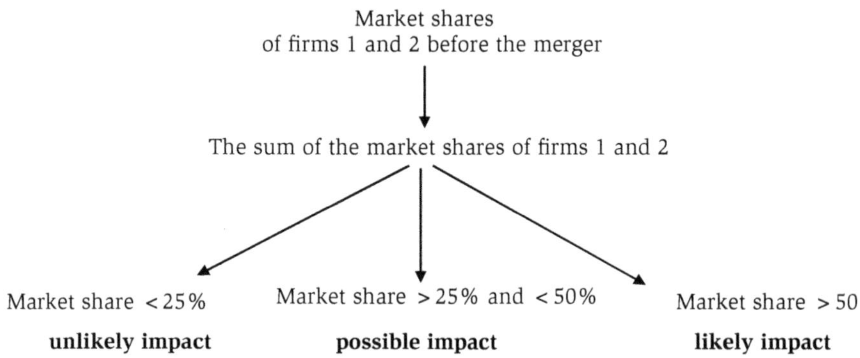

However, the simple sum of market shares does not provide any information about the distribution of market shares between all firms. Indeed, if the merger between Firms 1 and 2 leads to a market share of 38%, it remains to be seen how the remaining 62% of market shares are distributed. For instance, if 62% were spread over 62 firms (each with a 1% market share), the competitive configuration is quite different from a market in which a single firm has a 62% market share.

The concentration ratio: Beyond the mere sum of market shares of the merging firms, we can calculate a concentration ratio (CR). It consists of ranking all firms present on the market (N firms) in a descending order of size and summing the market shares of the M largest firms among the N (with M < N):

$$CR_M = \sum_{i=1}^{m} s_i \times 100 \qquad \text{with } s_i \in [0, 1] \text{ and } i = 1, \ldots, m, \ldots n$$

Thus, it is usual to calculate the CR_4, which is the sum of the market shares of the top four firms in a market.

For example, American antitrust authorities used this indicator during the period spanning 1968-1982, with three thresholds:

- a market with a $CR_4 < 50\%$ was considered to have a low concentration rate;
- a market had a moderate concentration rate if: $50 < CR_4 < 70\%$;
- a market was described as highly concentrated if: $CR_4 > 70\%$.

However, the concentration ratio has several limitations:

- it does not provide any information on (N – M) firms: Two markets with the same CR_4 do not necessarily have the same competitive intensity if the market shares of the (N – M) firms are distributed differently;
- it does not take into account the heterogeneity of market shares among the top M firms for a same value of the ratio. For example, a CR_4 equal to 60% can be obtained with four firms with an identical size (15% each) or through a very unequal distribution of sizes (45% for the first firm and 5% for each of the following three).

The Herfindahl-Hirschman index: Beyond the simple sum of market shares, a concentration index is used to analyze the evolution of a market before and after the merger.

A common index is the HHI, which is defined as the sum of the squared market shares of each firm on the market:

$$HHI = \sum_{i=1}^{n} s_i^2 \times 100 \text{ with } s_i \in [0, 100] \text{ and } i = 1, 2, \ldots, n.$$

The HHI index is equal to 10,000 in the case of a monopoly (100^2) and tends towards 0 when the number of firms is infinite, with symmetrical market shares. Indeed, when the number of firms increases, the market share of each firm (with symmetrical market shares) tends towards 1/N and the value of the HHI index is:

$$HHI = N\,(1/N)^2 = 1/N$$

with N, the total number of firms.

By using the variance of market shares (noted σ^2), the HHI can be rewritten:

$$H = N\sigma^2 + 1/N$$

We see that the value of the index depends both on the total number of firms N and the distribution of their market shares: For a given number of firms, the index gets higher as the market share distribution becomes more and more unequal.

This property can be illustrated by comparing several markets (Table 6.7). Market 1 includes three firms of identical size: Herfindahl's index is therefore equal to (3×33.3^2) or 3326. In Market 2, there are also three firms, but with the two leaders accounting for 98% of the market: The Herfindahl index, equal to 4,806, is higher given the asymmetry of market shares. Let us now consider markets 3 and 4: In Market 3 there are seven firms, but market shares are asymmetric. In Market 4, the number of players is only five, but market shares are symmetric. If the CR_4 is calculated, the two markets appear identical with a market share of 80% for the top four players. Although the number of firms is higher in Market 3, it appears more concentrated than Market 4, taking into account the market share of the first firm.

Table 6.7 Example of HHI Values

	Number of Firms and Distribution of Market Shares (in descending order)	*HHI Value*
Market 1	Three firms: 33.3% each	3,326
Market 2	Three firms: 49%, 49%, 2%	4,806
Market 3	Seven firms: 70%, 5% for the following six firms	5,050
Market 4	Five firms with identical size: 20%, 20%, 20%, 20%, 20%	2,000

Herfindahl-Hirschman Index and market power: The increase in market concentration provides a useful indicator to assess the risk of negative impact on competition. Indeed, as we saw in Chapter 1, the Cournot's competition model shows that there is a clear relationship between market power and the number of firms (N). A reduction of N results in an increase in price and profits in the Cournot's model:

$$P^{cour} = (a + Nc)/(N + 1) = c + [(a - c)/(N + 1)]$$

$$\Pi^{cour} = (a - c)^2/(N + 1)^2$$

In Cournot's model, a decrease in the number of firms results in an increase in market shares, which leads to an increase in market power. This result is also reflected when the HHI is included in Cournot's model with N firms. Indeed, the average margin rate increases with the HHI index, for a given level of price elasticity of demand:

$$\sum_{=1}^{n} s_i \left(\frac{P - c_i}{P}\right) = \frac{HHI}{\varepsilon}$$

We can therefore deduce that:

- the higher the firm's market share after the merger compared to that of its competitors, the greater the likelihood that it will strengthen its market power;
- the more concentrated the market is after the transaction, the greater the risk of competition being affected.

However, the relationship between market share and market power is not automatic and necessary:

- an increase in market share does not necessarily lead to an increase in market power, for example when firms are in a Bertrand's competition;

- conversely, in exceptional cases, a small increase in market share can have a significant impact on market power. For example, a firm may buy a small but highly innovative competitor or "*maverick,*" having a strong price impact.

The use of the Herfindahl-Hirschman Index by antitrust authorities: The HHI index has been used by U.S. antitrust authorities since 1982. Thus, the Horizontal Mergers Guidelines (2010) define three threshold values for the index and threshold changes, below which, mergers are considered not to have a negative impact on competition:

- HHI < 1,500 after the merger: The merger takes place in an unconcentrated market and is therefore unlikely to harm competition.
- 1,500 < HHI < 2,500 after the merger and the absolute change in HHI (rated ΔHHI) is less than 100: The market after the merger is moderately concentrated, but the merger is carried out with a small firm, resulting in a limited change in the value of the index.[45]
- HHI > 2,500 after the merger and ΔHHI < 100: The market is highly concentrated after the merger, but the merger has a marginal impact on the level of concentration.

It should be noted that:

- the calculation of the change in the HHI is based on market shares before the merger; any changes in market shares after the merger are therefore not taken into account;
- the threshold values are at a relatively low level, which means that they are generally reached quite quickly;
- when the values are beyond the safety zone, there is a presumption of negative impact on competition.

In Europe, the Merger Regulation 139/2004 also recommends the use of the Herfindahl index and defines two thresholds for horizontal mergers:

- a HHI value less than 1,000 after the merger makes it unlikely that competition will be negatively affected;
- when the value of HHI is between 1,000 and 2,000 after the merger and the change in the index is less than 250, or when the value of HHI is greater than 2,000 after the merger and the change in the index is less than 150, it is also unlikely that the European Commission will be concerned with the effects of the merger, except in special cases.

In the case of vertical or conglomerate mergers, the European Commission considers that it is unlikely that the project will raise competition concerns when the

45. In the case of two Firms 1 and 2 each with a market share s_i (with i = 1.2):

$$\Delta H = (s_1 + s_2)^2 - s_1^2 - s_2^2 = 2s_1s_2$$

market share after the merger is less than 30 % and the HHI after the merger is less than 2,000.

The use of a concentration index and its variations provides a first approximation of the risks that a merger poses to competition. However, this does not exempt competition authorities, when the post-merger market exceeds the thresholds, from carrying out an in-depth and case-by-case analysis of the merger's effects on competition.

SECTION 4 THE IMPACT OF A MERGER ON COMPETITION

The delineation of the relevant market and the measure of market concentration provide a first approximation of the merger's impact on competition. However, these two steps are not sufficient to accurately assess the future market power of the merging firms. While small market shares make it unlikely that merging firms will benefit from high market power, large market shares do not necessarily imply they will have significant market power either.

Competition authorities must assess the extent of market power after the merger by creating a damage scenario ("*theory of harm*"). Competition authorities focus mainly on the merger's impact on prices. But they may also take into account other impacts on competition, such as the impact on product diversity, quality, or the incentive to innovate.

We can identify different types of harm a merger can have on competition depending on the type of merger (Table 6.8). We will first analyze mergers between competitors (so-called "*horizontal*" mergers): They can lead to a "*unilateral effect*" or a "*coordinated effect*" (§1). We will continue by studying vertical and conglomerate mergers: Vertical mergers can foreclose the market; conglomerate mergers can favor a leverage effect or a multi-market contact effect (§2). Once the competitive impact of a merger has been identified, it remains to be seen whether it will occur after the merger: Competition authorities then examine the incentives and opportunities for merging firms to raise prices. To do this, the analysis of entry barriers and demand characteristics is essential (§3).

Table 6.8 Type of Merger and Theory of Harm

Type of Merger	*Type of Harm*	*Explanation*
Horizontal	Unilateral effect	The reduction in the number of firms leads to a price increase, which depends on the reaction of outsiders. Beyond the price increase, the merger may reduce product diversity or the incentive to innovate.
Horizontal	Coordinated effect	The reduction in the number of firms may encourage collusion (tacit or explicit) between competitors.
Vertical	Foreclosure of the market	A vertical merger can reduce the access of non-integrated competitors to scarce resources (upstream or downstream).
Conglomerate	Leverage or conglomerate effect	The merger may lead to tying sales, to the detriment of competitors without an equivalent product portfolio.
Conglomerate	Multi-market contact	A conglomerate merger can reduce the intensity of competition, each firm fearing retaliation in other markets.

§1 The Impact of a Horizontal Merger on Competition

A merger between competing firms leads to an overlap of market shares. For example, if the market is initially a duopoly, the merger simply leads to a monopoly situation and prices will go up. For instance, when Ryanair decided in 2007 to take over its Irish competitor Aer Lingus, the European Commission found that the new entity would obtain a monopoly situation on 22 routes from Dublin, which would result in price increases.

In fact, a merger does not suppress all competition in the market, as it does not concern all firms: Mergers are most often between two or three operators in an oligopolistic market. Therefore, in such a case, the final impact of the merger on prices will significantly depend on the reaction of firms outside the merger (called "*outsiders*").

We will distinguish below two main different effects: the unilateral effect and the coordinated effect. We will also present the case of a horizontal merger aimed at preventing the entry of a new competitor on the market.

Horizontal mergers and the unilateral effect: A merger between competitors can lead to an increase in prices through a so-called "*unilateral*" effect: As there is less competitive pressure on the market, prices will increase.

Suppose we have a Cournot's oligopoly, with three firms A, B, C, each with a symmetrical market share of 33%. At equilibrium, each firm makes a profit of $8 (Figure 6.9) and the total profit is $24. Firm A decides to take over its competitor Firm B: The market share of the new entity (A + B) increases to 66%; the market is now a duopoly, with less competitive pressure. By acquiring Firm B, Firm A not only gain Firm B's market share and profit (equal to $8), it also benefits from reduced competition, with total profits rising from $24 to $30. The total gain of the merger for Firm A is therefore ($20 – $8) = $12.

Figure 6.9 The Competitive Impact of an Horizontal Merger: An Example with 3 Firms

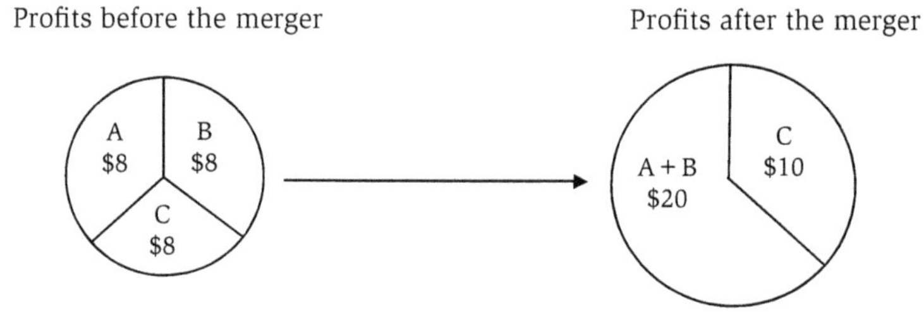

The reduction of competition can be explained: After the merger, the new entity (A + B) has an incentive to reduce its production in order to raise prices. In response, Firm C will increase its production level, but this effect will not be sufficient to compensate for the first effect, so the price on the market will increase.

The mechanism can be represented graphically (Figure 6.10) through the reaction function of Firm C (R_C) and the reaction function of firms A and B before the merger ($R_{A,\ B}$) and after the merger ($R'_{A,\ B}$). Before the merger, the Cournot's equilibrium is at point X, at the intersection of the two reaction functions: Firms A and B each produce the quantity Q_{A+B} while Firm C produces Q_C. The merger does not change the reaction function of Firm C but that of the new firm (A + B). Indeed, whatever the level of production of Firm C, the new entity reduces its production, taking into account the reduction of competition on the market. The firm's reaction function of Firm (A + B) moves downward from $R_{A,\ B}$ to $R'_{A,\ B}$. The new equilibrium is at point Z and not at point Y: Faced with the reduction in the (A + B) production, Firm C's best response is to increase its production level from Q_C to Q'_C, which limits the price increase.

Figure 6.10 The Unilateral Effect in a Cournot's Oligopoly

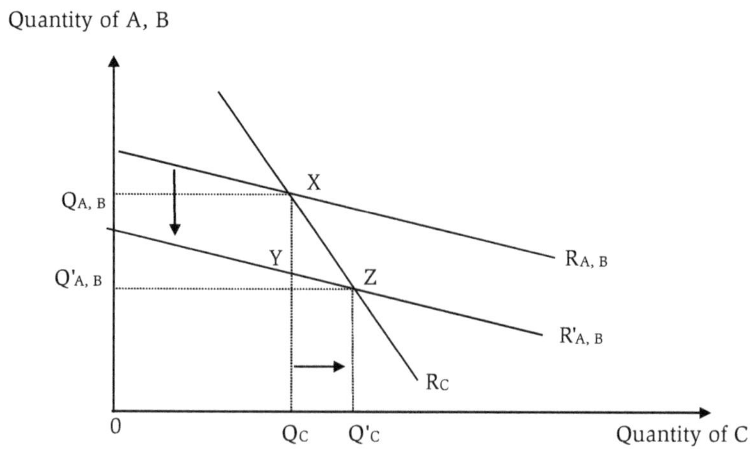

In a Bertrand's oligopoly with differentiated products, a merger also leads to an increase in price but through a different mechanism: Firms A and B increase the price after the merger and Firm C reacts by doing the same. This mechanism can be represented graphically (Figure 6.11) through the reaction function of Firm C (R_C) and the reaction function of firms A and B before the merger ($R_{A,\ B}$) and after the merger ($R'_{A,\ B}$). Before the merger, the Bertrand's equilibrium is at point X, at the intersection of the two reaction functions. The merger does not change the reaction function of Firm C but that of the new Firm (A + B). Indeed, whatever the price of Firm C, the new entity increases its price, taking into account the lower competition on the market. The reaction function of Firm (A + B) moves upwards from $R_{A,\ B}$ to $R'_{A,\ B}$. The new equilibrium point is at point Z and not at point Y: After the price increase of Firm (A + B), the best response for Firm C is to increase its price P_C to P'_C but less than Firm (A + B), in order to gain market share.

Figure 6.11 The Unilateral Effect in a Bertrand's Oligopoly (with Differentiated Products)

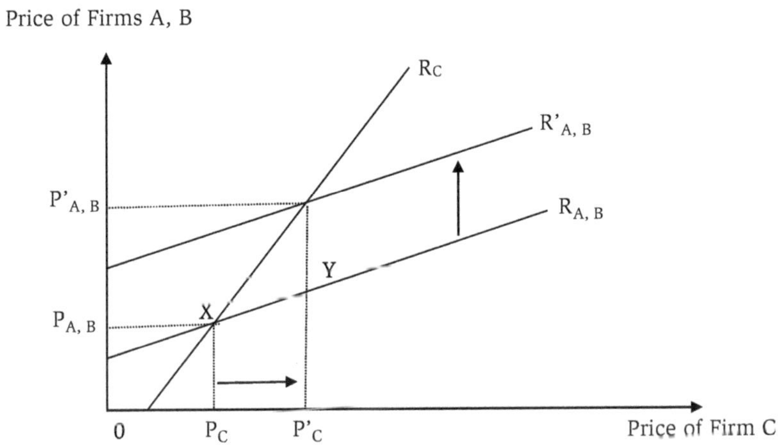

We can observe that the merger always benefits the outsiders. In the case of a Cournot's oligopoly, the outsiders increase their production and also benefit from an increase in the price. Similarly, in a Bertrand's oligopoly with differentiated products, outsiders increase their prices. It can even be shown, under certain conditions, that the merger can hurt the undertakings if they do not have a sufficient market share after the merger. Indeed, the merger is only profitable for merging firms if they hold a market share of more than 80% after the merger. However, this paradox is only valid if the merger does not lead to efficiencies; otherwise, the merger will reduce the profit of outsiders (*see* below).

Once the unilateral effect has been identified, its magnitude remains to be assessed. Several factors influence this unilateral effect:

- the market share of the merging firms: The larger the market share, the greater the risk of a unilateral effect;
- the possibilities for outsiders to increase their production (in the case of a Cournot competition): If capacity constraints are high, it will be difficult to increase the level of production. Similarly, if there are switching costs, it will be difficult for outsiders to capture customers from the merging firms;
- the presence of a "*maverick firm*" on the market can counter the price increase by keeping prices low;
- the relative size of the merging firms: In a Bertrand's competition model, the price of the firm with the lowest initial market share will increase more than that of other firms;
- the distribution of market shares between outsiders: Among outsiders, those with the largest market share increase their prices more than smaller outsiders. Consequently, when the market of outsiders is concentrated, outsiders will increase the prices sharply;
- the probability of new competitors entering the market;
- the efficiencies resulting from the merger;
- the countervailing power of customers;
- the degree of competition between the products of the merging firms: When firms operate in a differentiated product market (i.e., a chain of imperfectly substitutable goods), it is crucial to know the degree of substitutability between the products of the merging firms. We develop this point below.

The unilateral effect with differentiated products: When two firms merge, the risk of prices increasing is greater if the products of the two firms are strongly substitutable.

Suppose that three firms A, B, C each produce a differentiated good, respectively good X, Y and Z. Firms A and B each have a market share of 25% and Firm C has a market share of 50%. It could be assumed that a merger between Firm A and Firm C is riskier for competition than a merger between A and B: In the former case, the market share of the new entity would be 75% compared to only 50% in the latter case. In reality, it is necessary to assess the degree of proximity between products X, Y and Z.

Suppose that customers consider that products X and Y are very substitutable, while Product Z is quite far from products X and Z. In such a case, the merger between firms A and B presents more risk of unilateral effect than a merger between A and C. Indeed, after the merger, the new entity will increase the price of Product X, as a significant proportion of customers will switch to Product Y. The "diversion ratio" (DR) measures the proportion of consumers who shift from X to Y: The higher the diversion ratio, the more profitable the price increase will be post-merger. We see here that in industries with differentiated products, the relevant indicator for assessing the risk of unilateral effect is more the closeness of products between merging firms than their market shares.

Thus, in the FNAC/Darty case (2016), the French Competition Authority concluded that in case of a 10% price increase on FNAC products, customers who had purchased a laptop, tablet, smartphone, camera, television, or image and sound accessory would switch to Darty's products. FNAC therefore would have an incentive to increase its prices after the merger, given a high diversion ratio to Darty's products.

Measuring the unilateral effect: Several quantitative tests have been proposed to assess the risk of a unilateral effect when firms have differentiated products. It should be noted that these tests are used as an indicator and do not replace the qualitative analysis carried out by competition authorities.

A first test—the UPP ("*Upward Pricing Pressure*") test—consists of analyzing a firm's incentive to increase the price after the merger by taking into account both the reduction of competition and costs resulting from the merger (Farrell & Shapiro, 2010). Suppose that two firms A and B, which produce products 1 and 2 respectively, decide to merge. Firm A's incentive to increase the price of Product 1 after the merger depends on three factors:

- the diversion ratio between product 1 and 2: The higher it is, the higher the probability of a price increase will be, because the lost sales on Product 1 are transferred to Product 2;
- the margin of Firm B: When this margin is high, Firm A has incentive to increase the price of Product 1 after the merger;
- the efficiencies resulting from the merger: When efficiencies are high, Firm A has low incentive to increase the price of Product 1 after the merger.

Firm A's incentive to increase the price of Product 1 is equal to:

$$UPP_1 = [P_2 - c_2]\ DR_{1/2} - (e_1\ c_1)$$

with:
P_2 the price of the Product 2.
e_1, the efficiencies on the Product 1.
c_1, c_2 the marginal cost of Product 1 and Product 2.
$DR_{1/2}$, the diversion ratio from Product 1 to Product 2.

The first part of the equation represents the increase in profit resulting from customers switching from Product 1 to Product 2, which is equal to the margin on Product 2 (i.e., the difference between the price P_2 and the cost C_2) multiplied by the diversion ratio from Product 1 to Product 2. The second part of the equation represents the decrease in profit resulting from the fact that the merger lowers the cost of Firm A and thus increases its margin on each unit of Product 1. As sales of Product 1 decrease due to the price increase, Firm A loses a margin on each unsold unit.

If UPP1 > 0, the new entity has an incentive to raise the price after the merger. It should be noted that the UPP test does not say how much the price will rise; it simply indicates, for different efficiency scenarios, that a risk exists, which justifies further analysis of the case.

A second test—the GUPPI ("*Gross Upward Pricing Pressure Index*") test—was introduced by Salop and Moresi (2009) and then included in the Horizontal Merger Guidelines (2010) in the United States. It has also been used in Europe by competition authorities, particularly in France in the FNAC/Darty (2016) and Cofigeo/Agripole (2018) cases. Suppose that two firms A and B produce respectively Product 1 and

Product 2. Firms A and B decide to merge and continue after the merger to sell both products 1 and 2.

The GUPPI index on Product 1 measures the incentive of the new entity (A + B) to increase the price of Product 1 after the merger. This incentive is defined as the ratio between the additional profit earned by the switch of some consumers from Product 1 to Product 2 and the decline in sales on Product 1 after the price increase:

$$GUPPI\ of\ product\ 1 = \frac{profit\ resulting\ from\ transfer\ of\ sales\ to\ product\ 2}{value\ of\ sales\ lost\ on\ product\ 1}$$

$$\Leftrightarrow \text{GUPPI of Product 1} = \frac{\Delta Q_2(P_2 - C_2)}{\Delta Q_1 P_1}$$

$$\Leftrightarrow \text{GUPPI of Product 1} = \frac{\Delta Q_2}{\Delta Q_1}\frac{(P_2 - C_2)}{P_1}$$

$$\Leftrightarrow \text{GUPPI of Product 1} = \text{diversion ratio from 1 to 2} \times \frac{(P_2 - C_2)}{P_1}$$

$$\Leftrightarrow \text{GUPPI of Product 1} = RD_{1,2} \times \frac{(P_2 - C_2)}{P_2} \times \frac{P_2}{P_1}$$

$$\Leftrightarrow \text{GUPPI of Product 1} = RD_{1,2} \times \text{margin in \% on product 2} \times \text{price ratio}$$

We see that the empirical estimation of a GUPPI requires three types of data: the diversion ratio from Product 1 to Product 2, the margin on Product 2, and the prices of products 1 and 2.

If firms A and B are symmetrical (i.e., same diversion ratio, same price, same cost), the GUPPI index is equal to:

$$\text{GUPPI} = \text{RD} \times \text{m}$$

with m, the margin before the merger.

If the GUPPI index has a value below 5%, competition authorities consider that it is unlikely that the merger will lead to a unilateral effect. Conversely, if the GUPPI value is higher than 10%, it can be assumed that a unilateral effect is possible, leading to a price increase. It should be noted that the GUPPI index does not take into account possible efficiencies (unlike the UPP test) nor the reaction of outsiders.

Horizontal mergers and the coordinated effect: A horizontal merger can also favor a collusive behavior in the market: In a Cournot's oligopoly, for example, firms that are outside the merger can react in the same way as the merging firms by reducing their production. This coordinated effect results solely from the oligopolistic interaction between firms; it does not imply an explicit coordination between competitors, as in a cartel. The risk of a coordinated effect can be illustrated by an example.

Suppose that firms A and B each have a 25% market share, while Firm C has a market share of 50%. Firm A decides to merge with Firm B. The new entity

(A + B) obtains a 50% market share: We have a symmetrical duopoly between (A + B) and C. This symmetrical market structure may favor the emergence of a tacit collusion.

In addition to the symmetry of market shares, several factors can favor a coordinated effect:

- the number of firms on the market: A small number of firms facilitates a tacit collusion and its stability, because it is easier to detect (and therefore punish) "*cheaters*";
- the market transparency: Firms can easily converge on the same price without any explicit agreement;
- the type of merger: For example, the acquisition of a maverick firm will stabilize the collusion;
- the existence of a credible, rapid and viable sanction mechanism if a firm cheats;
- the low probability of entry: If entry barriers are high, the stability of the collusion is more likely.

The European Commission has used the coordinated effect argument several times (Table 6.9), in particular, in the Airtours/First Choice case. Airtours and First Choice operated in the U.K. short-haul package holiday market and decided to merge in 1999. In this market, the new entity would have had a 32% market share, compared to the two main competitors Thomson (27%) and Thomas Cook (20%). The European Commission blocked the merger in September 1999 on the grounds of a coordinated effect; its decision was overturned on appeal in June 2002 by the European Court of First Instance. According to the Court, several elements suggested that collusion would have been difficult to sustain:

- holiday packages are highly differentiated products, depending on their location, date, etc.;
- market shares and demand for holiday packages are quite volatile from one year to the next;
- small competitors, potential competitors, customers can counter any attempt to collude;
- the possibilities of retaliation (after cheating behavior) are low because production capacities are fixed 18 months in advance and are rigid. As a result, a firm that wants to punish cheating behavior by lowering its price would not gain clients in the short term. The only way to retaliate is to significantly increase its capacities in the next season. But, as retaliation is in the future, each firm has incentive to cheat today, because the losses due to retaliation are lower than short-term profit resulting from deviation.

More generally, the Airtours decision was an opportunity for the European Court of First Instance to set out the three conditions necessary for a coordinated effect to emerge, which are now exposed in the Horizontal Merger Guidelines (2004):

- a strong market transparency between competitors;
- a threat of credible retaliation in case of deviation from the collusive equilibrium;
- no market contestability by residual or potential competitors.

Table 6.9 Merger and the Risk of Coordinated Effect in Europe

Merger Case	*European Commission's Analysis*	*Decision*
Nestlé/Perrier (UE 1992)	Risk of a coordinated effect on the French bottled spring water market between Nestlé and BSN.	Merger approved with commitments (resale of Volvic and other assets).
Gencor/Lonrho (UE 1997)	Risk of a coordinated effect because of a duopoly in the platinum market (70% market share for the two leaders).	Merger prohibited, confirmed on appeal.
Mitteldeutsche Kali/ Kali + Salz (UE 1998)	Risk of a coordinated effect with the French firm SCPA, due to structural links.	Merger approved with structural commitments (termination of links with SCPA).
First Choice/Airtours (UE 1999)	Risk of a coordinated effect because of an oligopoly dominated by three actors (Airtours, Thompson and Thomas Cooke).	Merger prohibited, overturned on appeal.
Teliasonera/Telenor/JV (UE 2015)	The merger would reduce the number of Mobile Network Operators in Denmark from four to three, leading to coordination between the remaining operators.	The undertakings decided to abandon the proposed merger.
Hutchison 3G Italy/Wind/JV (UE 2016)	The merger would have created a market with three competitors having similar market shares in Italy. These factors would have facilitated coordinated behavior.	Merger approved with structural remedies the (market entry of French telecom operator Iliad).
AB Inbev/SAB Miller (UE 2016)	Risk of tacit price coordination among brewers in Europe through an increase in the number of multi-market contacts.	Merger approved with structural remedies (resale of AB InBev beer business in Europe)

Horizontal merger, new products and innovation*:* A merger can also have a negative impact on the launch of new products and the incentive to innovate.

A first situation is when the merger leads to removing competition from a new product that is about to be launched on the market. Suppose, for example, that three pharmaceutical companies A, B and C, each of which sells a drug, are in a Cournot competition. A new Firm D has completed clinical phase 3 trials on a new drug and is about to enter the market. The entry will increase competition and lower prices. If Firm A preventively buys Firm D, it can coordinate the price of its two drugs to avoid new competition on the market. The impact of the merger will be negative, as consumers will be deprived of a future price reduction. The magnitude of this impact will depend on the intensity of competition that firms B and C exert on Firm (A + D). In an extreme case, Firm A may even decide, after the merger, not to launch Firm D's product on the market, thereby depriving consumers of a greater variety of products.

An extreme case is when the sole purpose of the merger is to block the launch of a new product on the market: This situation is known as a "*killer acquisition.*" It can be illustrated by a simple example (Figure 6.12). Suppose that Firm A is in a monopoly position and makes a profit of $50. Firm B has developed a new product that competes directly with the product of Firm A and plans to enter the market: After the entry, the market situation will evolve into a Cournot's duopoly, with a decrease in total profits from $50 to $30. In order to avoid the entry of competitor B, Firm A has a strong incentive to buy it: It is willing to spend the difference between the monopoly profit and its profit in a duopoly, i.e., ($50 - $15) = $35. The purpose of Firm B's acquisition is to prevent the entry of a new competitor: Sometimes referred to as a killer acquisition, this type of strategy is difficult to detect by antitrust authorities, even if these practices have been highlighted in the pharmaceutical industry.

Figure 6.12 A Preemptive Merger

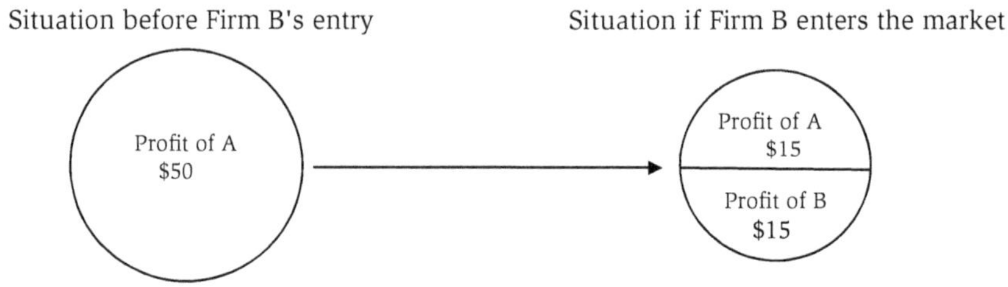

In several merger decisions, the European Commission has identified some negative impact of a merger on the launch of new products, capable of exerting a significant competitive constraint in the market. Under this approach, the assessment of mergers is typically conducted from the angle of pipeline products resulting in potential competition. In this respect, only products in late stages of development come into the picture, for only those products whose market entry is imminent can be found to exert—as potential competitors—significant competitive constraint over existing products of the acquiring party. In particular, a merger with a potential competitor can have horizontal anti-competitive effects if two cumulative conditions apply: First, the potential competitor significantly constrains the behavior of the firms active in the market; and second, there is not a sufficient number of other potential competitors capable of maintaining post-merger competitive pressure. This well-established practice of analyzing potential competition through pipeline products has been illustrated in numerous past cases, such as the Johnson & Johnson/Guidant case in 2005.

A second situation is related to mergers in which the merging parties compete over innovation at earlier stages, that is, over early R&D efforts of the parties that have not yet materialized into concrete products, or which do not yet have a high probability of successful commercialization.

The risk of a merger is then to slow down or stop the research effort, reducing competition in the innovation market. Indeed, if the race for innovation leads to a temporary monopoly (through a patent) for the first firm that discover the product, competition is a powerful incentive to innovate since each firm fears losing the race. Consequently, if two competing firms in a duopoly situation merge, their incentive to innovate decreases as the risk of being overtaken by their competitor disappears: The pace of innovation will slow down.

Suppose that two firms A and B are in a Cournot competition on an existing drug. They each make a profit of $15. If one of the two firms is the first to discover a new therapy, it excludes its competitor from the market and finds itself in a monopoly position. It then obtains a profit of $50 and its competitor is excluded from the market and therefore loses $15. Each firm's incentive to innovate is therefore equal to ($50 – $15) or $35. If the two firms merge, they obtain a monopoly on the old drug and make a profit of $40. Their incentive to find a new therapy is only ($50 – $40), or $10. This incentive is lower than that of the two firms in a duopoly situation, since the monopoly already enjoys a high profit: By innovating, it will simply replace itself. The merger will therefore slow down the pace of R&D.

In several recent merger decisions, culminating in the Dow/DuPont case, the European Commission broadened its approach by looking further into the development stages of a company's pipeline products, requiring that products in early stage development should be divested (Table 6.10). For instance, in the case of pharmaceutical industry, the Commission is increasingly looking beyond near-to-market pipeline products (i.e., those in phase III clinical trials) and focusing on products in phase I or phase II of development. It does not look only at harm to innovation on a specific product market in which parties are developing similar pipeline products, but adopts a general assessment of harm to innovation, unrelated to a specific product market.

Table 6.10 Mergers and Innovation (EU)

Merger Case	*Risks Concerning Innovation*	*Decision*
Medtronic/Covidien (EU, 2015)	Covidien had a late-stage pipeline product that was expected to compete in the near future with existing products of the acquirer.	Divestiture of the pipeline product of Covidien.
GSK/Novartis (EU, 2015)	Risk of ceasing to develop two early stage pipeline drugs. Two competing drugs, regarding skin and ovarian cancer treatment, were at their later stages of development.	Cooperation with a third company to continue along the path to commercialization of the two early stage drugs. Divestiture of one of the two skin and ovarian cancer treatments to the original developer.
Pfizer/Hospira (EU, 2015)	Pfizer would have delayed or discontinued two competing biosimilar drugs that could treat certain autoimmune diseases.	Divestiture of one of the two biosimilar drugs to another company.
General Electric/Alstom (EU, 2015)	GE would eliminate most of Alstom's R&D capabilities related to heavy-duty gas turbines. This would have reduced innovation pressure also on the remaining players.	The approval is conditional upon the divestiture of central parts of Alstom's heavy-duty gas turbines business to Ansaldo of Italy.

Merger Case	*Risks Concerning Innovation*	*Decision*
Dow/DuPont (EU, 2017)	The merger would have had a significant impact on innovation competition by: - removing the parties' incentives to continue to pursue ongoing parallel innovation efforts in a number of important herbicide, insecticide and fungicide innovation areas; - removing the parties' incentives to develop and bring to market new pesticides.	Divestiture of major parts of DuPont's global pesticide business, including its global R&D organization.
Johnson & Johnson/Actelion (EU, 2017)	Johnson & Johnson and Actelion are competitors in the development of new insomnia drugs.	Commitment to pursue the development of different insomnia drugs.
Monsanto/Bayer (EU, 2018)	Monsanto, the largest seed supplier in the world, was acquired by Bayer, a comparatively smaller player but with extensive R&D activities. The Commission found that the transaction would have eliminated innovation competition in herbicides.	Commitment of Bayer to divest the entire vegetable seed business, including its R&D organization.

§2 The Impact of a Vertical or Conglomerate Merger

We will first study the case of a vertical merger, which can lead to a foreclosure effect, and then we'll analyze the effect of a conglomerate merger.

Vertical mergers and market foreclosure: In the case of a vertical merger, the new entity is present at several stages of the value chain. The risk is that it may restrict the access of non-vertically integrated competitors to resources under its control, whether upstream or downstream.

A first scenario is that of an input market foreclosure: An upstream firm with market power may decide to buy a downstream firm. After the merger, the new entity may have an incentive to restrict access to its inputs to other downstream firms. Access restrictions can take several forms: price increases, quantity limitations, deterioration in the quality of inputs.

Let's take the case of an upstream dominant firm (Firm A), which supplies downstream Firms 1, 2, 3 ... at price P (Figure 6.13). If Firm A buys Firm 1, the new entity (A + 1) can harm downstream competitors by setting a higher price P'. Since their cost is now higher than that of Firm (A + 1), Firms 2 and 3 will see their profits fall.

Figure 6.13 Vertical Merger and Input Access Foreclosure

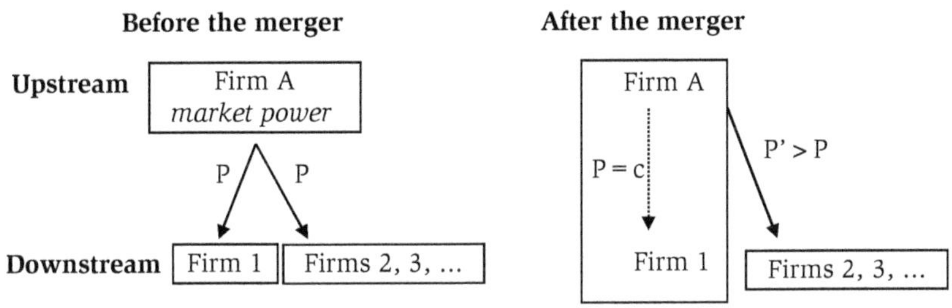

Firm A's incentive to block access to its inputs will depend on a trade-off between two opposing effects:

- the increase in input prices reduces sales and therefore profits for Firm A. The lower the upstream margins are, the lower the loss will be;
- increased profits resulting from a larger share of the downstream market and a higher price. The higher the downstream margins are, the higher the profits will be.

This arbitration can be illustrated graphically by comparing the situation before and after the vertical merger (Figure 6.14). Before the merger, Firm A, located upstream, supplies Firm 1 and its competitors downstream. Firm A makes a margin on these two types of sales, which corresponds in Figure 6.14 to areas X and Y. Firm 1 achieves a downstream margin on its sales, represented by area W. Before the merger, the cumulative profits of firms A and 1 are therefore equal to (X + Y + W).

Figure 6.14 The Vertical Situation Before the Merger

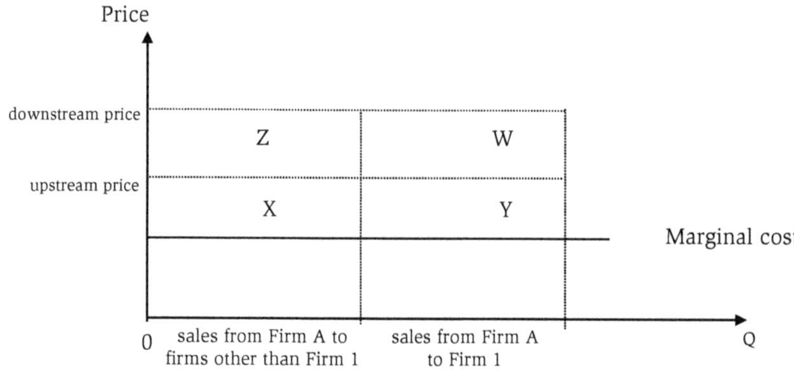

Suppose that Firm A merges with Firm 1 and decides, after the merger, to no longer supply competitors downstream. The latter will have to turn to other less efficient suppliers, which will increase their costs (Figure 6.15). The new entity (A + 1) increases its downstream market share, as well as its selling price: It gains the areas G (margin on new downstream sales) and F (price increase on existing sales). But the new entity (A + 1) loses a margin on sales it no longer makes with competitors of Firm 1. This loss of margin is represented by the area E (whose amount is smaller than area X because of the reduction in the market share of Firm 1's competitors). Firm A has an incentive to merge with Firm 1 in order to foreclose the market, if:

$$(G + F) > E.$$

Figure 6.15 The Situation after the Merger

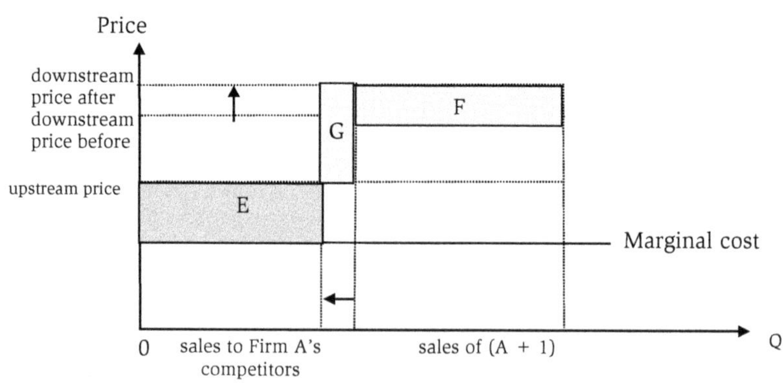

The incentive to foreclose the market will be strong if upstream margins are low; similarly, foreclosure will be more profitable if Firm A recovers a large proportion of sales lost by its competitors downstream and if the retail price increases significantly.

A second scenario is that of a customer foreclosure: a downstream firm (e.g., a distributor) having some market power may decide to buy its supplier, in order to restrict downstream access to upstream competitors.

Suppose that Firm 1, located downstream and having market power, decides to integrate upstream by buying Firm A (Figure 6.16). The incentive for Firm 1 to foreclose access to its downstream distribution network will depend on a trade-off between two opposing effects:

- the increase in its costs resulting from ceasing to source from upstream competitors (especially if they are efficient);
- the increase in profits, resulting from a larger share of the downstream market, because it is more difficult for upstream competitors to access the market.

The ability to block access to customers will depend in particular on the ability of upstream competitors to find alternative distribution channels.

Figure 6.16 Vertical Merger and Customer Foreclosure

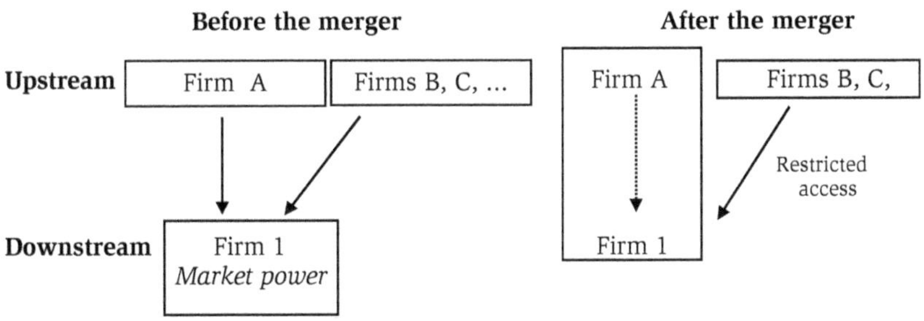

Mergers and the conglomerate effect: A merger is considered a conglomerate merger when the undertakings are not direct competitors and are not in a vertical relationship; for instance, they produce different goods which are complementary. Although the firms are not competitors, this type of merger may nevertheless affect competition through a "*conglomerate effect*" or "*leverage effect.*"

Suppose Firm A is in a monopoly situation on Product X (the "*tying product*"). Firm A acquires Firm B, which produces Y (the "*tied product*"), in competition with other products. After the merger, the new entity (A + B) can increase its market power by linking Product X with Product Y. This may take the form, for example, of a pure tying sale: The new entity exclusively offers X and Y together, without selling them separately. Similarly, the new entity may degrade the interoperability between its product X and Y's competing products, in particular by not providing sufficient information to ensure full compatibility.

The ability of the new entity to restrict competition through a leverage effect depends on several factors:

- Firm B's competitors cannot offer a product competing with Product X.

- The tying Product X must be considered by customers to be essential: There are no alternatives for this product, for example, because of its strong differentiation.
- A large majority of customers value buying both products X and Y at the same time, for example, because they are complementary.
- There are strong economies of scale in the production of Y: The reduction in sales of Firm B's competitors (which only produce Y) will lead to an increase in their production cost.

In the General Electric/Honeywell case (2001), the European Commission blocked the merger due to a conglomerate effect. Both GE and Honeywell were active in the market for large aircraft engines and business jets. Honeywell was also active in the avionics and non-avionics products market, while GE was a major player in the market for engine control systems and also operated an aviation finance and leasing business. The European Commission relied on three main arguments to infer a risk of a conglomerate effect:

- In the past, GE and Honeywell had practiced tying, either by marketing a different set of products at a reduced price (coupling discount) or by offering products exclusively in a tied manner.
- Customers were demanding this type of bundling when the package implied a lower overall price than the sum of its component prices.
- GE and Honeywell's competitors were not able to duplicate such a strategy, given the wide range of products offered by GE and Honeywell.

The analysis of conglomerate mergers has gained renewed interest in Europe since 2010, with seven mergers examined in terms of conglomerate effects (Table 6.11).

Table 6.11 Conglomerate Effect in Mergers (Europe)

Merger	*Conglomerate Effect*	*Remedy*
Intel/McAfee (2011)	Risk that McAfee's competitors, specialists in internet security software, may not have access to the same information about Intel processors.	Intel committed to ensure that McAfee's competitors would have access to the same information.
Dentsply/Sirona (2016)	Access by Dentsply's competitors, which offer dental consumables, to technical information on Sirona's dental equipment.	Extension of Sirona's licensing agreement with Dentsply's competitors.
Microsoft/LinkedIn (2016)	Microsoft will preinstall LinkedIn on all Windows PCs and thus marginalize competing professional social network applications.	Microsoft committed to not imposing on computer manufacturers the preinstallation of LinkedIn on Windows.
Broadcom/Brocade (2017)	Risk of degraded interoperability between interface cards and switching chips.	Broadcom committed to cooperate with competing interface card producers to ensure the same degree of interoperability.
Bayer/Monsanto (2018)	Risk of tying pesticides and seeds.	No remedy.
Essilor/Luxottica (2018)	Risk of imposing Essilor lenses on opticians that sell Luxottica frames.	No remedy because there was no incentive to make tied sales.
Qualcomm/NXP (2018)	Interoperability risk between Qualcomm chips and NXP competitors' products.	Qualcomm committed to ensuring interoperability between its chips and NXP competitors' products.

Conglomerate mergers and multi-market contact: When a firm in Market A decides to gain access to Market B through a merger, competition in these two markets may be affected if competitors have a similar portfolio of activities. Indeed, the contact of firms in markets A and B can reduce competition, because any aggressive behavior (e.g., price reduction) in Market A can lead the competitor to retaliate in Market B (Bernheim & Whinston, 1990).

Let's illustrate this principle with an example. Consider the following three air routes, connecting two points (Table 6.12): A-B, C-D and E-F. Route A-B is served by firms X and Y: Firm X holds a dominant position with 80% of market share, while Firm Y has 20%. Similarly, firms X and Y serve route C-D: Firm Y has 20% of market share and its competitor X holds 80%. On the third E-F route, Firms X and Y are not present and Firm Z represents 80% of the market. In order to increase its market share on route A-B, Firm Y could lower its fares, but Firm X can react by doing the same thing on route C-D. On the other hand, Firm Y can enter route E-F (by lowering the price) without fear of retaliation in other markets from firms X or Z.

Suppose now that firms X and Z merge; in this case, Firm Y will hesitate to enter route E-F, fearing retaliation from the new entity (X + Z) on other routes. A merger that creates a portfolio of air routes can favor a multi-market contact behavior, which has a disciplinary effect on firms staying out of the merger.

Table 6.12 Merger and Multi-Market Contact

	Route A-B	*Route C-D*	*Route E-F*
Firm X	80%	20%	0%
Firm Y	20%	80%	0%
Firm Z	0%	0%	80%

The empirical study of Kim and Singal (1993) on the impact of air transport mergers in the United States confirms this result. On the basis of a sample of 8,109 routes, over the period spanning 1985-1988, the authors compared the ticket price on each route affected by the merger with the ticket price on a sample of routes that were not affected by the merger. The effect that the merger had on price appears significant on routes that were not served simultaneously by both undertakings before the merger.

§3 What Are the Main Obstacles to Market Power?

After characterizing the competitive impact of a merger and examining the incentive for merging firms to restrict competition, it remains to be seen whether they will be able to increase their market power. Several factors may hinder this, including: the demand characteristics (price elasticity and customer counterpower), the product durability, the role of entry barriers and the degree of market contestability, and the reaction of firms that stay out of the merger (Figure 6.17).

Figure 6.17 Main Obstacles to the Market Power

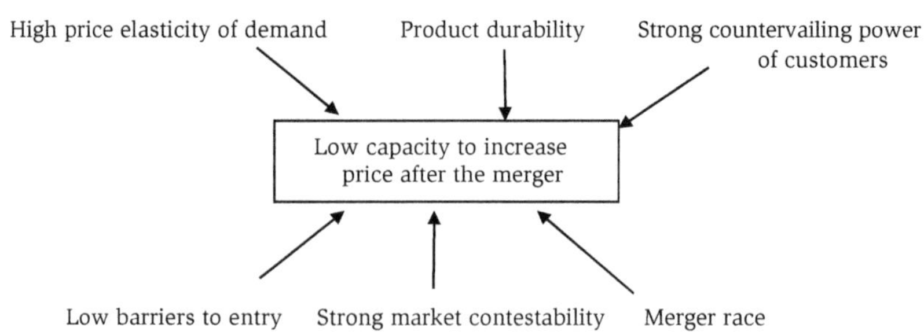

Demand characteristics: The extent of the merger's market power depends on the characteristics of the demand.

First, the extent of market power—whatever the market structure after the merger—depends on the price elasticity of demand: If price elasticity (in absolute terms) is high, then market power is low. In the case of a monopoly, we can consider that this market structure necessarily leads to a significant price increase. In reality, the ability of a monopoly to increase the price after a merger will depend on the value of the price elasticity of demand.

Remember that the marginal revenue of a monopoly is:

$$R_M = \frac{\partial[p(Q)Q]}{\partial Q}$$

$$\Leftrightarrow = p + Q\frac{\partial p}{\partial Q}$$

$$\Leftrightarrow = p(1 + \frac{1}{\varepsilon})$$

with ε, the price elasticity of demand.

Profit maximization leads the monopoly to equalize its marginal revenue with its marginal cost, i.e.:

$$p\left(1 + \frac{1}{\varepsilon}\right) = c$$

$$\Leftrightarrow \frac{(p-c)}{p} = \frac{1}{\varepsilon} \qquad (1)$$

The equation (1) shows that the market power (measured by the Lerner index) of a monopoly depends negatively on the price elasticity of demand: The higher it is, the closer the price is to marginal cost.

We also saw in Chapter 2 that in a Cournot's oligopoly situation, the average value of the Lerner index at the industry level was negatively linked with the price elasticity of demand:

$$\sum_{i=1}^{n} s_i \left(\frac{p - c_i}{p}\right) = \frac{HHI}{\varepsilon}$$

Second, the ability of the new entity to increase prices may be constrained by the countervailing power of customers: If there are few buyers (a situation referred as an "*oligopsony*"), it will be difficult for the merging firm to increase prices. The European Commission's 2004 Horizontal Merger Guidelines state that: "Even firms with very high market shares may not be in a position, post-merger, to significantly impede effective competition, in particular by acting to an appreciable extent independently of their customers, if the latter possess countervailing buyer power. Countervailing buyer power in this context should be understood as the bargaining strength that the buyer has vis-à-vis the seller in commercial negotiations due to its size, its commercial significance to the seller and its ability to switch to alternative suppliers" (§64).

This argument of the customers' counter power is sometimes used in mergers between firms that sell their products through retail chains:

- retail chains are often the only way for producers of everyday consumer goods to sell on a large scale. Large retailers possess a scarce resource (i.e., access to shelves) and exert a downward pressure on prices. Thus, in the Nabisco/Philip Morris (2000) case, the European Commission found that the undertaking's high market shares after the merger did not constitute a threat to competition on the Dutch market, given the countervailing power of customers when purchasing chocolate products: "On the demand side, the main customer categories are supermarket chains (Ahold, Laurus, Superunie, Trade Service Nederland), discounters (Aldi, Lekkerland and Sligro) cash and carry outlets (Makro and Sligro) and convenience outlets (e.g., gas stations, cafeterias, etc.). All of these categories are in a position to exercise sufficient bargaining power for these types of products. Large retailers account for nearly [50% to 60]% of chocolate confectionary purchases in the Netherlands, of which Laurus accounts for approximately [27-30]%, Ahold for [25-30]%, TSN [20-30]% and Superunie for [10 to 15]%. Since the success of a chocolate confectionery manufacturer's products depends largely on access to shelf space, retailers can exercise strong buying power";
- distributors often develop their own brand (private labels), which strengthens their bargaining power, particularly on entry-level products: The threat of a producer being delisted becomes credible insofar as the distributor can offer its own products instead. However, the ability and the incentive of supermarkets to counter a price increase are variable: In the case of unavoidable brands, the bargaining power is not in favor of distributors. A prestigious supplier may threaten to boycott the shelf, especially when it owns a portfolio of major brands. Thus, in the Grand Metropolitan/Guinness case (1999), the European Commission found that the undertaking's spirits brands (whisky, vodka, gin, etc.) limited the bargaining power of distributors: "It follows that permanent delisting of major brands is generally not a realistic option for retailers; accordingly, suppliers of those brands can, if necessary, get tough in the knowledge that the worst they can expect is a temporary delisting, perhaps limited to the less important sizes. That could very well be survivable, especially if, like the parties, the supplier also supplies a wide range of other

brands and products. The stronger the brand and the portfolio in question, the less realistic the threat of delisting."

Product durability: When the product is durable, the firm's market power is weakened, even in a monopoly situation. Indeed, when a product is durable, the first customers who buy the product today will no longer buy tomorrow, unless they renew their purchase periodically. In order to continue to sell, the monopoly therefore has no choice but to lower its price over time in order to win over new consumers (Figure 6.18).

Consider the case of a monopoly which offers a durable Product X over two periods. The demand function of Product X in the first period is:

$$P_X = 100 - Q_X$$

We assume that each consumer buys, at most, one unit of Product X for both periods. The total production cost is:

$$C = 20Q$$

In the first period, the monopoly sets a price of \$60 and sells 40 units. In the second period, the demand function becomes:

$$P_X = 60 - Q_X$$

The monopoly is then forced to lower its price to attract new customers: Product price drops to \$40 and the quantities sold are 20.

Figure 6.18 A Monopoly with a Durable Product (Without Consumer Anticipation)

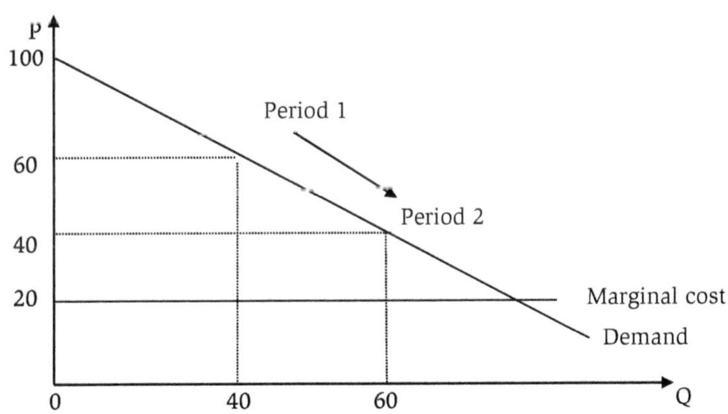

But in reality, the first customers (in period 1) can anticipate the future price decrease from \$60 to \$40. If they are patient, they will give up buying today, waiting for the price to drop. This wait-and-see attitude may force the monopoly to lower its price in the first period. Coase (1972) demonstrated that, under certain conditions, the equilibrium price for a monopoly is the competitive price: The monopoly loses all its market power.

The second characteristic of a durable good is that the producer has imperfect control over the flow of services generated by the use of the product, once sold. If the price of the product increases, consumers can, for example, use their existing equipment less intensively, extend the equipment's lifespan by spending more on maintenance, or buy a second-hand product. The existence of a stock of used goods increases the price elasticity of demand for new goods, which limits the market power of producers.

In the case of New Holland/Case (1999), firms invoked the durability of agricultural machinery as a constraint on market power, citing several arguments, which were not accepted by the European Commission:

- on the tractor market, the average depreciation rate is relatively low, which means a relatively long life of assets (more than 50% of the tractors sold are still in service 20 years later);
- technological progress remains limited: The second-hand market is a relevant channel to buy a tractor;
- there is an important and active second-hand market: Annual sales of second-hand tractors are two to three times higher than sales of new tractors;
- there is an active market for independent distributors of spare parts and services, allowing users to extend the lifespans of their tractors;
- few customers have a strong preference for new tractors. The price of the new tractor is strongly correlated with that of the second-hand tractor;
- in response to a price increase, users can extend the lifespans of their existing equipment rather than buying new tractors.

The role of entry barriers: The ability to raise prices after the merger also depends on entry barriers. If it's very easy to enter the market, any attempt to raise prices will be defeated. As highlighted in the U.S. Horizontal Mergers Guidelines (2010): "A merger is not likely to enhance market power if entry into the market is so easy that the merged firm and its remaining rivals in the market, either unilaterally or collectively, could not profitably raise prices or otherwise reduce competition compared to the level that would prevail in the absence of the merger. Entry is that easy if entry would be timely, likely, and sufficient in its magnitude, character, and scope to deter or counteract the competitive effects of concern."

There are different types of entry barriers (Table 6.13) with different origins:

Table 6.13 Typology of Entry Barriers

Barriers	*Explanation*
Legal barriers	Regulation (legal monopoly, quotas, marketing authorization, etc.) can limit or delay the entry of new competitors.
Technological innovation	Patents on a technology that reduces marginal cost make it more difficult for competitors to enter the market.
Learning by doing	The incumbent has a lower production cost, given its experience. The newcomer doesn't have any experience.
Economies of scope	The incumbent benefits from a large range of complementary products, which increases the entry cost for a newcomer.
Network effect	An incumbent possesses a standard with an installed base of consumers. It is difficult for a newcomer to launch a competing standard.
Well-known brands	An incumbent has a well-known brand. This implies that a newcomer has to invest in advertising to become as well-known.
Access to shelves	In retail distribution, controlling access to shelf space, which is a scarce resource, makes it difficult for a new competitor to enter the market.
Capacity investments	The existence of overcapacity owned by incumbent firms has a deterrent effect on the entry of new firms.

A competitor's entry into the market can take two main forms:

- supply substitution: A firm manufacturing related products may decide to modify its production to compete with those of the merging firm. The aim here is to estimate the extent of switching costs from one production to another. Thus, in the Nabisco/Philip Morris case, the European Commission found that the undertaking's high market shares after the merger did not constitute a real threat to competition in the chocolate bar market, given the possibility of supply substitution by agri-food giants: "Despite their currently modest presence in chocolate tablets, multinational competitors like Mars, Nestlé and Ferrero have the know-how, the brands, the manufacturing capability, the financial strength and the proven ability to launch new products. Considering their strong market shares in closely connected markets as bites (March [60-5]%; Nestlé [30-35]%) and bars (March [55-60]%; Nestlé [25-30]%) and the average 50% rate of capacity utilization in the overall chocolate confectionery industry, their ability to access the tablets' market will exercise a constraint on the new entity's competitive behavior in chocolate tablets (as well as in total chocolate confectionery) in the Netherlands";
- potential competition: New firms enter the market. The assessment of sunk costs plays a decisive role here; a new firm will enter if it is sure that it can exit the market without incurring huge losses. For example, the purchase of an

aircraft is a fixed cost for an airline, but an aircraft may be resold on the second-hand market or leased; it is therefore not a sunk cost. The specificity of an asset often constitutes an obstacle to its resale: Because it has been developed for a particular use, its value is difficult to transfer to another use or user.

The analysis of entry conditions is an important step in the merger assessment process, whether in the United States or Europe. Thus, in the U.S. Horizontal Mergers Guidelines (2010), three aspects of entry are taken into account:

- the speed of entry: Only a rapid entry—i.e., within less than two years—can prevent a lasting price increase after the merger;
- the entry probability: The entry will only be effective if the entrant can make a positive profit, taking into account the fixed entry costs;
- the sufficiency of entry: The entry process must be able to counteract a price increase. For example, in the case of a differentiated product industry, the products offered by the entrant must be sufficiently close to those of the merging firms to make a price increase unprofitable.

Similarly, at the European level, entry barriers are taken into account in the assessment of a merger. Thus, the Guidelines on the Assessment of Horizontal Mergers (2004) explain the European Commission's method of analysis, which is similar to that developed in the U.S. Mergers Guidelines: "When entering a market is sufficiently easy, a merger is unlikely to pose any significant anti-competitive risk. Therefore, entry analysis constitutes an important element of the overall competitive assessment. For entry to be considered a sufficient competitive constraint on the merging parties, it must be shown to be likely, timely and sufficient to deter or defeat any potential anti-competitive effects of the merger" (paragraph 68).

Contestable markets: In the case of a contestable market (*see* Chapter 2), market power is reduced to zero, because instantaneous entry and exit from the market are possible. This case, which seems a priori to be a theoretical economic one, has nevertheless found application in some merger decisions.

For example, in the United Kingdom, in the CHC Helicopters/HSG case (2000), the Competition Commission found that the market contestability, combined with buyer power, prevented any price increase after the merger. HSG and CHC offer helicopter services on offshore oil platforms in the U.K. part of the North Sea. The merger of the two operators would have led to a duopoly. However, the Competition Commission found that the conditions for a contestable market were met:

- there was a pool of potential entrants, consisting of helicopter firms operating in an offshore environment outside the North Sea. Oil firms, given their sizes and global presence, know these other firms;
- there were no specific entry costs: Whatever the continent on which they operate, helicopter firms bear the same operating costs, represented by the costs of crew, maintenance and purchase of aircraft;
- sunk costs were limited to the legal costs of obtaining an operating license;

- the reaction time of existing firms is always quite long after the entry of a new competitor. This is due to the fact that a newcomer will sign a contract with an oil company for a period of three to five years.

The Competition Commission also found that the absence of past entry into this market was the result of competitive prices and not entry barriers. In addition, the competition authority made a comparison with the situation in the Norwegian sector of the North Sea, where two helicopter firms operate. It was found that the existence of a duopoly led to a competitive situation as strong as that prevailing in the English area with three operators (before the merger).

Another example of contestable market can be found in France: In 2000, when the airline Air Liberté was acquired by another airline AOM, the French Competition Authority explicitly invoked the market contestability to authorize the merger. In particular, although the new entity AOM-Air Liberté was in a monopoly position on two air routes (Paris Orly-Perpignan and Paris Orly-Toulon), the French Competition Authority found that the threat of entry was strong. Indeed, the French leader Air France had 108,240 slots at Paris Orly airport, representing 49.3 % of total slots. These slots were not assigned to a specific route: It was therefore possible for Air France to use some of its slots on the Paris Orly-Toulon and Paris Orly-Perpignan routes if the new entity AOM/Air Liberté increased the prices on these two routes.

The reaction of outsiders: After the merger, the extent of market power also depends on the reaction of competitors (outsiders) that are not involved in the merger. They can react by merging too, defeating the potentially anti-competitive impact of the first merger.

Consider a vertical structure with two firms A and B upstream and two Firms 1 and 2 downstream (Figure 6.19). Both firms A and B produce at marginal cost c and compete in a Bertrand's duopoly with homogeneous products. They, therefore, make no profit at equilibrium and charge a price $P_A = P_B = c$. Firms A and B supply Firms 1 and 2, which have the same cost c and compete in a Cournot's duopoly in the downstream market. The prices of Firms 1 and 2 are therefore identical in the downstream market.

Figure 6.19 Vertical Situation Before the First Merger

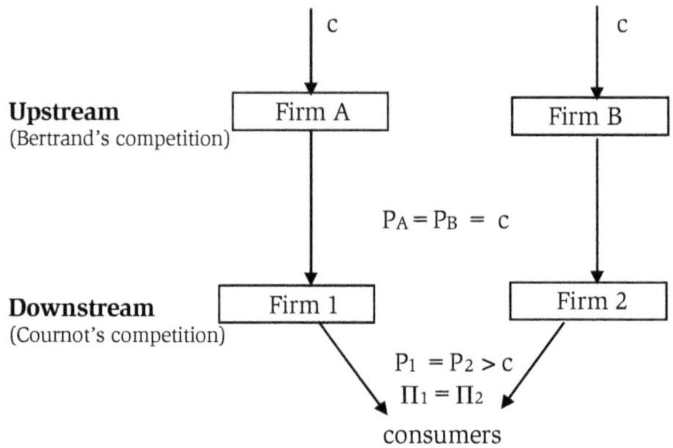

Suppose that Firm A merges with Firm 1 and decides to stop supplying to Firm 2. The latter is now faced with a single supplier (Firm B), which will act as a monopoly on the residual demand: It will sell at a price above marginal cost (Figure 6.20). Firm 1 is supplied at the cost c and therefore has a competitive advantage over its competitor Firm 2. Cournot's equilibrium on the downstream market is therefore changed: The profit of Firm 1 increases and that of Firm 2 decreases, while the final selling price increases.

Figure 6.20 Vertical Situation after the First Merger

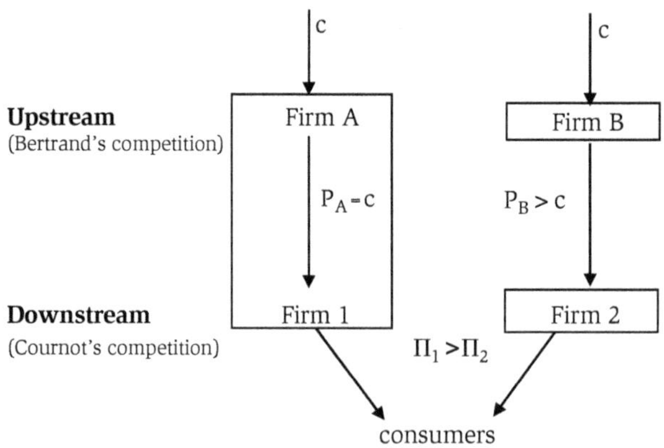

But Firm 2 can remedy this situation by merging with Firm B.[46] The market then returns to the initial situation, since both Firms 1 and 2 are sourcing again at the same

46. We can note that Firm B, which now has monopoly power, has no interest in the merger. The merger initiative must therefore come from Firm 2.

marginal cost c (Figure 6.21). This situation is a paradox for competition authorities: Either they block the first merger or they authorize the two successive mergers. The worst solution would be to allow the first merger and to block the second.

Figure 6.21 Vertical Situation after the Second Merger

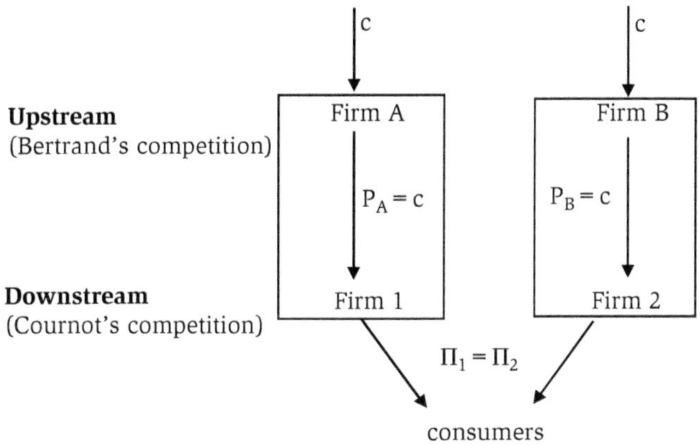

The previous result can also be illustrated algebraically. For simplicity, let us assume that the production cost of firms A and B is equal to 0. The two firms compete in a Bertrand's duopoly. The final demand function is linear:

$$P = a - Q_1 - Q_2$$

The reaction function of a firm i (i = 1, 2) in a Cournot duopoly is:

$$Q_i = (a - 2c_i + c_j)/3 \qquad (1)$$

Before the first merger between Firm A and Firm 1, the upstream equilibrium price is equal to 0 and profits are also nil. Downstream, Cournot's competition between Firms 1 and 2 leads to the following total equilibrium quantity, price and profits:

$$Q = Q_1 + Q_2 = 2a/3$$

$$P = a/3$$

$$\Pi_1 = \Pi_2 = a^2/9$$

Suppose that firms A and 1 merge and no longer supply Firm 2. The latter stays therefore alone with Firm B, which is now in a monopoly position.

Firm B maximizes its profit:

$$Max\ \pi_B = Max\ \frac{c_2(a - 2c_2 + c_1)}{3}$$

At equilibrium, Firm B charges a price P_B (which corresponds to the production cost of Firm 2) equal to:

$$P_B = c_2 = a/4$$

Firm 2 now bears a positive production cost, while its competitor benefits from a zero cost ($c_1 = 0$).

At equilibrium, we obtain the following quantities, prices and profits downstream:

$$Q_1 = 5a/12; Q_2 = a/6; Q = 7a/12$$

$$P = 5a/12$$

$$\Pi_1 = 25a^2/144; \Pi_2 = a^2/36$$

We can see that the merger of firms A and 1 increases the profit of the new entity, and decreases that of Firm 2. The total quantity at equilibrium decreases, which results in a higher price. Thanks to the merger, Firm B now makes a monopoly profit:

$$\Pi_B = a^2/24$$

But Firm 2 can react to the first merger by buying Firm B. In this case, the two downstream firms have the same production costs (equal to zero) and we find the initial result:

$$Q = Q_1 + Q_2 = 2a/3$$

$$P = a/3$$

$$\Pi_1 = \Pi_2 = a^2/9$$

SECTION 5 MERGERS AND EFFICIENCIES

A merger does not have the sole effect of reducing competition; it can also generate efficiencies by reducing production costs or promoting innovation. Unlike a cartel, whose sole object and effect is to restrict competition, a merger may result in synergies between the undertakings.

We will first analyze the trade-off between market power and efficiencies by using the Williamson's analysis (§1). We will then look for various sources of efficiencies (§2) before considering to what extent they should be taken into account by competition authorities (§3).

§1 The Trade-Off Between Market Power and Efficiencies

The idea that a merger has both a competitive and an efficiency effect has been highlighted by Williamson (1968).

A model without market power before the merger: Consider two firms with the same marginal cost function, equal to C_1; they are in a Bertrand's competition (Figure

6.22). Before they merge, the two firms sell the total quantity Q_1 at price P_1: They make no profit since the price is equal to the marginal cost. The two firms decide to merge, which has a double effect:

- the marginal cost of production decreases from C_1 to C_2, thanks to efficiencies;
- the price increases from P_1 to P_2, as the new entity is now in a monopoly position.

After the merger, the monopoly makes a profit, equal to the margin multiplied by the quantity Q_2:

$$\Pi = (P_2 - C_2) \times Q_2$$

Before the merger, the consumer surplus was equal to the abd area; since profits were nil, the welfare (defined as the sum of the consumer surplus and the profits) was equal to the abd triangle. After the merger, the consumer surplus decreases as consumers now pay more: They lose the gray triangle, represented by area D, as well as the rectangle A, which is a transfer of surplus from consumers to the monopoly. But the merger increases the profit, which is equal to area (A + B). If we add the profits and the consumers' loss (i.e.: A + B – D – A), the welfare change is equal to (B – D).

The final impact of the merger on welfare therefore depends on the comparison between area D (i.e., the net loss of consumers) and area B (i.e., the efficiency gain):

- if D > B, total welfare decreases;
- if D < B, the merger increases total welfare, even if it reduces the consumer surplus.

Figure 6.22 The Trade-Off Between Market Power and Efficiencies

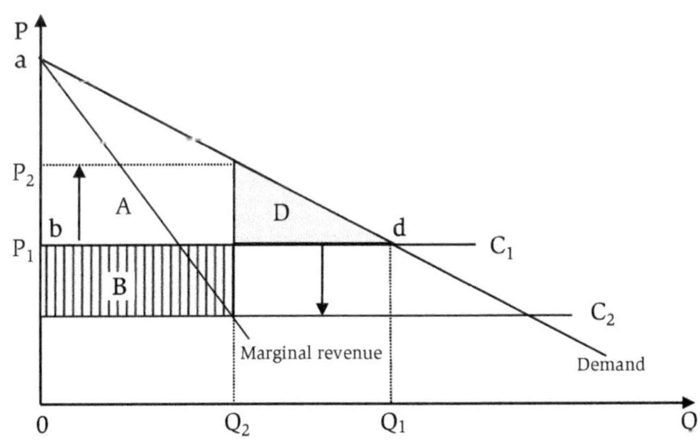

If we strictly apply Williamson's approach, a merger should be accepted if it increases total welfare and rejected if it does not. For example, a merger that will harm consumers (as a result of the price increase) but lead to significant efficiencies should be authorized. As we will see, this analysis does not exactly correspond to the one carried out by competition authorities, which mainly is focused on the consumer surplus.

The key role of price elasticity*:* If there is a trade-off between cost reduction and market power, it remains to be seen which factor influences this trade-off. To answer this question, we can start from Figure 6.23. Following the merger, the variation in quantities, price and cost is equal to:

$$\Delta Q = Q_2 - Q_1$$

$$\Delta P = P_2 - P_1$$

$$\Delta C = C_2 - C_1$$

Area D, which represents the net loss of consumers' surplus is equal to:

$$\text{Area D} = (Q_1 - Q_2)\ (P_2 - P_1)/2$$

$$\Leftrightarrow \text{Area D} = \frac{[|\Delta Q|\ \Delta P]}{2}$$

Similarly, area B, which represents the additional margin (resulting from the cost reduction), is equal to:

$$\text{Area B} = Q_2\ (C_1 - C_2)$$

$$\Leftrightarrow \text{Area B} = [Q_1 - (Q_1 - Q_2)]|\Delta C|$$

$$\Leftrightarrow \text{Area B} = [Q_1 - |\Delta Q|]|\Delta C|$$

The variation in quantity ΔQ can be rewritten as follows, by introducing the price elasticity of demand ε:

$$\Delta Q = \varepsilon Q_1 (\frac{\Delta P}{P_1})$$

The merger increases the welfare if area B is larger than area D, i.e.:

$$[Q_1 - |\Delta Q|]|\Delta C| > \frac{[|\Delta Q|\ \Delta P]}{2}$$

$$\Leftrightarrow \left[\frac{|\Delta C|}{C_1}\right] [Q_1 - |\Delta Q|]C_1 > \frac{[|\Delta Q|\ \Delta P]}{2}$$

$$\Leftrightarrow \frac{|\Delta C|}{C_1} > \frac{1}{2}\left[\frac{|\varepsilon|}{(1-\left|\varepsilon\left(\frac{\Delta P}{P_1}\right)\right|)}\right]\left(\frac{\Delta P}{P_1}\right)^2$$

In order to increase the total welfare, a merger should reduce the costs (equal to $\frac{|\Delta C|}{C_1}$) by more than half the square of the price increase (represented by $\left(\frac{\Delta P}{P_1}\right)$), weighted by the price elasticity of demand. This means that if the price elasticity of demand is low, the cost reduction doesn't have to be very high. Likewise, for a given cost reduction, the price increase can be high if the price elasticity of demand is low (Table 6.14). For example, if the price elasticity is 2 (in absolute terms), a 10% price increase could be offset by a decrease in the production cost of 1.25%, so that the welfare stays unchanged.

Table 6.14 Impact of Price Elasticity on the Williamson's Trade-Off

Value of Price Elasticity	*Cost Reduction to Compensate a 10% Price Increase*	*Price Increase That Does Not Change the Welfare for a 1% Cost Reduction*
-2	1.25%	9%
-1	0.55%	13%
-0.5	0.26%	19%

A model with market power before the merger: Until now, we've assumed that before the merger the two firms were in a situation of perfect competition and therefore did not make any profit.

Let's assume now that the two firms already had a market power before the merger. In this case, the conditions for a merger that doesn't reduce the total welfare become more restrictive.

Consider two Firms 1 and 2 are competing in a Cournot's duopoly. Before the merger, they charge a price P_1 higher than the marginal cost of production C_1 (Figure 6.23) and make a profit equal to area (E + F). After the merger, the two firms reduce their marginal cost from C_1 to C_2. They will be in a monopoly situation and will charge a price P_2. The decrease in the consumer surplus is represented by area (A + D). The profit increases by (A + B – F). Therefore, the merger increases the total welfare if:

$$(A + B - F) > (A + D)$$

$$\Leftrightarrow B > (F + D)$$

The condition is more restrictive, because, by increasing the price, the monopoly reduces the quantity sold from Q_1 to Q_2. However, before the merger, the firms were making a profit by selling a quantity Q_1, equal to area (E + F).

Figure 6.23 Williamson's Trade-Off with Market Power Before the Merger

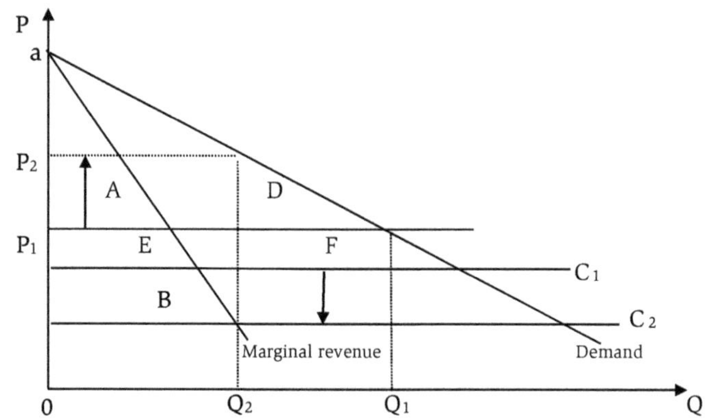

A numerical example: The fact that a merger can simultaneously increase the price and the welfare can be illustrated through a numerical example. Suppose two Firms 1 and 2 are competing in a Cournot's duopoly with a homogeneous good. Firm 1 has a lower production cost than its competitor:

$$C_1 = 1 \text{ and } C_2 = 4$$

The demand function is linear:

$$P = 10 - Q \quad \text{with} \quad Q = q_1 + q_2$$

At Cournot's equilibrium, we obtain:

$$q_1^{cour} = 4;\ q_2^{cour} = 1\ ;\ p^{cour} = 5\ ;\ \Pi_1^{cour} = 16\ ;\ \Pi_2^{cour} = 1$$

In this case, the consumer surplus (SC^{cour}) and the total profit of Firms 1 and 2 are equal:

$$SC^{cour} = 12.5$$

$$\Pi^{cour} = 17$$

We deduce the total welfare (W^{cour}), defined as the sum of the consumer surplus and profits:

$$W^{cour} = \Pi_1^{cour} + \Pi_2^{cour} + SC^{cour} = 29.5$$

Now suppose that Firms 1 and 2 merge and become a monopoly (M). The new entity adopts the production cost of Firm 1 ($C_1 = 1$). At the monopoly equilibrium, we obtain:

$$Q^M = 4;\ P^M = 5.5;\ \Pi^M = 20.25$$

$$SC^M = 10.125;\ W^M = 30.375$$

We note that the merger has three consequences:

- a decrease in the consumer surplus due to the increase in prices;
- an increase in the total profit of firms, the new entity being in a monopoly situation;
- an increase in total welfare: The loss of consumer surplus is less than the additional profits.

The impact of efficiencies on competitors: Previous developments have focused on a merger between two firms, which leads to a monopoly situation. In practice, such a scenario is unlikely and it is more realistic to assume that the merger between two firms (the insiders) will leave competitors outside the merger (the outsiders). In this case, it's interesting to analyze the impact that a merger has on competitors.

We have seen that without efficiencies the merger always benefits outsiders, whether in a Cournot's or Bertrand's situation. However, this result is no longer valid if the merger allows merging firms to sufficiently lower their costs: In this case, the merger will reduce the profits of outsider firms. This mechanism can be illustrated through a graphical example (Figure 6.24). Suppose that three firms A, B and C compete in a Bertrand's oligopoly with differentiated products. The equilibrium before the merger is at point X at the intersection of the two reaction functions. Firm A decides to merge with Firm B. Without efficiency gains, the firm's reaction function (A + B) would move upwards from $R_{A,B}$ to $R'_{A,B}$. The new equilibrium would move from point X to point Z. Facing a price increase of (A + B), Firm C's best response would be to increase its price from P_C to P'_C but less strongly than (A + B) in order to gain market share.

With efficiencies, the production cost of Firm (A + B) will decrease. Its reaction function therefore will move downwards from $R_{A,B}$ to $R^*_{A,B}$. The new equilibrium is at point Y and not Z: Thanks to efficiencies, the new entity has reduced its price from $P_{A,B}$ to $P^*_{A,B}$. Firm C has no choice but to adjust its price downwards, even though its production cost has not decreased: Its profit will therefore decrease.

Figure 6.24 The Effect of a Merger on Competitors with Efficiencies

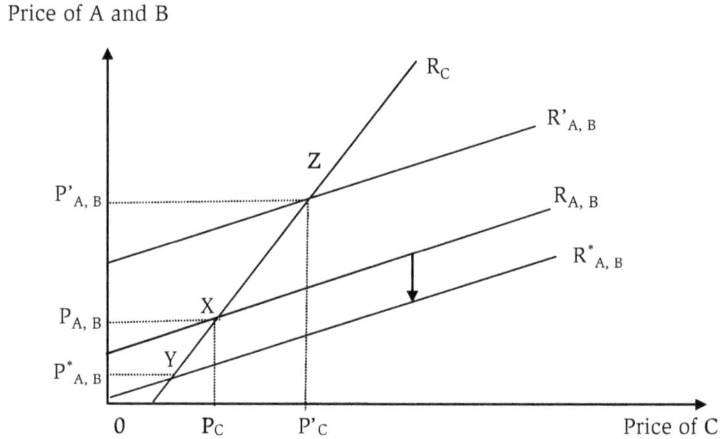

§2 Where Do Efficiencies Come From?

Efficiencies resulting from a merger are multiple, and we can identify them according to the type of merger (Table 6.15):

- in the case of a horizontal merger, efficiencies may come from economies of scale, economies of experience or from an absolute cost reduction;
- in the case of a diversification merger, efficiencies result mainly from a technological complementarity and economies of scope;
- in the case of a vertical merger, efficiencies are obtained by reducing transaction costs or by eliminating a double margin.

A merger can also have a positive impact on the incentive to innovate, even if there is no economic consensus on the meaning and magnitude of this effect.

Table 6.15 The Main Efficiencies of a Merger

Nature of the Efficiencies	*Type of Merger*	*Mechanism*
Economies of scale	horizontal	A merger increases the size of the firm, which allows it to better amortize fixed costs.
Appropriability	horizontal	A merger can increase the degree of appropriability by eliminating the risk of imitation between the two merging parties.
Learning curve	horizontal, conglomerate	The merging firms benefit from the experience of their partner and this enables them to lower their unit cost.
Adoption of an efficient technology	horizontal	A merger allows a firm with an obsolete technology to acquire a more efficient technology.
Economies of scope	conglomerate	A merger allows different goods to be produced simultaneously by using the same technology.
Technological complementarity	conglomerate	A merger allows firms to combine complementary products and thus avoid a multiplication of margins.
Elimination of the double margin	vertical	A merger allows firms to reduce successive margins from upstream to downstream.
Reduction of transaction costs	conglomerate, vertical	A merger avoids the risks associated with the use of contracts between firms.

Horizontal mergers: A horizontal merger can have three effects.

First, it can allow a Firm 2 with a high production cost C_2 to access a more efficient technology C_1. Graphically, for any level of production, Firm 1 has a lower marginal cost than Firm 2 (Figure 6.25). This argument is particularly relevant in industries where firms operate with different business models. For example, a low-cost airline may buy a high-cost airline to apply the low-cost model to it.

Figure 6.25 Mergers and Reducing Marginal Costs

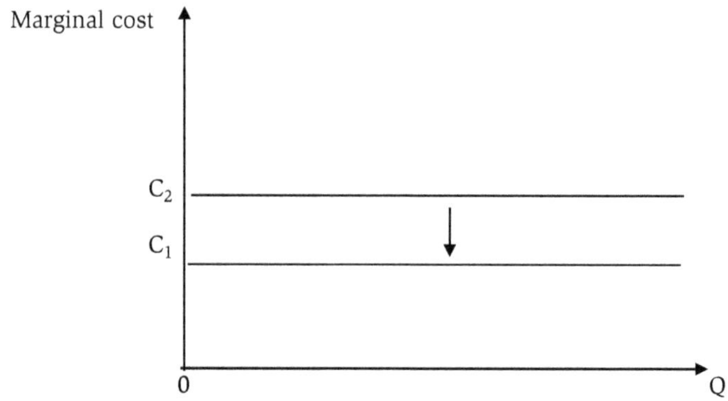

Second, thanks to the merger, merging firms will increase their sizes and lower their unit costs. This is due to the presence of fixed costs: When the production increases, fixed costs are spread over a larger quantity, which reduces the average cost. The level of production that minimizes the average cost is called the "*minimum efficient size.*" These economies of scale are not only in the production process, but can also be extended to other functions such as distribution, marketing or R&D.

Suppose two Firms 1 and 2 are each incurring a fixed cost F. Firms 1 and 2 also bear the same marginal cost of production c. The total cost function of each firm is:

$$\text{Total cost} = cQ + F$$

The average production cost is therefore equal to:

$$\text{Total cost}/Q = c + F/Q$$

We note that the average cost decreases with the quantity, because the fixed cost is spread over a higher level of production. The average cost tends asymptotically towards the marginal cost c, when the quantity increases.

Before the merger, each firm produces a quantity Q_A and incurs a high unit cost since each firm's production is low (Figure 6.26). After the merger, the two firms will concentrate the production in a single plant and will produce the quantity Q_B (greater than Q_A). They will benefit from economies of scale: The average cost of production will decrease from C_A to C_B.

Figure 6.26 Mergers and Economies of Scale

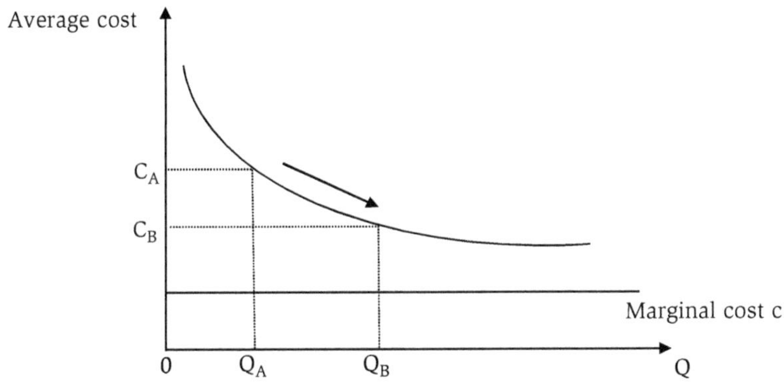

Third, with a horizontal merger, a firm will benefit from the learning curve of its competitor. A learning curve appears when the average production cost decreases with the cumulative quantity produced: The longer a firm has produced, the more experience it has accumulated in the way of producing, which lowers its average cost. In Figure 6.27, we have an experience curve of 90% and 80%. In the case of a 90% curve, each time the firm's cumulative production doubles, its unit cost decreases by 10%, thanks to the experience acquired.

Suppose that the firm produces only one unit per period. When the firm is in the second period it has therefore produced two units: Its unit cost will have decreased by 10% compared to the first unit. When it has produced four units (after four periods), its unit cost will be equal to $(0.9)^2$, or 0.81 of the cost of the first unit. In the case of an 80% curve, each time the cumulative production doubles, the unit cost decreases by 20%. The experience curve is very important in sectors such as aeronautics or semiconductors.

Let us take a Firm 1 that has been present on the market for four periods with a 10% experience curve: Its average production cost is therefore equal to 81% of that of the first unit. Firm 2 is in the same sector with the same technology, but for 32 periods: Its average production cost is therefore equal to $(0.9)^4$, or 65% of that of the first unit. Firm 1 therefore faces a cost disadvantage compared to its competitor because it entered the market later. Firm 1 has an incentive to merge with Firm 2 in order to benefit from its accumulated experience and thus reduce its unit cost of production.

Figure 6.27 The Learning Curve

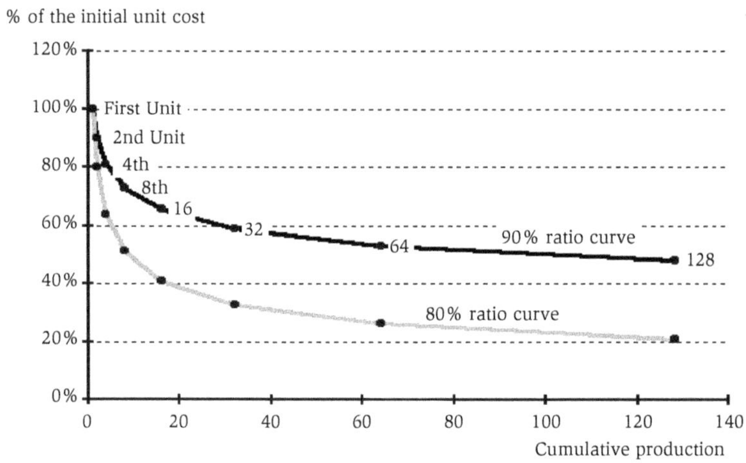

Source: http://www.maxwideman.com/papers/*resource*/theory.htm#table1.

Conglomerate mergers*:* A conglomerate merger can generate "*economies of scope*," when firms produce different goods with the same inputs. An economy of scope arises when the total cost of producing different goods is lower than the total cost of producing each good separately for a given quantity of products. In the case of two products 1 and 2, the economies of scope imply that:

$$C(q_1 + q_2) < C(q_1) + C(q_2).$$

To measure the extent of economies of scope, it is usual to calculate the following ratio:

$$\frac{C(q_1) + C(q_2) - C(q_1 + q_2)}{C(q_1 + q_2)}$$

If there are economies of scope in the production of products 1 and 2, this ratio will be positive; indeed, since the cost of the joint production $C(q_1 + q_2)$ is smaller than the cost of producing each product separately, the numerator is positive. By dividing the numerator by the cost of the joint production, we obtain a measure (in percentage) of the cost savings. Economies of scope can be represented graphically (Figure 6.28): The unit cost of production decreases with the number of products manufactured.

Figure 6.28 Merger and Economies of Scope

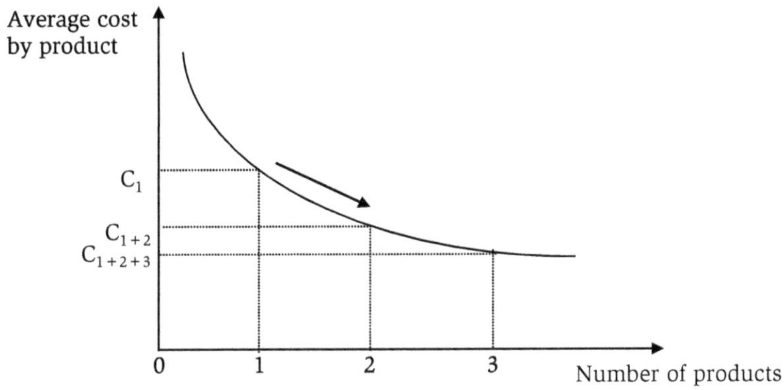

Second, a conglomerate merger can enable firms to better coordinate themselves when they sell perfectly complementary goods. This phenomenon is known as the "*Cournot effect*" (1838).

Suppose that Firm 1 produces Product X and Firm 2 produces Product Y. Both products X and Y are perfect complements: Consumers want to consume one unit of X with one unit of Y (e.g., think of a central computer unit and a screen). Each of the two firms, which are in a monopoly on their own product, will charge a high price and thus limit the other firm's sales. Indeed, since Firm A is charging a margin on Product X, the demand for Product X is limited, which limits the sales of Product Y. Symmetrically, since Firm B is charging a margin on Product Y, this limits the sales of Product X. A merger remedies this situation by leading both to a decrease in price of (X + Y), which is beneficial to consumers, and leads to an increase in profits.

Suppose there is a producer of computer central units (Firm 1) and a producer of screens (Firm 2); for simplicity, we assume that the cost of production is zero. A computer is composed of two complementary products: a central unit (noted X), sold at price P_X and a screen (noted Y), sold at price P_Y. The price of a computer, noted P_S, is therefore:

$$P_S = P_X + P_Y$$

As the two products are perfectly complementary, consumers never buy them separately: The number of central units sold is equal to the number of screens. The computer demand function is equal to:

$$Q = a - P_S$$

Let us assume that there is no coordination between the two firms. Firm 1 maximizes its profit, taking as given the price of a screen:

$$Max\ \Pi_x = Max\ [p_x\ (a - p_x - p_y)]$$

The optimal price P_X of Firm 1 (which produces central units) depends on the price P_Y of Firm 2 (which produces screens):

$$P_X = (a - P_Y)/2$$

By symmetry, the optimal price P_Y of Firm 2 depends on the price P_X of Firm 1:

$$P_Y = (a - P_x)/2$$

We obtain:

$$P_X = P_Y = a/3; Q_X = Q_Y = a/3 ; \Pi_1 = \Pi_2 = a^2/9$$

Assume now that Firms 1 and 2 merge. The new entity has a monopoly situation on the production of computers (central units plus screens) and maximizes its profit:

$$\text{Max } \Pi = \text{Max } [p_s (a - p_s)]$$

We obtain:

$$P^*_S = a/2; Q^* = a/2; \Pi^* = a^2/4 \qquad (2)$$

We can see that the merger, which leads to a multi-product monopoly, increases welfare: It increases not only the consumer's surplus but also the total profit. Indeed, we have:

$$P^*_S = a/2 < P_S = (P_X + P_Y) = 2a/3$$

$$\Pi^* = a^2/4 > (\Pi_1 + \Pi_2) = 2a^2/9$$

Vertical mergers: A vertical merger can reduce costs by eliminating certain stages in the production process. For example, canned fish manufacturers can buy fishing firms in order to transform them into factory boats and to eliminate the freeze-thaw stage.

Second, a vertical merger reduces transaction costs, especially when using the market is risky. For example, in the aluminum industry, the number of bauxite suppliers is limited, while the assets of aluminum producers are very specialized. Under these conditions, there is a high risk of suppliers behaving opportunistically and suddenly raising the price of bauxite. Long-term supply contracts may not be sufficient to secure supply; consequently, an aluminum firm has a strong incentive to buy a bauxite producer. Similarly, in the banana trade, there is an asymmetry of information on product quality between the banana producer and the distributor. The quality—and in particular, the degree of ripeness of the bananas—is difficult to control ex-ante by the distributor. The risk is that market contracts lead to an inefficient result in which distributors offer a low price and producers reduce the quality of bananas. To avoid this situation, the distributor may decide to buy a banana plantation.

Third, a vertical merger can eliminate a double margin situation (Figure 6.29). Suppose that Firm 1, in a monopoly situation, produces at a marginal cost C_1. It sells its product to Firm 2 at price P_1. Price P_1 therefore constitutes for Firm 2 its production cost C_2. Firm 2 is itself in a monopoly situation and charges customers price P_2 (with $P_2 > P_1$). This situation is not only harmful for final consumers, since they bear a "*double margin,*" but also for both firms: Since Firm 2 charges a monopoly price downstream, end demand is low, which hampers Firm 1's upstream sales. Symmetrically, since Firm 1 sets a monopoly price, Firm 2 bears a high cost, which impacts its own price downstream. In reality, in the absence of coordination, the two firms harm each other: Each ignores the negative influence of its behavior on the profit of its partner. This situation is qualified in economics as a "*cross negative externality.*" To remedy this situation, both firms have an interest in merging: a merger will lead to a lower price, beneficial for consumers and firms. For example, Firm 2 can buy Firm 1, which becomes its subsidiary and now supplies the downstream entity at a marginal cost C.

Figure 6.29 Mergers and Double Marginalization

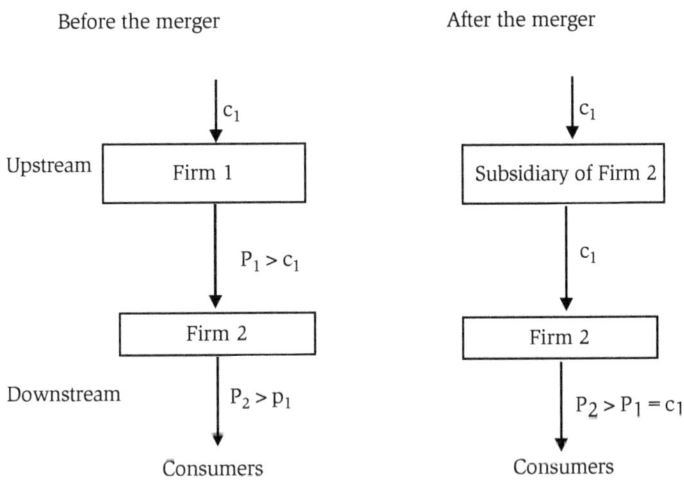

The fact that the double margin has been eliminated can be demonstrated with a two-step model. In the second stage, Firm 2 faces a final demand equal to:

$$Q(P_2) = a - P_2$$

Firm 2 sets price P_2, which maximizes its profit:

$$\Pi_2 = (a - p_2)\ (p_2 - p_1)$$

We deduce from this:

$$P^*_2 = (P_1 + a)/2$$

$$\Pi^*_2 = (a - P_1)^2/4$$

$$Q^*_2 = (a - P_1)/2$$

At the first stage of the game, Firm 1 maximizes its profit by taking into account the quantity offered by Firm 2 to final consumers:

$$\text{Max}\,\Pi_1 = \text{Max}\,[(p_1 - c)\,(a - p_1)/2]$$

We deduce the price and profits of Firm 1:

$$P^*_1 = (c + a)/2$$

$$\Pi^*_1 = (a - c)^2/8$$

We obtain the price of Firm 2:

$$P^*_2 = (c + 3a)/4 > P^*_1 = (c + a)/2 > c$$

There is a double margin phenomenon: Each firm behaves as a monopoly and therefore charges a price above its marginal cost. Without any coordination, each firm does not take into account the negative effect of its monopoly behavior on the other firm.

Now suppose that Firms 1 and 2 merge. The new entity maximizes its profit:

$$\text{Max}\,\Pi = \text{Max}\,(a - p^*)\,(p^* - c)$$

We obtain the price, the quantity and the profit of an integrated monopoly:

$$P^* = (c + a)/2$$

$$\Pi^* = (a - c)^2/4$$

$$Q^* = (a - c)/2$$

We see immediately that the profit of the integrated monopoly is higher than the sum of the profits of the two firms when they do not coordinate their behavior. Similarly, the price of the final product decreases, which benefits consumers. In other words, the total welfare increases and this benefits both the producer/distributor and the consumers.

Mergers and the incentive to innovate: Beyond static gains, a merger can also have a positive effect on the incentive to innovate. This idea was initially developed by Schumpeter (1942) and is based on several arguments:

- R&D activity is characterized by threshold effects, below which the probability of discovery is nil. Suppose, for example, that it is necessary to invest at least €1 billion to find a new vaccine. There are two firms on the market and each has an investment capacity of €500 million. Without any coordination, none of them will invest in R&D. On the other hand, if the two firms merge (or cooperate in R&D), they will pool their investment capacity and the probability of discovering a new vaccine will become highly likely.
- The incentive to innovate would be higher in concentrated sectors because the small number of firms makes it easier to capture the benefits of an innovation. A greater appropriability enhances the incentives to innovate by allowing the innovator to obtain a higher reward from its invention. In contrast, in an environment with low appropriability, firms have an incentive to "free ride"

on each other's innovation, resulting in lower innovation incentives. A merger can affect the degree of appropriability by eliminating the risk of imitation between the two merging parties. Effectively, with imperfect appropriability, there is a positive innovation externality: Firm A does not take into account the positive impact on Firm B's profits resulting from its innovation, and vice versa. The merger internalizes this positive externality, thus increasing innovation incentives.
- A larger firm can conduct several research projects simultaneously and therefore diversify the risk. It can also benefit from positive spillovers between R&D projects: Research carried out in area A can benefit another area of research B. Downstream, the results of R&D activity can be applied to several product lines, as large firms are often more diversified.
- The existence of financial constraints may justify that large firms (or firms operating in concentrated markets) have greater incentive to innovate than firms in a competitive situation. Indeed, since innovating is a risky activity, it is difficult to finance it externally, either by bank loan or via financial markets. Under these conditions, only firms with significant internal financial resources can innovate. A merger between two firms can therefore improve innovation capacities: For example, in the Dolisos/Boiron case (2005), the French Competition Authority welcomed the undertaking's argument that the merger would free up additional financial resources to invest in R&D.

§3 Efficiencies and Competition Policy: A Cautious Approach

If Williamson's reasoning is strictly applied, a merger should be accepted if it increases total welfare, and rejected if it does not. This means that a merger that harms consumers (as a result of the price increase) but leads to strong efficiencies should be allowed (Table 6.16). This analysis, based solely on the criterion of total welfare, does not correspond to the one carried out by competition authorities.

Table 6.16 Implications of Williamson's Analysis

Effect on the Consumer's Surplus	*Efficiencies*	*Antitrust Approach*
Price decrease or unchanged price	Strong or nil	Unconditional acceptance
Price increase	Nil	Refusal
Price increase	Strong	Conditional acceptance, if the efficiencies offset the price increase

In practice, competition authorities are very cautious about taking efficiencies into account. Moreover, these efficiencies are only considered if they will potentially avoid a price increase and therefore a decrease in the consumer's surplus. Thus, in the

United States, the Horizontal Merger Guidelines (2010) recall that a merger with a negative impact on competition can be "saved" thanks to the efficiencies it will generate, but a reasonable proportion of these gains must benefit consumers. In addition, efficiencies are taken into account under strict conditions:

- their existence must be demonstrated: What is their magnitude, likelihood of occurrence, origin and time frame?
- the merger must be the only way to achieve the efficiencies. The aim here is to compare the merger choice with other alternatives (e.g., licensing);
- efficiencies must be "*sufficient*" to offset the harm done to competition: "The Agency considers whether cognizable efficiencies likely would be sufficient to reverse the merger's potential to harm consumers in the relevant market [...]. When the potential adverse competitive effect of a merger is likely to be particularly large, extraordinarily great cognizable efficiencies would be necessary to prevent the merger from being anti-competitive."

A fairly similar approach is adopted in Europe. Merger Regulation 139/2004 states that the Commission assesses the impact of a merger on competition by taking into account, in particular, "developments in technical and economic progress, provided that they are to the benefit of consumers and do not constitute an obstacle to competition." These efficiencies must be specific to the merger and their existence must be verifiable.

Why are competition authorities so cautious? Several factors may explain the caution of competition authorities when it comes to assessing efficiencies.

First, efficiencies are particularly difficult to estimate ex-ante, particularly in a context of asymmetric information between undertakings and antitrust authorities. This issue is particularly relevant when antitrust authorities need to analyze the dynamic gains of a merger: Since the time frame is very long, it's very difficult and risky to assess the impact of a merger on the incentive to innovate. Thus, in Europe, while the Horizontal Merger Guidelines mention dynamic gains, the Commission recalls that "the further in time the projected efficiencies are, the less weight the Commission will be able to give them" (paragraph 83).

In the American case, antitrust authorities consider also dynamic gains with caution: "Other efficiencies, such as those relating to research and development, are potentially substantial, but are generally less susceptible to verification [...]."

Second, many empirical studies show a high failure rate of mergers and an overestimation of their expected benefits: The value resulting from synergies between firms—summarized by the famous formula "1 + 1 = 3"—is often not achieved. Regardless of the methodology used, empirical studies show a merger failure rate of between 50% and 83%.

For example, a study by McKinsey (2004) measured the difference between the estimated cost reductions at the time of the merger and the cost reductions achieved after the merger, based on a sample of 92 M&As. While 66% of the mergers achieve more than 90% of the expected cost synergies, the promise of costs reduction is not achieved in 27% of cases, or is at least 20% lower than expected.

Several factors may explain this result: Forecasts are sometimes made on the basis of assumptions that are not relevant; there is a psychological bias of "*overconfidence*" among managers, leading them to overestimate the gains and minimize the obstacles. Purchasers do not always have sufficient information on the exact situation of the target firm when they launch their takeover.

Third, when horizontal mergers succeed in creating value, it may be through efficiencies but also through the reduction of competition on the market. Thus, Clougherty and Duso (2009) measured the impact of horizontal mergers on the share price of the undertakings and on that of their competitors (the outsiders). The methodology used is an "*event study*": It consists of studying the reaction of the stock price following the announcement of an unanticipated event. It is based on a comparison between the observed situation (increase or decrease in the share price) and a theoretical evolution of the share price if the event (here, the announcement of a merger) had not taken place. This counterfactual situation is based on the "*Capital Asset Pricing Model*": The return on a share i (R_i) at a given time t depends on how the return on the equity market (R_m) will evolve, corrected by a factor β_i, which measures the volatility of the share i compared to the market:

$$R^*_{i,t} = \alpha_i + \beta_i R_{m,t} + \varepsilon_{i,t}$$

The counterfactual return $R^*_{i,t}$ is compared to the observed return in order to identify a difference, qualified as "*abnormal return*" (AR):

$$RA_{i,t} = R_{i,t} - R^*_{i,t}$$

Four scenarios are possible (Table 6.17).

In the first case, there is a positive abnormal return for both the new entity and the competitors (case 1). This means that the merger benefits the undertakings and the competitors: the merger leads to an increase in market power.

In the second scenario, the abnormal return of undertakings is negative while that of the outsiders is positive: The market expects that the merger will increase costs and therefore benefit outsiders (case 2).

A third case is the one in which the merging firms obtain a positive abnormal return while the outsiders have a negative abnormal return (case 3): It is a merger with strong synergies, which lowers costs and therefore harms competitors.

A final case is the one in which merging firms and outsiders have an abnormal negative return (case 4): It is a pre-emptive merger, which destroys value for the entire market. This is the case, for example, if all firms have outbid each other to acquire the same firm. The winner overpays the target, while competitors see their share price fall because the merger represents a threat to their future business.

Table 6.17 Motives of M&As and Impact on Share Price

	Merging Firms Benefit from the Merger (Abnormal Increase in Their Share Price)	*Merging Firms Lose Post-Merger (Abnormal Decrease in Their Share Price)*
Competitors benefit from the merger (abnormal rise in their share price)	Merger motivated by market power	Merger that does not create synergies
Competitors lose post-merger (abnormal drop in their share price)	Merger motivated by efficiencies	Preemptive merger

The authors apply this grid to a sample of 165 transactions notified to the European Commission between 1990 and 2002: The advantage of this sample is that the identification of competitors is based on the market analysis that the European Commission carried out. They obtain several interesting results (Table 6.18):

- 21% of mergers benefit all market participants: These mergers are driven by the search for market power;
- in 36% of cases, the stock market value of merging firms decreases: This means that the financial markets do not believe in the announced synergies;
- mergers that create efficiencies represent only 16% of the sample: This is less than mergers motivated by increasing market power.

Table 6.18 Merger's Impact on Share Price

	Gain for Merging Firms	*No Effect on Merging Firms*	*Loss for Merging Firms*	*Total*
Gain for competitors	21.83% (market power)	5.9%	15.34% (no synergies)	43.07%
No effect on competitors	5.9%	3.83%	5.6%	15.34%
Loss for competitors	16.22% (synergies)	9.73%	15.63%	41.59%
Total	43.95%	19.47%	36.58%	

Source: Clougherty and Duso (2009).

Review Topics:

Under what conditions should competition authorities be notified of a merger?
What are the possible issues of a merger control?
What are the advantages and limitations of structural and behavioral remedies?
What elements are generally used to delimit the relevant market?
How is market concentration measured?
What are the main channels for exercising market power after a merger?
What factors limit market power?
What are the main efficiencies of a merger?
To what extent are efficiencies taken into account by antitrust authorities?

Recommended Readings:

John Kwoka, Mergers, *Merger Control, and Remedies: A Retrospective Analysis of U.S. Policy* (The MIT Press, 2014).
Louis Vogel, *European Merger Control* (Bruylant, 2017).

Conclusion: The Challenges of Competition Policy

While competition policy is based on well-known economic principles, it often sparks debate and must now face several new challenges.

The first challenge is the role it should or could play in the digital economy, a sector where oligopolies and monopolies are rapidly emerging. The second challenge concerns the effectiveness of national or regional competition policies in a globalized world. To be effective, for example, antitrust policies must be carried out hand in hand with trade defense policies that deal with "*unfair competition*" practices such as dumping or abusive public subsidies. The third challenge, essentially European, concerns the coordination—or sometimes the conflict—between an all-powerful antitrust policy and an industrial policy that is still underdeveloped within the EU.

In this conclusion, we set out the main terms of the debate, leaving it up to the reader, now fully equipped to understand the fundamentals of competition economics, to explore the issues in greater depth and form his or her own opinion.

SECTION 1 COMPETITION POLICY FACING THE DIGITAL CHALLENGE

Numerous empirical studies have shown a return of industrial concentration in countries such as the United States since the 2000s. Thus, Philippon (2018) notes an increase in the concentration ratio (CR_8) and the HHI, whatever the indicator chosen (Figure 1). This trend towards concentration is also coupled with an increase in U.S. margins and a decline in entrepreneurial dynamism—clearly illustrated by the steady decrease of the entry rate of new firms over the past few years. This high level of market concentration appears to be particularly true in the digital sector, with the development of "*tech giants*" that play pivotal roles in the American economy.

Figure 1 Concentration Ratios (CR_8) and HHI in the United States (2000-2015)

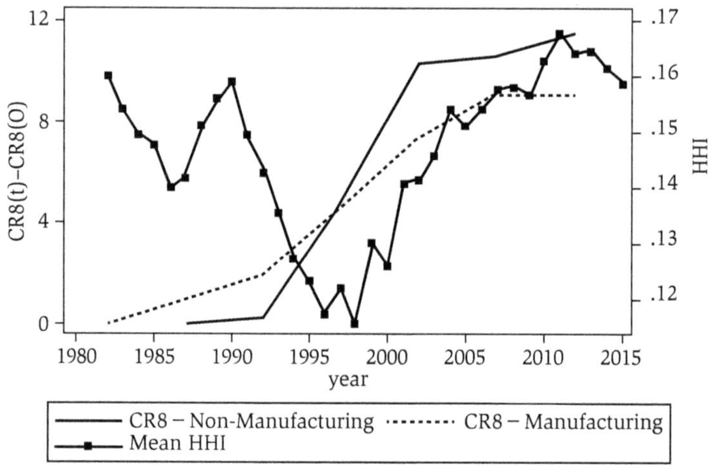

Source: Philippon (2018).

The main characteristics of the digital economy: It is true that the digital economy appears to be conducive, by way of its intrinsic characteristics, to the emergence of oligopolistic—even monopolistic—market structures.

First, it is a sector with high fixed costs: Digital technology requires significant R&D investments, particularly in algorithms and data processing. The presence of high fixed costs fuels economies of scale, which are all the more important when variable costs are low. Indeed, in most-digital activities, the marginal cost—the cost of serving an additional consumer—is close to zero. This limited marginal cost allows digital firms to operate globally, as illustrated by the social network Facebook, which had more than 2.3 billion users worldwide in 2020.

Second, digital players often operate in several business segments at the same time with complementary links: They form open or closed ecosystems. This characteristic gives them a clear competitive advantage: For example, it allows them to benefit from leverage effects from one activity to another, and to take advantage of synergies and economies of scope by focusing on complementarities between upstream and downstream markets. All this makes it more difficult for a new player to enter a single market segment.

Third, the digital economy is characterized by strong network effects, both direct and indirect. For example, the more a search engine is used, the more efficient it will be and the more it will be used in the future. Similarly, the more suppliers an online booking platform brings together, the more attractive it is to customers, which, in turn, makes it more attractive to suppliers. This is also the case with social networks: The more people there are on the same social network, the more attractive it becomes to those who use it, which reinforces the market share of the social network. The network effects can also be crossed, as in the case of Uber or Booking: The utility that an individual gets from a service depends on the number of suppliers on the other side of the market and vice versa. In the case of ride-hailing, customer utility increases with the number of drivers using the same application as them: The wait time for a car will be shorter. For their part, drivers are more satisfied to work for an application if it's used by many customers: They'll have a better chance of getting a reservation.

Finally, the digital economy is based on the collection and processing of a large amount of personal data, which can lead to market-share strengthening mechanisms: The more personal data a digital platform has, in both quantity and quality, the more effective it becomes (e.g., for targeted advertising or recommendations), thereby making the platform more attractive to users.

The combination of these different characteristics leads to a "*snowball*" phenomenon, whereby a company quickly captures most of the market shares, as described in the famous saying: "winner takes all." For example, in the online search engine market, Google has a market share of more than 90% in Europe and is in a narrow oligopoly, with Facebook and Amazon, in the digital advertising market. The same applies to social networks such as Facebook, intermediation platforms such as Booking, Airbnb, and Uber, and operators such as Amazon—which, in the United States, represents 46% of online sales. In each of these markets, there are only a few players with high market shares.

For example, in the United Kingdom in 2018, the market share of the top two operators in business segments such as search engines, digital advertising, smartphone operators, or social networks all exceeded 50%, and sometimes even exceeded 90% (Figure 2). Their market shares have remained fairly constant over time, with the exception of the market share of mobile phone operating systems, which rose steadily to reach 99% in 2018.

Figure 2 Market Share of the Top Two Operators in Selected Digital Activities (United Kingdom, 2010-2018)

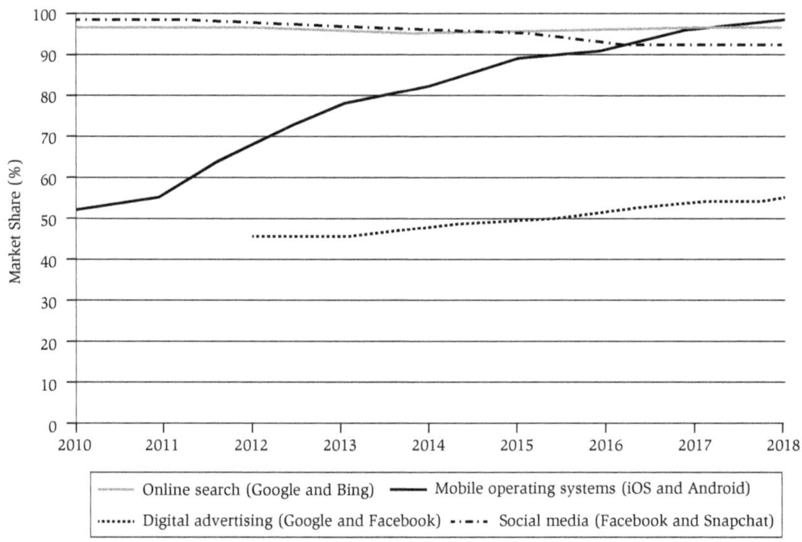

Source: Furman et al. (2019).

This snowball phenomenon can be illustrated through a simple numerical example. Suppose that two new firms A and B each launch a ride-hailing app with the same quality for consumers. The utility for a consumer who uses a ride-hailing app is an increasing function of the number of drivers. Symmetrically, the utility of an app for drivers depends on the number of consumers using it. Consumers arrive in cohorts of 1,000 in each period. There are 5,000 potential consumers. Since apps A and B are of equivalent quality (e.g., their location algorithm is just as efficient), the first 1,000 users are indifferent between choosing App A or App B. In both cases, their utility is 10 (Table 1). Suppose that, as a result of an effective advertising action by Firm A, the first 1,000 consumers choose to download App A. The drivers on the other side of the market will also use this app. The second cohort of consumers will naturally choose App A, with full knowledge of the facts: Since there are already drivers on App A, the utility of App A is 12, whereas if they download the App B, which has not yet "taken off," their utility is only 10. They will choose to download App A, which will increase its attractiveness for new drivers. Through a cumulative mechanism, App A will conquer the entire market, and its performance will increase over time with the number of users and drivers. App B will never be able to "get out of the starting gate" of the race. At the end of the race, App A will give consumers a utility of 17, as opposed to 10 in the case of App B.

Table 1 A Standardization Race with Network Effects

Consumer Cohorts	*0-1,000*	*1,000-2,000*	*2,000-3,000*	*3,000-4,000*	*4,000-5,000*
Utility of A	10	12	14	16	17
Utility of B	10	12	14	16	17

Once App A has won the market, it becomes also very difficult for a new firm to enter the market, even if that firm is offering a better-quality app, C. This phenomenon is due to the fact that each user, even if she or he wishes to change, has an individual incentive to wait so as not to lose the existing indirect network effect. For instance, using new App C presents a huge risk: that of not having enough drivers on the other side of the market. But since consumers and drivers cannot coordinate their behavior, everyone waits and a situation of "excess of inertia|" appears: The new technology C fails to dethrone the old one.

We can illustrate this phenomenon with a numerical example (Table 2). Two consumers X and Y are present on App A, which gives them a utility of 18. If they both switch to the new app, C, their utility increases to 25 because it is of better quality. But the most damaging situation for a consumer is to find himself alone on new App C: In this case, the consumer's utility is very low (5) because there will not be enough drivers, and he will have to wait for a cab ride. On the other hand, the consumer who stayed on old App A increases her utility, because she is now the only one to use it and has many drivers (utility of 20 instead of 15). Each consumer has an incentive to wait and to stay on old App A. The Nash's equilibrium in this simultaneous game is (18, 18): Nobody moves and the two consumers stay on the old technology. This result stems from the lack of coordination between consumers (who are competing for access to a ride-hailing reservation) and drivers to collectively switch to new App C.

Table 2 Network Effect and Excess of Inertia

	Consumer X: Stay on the Old App A	*Consumer X: Switch to the New App C*
Consumer Y: Stay on the old App A	**(18, 18)**	(20, 5)
Consumer Y: Switch to the new App C	(5, 20)	(25, 25)

N. B.: The first number in each box of the matrix corresponds to the utility of consumer Y; the second number corresponds to the utility of consumer X.

The debate on the persistence of concentrated markets*:* A very important question is whether these high market shares, which persist over time, are first and foremost the result of a competition based on merit, or whether they're also the fruit of anti-competitive strategies (*see* in particular Furman et al. [2019], and Cremer et al. [2019] reports).

A first point of view considers that the dominant positions of certain digital players reflect above all the intrinsic superiority of their models, which are praised by consumers. This school of thought argues for a certain amount of caution when it comes to antitrust actions, particularly in the field of abuse of dominant position. For them, it is necessary to clearly identify a theory of harm: To what extent do the practices of the tech giants translate into higher prices, quantity restrictions, lower product diversity or altered incentives to innovate? (*see*, for example, Auer et al., 2018).

In addition, this approach finds that the dominant positions of these tech giants are not automatic and durable, because several factors may favor the entry of new competitors, such as:

- the degree of product differentiation: If products are highly differentiated, there is room for niche operators;
- the geographical dimension of network effects: When network effects are essentially valued by customers in a local dimension (such as a ride-hailing app), the cost of entry for a new operator is lower;
- the existence of markets related to the main market: If an operator has significant market power in Market A which uses an app similar to that used in Market B, it will be easier for it to enter Market B;
- the "multi-homing" behavior of users: If customers have several applications—particularly those that compare performance in terms of price or quality—it will be more difficult for a firm to conquer the entire market. Internet users can easily switch from one application to another whenever something new comes out, making competition always just "a mouse click away."

A second point of view finds that the dominant positions of the tech giants cannot simply be explained by their competitive merits, but are also the result of recent anti-competitive strategies facilitated by the lull in antitrust policy in the United States since the early 2000s.

In particular, the debate was sparked by the publication of a resounding article by Kahn (2016) on the Amazon case. According to the author, Amazon built its market power with a predatory pricing strategy, i.e., it developed its market shares at the expense of profitability. This practice would have therefore escaped antitrust scrutiny until now, as it is a long-lasting strategy, unlike typical short-term predatory pricing strategies. In addition, Kahn finds that Amazon's diversification of its distribution activities creates a conflict of interest and possible anti-competitive practices. Indeed, Amazon is both a direct player in online sales and also a marketplace for independent sellers (producers and distributors). Amazon therefore has asymmetric access to the data of these third-party distributors, which are both its customers and competitors. This dual position that Amazon holds makes it possible to implement exploitative abuses: for example, in the form of excessive commissions or discrimination, particularly in the commercial conditions of use of its marketplace. We can also consider other possible eviction practices such as abusive de-referencing. Khan argues for a return to the structuralists' antitrust approach, in order to limit the diversification of activities.

Otherwise, Kahn suggests that Amazon should be considered as a natural monopoly and therefore, the company should be regulated.

Tech giants and antitrust enforcement: A concern in Europe: Regarding antitrust enforcement, the United States has so far remained very cautious when it comes to digital issues. Whereas in Europe, the EU has recently launched several large investigations: For example, it conducted a broad sectorial investigation on e-commerce published in 2016, and has opened a handful of litigation cases.

One particular practice currently under close scrutiny is "*Platform Price Parity Agreements*" (APPA). Fairly standard on e-platforms, these agreements require suppliers to always offer a price equal to, or lower than, the price offered on a competing platform. While platform price parity agreements may be explained by the need to protect specific investments (as discussed in Chapter 4), they also make it more difficult for a new platform to enter the market, as it cannot charge a lower price to attract its first customers. Several of these APPAs have led to the opening of antitrust investigations, such as the Booking case in France or the Digital Books case at the European level. Thus, in 2011, the European Commission initiated proceedings against Apple and several book publishers that had simultaneously decided to switch from a wholesale distribution model, in which the retailer set the retail price of digital books, to a model based on agency agreements containing the same clauses for retail prices—including an unusual so-called "*most favored nation*" (MFN) clause for retail prices and the same 30% commission rate for Apple. The European Commission considered that this change was part of a joint strategy between publishers and Apple to increase the retail price of digital books, or at least to prevent them from falling.

In 2012, the European Commission accepted commitments from Apple and four international publishers to terminate all existing agency contracts.

With regards to abuse of dominant position, several cases have also been dealt with by the European Commission since 2010, sometimes leading to severe sanctions and injunctions.

In recent years, Google has been condemned three times:

(1) in 2017, after seven years of investigation, the European Commission condemned Google for having favored its own Google Shopping price comparison system to the detriment of its competitors, thanks to its dominant position on the search engine market;
(2) in 2018, the European Commission again concluded that Google had engaged in an abusive tying practice, requiring mobile phone manufacturers to preinstall the Google Search application and its Chrome browser as a condition for licensing its Play Store online application shop;
(3) in 2019, the European Commission fined Google €2.42 billion for abusive online advertising practices, for having imposed a number of restrictive clauses in contracts with third-party websites, preventing its competitors from placing their ads on these websites.

In addition to eviction practices, exploitative abuses have also been sanctioned in Europe. For example, in France, in 2019, the French Competition Authority ordered emergency measures against Google, aimed at clarifying the rules of its Google Ads advertising network, in order to make them more precise and to guarantee their non-discriminatory application.

Competition authorities have also focused their attention on merger control. As we have seen in Chapter 6, mergers can reduce competition in the market—whether through a unilateral or coordinated effect—but also can impede the development of future competition, in particular if the acquired entity is likely to launch an innovative product. This case is explicitly mentioned in Europe in the Horizontal Merger Guidelines (2004): "A company with a relatively small market share can nevertheless be an important competitive driver if the products under development are promising."

Some mergers can prevent new competitors from entering the market. Sometimes referred to as "*killer acquisitions*," these types of mergers have been highlighted in a sector such as the pharmaceutical industry. Cunningham et al. (2018) have shown that 6% of acquisitions in this sector have stopped all R&D efforts of the targeted firm on projects competing with those carried out by the acquiring company.

However, this type of strategy remains difficult to detect ex-ante by competition authorities. When a big firm takes control of a small innovative company with a low turnover, these mergers fall under the merger control thresholds. To remedy this problem, a first solution, implemented in particular in Germany, is to lower the thresholds. However, the risk is that a large number of mergers that do not pose any competitive concerns will then have to be controlled. A second solution would be to create new thresholds by using the transaction's value. Indeed, innovative start-ups are often bought up for very large amounts, even though they have little or no turnover. However, this solution is hampered by the fact that the value of a transaction can easily be manipulated. In order to avoid merger controls, the acquirer can ensure that the purchase price is different from the final price. A third solution, which already exists in countries such as the United Kingdom or the United States, is to introduce an ex-post control: Within a fairly short period of time after the transaction, the competition authority could carry out an ex-post merger control, whereas this control is normally carried out ex-ante.

Digital economy: Some practical challenges for the antitrust authorities*:* On digital issues, competition authorities face several practical challenges.

First, the digital economy requires specialized skills in algorithm analysis as well as sufficient investigative skills to detect complex practices. In addition, digital markets are characterized by the speed of change, which requires a high degree of responsiveness if competition authorities want their decisions to have useful impacts.

For example, in the case of Google Shopping, between the first complaint filed with the European Commission and the final ruling was a seven-year period, during which time most price comparison systems in the market had already disappeared. It would therefore be useful if competition authorities took provisional measures, as they do in France. The objective of these measures is to freeze the market in a state compatible with maintaining a certain level of competition until the case is dealt with.

At the European level, it is currently difficult to pronounce provisional measures, as the legal conditions for their implementation are too demanding (*see* IGF, 2019).

Second, the digital economy calls into question the ability of competition authorities to detect anti-competitive practices as they are being applied. This is the case, for example, of collusive behaviors, which can be implemented through algorithms without any explicit human intervention (*see* Stucke & Ezrachi, 2016; and OECD, 2017).

To demonstrate this issue, Calvano et al. (2018) assigned two distinct algorithms (red and blue in Figure 3) the task of setting a price at each period in order to maximize profit in a repeated game. Both algorithms have the ability to modify their behavior (and therefore the price) depending on the reaction of the other algorithm. A collusive price is set at the beginning of the game at 1.68. In the first period of the game, the researchers voluntarily lowered the price of the first algorithm down to the competitive price (1.62). The second algorithm reacted by lowering its price in Period 2, in order to limit the gain of its competitor. The first algorithm then gradually returned to the starting price of 1.68 and no longer deviated from this price. We see that without any explicit communication between both entities, the two-price algorithms automatically led to the initial collusive strategy. The main difficulty for antitrust authorities here is to detect and condemn this type of practice, which is, in fact, a tacit collusion.

Figure 3 Behavior of Two Price Algorithms

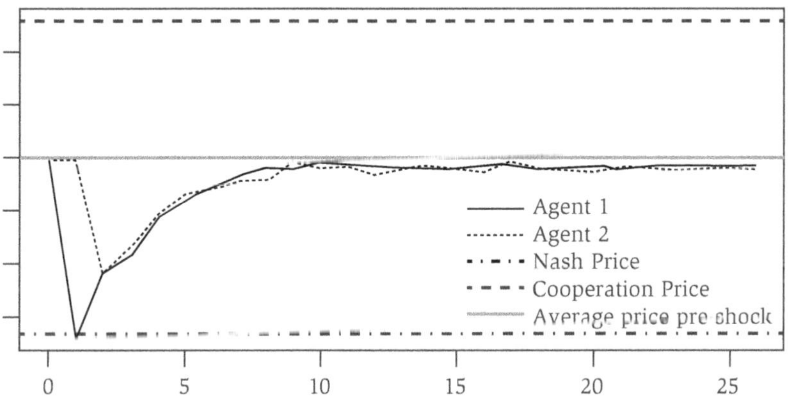

Source: Calvano et al. (2018).

Third, the development of new technologies such as blockchains can help firms form cartels and/or abuse of their dominant positions (Schrepel, 2019a and 2019b). A blockchain can be defined as a large digital ledger that irreversibly records all kinds of transactions between users according to a consensus rule that guarantees the authenticity of the validated information. For example, firms engaged in collusive practices could use the blockchain as an instrument to monitor cartel members by setting up an automatic punitive mechanism if ever a member deviated from the agreement. Moreover, private blockchains lead to a certain opacity in transactions insofar as their access is restricted to its members only, making the detection of collusion by antitrust authorities even more complex.

SECTION 2 COMPETITION POLICY IN A GLOBALIZED WORLD

Despite the resurgence of protectionism and the deadlock in the WTO negotiations since the Doha Round (2001), most countries today remain largely open to international trade and capital flows: In 2020, 164 countries belonged to the WTO and many bilateral free trade agreements are concluded each year, like the one concluded between the EU and Japan in 2018.

In accordance with international trade theory, countries expect a mutual benefit from trade. Gains can come first of all from an improvement in allocative efficiency: The threat of imports reduces the rents that domestic firms enjoy in a closed economy and brings prices down. This effect is beneficial for both consumers and welfare. Second, international trade favors economies of scale: When the market size increases, firms specialize; as a consequence, the production level increases, generating economies of scale. Finally, the threat of foreign competition pushes companies to be more innovative and efficient.

Anti-competitive strategies in a globalized world*:* The benefits expected from opening local markets to international trade are not automatic and can be quashed by anti-competitive strategies.

First, as we saw in Chapter 4, the market integration goal in Europe has sometimes been thwarted by geographic discrimination strategies aimed at preventing customer arbitrage between countries. For example, some producers introduce in their distribution contracts a clause prohibiting distributors located in Country X from supplying customers located in Country Y. The European Commission sanctioned this clause limiting passive sales several times during the 1990s, particularly in the car industry. With development of e-commerce, these spatial discrimination strategies have been transposed online. For example, producers practice geographical online blocking to ensure that each consumer in a given country buys their products at the price that has been defined for that given country, as highlighted by the Sector Inquiry on Electronic Commerce (2017).

Second, cartel strategies can undermine the gains expected from opening up to international trade: Firms from developed countries can, for example, organize an export cartel in developing or emerging countries; Ivaldi et al. (2016) measured the impact of 200 cartels on a sample of 20 developing and emerging countries during the period spanning 1995-2013. They show that sales affected by these practices represent on average 0.9% of a country's Gross Domestic Product (GDP), but can reach up to 6.38%. The damage caused to consumers through higher prices can reach up to 0.8% of GDP. This negative impact of international cartels has prompted emerging and developing countries to adopt antitrust policies since the 2000s, as we saw in Chapter 2. However, the effectiveness of such policies remains limited, given the difficulty of proving the illicit wrongdoings of international cartels when their headquarters are located in developed countries. Cooperation with the authorities of developed countries seems unlikely given the asymmetry of interests.

Third, opening up to international trade can also favor some "*unfair competition*" practices, such as "*dumping*" or public subsidies. Dumping is a strategy whereby a company sets an export price lower than the price applied in its domestic market. Dumping can be economically justified if international competition is more intense for exports than in the domestic market. In this case, it's rational for a producer to lower export prices, despite transport costs. But a firm can also sell its products for export below its variable costs with the sole aim of eliminating efficient competitors on the world market. After the price war, that firm will obtain a monopoly position and will increase its price. However, predatory dumping is difficult to prove due to the lack of information regarding foreign operators' production costs.

Fighting dumping practices is mainly the aim of the trade defense policy, which has objectives and instruments that are quite different from those of competition policies. Indeed, anti-dumping rules are set within the multilateral framework of the WTO. These rules are not limited to the case of predatory dumping: Any action of setting export prices below the price charged by the exporter on its domestic market could be considered dumping. This results in a proliferation of anti-dumping complaints before the WTO, which often leads countries to impose countervailing duties: In Europe, there were no fewer than 94 anti-dumping measures in force in 2018, two-thirds of which concerned China. There is a risk that anti-dumping tools—which are legitimate when used against a predatory behavior—turn into a protectionist instrument designed to curb competition from more-efficient foreign producers (*see*, for example, Blonigen & Prusa, 2016).

Public subsidies are a second form of unfair competition: A foreign firm that benefits from public funds obtains an "*artificial*" competitive advantage over its main competitors. For this reason, public subsidies are strictly regulated by the WTO: WTO members must report the public subsidies they grant to national firms. The WTO also considers that certain subsidies are prohibited: This covers subsidies indexed to export performance or conditional to the use of domestic inputs in the production of a good.

If a WTO member considers that it has been injured by a foreign subsidy, it may file a complaint before the WTO. If the plaintiff succeeds in demonstrating the existence of a public subsidy, the injury it has suffered from it, and a direct link between the subsidy and the injury, it can obtain the right to impose, in retaliation, countervailing measures, such as tariffs on imports.

In practice, however, the WTO subsidy complaint procedure is quite complex and lengthy, because not all countries report the public subsidies they have allocated. Moreover, in the absence of coercive powers, it's difficult to obtain direct proof of a public subsidy and plaintiffs must therefore make their own estimates, based on available, sometimes limited, data resources. Finally, the definition of a subsidy adopted by the WTO is quite restrictive: It is direct aid from the State. The WTO agreement excludes aid that takes more indirect forms, such as access to a resource at a preferential price or the use of a soft loan.

In view of these difficulties, anti-subsidy measures are less frequently used than anti-dumping proceedings (Figure 4).

Figure 4 Trade Defense Measures Applied by WTO Members (1994-2018)

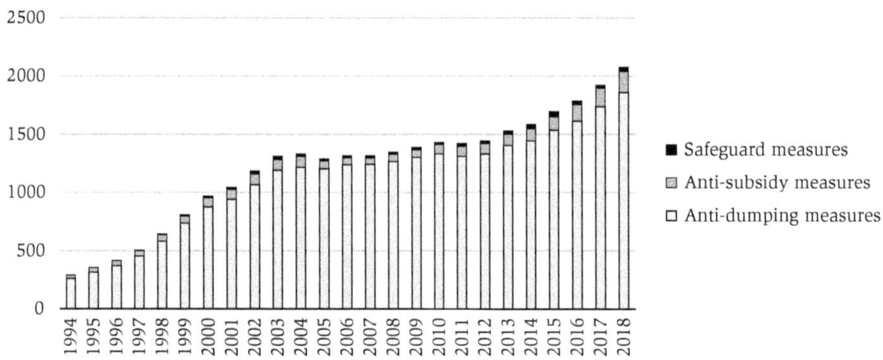

Source: WTO (2019).

The question that is being asked today is how to strengthen the WTO anti-subsidy system, which is not sufficiently binding for countries. It should be noted, however, that the EU has chosen to go beyond the WTO rules; while WTO rules require three conditions for countervailing measures to be put in place, Europe has added an "*Union interest*" criterion, which requires taking into account not only the interests of injured producers, but also those of consumers. While this additional criterion is economically justified—insofar as it is based on a total welfare approach—it appears problematic because other WTO members do not apply it.

SECTION 3 COMPETITION POLICY AND INDUSTRIAL POLICY

The link between competition policy and industrial policy is under debate in Europe; the European Commission is accused by some of being too rigid in its competition policy, a rigidity that prevents the emergence of "European champions" capable of competing with American and Chinese giants.

A strong debate in Europe: This debate resurfaced in 2019 when the merger between Siemens and Alstom was blocked by the European Commission, triggering a Franco-German political reaction in the form of a "*Manifesto for an Industrial Policy for the 21st Century.*" The European competition policy is repeatedly criticized on the following three points.

A first criticism is that competition policy is excessively consumer oriented and does not sufficiently take into account producers' interests. However, we have seen in Chapters 3 and 5 that by fighting against cartels and abuses of dominant position, competition policies put an end to harmful practices that affect first and foremost companies and not end consumers. For example, in March 2019, the European

Commission imposed a fine of €368 million on three suppliers of vehicle safety equipment: The direct victims were European car manufacturers, which had suffered an increase in price of components such as seat belts, airbags or steering wheels. These practices had been implemented by non-European companies—in particular, by American and Japanese producers. By fighting cartels, competition policy therefore indirectly contributes to maintaining the internal and external competitiveness of European companies.

A second criticism more specifically concerns merger controls: In a context of market globalization, Europe needs to have European champions. While it is indeed crucial in a globalized world that European companies reach a critical size sufficient to compete on an equal footing with their Chinese and American competitors, we have seen in Chapter 6 that these mergers must not, however, lead to substantial price increases. Thus, for example, in February 2019, the European Commission blocked the merger between Alstom and Siemens because this operation would have led to the new entity gaining a dominant position in Europe on certain markets for rail-signaling and very high-speed trains. This merger would have significantly reduced competition in the markets of these two types of products, restricting the customers' (particularly railway operators and rail infrastructure managers) choice of suppliers and products. Alstom and Siemens failed to demonstrate that the merger would generate sufficient efficiencies to counterbalance this negative effect on competition. Moreover, the birth of a European giant in the railway sector would not have solved the question of access to the Chinese market, which remains closed to foreign companies. Finally, it has never really been proven that being big enables firms to generate efficiencies, as demonstrated by the high failure rate of M&As.

Beyond the Siemens-Alstom case, we saw in Chapter 6 that mergers are rarely prohibited in Europe, although they are usually subject to a lot of media coverage: During the period spanning 2010-2019, a total of 30 bans were imposed, representing less than 1% of the notified cases. On the other hand, it may be noted that the European Commission has controlled many merger projects initiated by non-European companies, but which were likely to hinder competition in the European market. For example, in June 2013, the European Commission accepted the merger between American Airlines and U.S. Airways—two American airlines operating on European soil—with some commitments in order to preserve competition on several transatlantic routes from London.

A third criticism concerns the asymmetry of competition policies in the world: Why should Europe impose antitrust rules on its companies when its non-European partners—first and foremost emerging countries—do not always apply these rules to themselves with the same rigor. In response to this argument, one should note that European competition policy is applied to any company present on the European continent, whatever its nationality: It protects Europe against anti-competitive practices implemented in its territory, particularly in the field of cartels. Furthermore, maintaining competition within the European market pushes firms to be more productive and innovative. It is therefore in the EU's interest to have strong competition in its internal market.

Competition policy: A subtle industrial policy?: Unlike the critical school of thought seen above, competition policy can also be considered a form of industrial policy, especially in today's high-tech race (Combe, 2014): Europe has indeed been closing its technological gap since the 1980s, and the challenge today is no longer to simply imitate existing technologies, but to innovate and come up with radical new ones. Empirical studies show that productivity growth is mainly driven by the entry of new firms as they introduce disruptive innovations and have a contestability effect on established operators, encouraging them to be more productive and to renew their business model. Market entry and the rapid growth of new companies are therefore becoming crucial issues for Europe's economic dynamism, just as much as the consolidation of large companies.

From this perspective, competition policy can play a useful role: By fighting against abuses of dominant position and "*killer acquisitions*," competition policy promotes the entry and development of new market players. Indeed, when a dominant company commits an exclusionary abuse, it limits the growth or even compromises the very existence of a small but threatening competitor. Thus, Google's practices in the price comparison market, condemned in 2017 by the Commission, had the purpose and effect of disadvantaging operators such as Kelkoo or Liligo by favoring its own price comparison service in its search results.

The need for an R&D policy: However, competition policy cannot replace an active industrial policy that has the primary objective of remedying clearly identified market failures (Tirole, 2016). This is particularly the case for R&D, a risky, long-term activity that generates strong positive externalities that go beyond the sole private benefit of the innovator. If public policy does not intervene to support R&D activities, the risk is that the total level of investment will fall short of its optimal level.

In this respect, we can see that the EU is characterized, within OECD countries, by a low level of private investment in R&D when compared to similar regions of the world. Over a 20-year period (1995-2015), despite a catch-up effort, the EU invests on average less than other OECD countries (Figure 5): In 2017, R&D expenditure amounted to 2.07% of the European GDP, which was lower than in South Korea (4.22% in 2015), Japan (3.28% in 2015), and the United States (2.76% in 2015); in 2015, Europe was at the same level as China (2.06%).

In absolute terms, the level of R&D spending in the EU is €320 billion, much less than countries such as the United States ($550 billion) or China ($475 billion). In view of this lack of private R&D effort in Europe, it is undoubtedly appropriate to conduct a public policy to boost R&D.

Figure 5 R&D Expenditure in Several Countries (as a % of GDP) Between 1995 and 2015

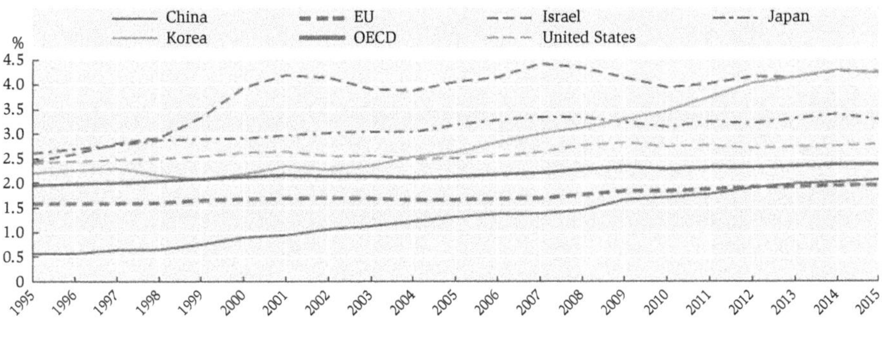

Source: OECD (2018).

Regarding governmental support for R&D, competition policy can play a role of facilitator. In this respect, the European state aid control system—the only one of its kind in the world—is often criticized for preventing and slowing down the implementation of proactive industrial policies by limiting sectorial aid and imposing excessive delays and procedures.

However, it should be noted that since 2014 the EU has reduced Member States' notification obligations by adding categories of aid exempted from notification, particularly in the field of innovation. In addition, the Union authorizes the development of Important Projects of Common European Interest, bringing together several Member States around an innovative industrial project co-financed by companies.

For example, in December 2018, the Commission authorized, for the first time in a technology sector, the plan of France, Germany, Italy, and the United Kingdom to provide public support of €1.75 billion for a joint R&D project in the field of microelectronics ("*Nano 2022 plan*"). Another Franco-German project, called the "*European Battery Alliance*," focuses on the joint design and production of new generation battery cells and modules for electric vehicles. Called the "*Battery Airbus*" and launched in May 2019, this project will enable Europe to catch-up with China and provide for €5 billion of investment, including €1.2 billion in public subsidies.

Even if state aid rules were relaxed in 2014, one must note that public efforts in favor of R&D are still limited at the European level. In 2019, with a total budget of €148 billion, R&D policy is only the third largest spending item with €11 billion (or 7.4% of the total budget), far behind the common agricultural policy (€56 billion, or 33.7% of the total budget) and the cohesion policy (€47 billion, or 31.7%). Thus, Europe's lack of spending on R&D is not the result of an overly rigorous competition policy, but is rather the consequence of political choices when allocating the European budget.

Bibliography

Rosa Abrantes-Metz et al., *A Variance Screen for Collusion* (International Journal of Industrial Organization 467-486, 2006).

Philippe Aghion and Patrick Bolton, *Contracts as a Barrier to Entry* (American Economic Review 388-401, 1987).

Philippe Aghion et al., *Competition and Innovation: An Inverted-U Relationship* (The Quarterly Journal of Economics 701-728, 2005).

Philippe Aghion et al., *The Effects of Entry on Incumbent Innovation and Productivity* (The Review of Economics and Statistics 20-32, 2009).

Umut Aydin and Tim Büthe, *Competition Law & Policy in Developing Countries: Explaining Variations in Outcomes—Exploring Possibilities and Limits* (Law and Contemporary Problems 1-36, 2016).

Alice Amsden and Ajit Singh, *The Optimal Degree of Competition and Dynamic Efficiency in Japan and Korea* (European Economic Review 941-951, 1994).

Bharat Anand and Tarun Khanna, *The Structure of Licensing Contracts* (Journal of Industrial Economics 103-133, 2000).

Phillip Areeda and Donald Turner, *Predatory Pricing and Related Practices under Section 2 of the Sherman Act* (Harvard Law Review 697-733, 1975).

Dominick Armentano, *Antitrust and Monopoly: Anatomy of a Policy Failure* (The Independent Institute, 1996).

Mark Armstrong, Chris Doyle and John Vickers, *The Access Pricing Problem: A Synthesis* (Journal of Industrial Economics 131-150, 1996).

Mark Armstrong and Steffen Huck, *Behavioral Economics and Antitrust*, in *The Oxford Handbook of International Antitrust Economics* [R. Blair and D. Sokol (eds.) Oxford University Press, 2014].

Kenneth Arrow, *Economic Welfare and the Allocation of Resources for Invention*, in *The Rate and Direction of Inventive Activity* [R. Nelson (ed.) Princeton University Press, 1962].

Peter Asch and J.J. Seneca, *Is Collusion Profitable?* (Review of Economics and Statistics 1-12, 1976).

Dirk Auer et al., *Why Sound Law and Economics Should Guide Competition Policy in the Digital Economy* (Report ICLE, 2018).
David Autor et al., The Fall of the Labor Share and the Rise of Superstar Firms (NBER Working Paper, 2017).
Autorité de la Concurrence, *Rapport Annuel* (La Documentation Française, 2009-2018).
Autorité de la Concurrence, *Droit de la Concurrence et Données* (2016).
Autorité de la Concurrence. *Remises Fidélisantes* (La Documentation Française, 2018).
Jonathan Baker, *The Case for Antitrust Enforcement* (Journal of Economic Perspectives 27-50, 2003).
Joe Bain, *Relation of Profit Rate to Industry Concentration: American Manufacturing, 1936–1940* (Quarterly Journal of Economics, 1951).
Joe Bain, *Barriers to New Competition* (Cambridge University Press, 1956).
Joe Bain, *Industrial Organization* (J. Wiley & Sons, 1969).
David Balto and Richard Parker, *The Evolving Approach to Merger Remedies* (Antitrust Report, 2000).
William Baumol, *Quasi Performance of Price Reductions: A Policy for Prevention of Predatory Pricing* (Yale Law Journal 1-26, 1979).
William Baumol, John Panzar and Robert Willig, *Contestable Markets and the Theory of Industry Structure* (Harcourt, Brace & Jovanovich, 1982).
Gary Becker, *Crime and Punishment: An Economic Approach* (Journal of Political Economy 169-217, 1968).
William Baumol and Gregory Sidack, *The Pricing of Inputs Sold to Competitors* (Yale Journal of Regulation 171-202, 1994).
Paul Beckner and Erick Gustafson, *Trial and Error: United States Versus Microsoft* (Citizen for a Sound Economy Foundation, 2000).
Jean Pierre Benoit, *Financially Constrained Entry in a Game with Incomplete Information* (Rand Journal of Economics 490-499, 1984).
B. Douglas Bernheim and Michael Whinston, *Multimarket Contact and Collusive Behavior* (Rand Journal of Economics 1-26, 1990).
B. Douglas Bernheim and Michael Whinston, *Exclusive Dealing* (Journal of Political Economy 64-103, 1988).
Joseph Bertrand, *Revue de la Théorie Mathématique de la Richesse Sociale* (Journal des Savants 499-508, 1883).
BEUC, *The Role of Competition Policy in Protecting Consumers' Well-Being in the Digital Era* (Report, 2019).
Alain Bienaymé, *Principes de Concurrence* (Economica, 1998).
Bruce Blonigen and Thomas Prusa, *Dumping and Antidumping Duties*, in *The Handbook of Commercial Policy* [K. Bagwell and R. Staiger (eds.) Elsevier, 2016].
Fred Boadu and Tolulope Olofinbiyi, *Regulating the Market: Competition Law and Policy in Kenya and Zambia* (World Competition 75-99, 2003).
Patrick Bolton, Joseph Brodley and Michael Riordan, *Predatory Pricing: Strategic Theory and Legal Policy* (Georgetown Law Journal 2239-2330, 2000).

Severin Borenstein, *Rapid Price Communication and Coordination: The Airline Tariff Publishing Case*, in *The Antitrust Revolution* [J. Kwoka and L. White (eds.) Oxford University Press, 1999].
Robert Bork, *The Antitrust Paradox* (The Free Press, 1993).
David Bosco and Catherine Prieto, *Droit Européen de la Concurrence* (Bruylant, 2013).
Marcel Boyer and Rachidi Kotchoni, *How Much Do Cartels Overcharge?* (Review of Industrial Organization 119-153, 2015).
Peter Bryant and Edwin Eckard, *Price Fixing: The Probability of Getting Caught* (The Review of Economics and Statistics 531-536, 1991).
Paolo Buccirossi, *Handbook of Antitrust Economics* (The MIT Press, 2008).
Paolo Buccirossi et al., *Competition Policy and Productivity Growth: An Empirical Assessment* (The Review of Economics and Statistics 1323-1336, 2013).
Guy Canivet, *La Modernisation du Droit de la Concurrence* (LGDJ, 2006).
Guy Canivet and François Brunet, *Le Nouveau Droit Communautaire de la Concurrence* (LGDJ, 2008).
Dennis Carlton and Jeffrey Perloff, *Industrial Economics* (De Boeck, 2015).
Richard Caves and Michael Porter, *From Entry Barriers to Mobility Barrier: Conjectural Decisions and Contrived Deterrence to New Competition* (Quarterly Journal of Economics 241-261, 1977).
Edward Chamberlin, *La Théorie de la Concurrence Monopolistique* (PUF, 1953).
Alfred Chandler, *The Visible Hand* (Harvard University Press, 1977).
John B. Clark and John M. Clark, *The Control of Trusts* (MacMillan, 1912).
Julian Clarke and Simon Evenett, *The Deterrent Effects of National Anticartel Laws: Evidence from the International Vitamins Cartel* (The Antitrust Bulletin 689-726, 2003).
Joseph Clougherty and Tomaso Duso, *The Impact of Horizontal Mergers on Rivals: Gains to Being Left Outside a Merger* (Journal of Management Studies 1365-1395, 2009).
CMA, *Productivity and Competition: A Summary of the Evidence* (Report, 2015).
UNCTAD, *Can Developing Economies Benefit from WTO Negotiations on Binding Disciplines for Hard Core Cartels?* (Work Report, 2003).
Ronald Coase, *The Nature of the Firm* (Economica 386-405, 1937).
Ronald Coase, *Durability and Monopoly* (Journal of Law & Economics 143-149, 1972).
Harold Cole and Lee Ohanian, *New Deal Policies and the Persistence of the Great Depression: A General Equilibrium Analysis* (Journal of Political Economy 779-816, 2003).
Norman Collins and Lee Preston, *Price-Cost Margins and Industry Structure* (Review of Economics and Statistics 271-286, 1969).
Emmanuel Combe, *Cartels et Ententes* (PUF Que-sais-je?, 2004).
Emmanuel Combe, *La Politique de Concurrence: Un Atout Pour Notre Industrie* (Fondapol, 2014).
Emmanuel Combe, *La Politique de Concurrence* (La Découverte, 2016).
Emmanuel Combe, *Vers des Prix Personnalisés?* (Fondapol, 2019).

Emmanuel Combe, Constance Monnier and Renaud Legal, *Cartels: The Probability of Getting Caught in the European Union*, 2008, https://ssrn.com/abstract=1015061.

Emmanuel Combe and Constance Monnier, *Fines Against Hard Core Cartels: The Myth of Overenforcement* (Antitrust Bulletin 235-276, 2011).

Emmanuel Combe and Constance Monnier, *Les Cartels en Europe: Un Portrait-Robot* (Revue Française d'Economie1-40, 2012).

Emmanuel Combe and Constance Monnier, *Quelle est l'Ampleur de la Sous-Dissuasion des Cartels en Europe?* (Concurrences 16-26, 2013).

Emmanuel Combe and Etienne Pfister, *Licence et Politique Antitrust* (Revue d'Économie Industrielle 23-46, 2003).

European Commission, *Rapport sur la Politique de Concurrence* (2003-2018).

John Connor and Robert Lande, *Cartels as Rational Business Strategy: Crime Pays* (Cardozo Law Review 455-462, 2012).

Thomas Cooper, *Most-Favored-Customer Pricing and Tacit Collusion* (Rand Journal of Economics 377-388, 1986).

Augustin Cournot, *Recherches sur les Principes Mathématiques de la Théorie des Richesses* (Hachette, 1838).

Matias Covarrubias, Germán Gutiérrez and Thomas Philippon, From Good to Bad Concentration? U.S. Industries over the Past 30 Years (NBER Working Paper, 2019).

Keith Cowling and Michael Waterson, *Price-Cost Margins and Market Structure* (Economica 267-74, 1976).

Keith Cowling and Dennis Muller, *The Social Cost of Monopoly Power* (Economic Journal 727-748, 1978).

Robert Crandall and Clifford Winston, *Does Antitrust Policy Improve Consumer Welfare? Assessing the Evidence* (Journal of Economic Perspectives 3-26, 2003).

Jacques Cremer, Yves-Alexandre de Montjoye and Heike Schweizer, *Competition Policy for the Digital Era* (European Commission, 2019).

Colleen Cunningham, Song Ma and Florian Ederer, *Killer Acquisitions* (Academy of Management Proceedings, 2018).

Herbert Davenport, *The Economics of Enterprise* (MacMillan, 1919).

Ryan Decker et al., *Declining Business Dynamism: What We Know and the Way Forward* (American Economic Review 203-207, 2016).

Ryan Decker et al., *Declining Dynamism, Allocative Efficiency, and the Productivity Slowdown* (American Economic Review 322-326, 2017).

Harold Demsetz, *Two Systems of Belief About Monopoly*, in *Industrial Concentration: The New Learning* [H. Goldschmid et al. (eds.) Little Brown, 1974].

Raymond Deneckere and Carl Davidson, *Incentives to Form Coalitions with Bertrand Competition* (Rand Journal of Economics 473-486, 1985).

Thomas DiLorenzo and Jack High, *Antitrust and Competition, Historically Considered* (Economic Inquiry 423-435, 1988).

Thomas DiLorenzo, *The Myth of Predatory Pricing* (CATO Policy Analysis, 1992).

Avinash Dixit, *The Role of Investment in Entry Deterrence* (Economic Journal 95-106, 1980).

Avinash Dixit, *Recent Developments in Oligopoly Theory* (American Economic Review 12-17, 1982).

Hervé Dumez and Alain Jeunemaître, *La Concurrence en Europe* (Le Seuil, 1991).

Mark Dutz and Maria Vagliasindi, *Competition Policy Implementation in Transition Economies: An Empirical Assessment* (European Economic Review 762-772, 2000).

Nicholas Economides, *The Economics of Networks* (International Journal of Industrial Organization 673-699, 1996).

Richard Ely, *Monopolies and Trusts* (MacMillan, 1900).

Kenneth Elzinga and Thomas Hogarty, *The Problem of Geographic Market Definition in Antimerger Suits* (Antitrust Bulletin 45-81, 1973).

David Encaoua, *Analyze Economique des Opérations de Concentration*, dans *La Pratique Communautaire Du Contrôle des Concentrations* [A. Winckler et al. (eds.) De Boeck, 1998].

Frank Easterbrook, *Predatory Strategies and Counters trategies* (University of Chicago Law Review 304-313, 1981).

Mukesh Eswaran, *Cross-Licensing as a Facilitating Device* (Canadian Journal of Economics 691-708, 1993).

Simon Evenett, Margaret Levenstein and Valerie Suslow, *International Cartel Enforcement: Lessons from the 1990s* (World Economy 645-660, 2002).

Ariel Ezrachi and Maurice Stucke, *Virtual Competition* (Harvard University Press, 2016).

Joseph Farrell and Carl Shapiro, *Horizontal Mergers: An Equilibrium Analysis* (American Economic Review 107-125, 1990).

Joseph Farrell and Carl Shapiro, *Antitrust Evaluation of Horizontal Mergers: An Economic Alternative to Market Definition* (The B.E. Journal of Theoretical Economics, 2010).

Joseph Farrell and Carl Shapiro, *Scale Economies and Synergies in Horizontal Merger Analysis* (Antitrust Law Journal 685-710, 2001).

Chaim Fershtman and Morton Kamien, *Cross Licensing of Complementary Technologies* (International Journal of Industrial Organization 329-348, 1992).

Harry First, *Vitamins Case: Cartel Prosecutions and the Coming of International Competition Law* (Antitrust Law Journal 711-729, 2001).

Drew Fudenberg and Jean Tirole, *A Signal Jamming Theory of Predation* (RAND Journal of Economics 366-376, 1986).

Jason Furman, *Unlocking Digital Competition: Report of the Digital Competition Expert Panel,* (Report for the U.K. Government, 2019).

John Haltiwanger, Ian Hathaway and Javier Miranda, *Declining Business Dynamism in the U.S. High-Technology Sector* (Ewing Marion Kauffman Foundation, 2014).

Richard Gilbert, *Mobility Barriers and the Value of Incumbency*, in *Handbook of Industrial Organization* [R. Schmalensee and R. Willig (eds.) Chapter 8, North Holland, 1996].

Richard Gilbert, Economics, Law and History of Patent Pools and Cross-Licensing Agreements (UC Berkeley Working Paper, 2001).

Richard Gilbert and David Newbery, *Preemptive Patenting and the Persistence of Monopoly* (American Economic Review 514-525, 1982).

Richard Gilbert and Carl Shapiro, *Antitrust Issues in the Licensing of Intellectual Property: The Nine No-No's Meet the Nineties* (BPEA Microeconomics 283-336, 1997).

Richard Gilbert and Xavier Vives, *Entry Deterrence and the Free Rider Problem* (Review of Economic Studies 71-83, 1986).

Maurice Glais, *Économie Industrielle: Les Stratégies Concurrentielles des Firmes* (Litec, 1992).

Maurice Glais, *Infrastructures Essentielles et Autres Ressources Essentielles au Regard du Droit de la Concurrence* (Revue d'Économie Industrielle 85-116, 1998).

Maurice Glais and Philippe Laurent, *Traité d'Économie et de Droit de la Concurrence* (PUF, 1983).

Vivek Goshal and Joseph Gallo, *The Cyclical Behavior of the Department of Justice's Antitrust Enforcement Activity* (International Journal of Industrial Organization 27-54, 2001).

Edward Graham, *Internationalizing Competition Policy: An Assessment of the Two Main Alternatives* (Antitrust Bulletin 947-972, 2003).

Germán Gutiérrez and Thomas Philippon, Declining Competition and Investment in the US (NBER Working Paper, 2017).

Germán Gutiérrez and Thomas Philippon, How EU Markets Became More Competitive than U.S. Markets: A Study of Institutional Drift (NBER Working Paper, 2018).

Germán Gutiérrez and Thomas Philippon, The Failure of Free Entry (NBER Working Paper, 2019).

Arnold Harberger, *Monopoly and Resource Allocation* (American Economic Review 77-87, 1954).

Scott Hammond, *The Evolution of Criminal Antitrust Enforcement over the Last Two Decades*, 2010, http://www.justice.gov/atr/public/speeches/255515.htm.

Joseph Harrington, *How Do Cartels Operate?* (Foundations and Trends in Microeconomics 1-105, 2006).

George Hay and Daniel Kelley, *An Empirical Survey of Price Fixing Conspiracies* (Journal of Law and Economics 13-38, 1974).

Friedrich Hayek, *The Meaning of Competition in Individualism and Economic Order* (University of Chicago Press, 1948).

Roberto Hernan Gonzalez, Pedro Marin and Georges Siotis, *An Empirical Evaluation of the Determinants of Research Joint Venture Formation* (Journal of Industrial Economics 75-90, 2003).

John Hicks, *The Theory of Monopoly* (Econometrica 1-20, 1935).

Jack High (ed.), *Competition* (Elgar, 2002).

Bernard Hoekman and Petros Mavroidis, *Economic Development, Competition Policy and the World Trade Organization* (Journal of World Trade 1-27, 2003).

Simon Horobin, John Kwoka and Lawrence White, *The Antitrust Revolution: Economics, Competition, and Policy* (4th ed., Oxford University Press, 2003).

Herbert Hovenkamp, *Principles of Antitrust* (Foundation Press, 2017).

Inspection Generale des Finances, *La Politique de la Concurrence et les Intérêts Stratégiques de l'Union* (Report 82, 2019).

Pauline Ippolito, *Resale Price Maintenance: Empirical Evidence from Litigation* (Journal of Law and Economics 263-294, 1991).

Pauline Ippolito and Thomas Overstreet, *Resale Price Maintenance: An Economic Assessment of the Federal Trade Commission's Case Against the Corning Glass Works* (Journal of Law and Economics 285-328, 1996).

Marc Ivaldi, Frédéric Jenny and Aleksandra Khimich, Cartels Damages to the Economy: An Assessment for Developing Countries (Work Report PEDL, 2016).

Alexis Jacquemin (ed.), *Competition Policy in Europe and North America: Economic Issues and Institutions* (Harwood Publishers, 1990).

Alexis Jacquemin and Claude d'Aspremont, *Cooperative and Noncooperative R&D in Duopoly with Spillovers* (American Economic Review 1133-1137, 1988).

Alexis Jacquemin and Margaret Slade, *Cartels, Collusion, and Horizontal Merger*, in *Handbook of Industrial Organization* [R. Schmalensee and R. Willig (eds.) Elsevier, 1989].

Sébastien Jean, Anne Perrot and Thomas Philippon, *Concurrence et Commerce: Quelles Politiques Pour l'Europe?* (Note du Conseil d'Analyse Économique, 2019).

Frédéric Jenny and André-Paul Weber, *La Concurrence et les Marchés* (Entreprise Moderne D'Edition, 1980).

Frédéric Jenny, *Competition Law and Policy: Global Governance Issues* (World Competition 609-624, 2003a).

Frédéric Jenny, *International Cooperation on Competition: Myth, Reality and Perspective* (Antitrust Bulletin 973-1003, 2003b).

Paul Joskow and Alvin Klevorick, *A Framework for Analyzing Predatory Pricing Policy* (Yale Law Journal 213-270, 1979).

Yun Joo Jung, John Kagel and Dan Levin, *On the Existence of Predatory Pricing: An Experimental Study of Reputation and Entry Deterrence in the Chain-Store Game* (RAND Journal of Economics 72-93, 1994).

Lina Khan, *Amazon's Antitrust Paradox* (Yale Law Journal 710-805, 2016).

E. Han Kim and Vijay Singal, *Mergers and Market Power: Evidence from the Airline Industry* (American Economic Review 549-569, 1993).

Thierry Kirat and Frédéric Marty, The Late Emerging Consensus Among American Economists on Antitrust Laws in the Second New Deal (CIRANO Scientific Paper, 2019).

Israel M. Kirzner, *Competition and Entrepreneurship* (University of Chicago Press, 1973).

Roland Koller, *The Myth of Predatory Pricing: An Empirical Study* (Antitrust Law and Economic Review 105-123, 1971).

William Kovacic, *Criminal Enforcement of Competition Law: Implications of U.S. Experience* (Concurrences 33-40, 2016).

William Kovacic and Marianela Lopez-Galdos, *Lifecycles of Competition Systems: Explaining Variation in the Implementation of New Regimes* (Law and Contemporary Problems 85-122, 2016).

William Kovacic and Carl Shapiro, *Antitrust Policy: A Century of Economic and Legal Thinking* (Journal of Economic Perspectives 43-60, 1999).

David Kreps and Robert Wilson, *Reputation and Imperfect Competition* (Journal of Economic Theory 253-279, 1982).

John Kwoka and Lawrence White, *The Antitrust Revolution: Economics, Competition and Policy* (4th ed., Oxford University Press, 2003).

John Kwoka, *Mergers, Merger Control, and Remedies: A Retrospective Analysis of U.S. Policy* (The MIT Press, 2014).

Jean Jacques Laffont and Jean Tirole, *Access Pricing and Competition* (European Economic Review 1673-1710, 1994).

Francine Lafontaine, *Agency Theory and* Franchising: *Some Empirical Results* (RAND Journal of Economics 263-283, 1992).

Robert Lande, *Wealth Transfers as the Original and Primary Concern of Antitrust*: *The Efficiency Interpretation Challenged* (Hastings Law Review 65-131, 1982).

Henri Lepage, *La Nouvelle Economie Industrielle* (Hachette-Pluriel, 1989).

François Lévêque and Yann Ménière, *Économie de la Propriété Intellectuelle* (La Découverte, 2003).

Margaret Levenstein and Valerie Suslow, What Determines Cartel Success? (University of Massachusetts Working Paper, 2001).

Margaret Levenstein, Lynda Oswald and Valerie Suslow, International Price-Fixing Cartels and Developing Countries: A Discussion of Effects and Policy Remedies (University of Michigan Business School Working Paper, 2002).

Richard Levin et al., *Appropriating the Returns from Industrial Research and Development* (Brookings Papers on Economic Activity 783-820, 1987).

Ping Lin, *Fixed-Fee Licensing of Innovations and Collusion* (Journal of Industrial Economics 443-449, 1996).

Ping Lin et al., *The U.S. Antitrust System and Recent Trends in Antitrust Enforcement* (Journal of Economic Surveys 255-306, 2000).

Jeffrey Mackie-Mason and John Metzler, *Links Between Vertically Related Markets: ITS v. Kodak (1992)*, in *The Antitrust Revolution: Economics, Competition and Policy* [J. Kwoka and L. White (eds.) 4th ed., Oxford University Press, 2003].

Stephen Martin, *Industrial Economics* (2nd ed., MacMillan, 1994).

Frédéric Marty, *Plateformes Numériques, Algorithmes et Discrimination* (Revue de l'OFCE 1-40, 2019).

Edwin Mansfield, Mark Schwartz and Samuel Wagner, *Imitation Costs and Patents*: *An Empirical Study* (Economic Journal 907-918, 1985).

Edward Mason, *Economic Concentration and the Monopoly Problem* (Harvard University Press, 1957).

Akihiko Matsui, *Consumer-Benefited Cartels under Strategic Capital Investment Competition* (International Journal of Industrial Organization 451-470, 1989).

G. Frank Mathewson and Ralph Winter, *The Economics of Franchise Contracts* (Journal of Law and Economics 503-526, 1985).

John McGee, *Predatory Price Cutting: The Standard Oil Case* (Journal of Law and Economics 137-169, 1958).

John McGee, *In Defense of Industrial Concentration* (Praeger Publishers, 1971).

John McGee, *Predatory Pricing Revisited* (Journal of Law and Economics 289-300, 1980).

Paul Milgrom and John Roberts, *Limit Pricing and Entry under Incomplete Information: An Equilibrium Analysis* (Econometrica 443-459, 1982a).

Paul Milgrom and John Roberts, *Predation, Reputation and Entry Deterrence* (Journal of Economic Theory 280-312, 1982b).

Paul Milgrom and John Roberts, *New Theories of Predatory Pricing*, in *Industrial Structure in the New Industrial Economics* [G. Bonanno and D. Brandolini (eds.) 112-136, Clarendon Press, 1990].

Franco Modigliani, *New Developments on the Oligopoly Front* (Journal of Political Economy 215-232, 1958).

Massimo Motta and Michele Polo, *Leniency Programs and Cartel Prosecution* (International Journal of Industrial Organization 347-379, 2003).

Massimo Motta, *Competition Policy: Theory and Practice* (Cambridge University Press, 2004).

Dennis Mueller, *Lessons from the United States's Antitrust History* (International Journal of Industrial Organization 415-445, 1996).

Barry Nalebuff, *Bundling as an Entry Barrier* (Quarterly Journal of Economics 159-184, 2004).

Manfred Neumann, *Competition Policy: History, Theory and Practice* (Edward Elgar, 2001).

Damien Neven, *Strategic Entry Deterrence: Recent Developments in the Economics of Industry* (Journal of Economic Surveys 213-233, 1989).

Stephen Nickell, *Competition and Corporate Performance* (Journal of Political Economy 724-746, 1996).

OECD, *Failing Firm Defence* (1996).

OECD, *Leniency Programs to Fight Hard Core Cartels* (2001a).

OECD, *Les Ententes Injustifiables: Progrès Récents et Défis Futurs* (2003).

OECD, *Competition and Poverty Reduction* (2013).

OECD, *Vertical Restraints for Online Sales* (2013).

OECD, *Price Discrimination* (2016).

OECD, *Algorithms and Collusion* (2017).

OECD, *Personalized Pricing in the Digital Era* (2018).

OECD, *Excessive Pricing in Pharmaceutical Markets* (2018).

Daniel Okimoto, *Between the MITI and the Market* (Stanford University Press, 1989).

Cath O'Neil, *Weapons of Math Destruction* (Crown, 2016).

José Manuel Ordóñez-De-Haro, Joan-Ramon Borrell and Juan Luis Jimenez, *The European Commission's Fight Against Cartels (1962–2014): A Retrospective and Forensic Analysis* (Journal of Common Market Studies 1087-1107, 2018).

Richard Parker and David Balto, *The Evolving Approach to Merger Remedies* (Antitrust Teport 228, 2000).

Sam Peltzman, *Toward a More General Theory of Regulation* (Journal of Law and Economics 211-240, 1976).

Anne Perrot, *Réglementation et Concurrence* (Economica, 1997).

Nicolas Petit, *Droit Européen de la Concurrence* (2nd ed., LGDJ, 2018).

Nicolas Petit, *American Tech Giants Are Fiercely Competitive Monopolies* (ESB Market Power 82-87, 2018).

Nicolas Petit, Are "FANGs" Monopolies? A Theory of Competition under Uncertainty (Working Paper, 2019).

Jerome Philippe, *La Mesure du Marché Pertinent* (Revue Française d'Économie 125-160, 1998).

Thomas Philippon, A Primer on Concentration, Investment and Growth (Working Paper for the Jackson Hole Economic Policy Symposium, 2018).

Thomas Philippon, *The Great Reversal: How America Gave Up on Free Markets* (Harvard University Press, 2019).

Louis Phlips, *Competition Policy: A Game-Theoretic Perspective* (Cambridge University Press, 1995).

Louis Phlips, *Applied Industrial Economics* (Cambridge University Press, 1998).

Arthur Pigou, *The Economics of Welfare* (McMillan, 1920).

Christopher Pleatsikas and David Teece, *The Analysis of Market Definition and Market Power in the Context of Rapid Innovation* (International Journal of Industrial Organization 665-693, 2001).

Richard Posner, *A Statistical Study of Antitrust Enforcement* (Journal of Law and Economics 365-419, 1970).

Richard Posner, *Antitrust Law: An Economic Perspective* (University of Chicago Press, 1976).

Michael Porter and Mariko Sakakibara, *Competition in Japan* (Journal of Economic Perspectives 27-50, 2004).

George Priest, *Cartels and Patent Licence Arrangements* (Journal of Law and Economics 309-78, 1977).

Carlos Ramirez and Christian Eugen-Zucchi, *Understanding the Clayton Act of 1914: An Analysis of the Interest Group Hypothesis* (Public Choice 157-181, 2001).

Eric Rasmusen, J. Mark Ramseyer and John Wiley, *Naked Exclusion* (American Economic Review 1137-1145, 1991).

Jennifer Reinganum, *The Timing of Innovation: Research, Development, and Diffusion*, in *Handbook of Industrial Organization* [R. Schmalensee and R. Willig (eds.) North Holland, 1989].

Patrick Rey, *Impact des Accords Verticaux Entre Producteurs et Distributeurs* (Revue Française d'Économie 3-55, 1997).

Patrick Rey and Jean Tirole, *Analyze Economique de la Prédation* (Revue Française d'Économie 3-32, 1997).

Jean-Christophe Roda, *Droit de la Concurrence* (Dalloz, 2019).

Armando Rodriguez, *The Lessons of Mexico's Antitrust Initiative*, in *Competition Policy, Deregulation and Modernization in Latin America* [M. Naim and J. Tulchin (eds.) Lynne Rienner, 2001].
Murray Rothbard, *Man, Economy, State* (Nash Publishing, 1962).
Stephen Salant, Sheldon Switzer and Robert Reynolds, *Losses from Horizontal Mergers: The Effects of an Exogenous Change in Industry Structure on Cournot-Nash Equilibrium* (Quarterly Journal of Economics, 1983).
Steven Salop, *Practices That (Credibly) Facilitate Oligopoly Coordination*, in *New Developments in the Analysis of Market Structure* [J. Stiglitz and G. Mathewson (eds.) The MIT Press 265-290, 1986].
Steven Salop and David Scheffman, *Raising Rivals' Costs* (American Economic Review, Papers and Proceedings 267-271, 1983).
Steven Salop and Serge Moresi, *Updating the Merger Guidelines: Comments* (Horizontal Merger Guidelines Review Project, 2009).
Steven Salop and Carl Shapiro, *Jean Tirole's Nobel Prize in Economics: The Rigorous Foundations of Post-Chicago Antitrust Economics* (Antitrust 78-81, 2015).
Stéphane Saussier and Anne Yvrande-Billon, *Economie des Coûts de Transaction* (La Découverte/Repères, 2007).
Frederic Scherer and David Ross, *Industrial Market Structures and Economic Performance* (3rd ed., Houghton Mifflin, 1990).
Richard Schmalensee, *Entry Deterrence in the Ready-To-Eat Breakfast Cereal Industry* (Bell Journal of Economics 305-327, 1978).
Richard Schmalensee, *Advertising and Entry Deterrence: An Exploratory* Model (Journal of Political Economy 636-653, 1983).
Klaus Schmidt, *Managerial Incentives and Product Market Competition* (Review of Economic Studies 191-213, 1997).
Thibault Schrepel, *Collusion by Blockchain and Smart Contracts* (Harvard Journal of Law and Technology, 2019a).
Thibault Schrepel, *Is Blockchain the Death of Antitrust Law?* (Georgetown Law Technology Review 281-338, 2019b).
Joseph Schumpeter, *Capitalism, Socialism and Democracy* (Harper and Row Publishers, 1942).
Reinhard Selten, *A Simple Model of Imperfect Competition Where 4 Are Few and 6 Are Many* (International Journal of Game Theory 141-201, 1973).
Reinhard Selten, *The Chain Store Paradox* (Theory and Decision 127-159, 1978).
Carl Shapiro, *Patent Licensing and R&D Rivalry* (American Economic Review 25-30, 1985).
Carl Shapiro, *Navigating the Patent Thicket: Cross Licenses, Patent Pools, and Standard Setting*, in *Innovation Policy and the Economy* [A. Jaffe, J. Lerner and S. Stern (eds.) The MIT Press, 2001].
Carl Shapiro and Hal R. Varian, *L'Économie de l'Information* (De Boeck, 2000).
Oz Shy, *Industrial Organization: Theory and Applications* (The MIT Press 1996).
Ajit Singh and Rahule Dhumale, Competition Policy, Development, and Developing Countries (South Centre Working Paper, 1999).

Giancarlo Spagnolo, Optimal Leniency Programs (Fondazione Eni Enrico Mattei Work Report, 2000).

Michael Spence, *Entry, Capacity, Investment and Oligopolistic Pricing* (Bell Journal of Economics 49-70, 1977).

Joseph Spengler, *Vertical Integration and Antitrust Policy* (Journal of Political Economy 347-352, 1950).

Christodoulos Stefanadis, *Selective Contracts, Foreclosure, and the Chicago School View* (Journal of Law and Economics 429-450, 1998).

Andreas Stephan, *Is There Public Support for Cartel Criminalization?* (Concurrences 40-44, 2016).

George Stigler, *Monopoly and Oligopoly by Merger* (American Economic Review 23-34, 1950).

George Stigler, *A Theory of Oligopoly* (Journal of Political Economy, republished in The Organization of Industry, Irwin, 1964).

George Stigler and Robert Sherwin, *The Extent of the Market* (Journal of Law and Economics 555-585, 1985).

Stigler Committee on Digital Platforms, *Final Report* (Stigler Center, 2019).

Allyn Strickland and Leonard Weiss, *Advertising, Concentration and Price-Cost Margins* (Journal of Political Economy 1109-1121, 1976).

Maurice Stucke, *Am I a Price-Fixer? A Behavioral Economics Analysis of Cartels*, in *Criminalizing Cartels: A Critical Interdisciplinary Study of an International Regulatory Movement* [C. Beaton-Wells and A. Ezrachi (eds.) Hart Publishing, 2011].

E. Thomas Sullivan (ed.), *The Political Economy of the Sherman Act: The First One Hundred Years* (Oxford University Press, 1991).

Paolo Sylos-Labini, *Oligopoly and Technical Progress* (Harvard University Press, 1962).

Lester Telser, *Why Should Manufacturers Want Fair Trade?* (Journal of Law and Economics 86-105, 1960).

Lester Telser, *Cutthroat Competition and the Long Purse* (Journal of Law and Economics 259-277, 1966).

Jonathan Tepper, *The Myth of Capitalism* (Wiley, 2019).

Jean Tirole, *Industrial Organization* (Economica 2015).

Jean Tirole, *Économie du Bien Commun* (PUF, 2016).

Michael Utton, *Market Dominance and Antitrust Policy* (2nd ed., Elgar, 2003).

Theon van Dijk and Frank Verboven, A Practical Guide to Computing Cartel Damages in Private Actions (Working Paper, 2010).

W. Kip Viscusi, John Vernon and Joseph Harrington, *Economics of Regulation and Antitrust* (3rd ed., The MIT Press, 2005).

Louis Vogel, *Contrôle Européen des Concentrations* (Bruylant, 2017).

Ludwig von Mises, *Human Action: A Treatise on Economics* (4th ed., Irvington, 1896).

Nicholas Vonortas, *Research Joint Ventures in the U.S.* (Research Policy 577-595, 1997).

Leonard Weiss (ed.), *Concentration and Price* (The MIT Press, 1987).

Michael Whinston, *Tying, Foreclosure, and Exclusion* (American Economic Review 837-859, 1990).

Oliver Williamson, *Wage Rates as a Barrier to Entry* (Quarterly Journal of Economics, 1968a).

Oliver Williamson, *Economies as an Antitrust Defense: The Welfare Tradeoffs* (American Economic Review 18-36, 1968b).

Oliver Williamson, *Predatory Pricing: A Strategic and Welfare Analysis* (Yale Law Journal 284-340, 1977).

Oliver Williamson, *Market and Hierarchies: Analysis and Antitrust Implications* (The Free Press, 1975).

Oliver Williamson, *Comparative Economic Organization: The Analysis of Discrete Structural Alternatives* (Administrative Science Quarterly 269-296, 1991).

Useful Websites and Resources on Competition Policy

There are several reference reviews on competition policy, including:

- *Antitrust Bulletin* (academic journal): https://journals.sagepub.com/home/abx.
- *Antitrust Law Journal* (academic journal): https://www.americanbar.org/groups/antitrust_law/publications/antitrust_law_journal/.
- *World Competition* (academic journal): http://www.kluwerlawonline.com/toc.php?pubcode=WOCO.
- *European Competition Law Review*: https://www.sweetandmaxwell.co.uk/Catalogue/ProductDetails.aspx?productid=30791406ecordid=455.
- *Concurrences* (academic and practical review): www.concurrences.com.
- *Competition Policy Brief* (European Commission publication): https://ec.europa.eu/competition-policy/publications/competition-policy-briefs_en
- *Lamy Concurrence* (predominantly legal review): http://lamyconcurrence.fr.

Several websites provide information on competition policy, including:

- https://www.autoritedelaconcurrence.fr/fr (French Competition Authority website, presenting its opinions and decisions, available online).
- http://www.economie.gouv.fr/dgccrf/concurrence (DGCCRF website, in charge of local anti-competitive practices in France).
- http://ec.europa.eu/competition/index_en.html (European Commission's DG Competition website, presenting in detail the texts and decisions on European competition policy).
- www.usdoj.gov/atr/ (U.S. Department of Justice's Antitrust Division website).
- www.ftc.gov (Federal Trade Commission website, which includes a section on antitrust).

- http://www.oecd.org/competition/ (OECD website, with a page dedicated to competition policy; many reports and round tables are available online).
- http://unctad.org/en/Pages/DITC/CompetitionLaw/Competition-Law-and-Policy.aspx (UNCTAD website, which includes a division on competition law and consumer and consumer protection policy. Many reports and working papers, focusing on developing countries, can be consulted online).
- https://www.internationalcompetitionnetwork.org/ (ICN website, which brings together in 2019 no fewer than 104 competition authorities from 92 jurisdictions; it is a forum for discussion and exchange of best practices between competition authorities. Several working groups report on their discussions, including on cartels, mergers and acquisitions or advocacy).
- https://www.antitrustinstitute.org (American Antitrust Institute website).

Index

www.ingramcontent.com/pod-product-compliance
Ingram Content Group UK Ltd.
Pitfield, Milton Keynes, MK11 3LW, UK
UKHW020846290926
15470UKWH00004B/1576

9 789403 537313